Story and Art by
Rumiko Takahashi

RIN-NE りんね

Characters

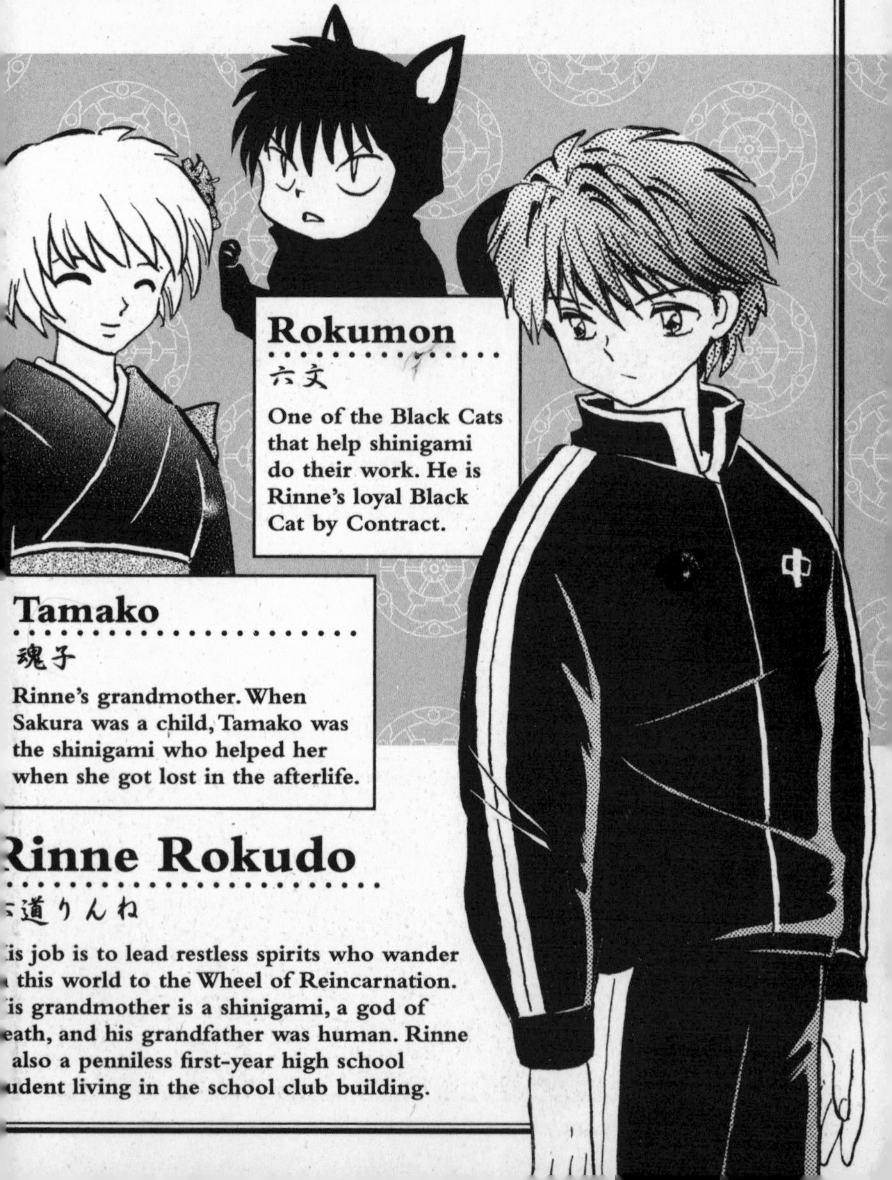

Rokumon

六文

One of the Black Cats that help shinigami do their work. He is Rinne's loyal Black Cat by Contract.

Tamako

魂子

Rinne's grandmother. When Sakura was a child, Tamako was the shinigami who helped her when she got lost in the afterlife.

Rinne Rokudo

六道りんね

is job is to lead restless spirits who wander this world to the Wheel of Reincarnation. is grandmother is a shinigami, a god of eath, and his grandfather was human. Rinne also a penniless first-year high school udent living in the school club building.

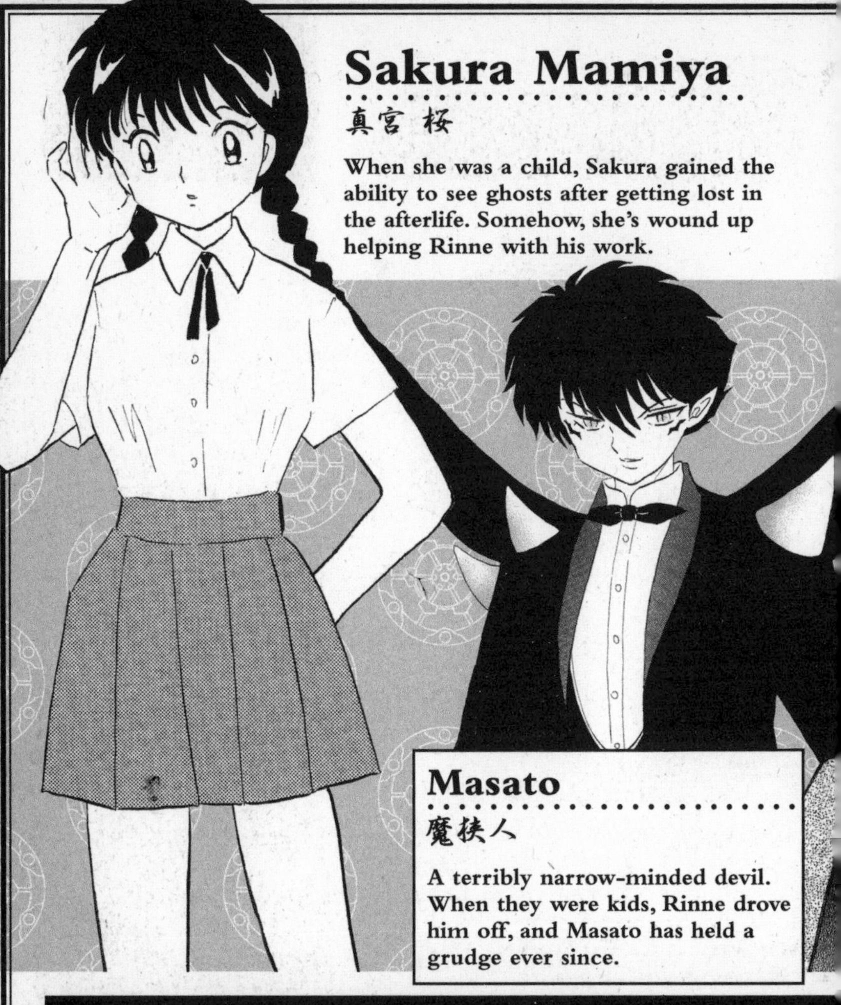

Sakura Mamiya

真宮 桜

When she was a child, Sakura gained the ability to see ghosts after getting lost in the afterlife. Somehow, she's wound up helping Rinne with his work.

Masato

魔挟人

A terribly narrow-minded devil. When they were kids, Rinne drove him off, and Masato has held a grudge ever since.

The Story So Far

Sakura and Rinne have had their hands full dealing with the earthbound spirits of people who can't pass on into the afterlife. Solving a samurai ghost's case of mistaken identity, and saving the wounded pride of the ghost of the most popular girl in school were just a warm-up.

The strange case of the angry spirit of a boy who isn't dead yet leads Rinne to a confrontation with Masato, an old rival from when Rinne was in elementary school. Masato plans to trap Rinne in debt hell, but his clumsy plan backfires and Rinne (with some help from Sakura and Rokumon) defeats Masato and manages to escape from hell.

With an after-school schedule like this, how does Sakura get her homework done?

Contents

CHAPTER 19: THE TRANSFER STUDENT

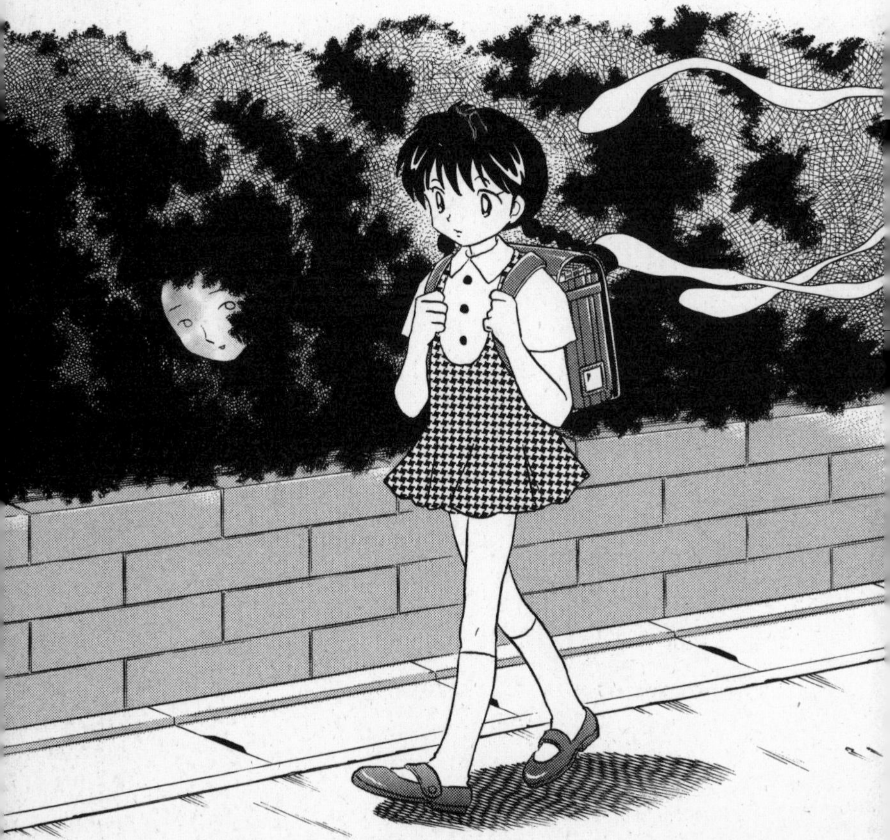

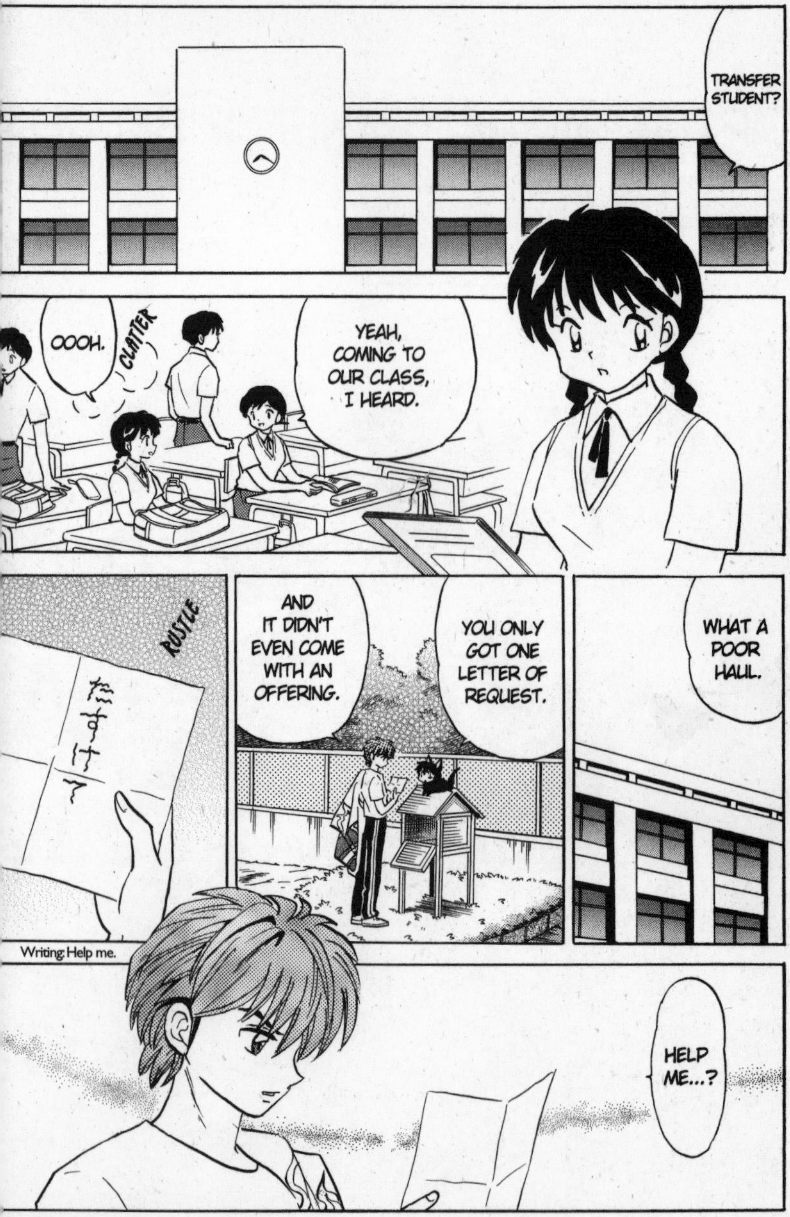

TRANSFER STUDENT?
YEAH, COMING TO OUR CLASS, I HEARD.
CLATTER
OOOH.
WHAT A POOR HAUL.
YOU ONLY GOT ONE LETTER OF REQUEST.
AND IT DIDN'T EVEN COME WITH AN OFFERING.
RUSTLE
たすけて
Writing: Help me.
HELP ME...?

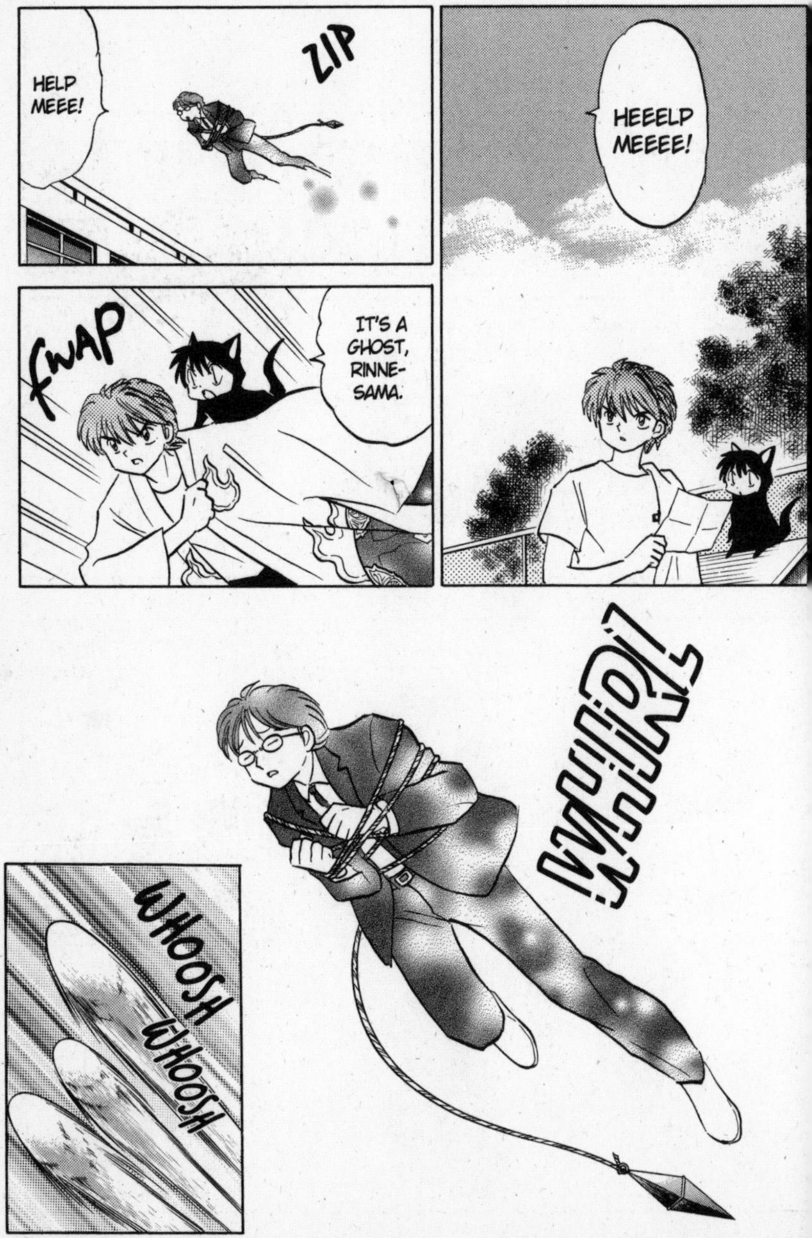
HEEELP MEEEE!
ZIP
HELP MEEE!
FWAP
IT'S A GHOST, RINNE-SAMA.
WHiiiRL!
WHOOSH
WHOOSH

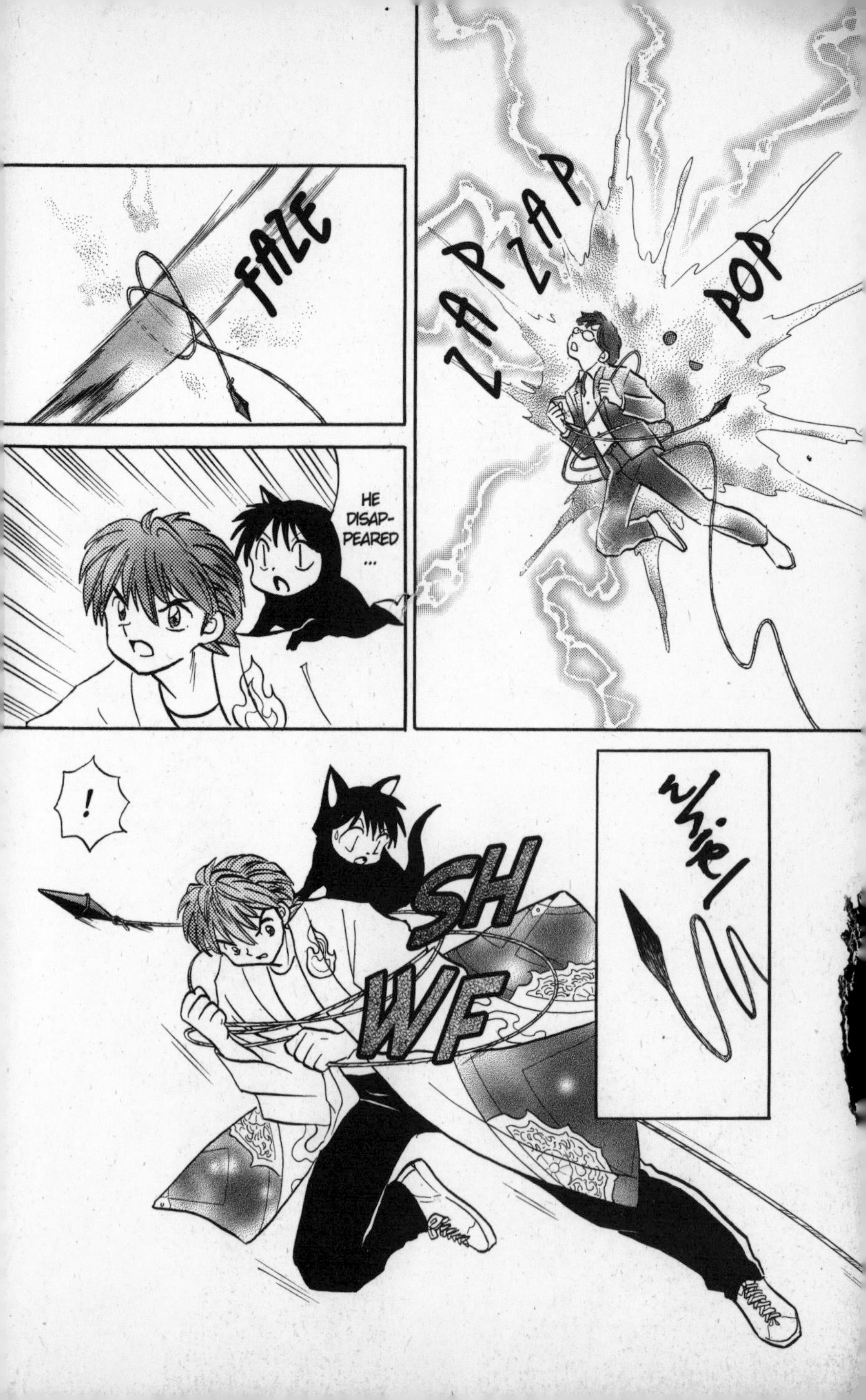
ZAP ZAP
POP
FAZE
HE DISAP-PEARED...
whirl
!
SHWF

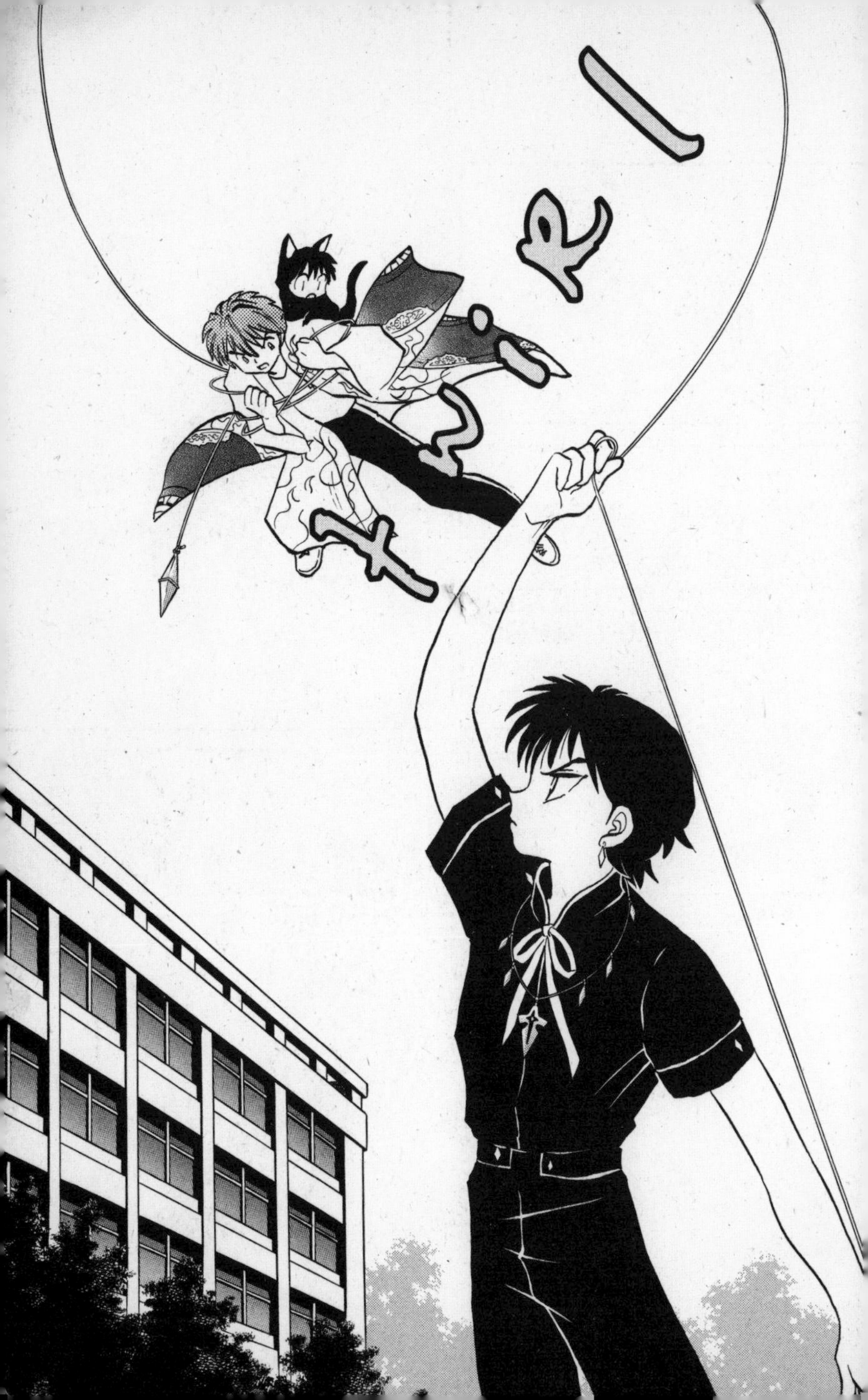

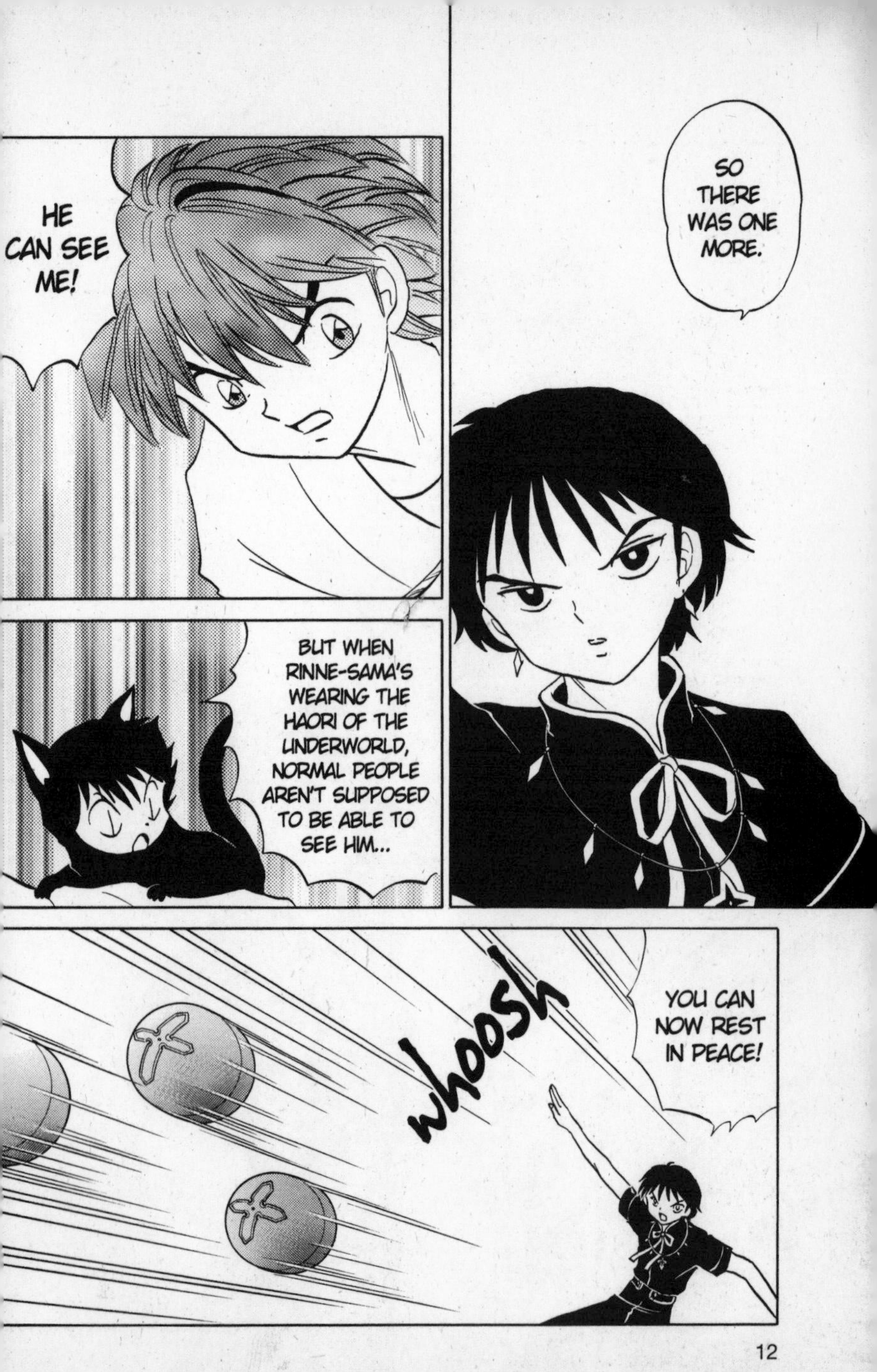
SO THERE WAS ONE MORE.
HE CAN SEE ME!
BUT WHEN RINNE-SAMA'S WEARING THE HAORI OF THE UNDERWORLD, NORMAL PEOPLE AREN'T SUPPOSED TO BE ABLE TO SEE HIM...
YOU CAN NOW REST IN PEACE!
whoosh

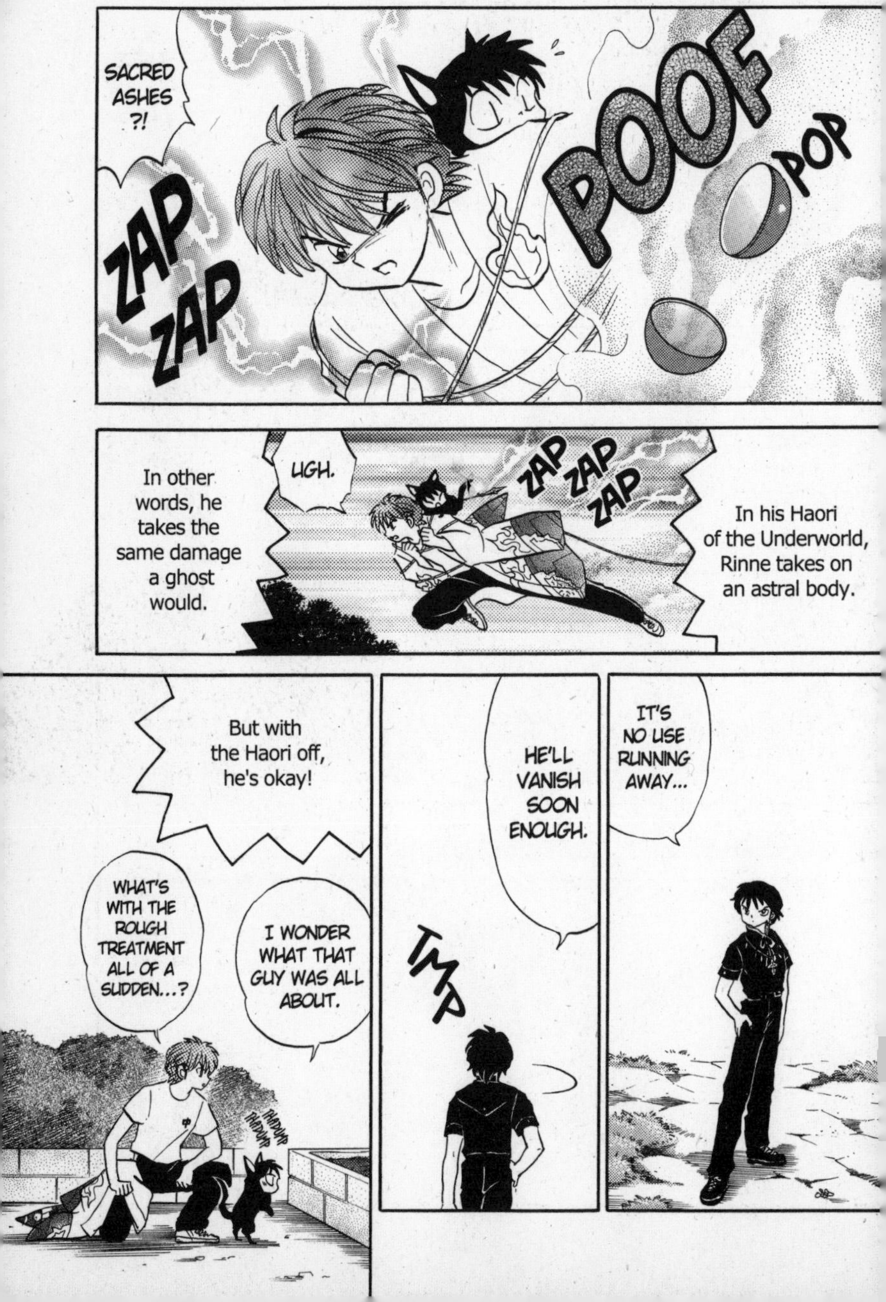
POOF
POP
SACRED ASHES ?!
ZAP ZAP
In his Haori of the Underworld, Rinne takes on an astral body.
ZAP ZAP ZAP
UGH.
In other words, he takes the same damage a ghost would.
IT'S NO USE RUNNING AWAY...
HE'LL VANISH SOON ENOUGH.
TMP
But with the Haori off, he's okay!
I WONDER WHAT THAT GUY WAS ALL ABOUT.
WHAT'S WITH THE ROUGH TREATMENT ALL OF A SUDDEN...?

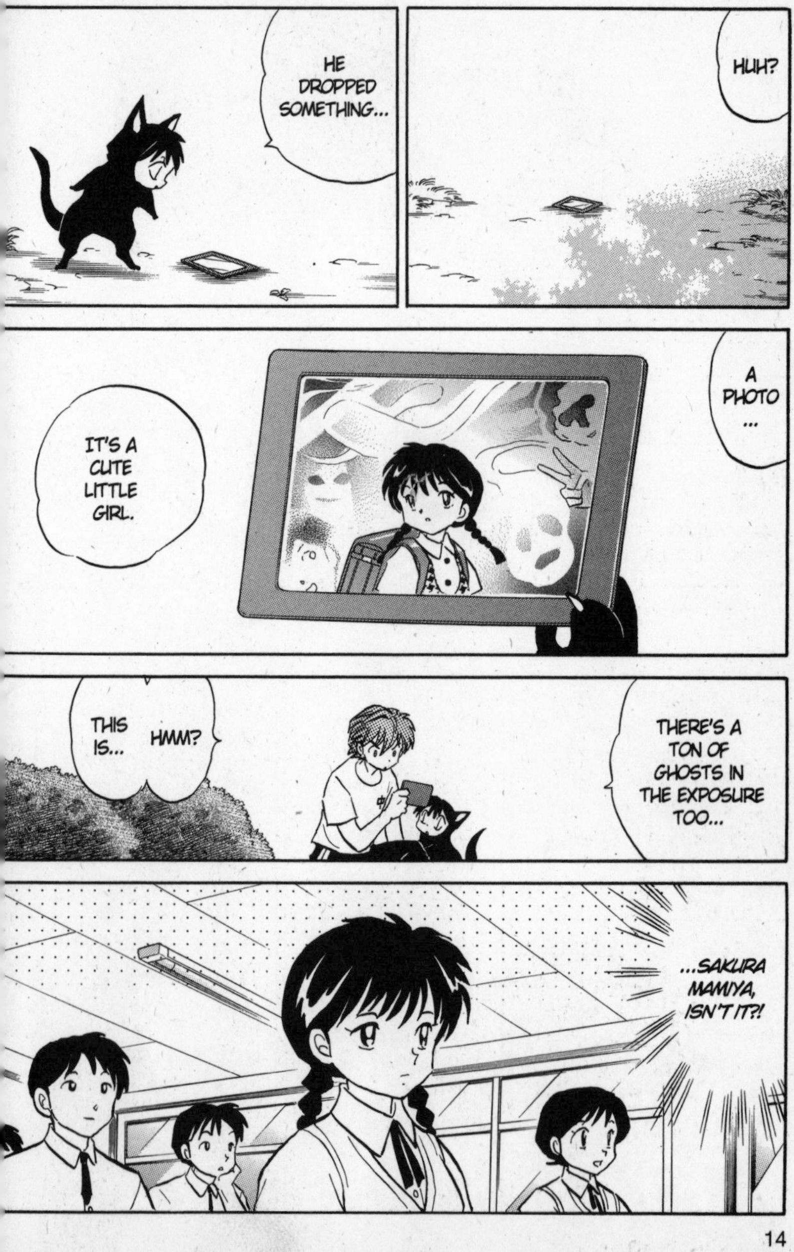
HUH?
HE DROPPED SOMETHING...
A PHOTO ...
IT'S A CUTE LITTLE GIRL.
THERE'S A TON OF GHOSTS IN THE EXPOSURE TOO...
HMM?
THIS IS...
...SAKURA MAMIYA, ISN'T IT?!

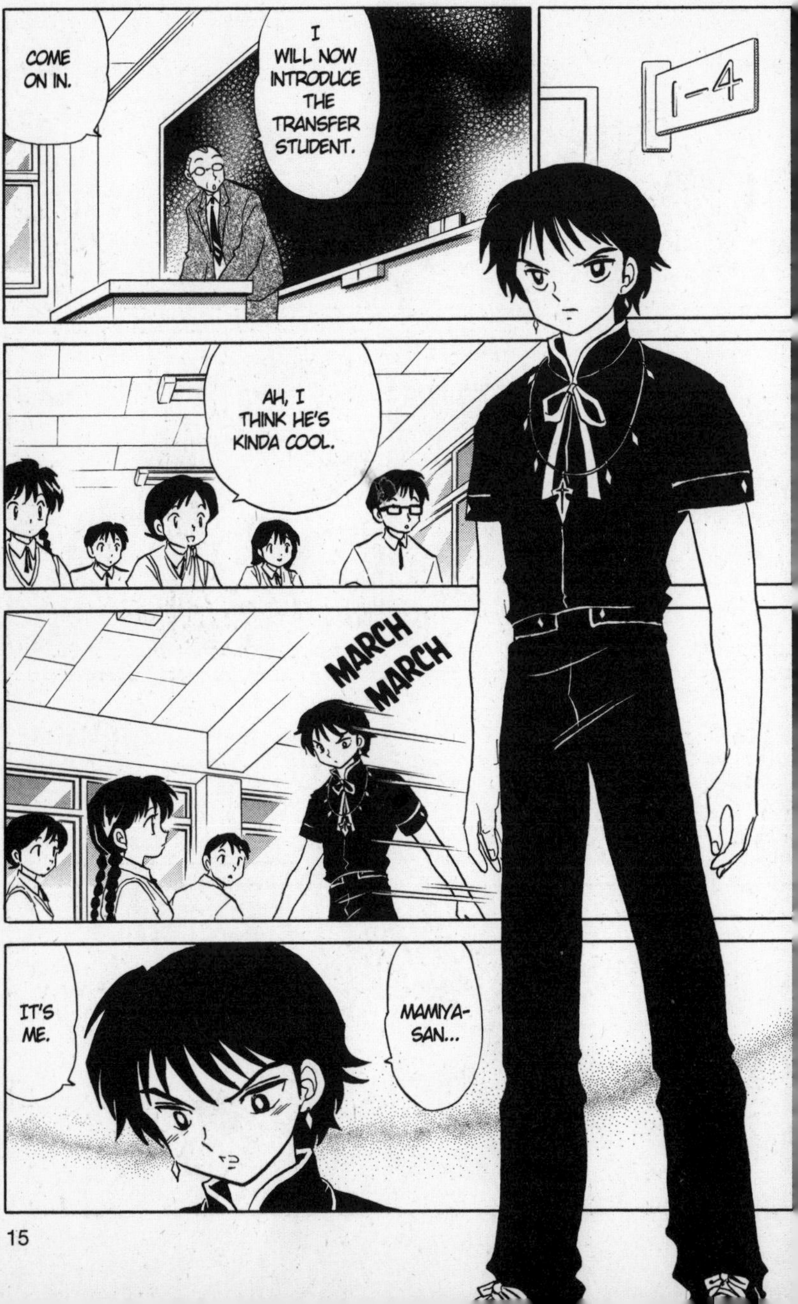
I WILL NOW INTRODUCE THE TRANSFER STUDENT.
COME ON IN.
AH, I THINK HE'S KINDA COOL.
MARCH MARCH
MAMIYA-SAN...
IT'S ME.

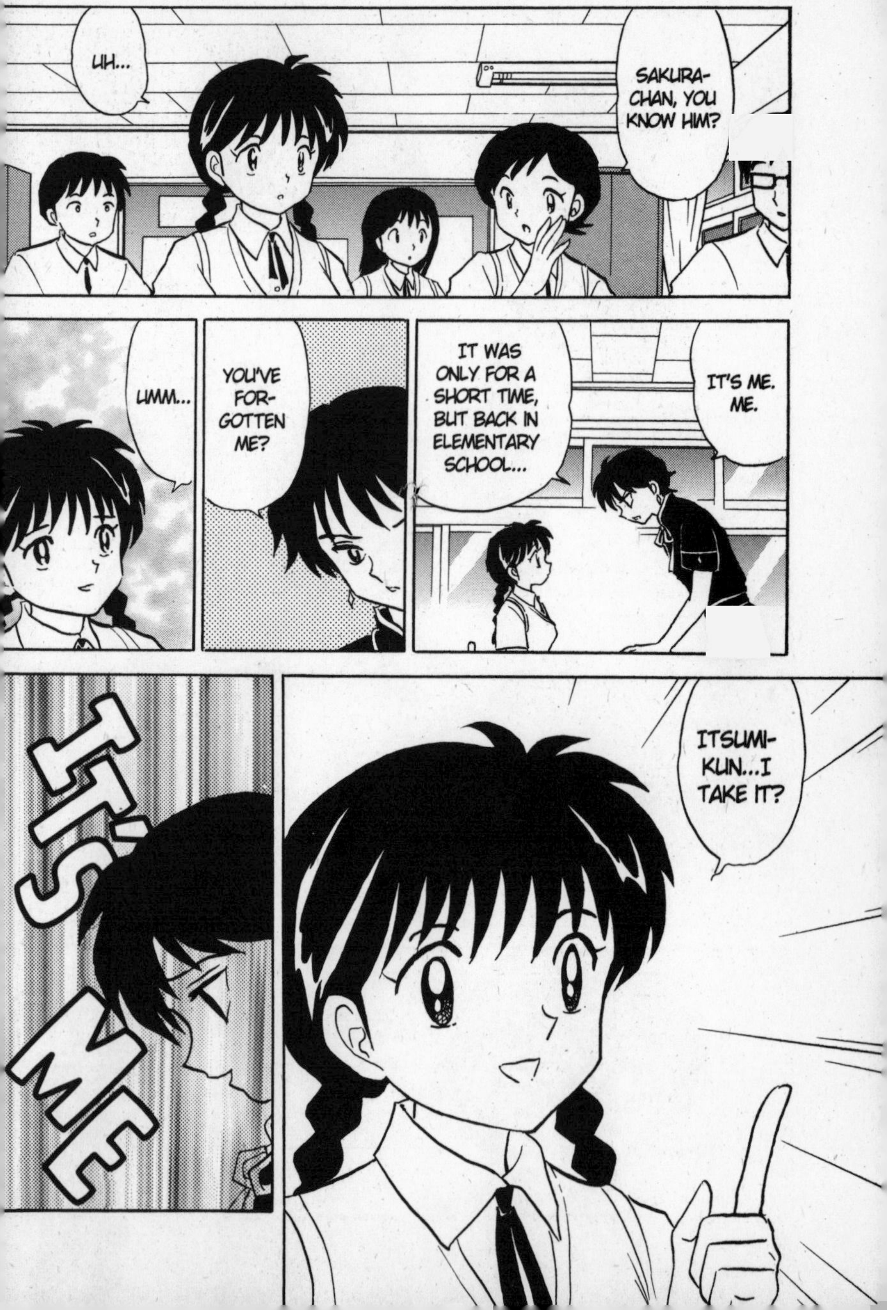
SAKURA-CHAN, YOU KNOW HIM?
UH...
IT'S ME. ME.
IT WAS ONLY FOR A SHORT TIME, BUT BACK IN ELEMENTARY SCHOOL...
YOU'VE FOR-GOTTEN ME?
UMM...
ITSUMI-KUN...I TAKE IT?
IT'S ME

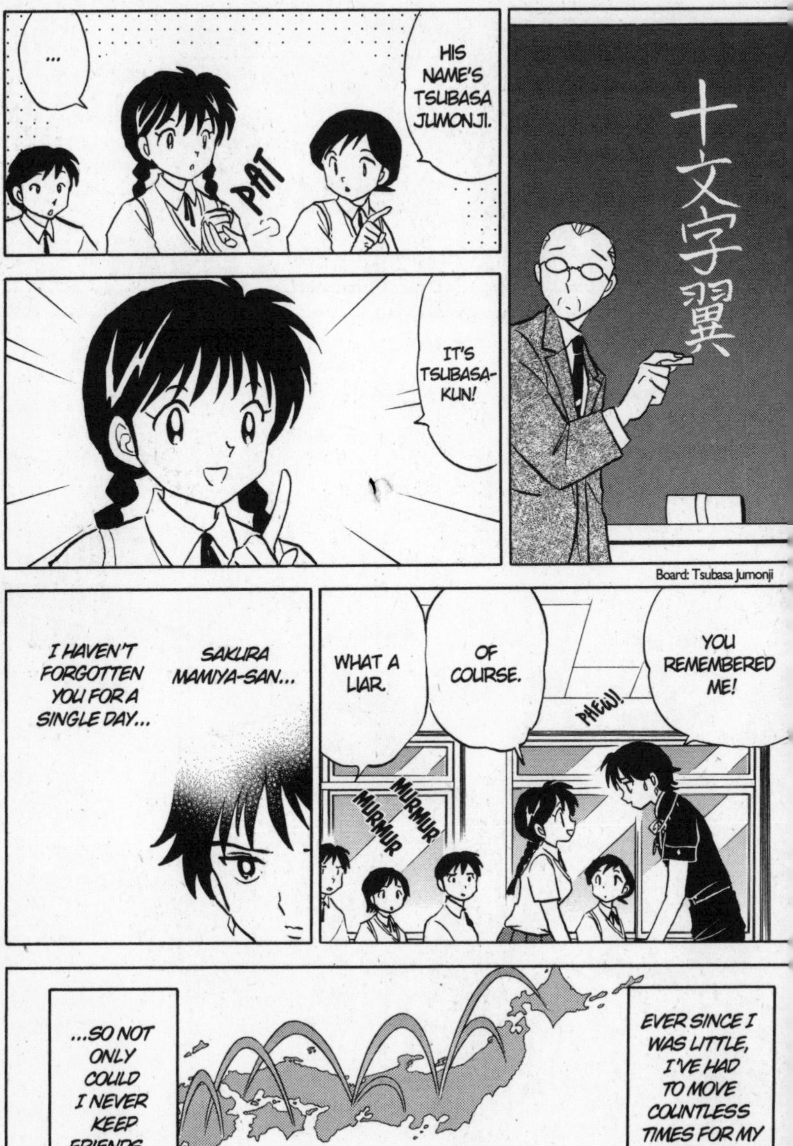
十文字翼
HIS NAME'S TSUBASA JUMONJI.
PAT
...
IT'S TSUBASA-KUN!
YOU REMEMBERED ME!
PHEW!
OF COURSE.
WHAT A LIAR.
MURMUR MURMUR
SAKURA MAMIYA-SAN...
I HAVEN'T FORGOTTEN YOU FOR A SINGLE DAY...
EVER SINCE I WAS LITTLE, I'VE HAD TO MOVE COUNTLESS TIMES FOR MY FAMILY...
...SO NOT ONLY COULD I NEVER KEEP FRIENDS...

Board: Tsubasa Jumonji

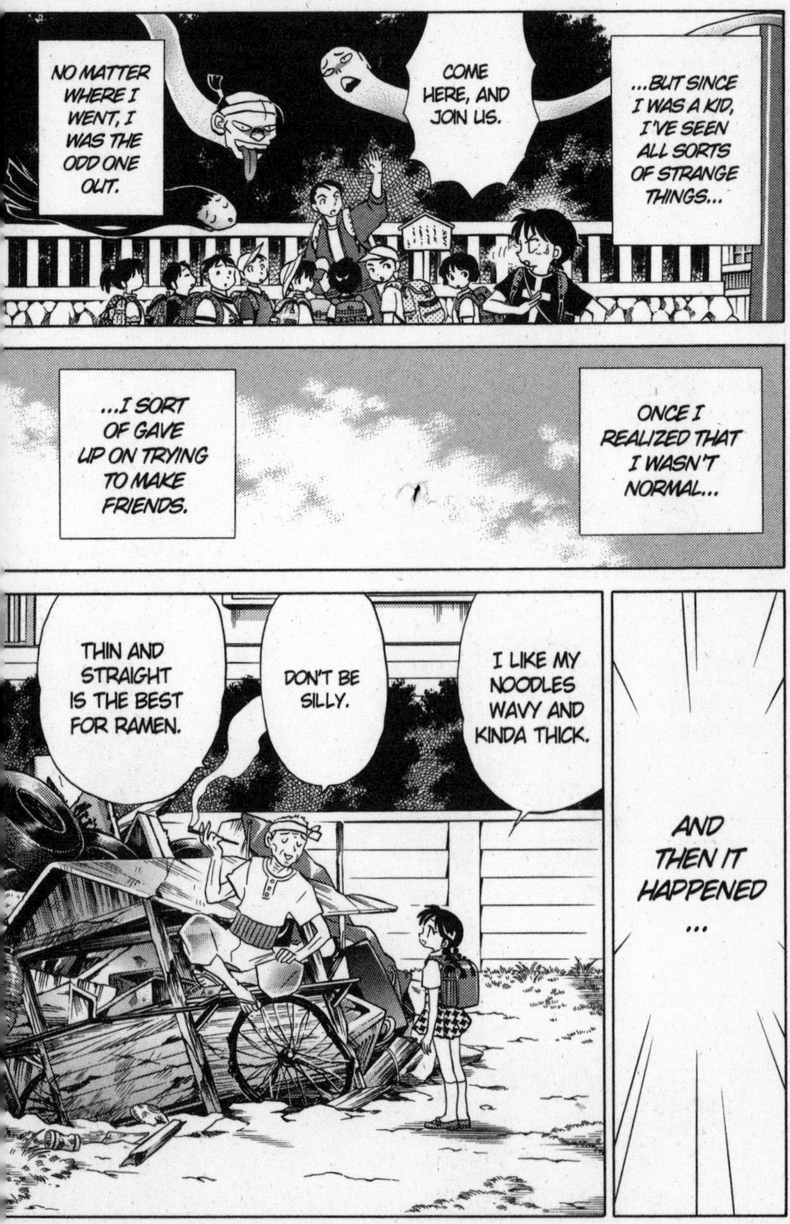
...BUT SINCE I WAS A KID, I'VE SEEN ALL SORTS OF STRANGE THINGS...
COME HERE, AND JOIN US.
NO MATTER WHERE I WENT, I WAS THE ODD ONE OUT.
ONCE I REALIZED THAT I WASN'T NORMAL...
...I SORT OF GAVE UP ON TRYING TO MAKE FRIENDS.
AND THEN IT HAPPENED ...
I LIKE MY NOODLES WAVY AND KINDA THICK.
DON'T BE SILLY.
THIN AND STRAIGHT IS THE BEST FOR RAMEN.

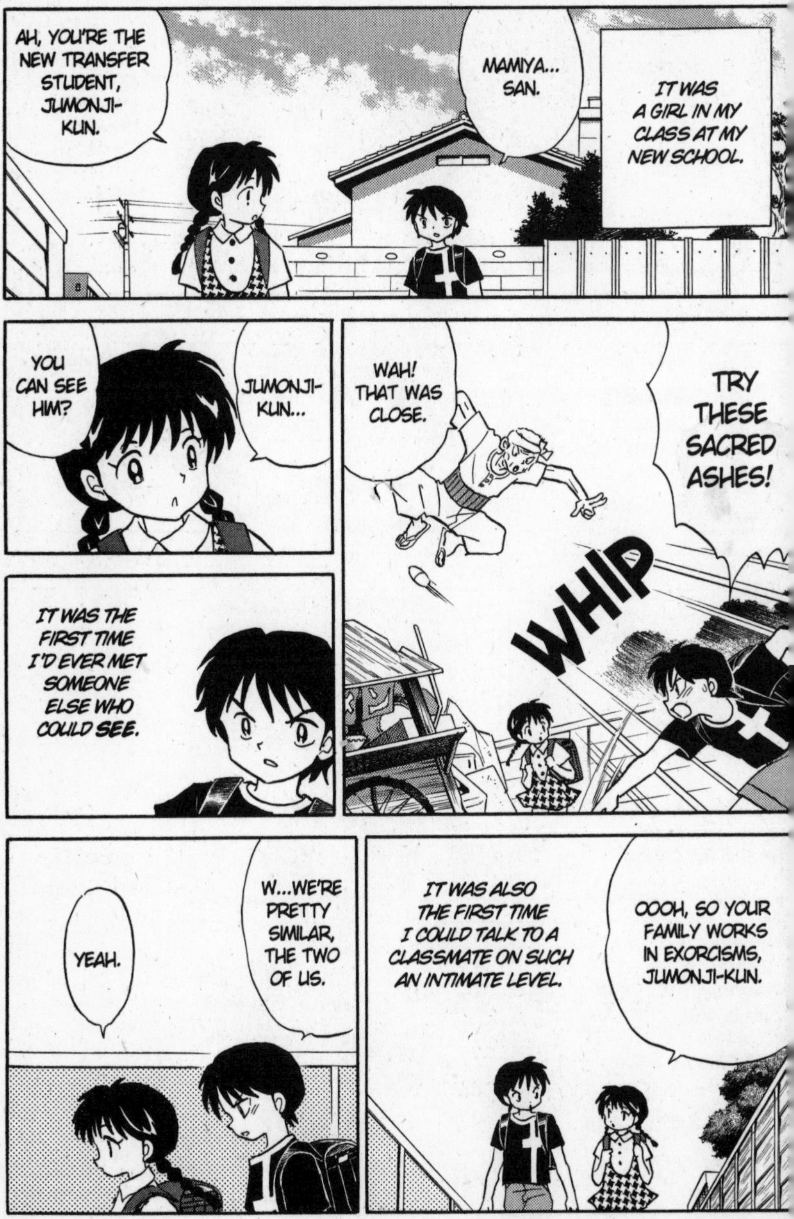
IT WAS A GIRL IN MY CLASS AT MY NEW SCHOOL.
MAMIYA... SAN.
AH, YOU'RE THE NEW TRANSFER STUDENT, JUMONJI-KUN.
TRY THESE SACRED ASHES!
WAH! THAT WAS CLOSE.
WHIP
JUMONJI-KUN...
YOU CAN SEE HIM?
IT WAS THE FIRST TIME I'D EVER MET SOMEONE ELSE WHO COULD SEE.
OOOH, SO YOUR FAMILY WORKS IN EXORCISMS, JUMONJI-KUN.
IT WAS ALSO THE FIRST TIME I COULD TALK TO A CLASSMATE ON SUCH AN INTIMATE LEVEL.
W...WE'RE PRETTY SIMILAR, THE TWO OF US.
YEAH.

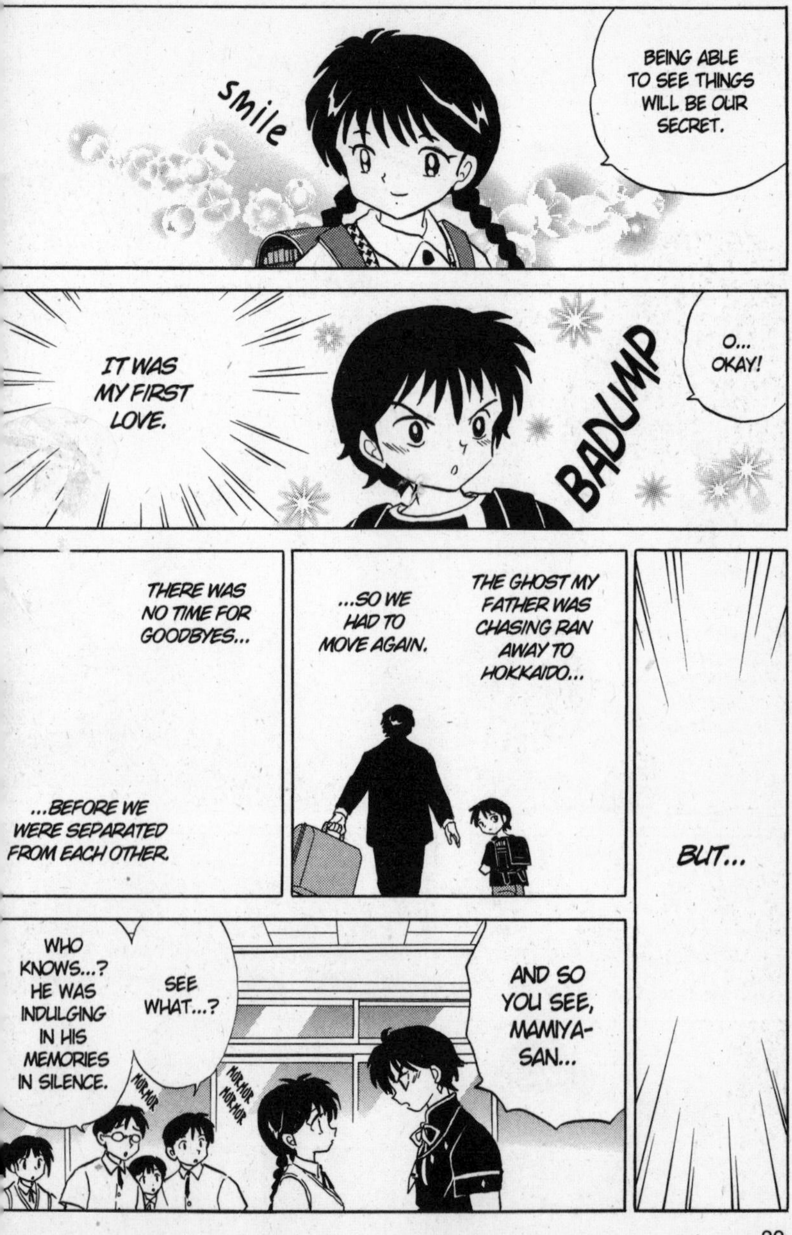

BEING ABLE TO SEE THINGS WILL BE OUR SECRET.
smile
O... OKAY!
BADUMP
IT WAS MY FIRST LOVE.
BUT...
THE GHOST MY FATHER WAS CHASING RAN AWAY TO HOKKAIDO...
...SO WE HAD TO MOVE AGAIN.
THERE WAS NO TIME FOR GOODBYES...
...BEFORE WE WERE SEPARATED FROM EACH OTHER.
AND SO YOU SEE, MAMIYA-SAN...
SEE WHAT...?
WHO KNOWS...? HE WAS INDULGING IN HIS MEMORIES IN SILENCE.
MORMOR MORMOR
MORMOR

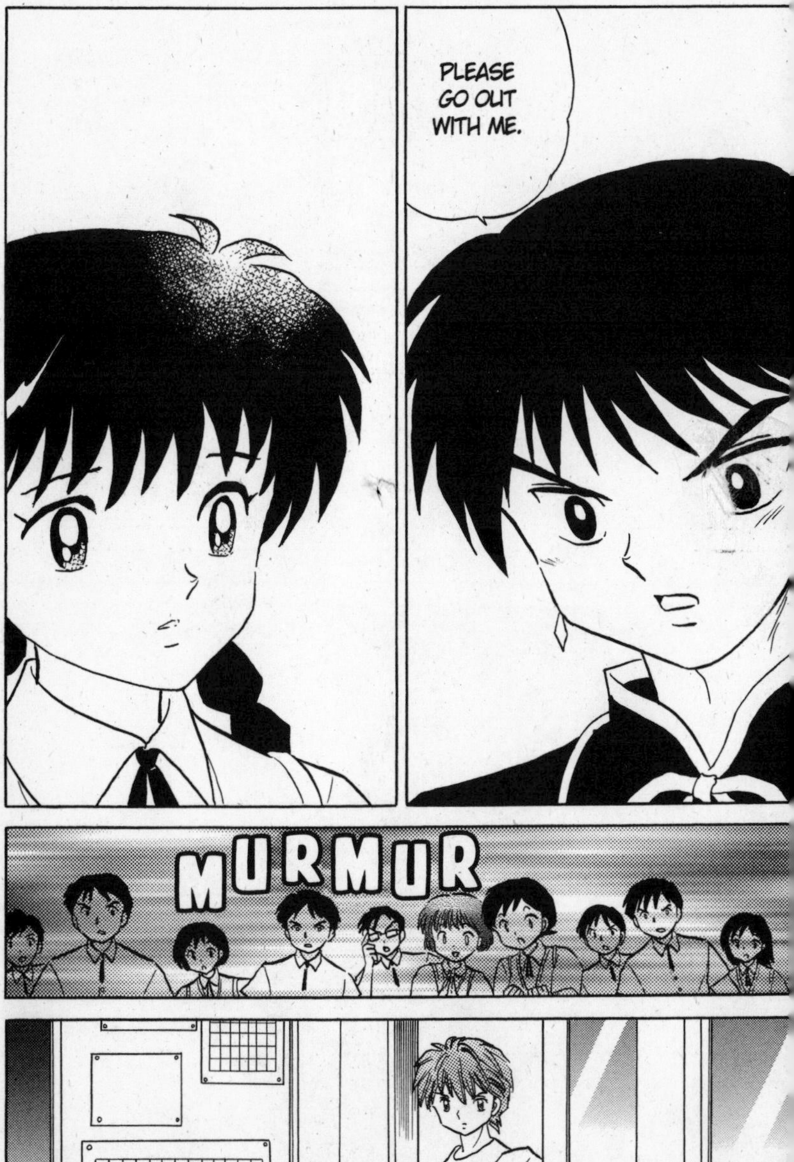
PLEASE GO OUT WITH ME.
MURMUR

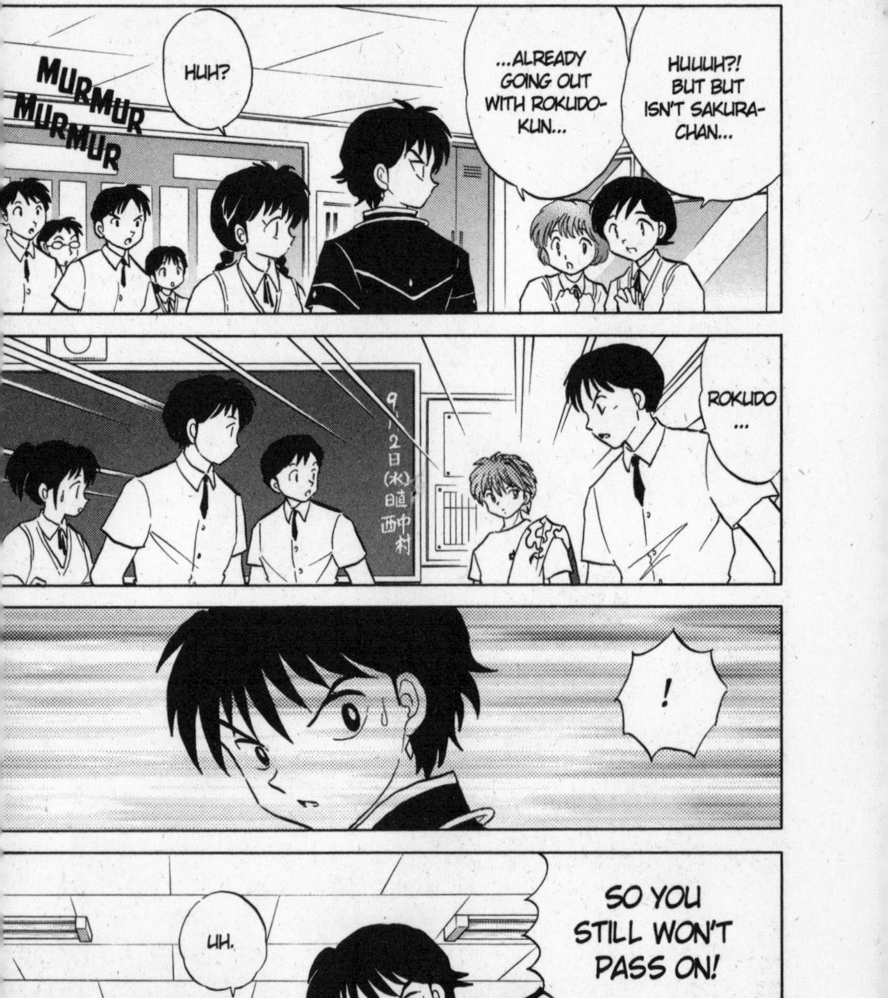
HUUUH?! BUT BUT ISN'T SAKURA-CHAN...
...ALREADY GOING OUT WITH ROKUDO-KUN...
HUH?
MURMUR MURMUR
ROKUDO ...
!
SO YOU STILL WON'T PASS ON!
UH.
WHIP

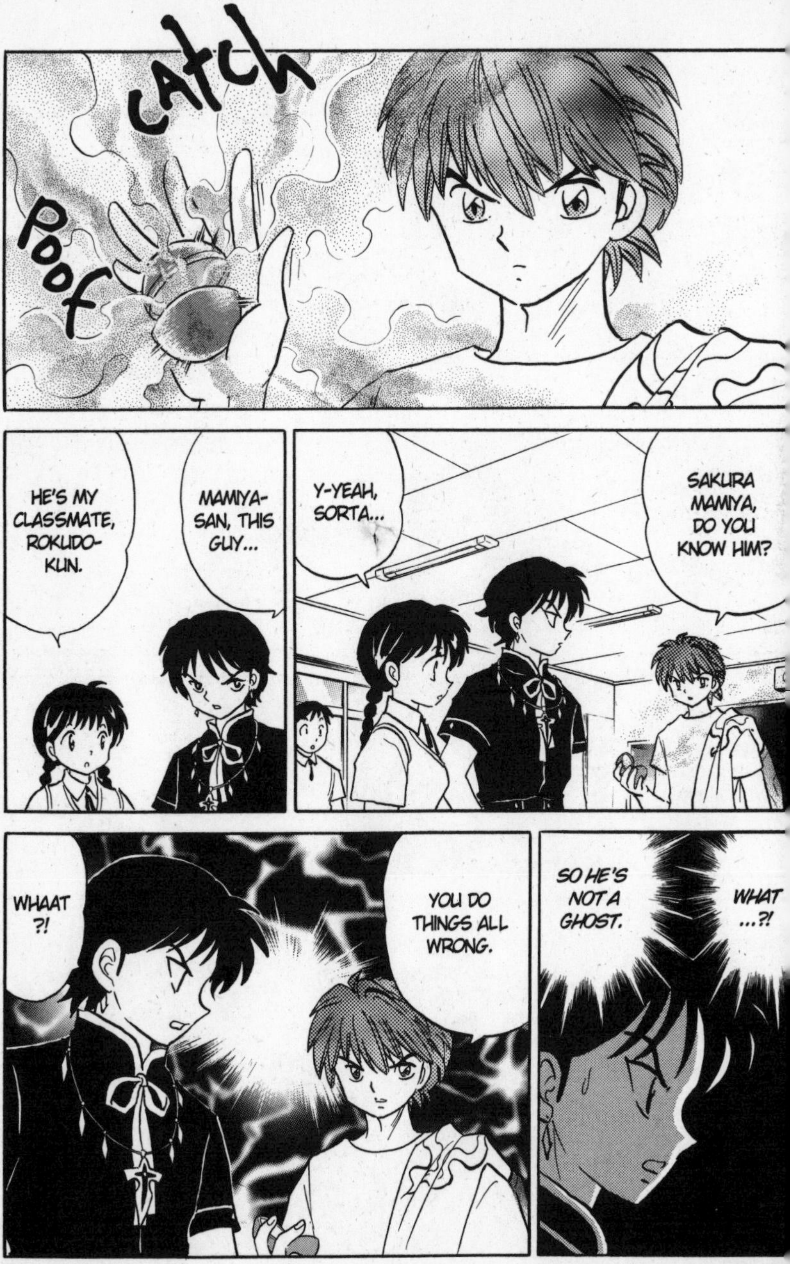
catch
Poof
SAKURA MAMIYA, DO YOU KNOW HIM?
Y-YEAH, SORTA...
MAMIYA-SAN, THIS GUY...
HE'S MY CLASSMATE, ROKUDO-KUN.
WHAT ...?!
SO HE'S NOT A GHOST.
YOU DO THINGS ALL WRONG.
WHAAT ?!

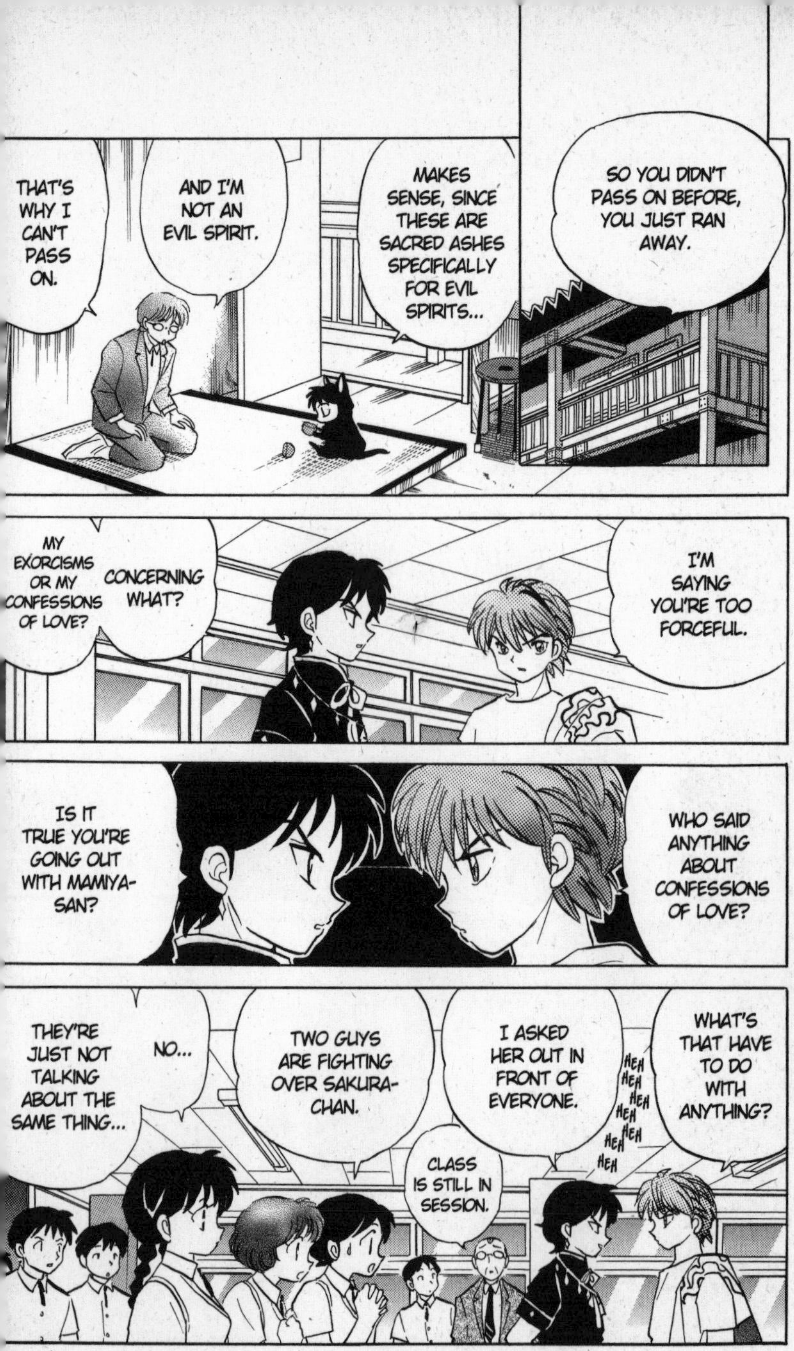

SO YOU DIDN'T PASS ON BEFORE, YOU JUST RAN AWAY.
MAKES SENSE, SINCE THESE ARE SACRED ASHES SPECIFICALLY FOR EVIL SPIRITS...
AND I'M NOT AN EVIL SPIRIT.
THAT'S WHY I CAN'T PASS ON.
I'M SAYING YOU'RE TOO FORCEFUL.
CONCERNING WHAT?
MY EXORCISMS OR MY CONFESSIONS OF LOVE?
WHO SAID ANYTHING ABOUT CONFESSIONS OF LOVE?
IS IT TRUE YOU'RE GOING OUT WITH MAMIYA-SAN?
WHAT'S THAT HAVE TO DO WITH ANYTHING?
HEH HEH HEH HEH HEH HEH HEH
I ASKED HER OUT IN FRONT OF EVERYONE.
CLASS IS STILL IN SESSION.
TWO GUYS ARE FIGHTING OVER SAKURA-CHAN.
NO...
THEY'RE JUST NOT TALKING ABOUT THE SAME THING...

CHAPTER 20: IF YOU DON'T MIND, LET'S BE FRIENDS FIRST

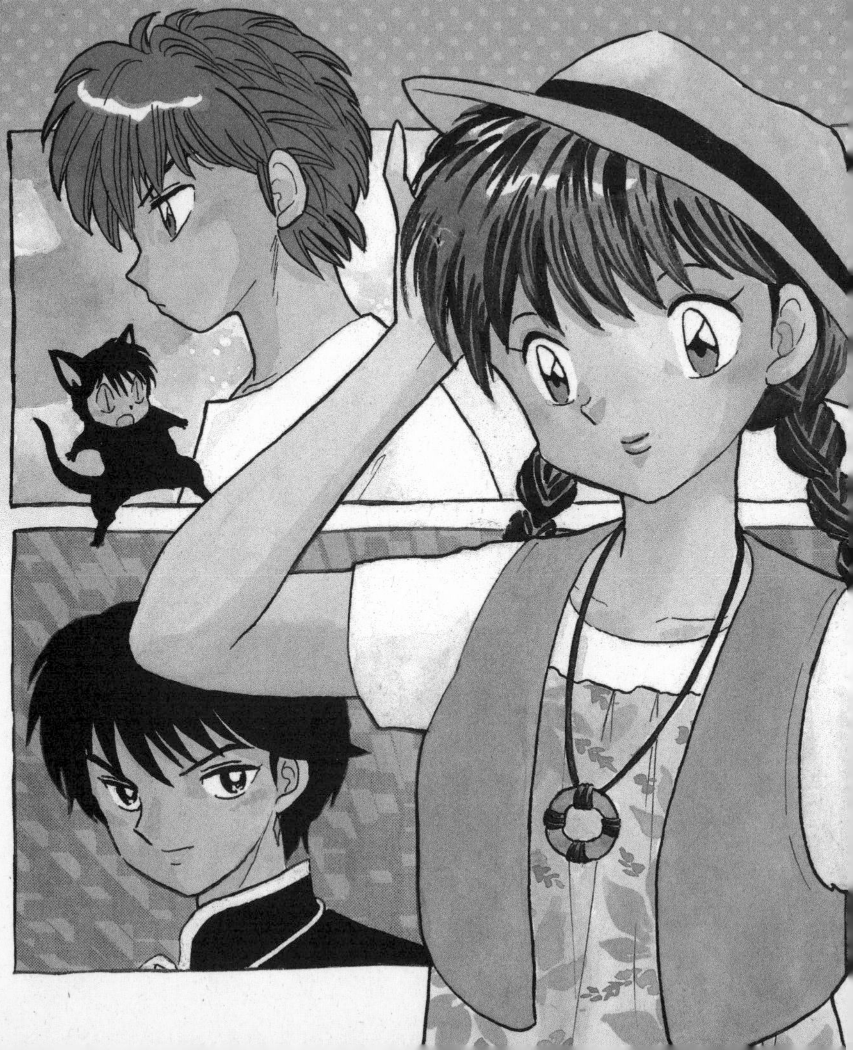

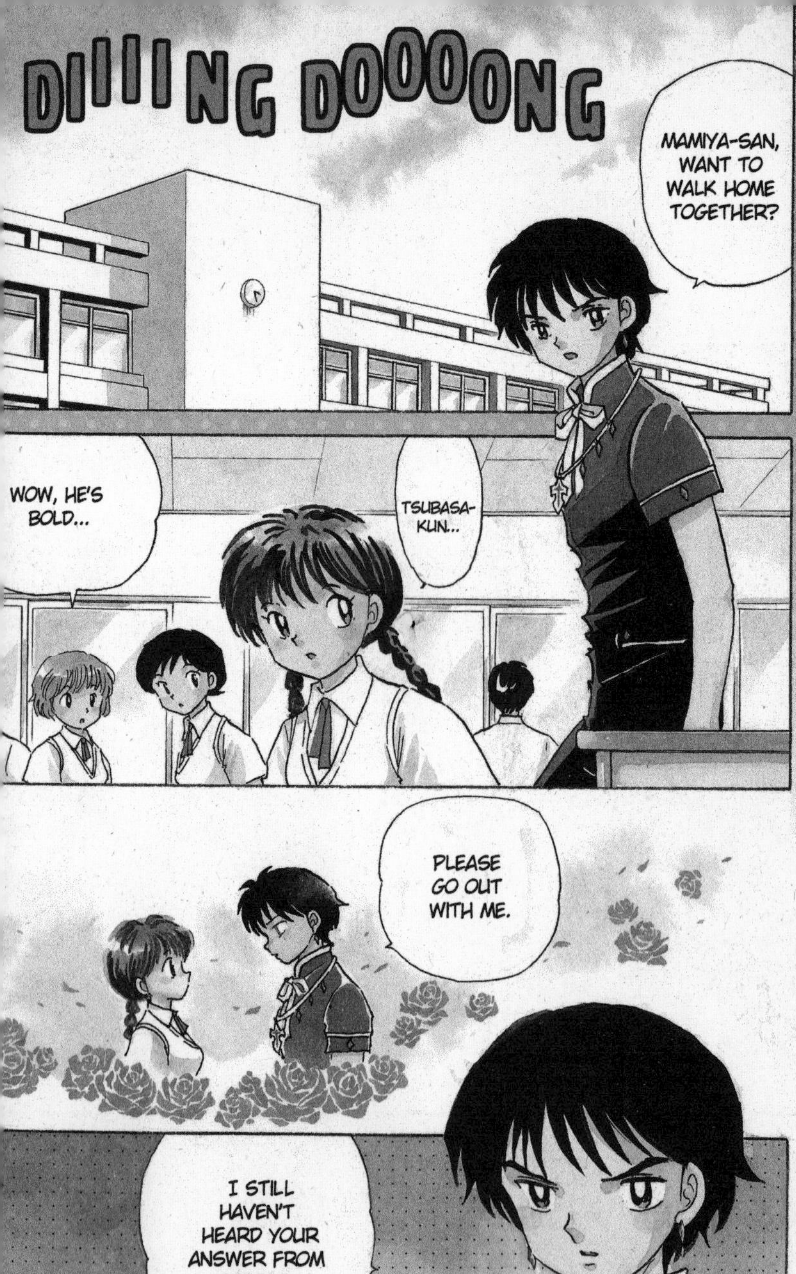
DIIIING DOOOOONG
MAMIYA-SAN, WANT TO WALK HOME TOGETHER?
TSUBASA-KUN...
WOW, HE'S BOLD...
PLEASE GO OUT WITH ME.
I STILL HAVEN'T HEARD YOUR ANSWER FROM BEFORE.

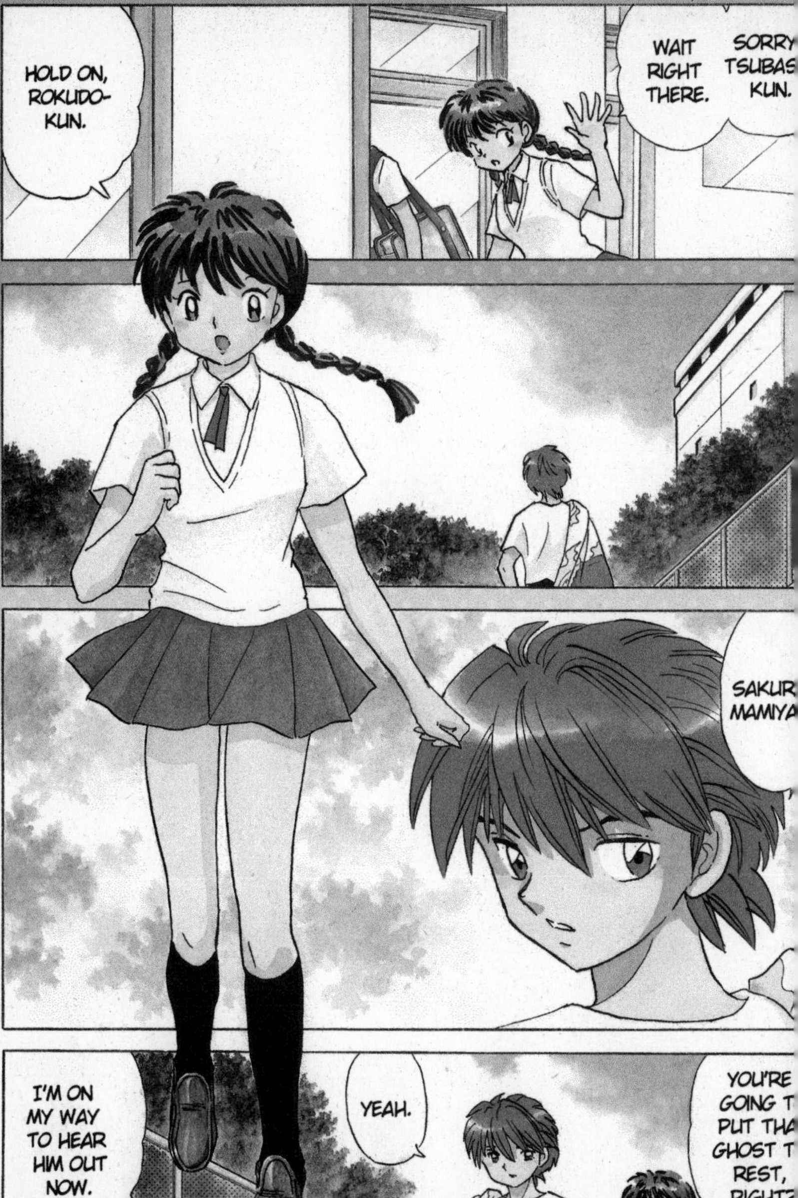
SORRY TSUBAS KUN.
WAIT RIGHT THERE.
HOLD ON, ROKUDO-KUN.
SAKUR MAMIYA
YOU'RE GOING T PUT THA GHOST T REST, RIGHT?
YEAH.
I'M ON MY WAY TO HEAR HIM OUT NOW.

RIN-NE

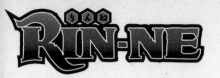

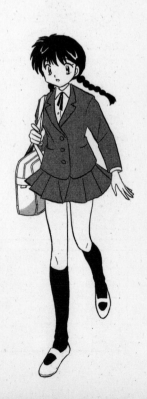

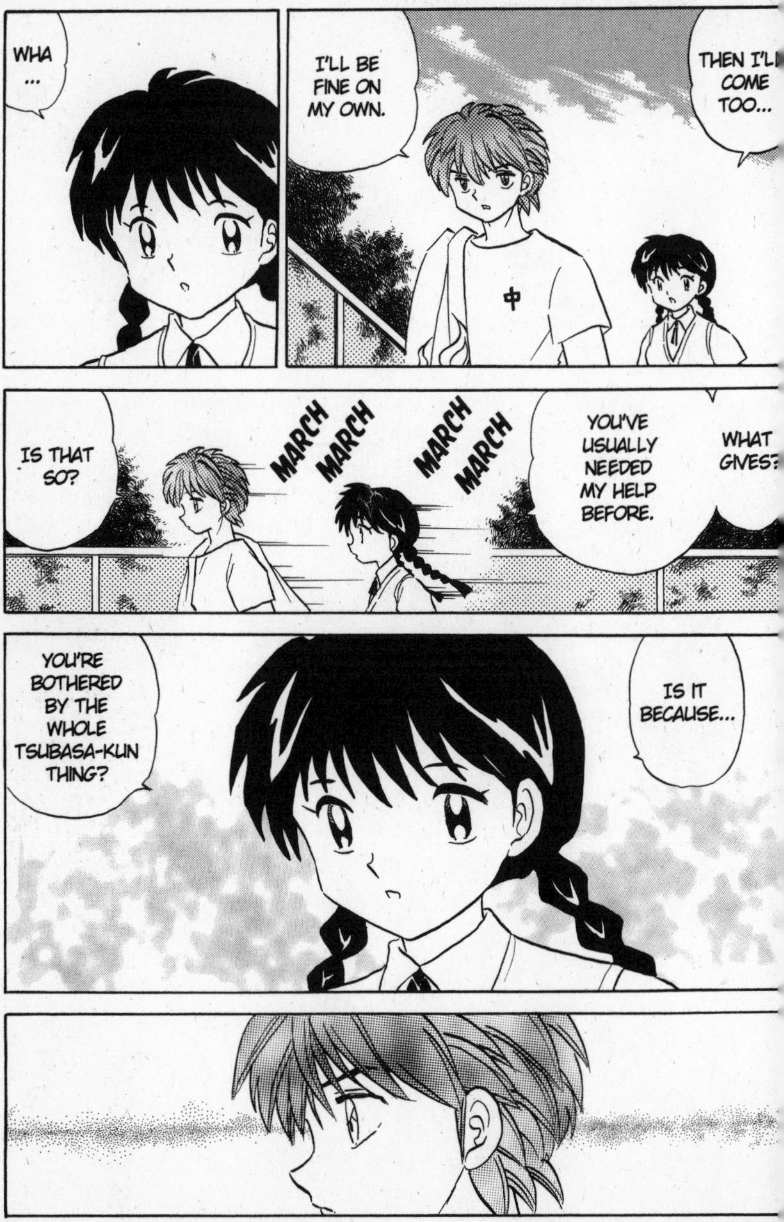
THEN I'L
COME TOO...
I'LL BE FINE ON MY OWN.
WHA ...
WHAT GIVES
YOU'VE USUALLY NEEDED MY HELP BEFORE.
MARCH MARCH
MARCH MARCH
IS THAT SO?
IS IT BECAUSE...
YOU'RE BOTHERED BY THE WHOLE TSUBASA-KUN THING?

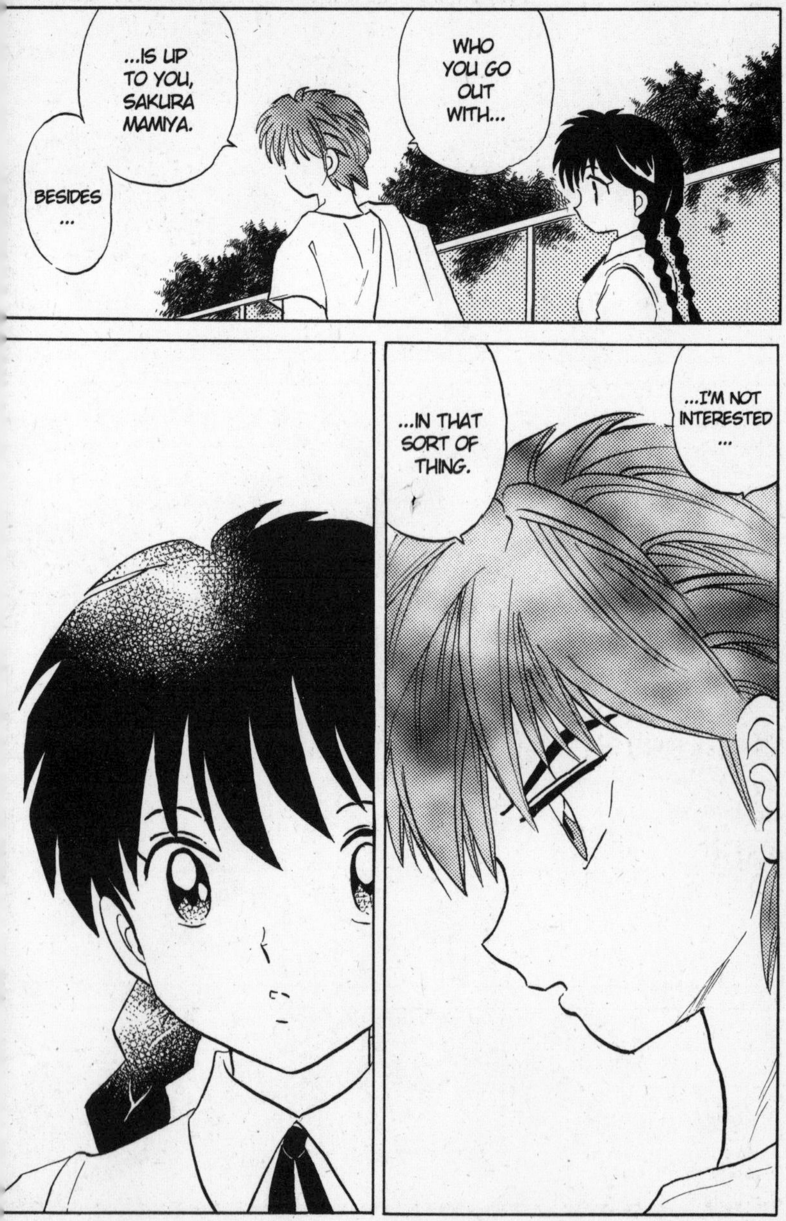
WHO YOU GO OUT WITH...
...IS UP TO YOU, SAKURA MAMIYA.
BESIDES ...
...I'M NOT INTERESTED ...
...IN THAT SORT OF THING.

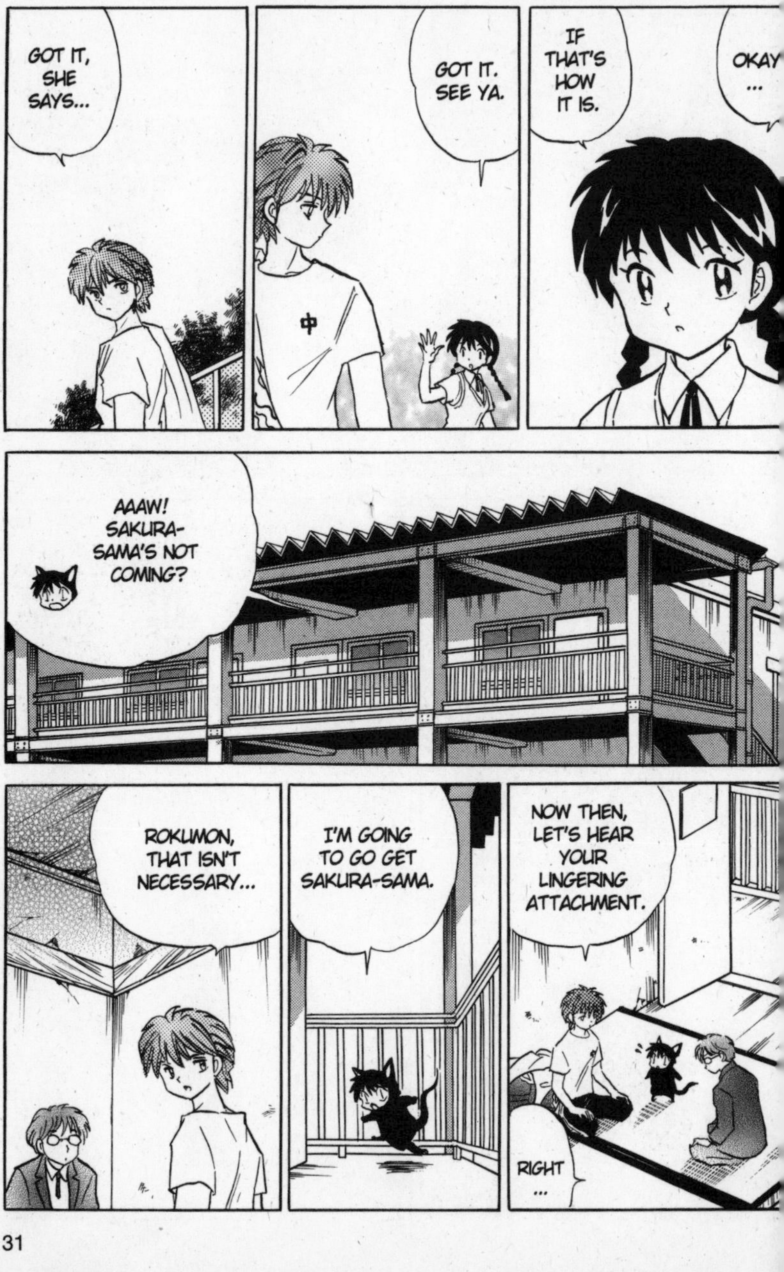
OKAY ...
IF THAT'S HOW IT IS.
GOT IT. SEE YA.
GOT IT, SHE SAYS...
AAAW! SAKURA-SAMA'S NOT COMING?
NOW THEN, LET'S HEAR YOUR LINGERING ATTACHMENT.
RIGHT ...
I'M GOING TO GO GET SAKURA-SAMA.
ROKUMON, THAT ISN'T NECESSARY...

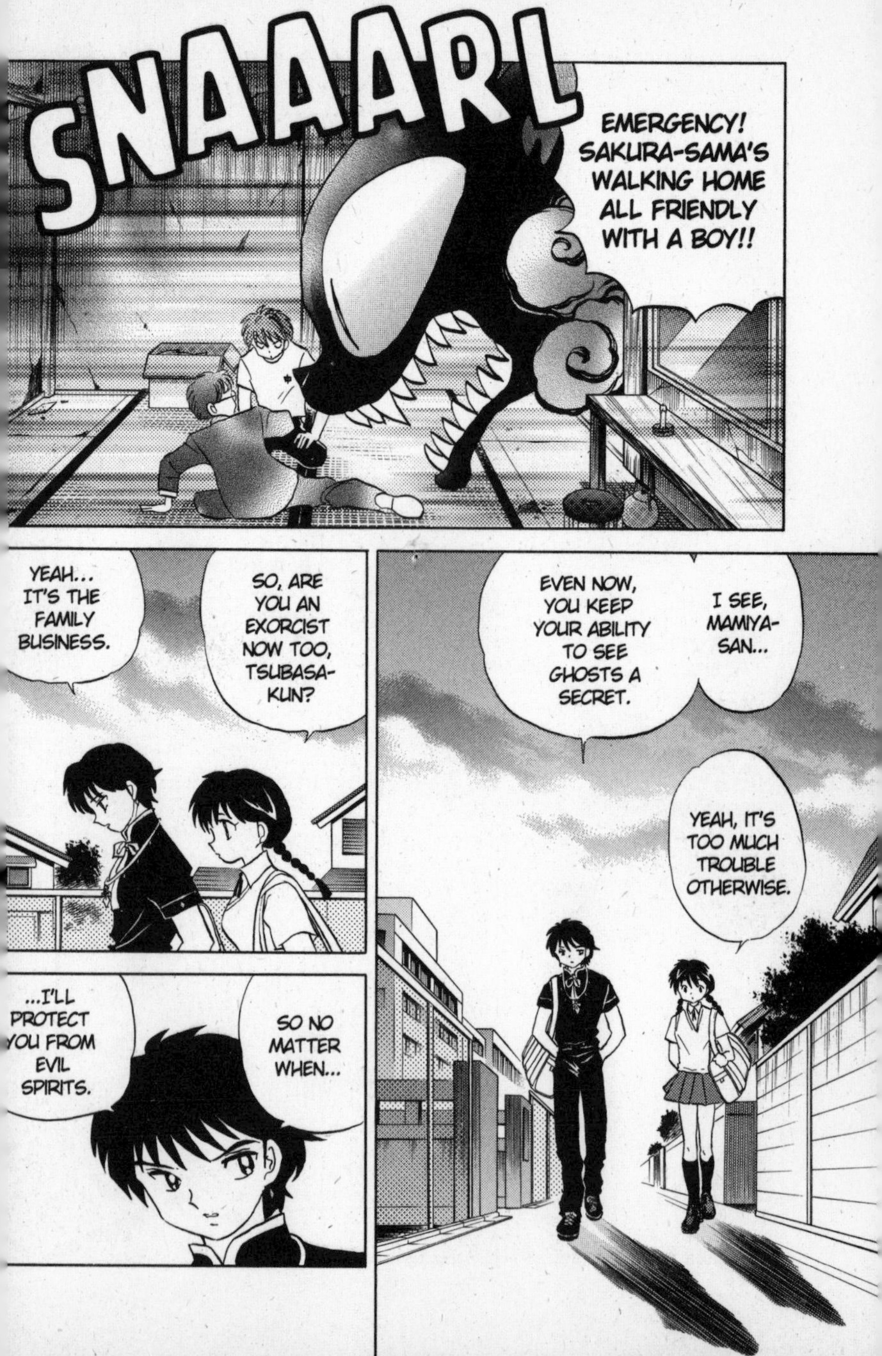
SNAAARL
EMERGENCY! SAKURA-SAMA'S WALKING HOME ALL FRIENDLY WITH A BOY!!
I SEE, MAMIYA-SAN...
EVEN NOW, YOU KEEP YOUR ABILITY TO SEE GHOSTS A SECRET.
YEAH, IT'S TOO MUCH TROUBLE OTHERWISE.
SO, ARE YOU AN EXORCIST NOW TOO, TSUBASA-KUN?
YEAH... IT'S THE FAMILY BUSINESS.
SO NO MATTER WHEN...
...I'LL PROTECT YOU FROM EVIL SPIRITS.

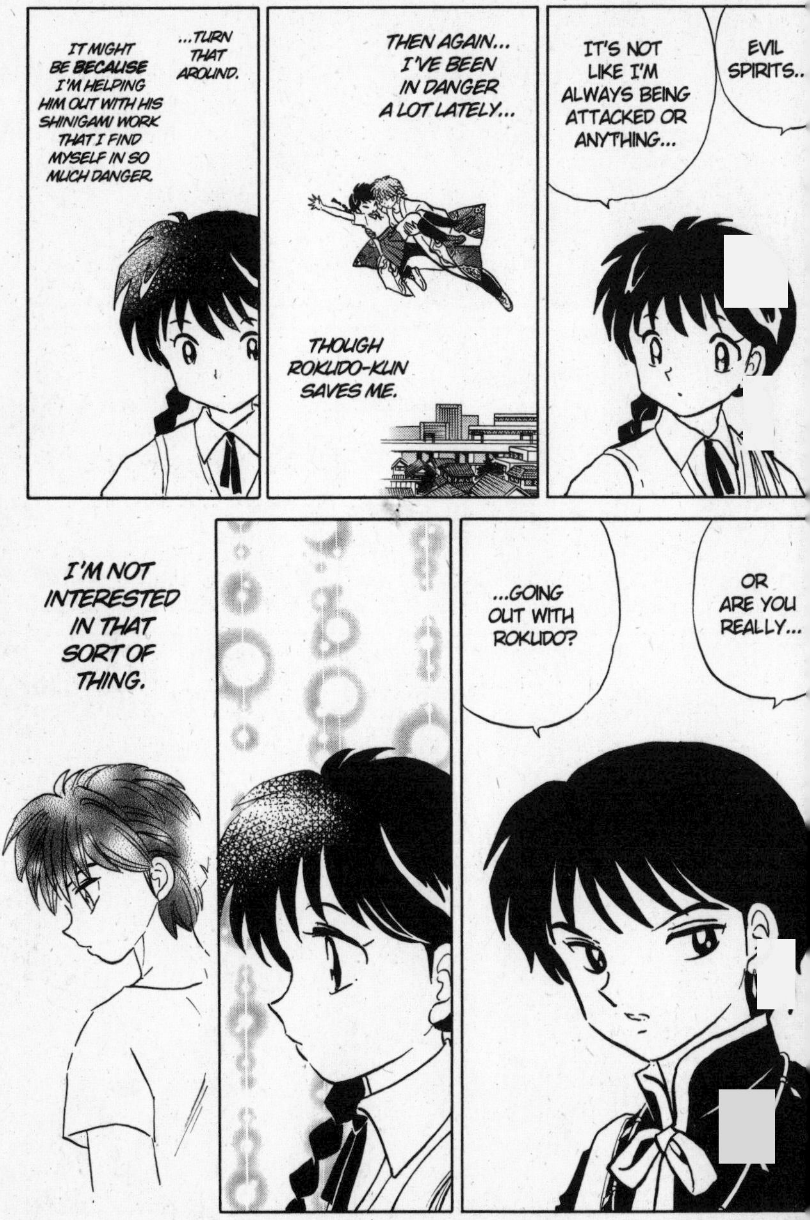
EVIL SPIRITS..
IT'S NOT LIKE I'M ALWAYS BEING ATTACKED OR ANYTHING...
THEN AGAIN... I'VE BEEN IN DANGER A LOT LATELY...
THOUGH ROKUDO-KUN SAVES ME.
...TURN THAT AROUND.
IT MIGHT BE BECAUSE I'M HELPING HIM OUT WITH HIS SHINIGAMI WORK THAT I FIND MYSELF IN SO MUCH DANGER.
OR ARE YOU REALLY...
...GOING OUT WITH ROKUDO?
I'M NOT INTERESTED IN THAT SORT OF THING.

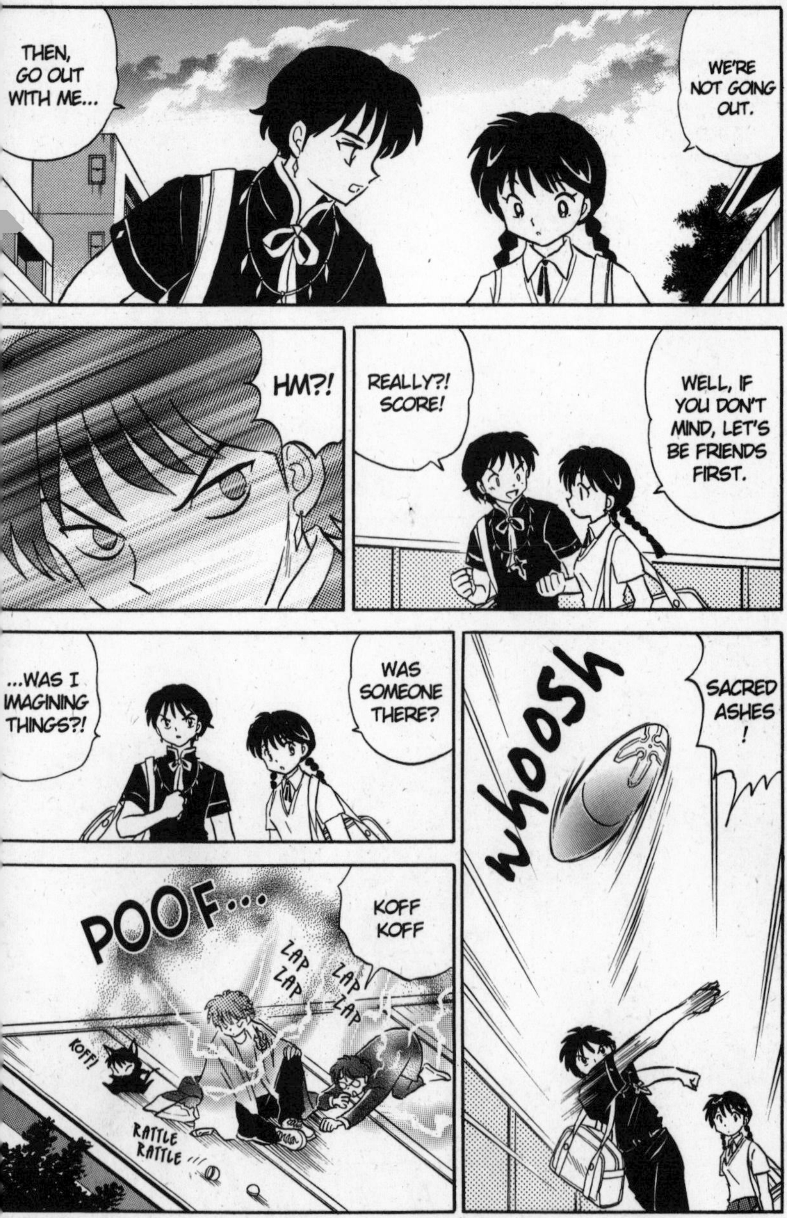
WE'RE NOT GOING OUT.
THEN, GO OUT WITH ME...
WELL, IF YOU DON'T MIND, LET'S BE FRIENDS FIRST.
REALLY?! SCORE!
HM?!
SACRED ASHES!
whoosh
WAS SOMEONE THERE?
...WAS I IMAGINING THINGS?!
POOF...
KOFF KOFF
ZAP ZAP
ZAP ZAP
KOFF!
RATTLE RATTLE

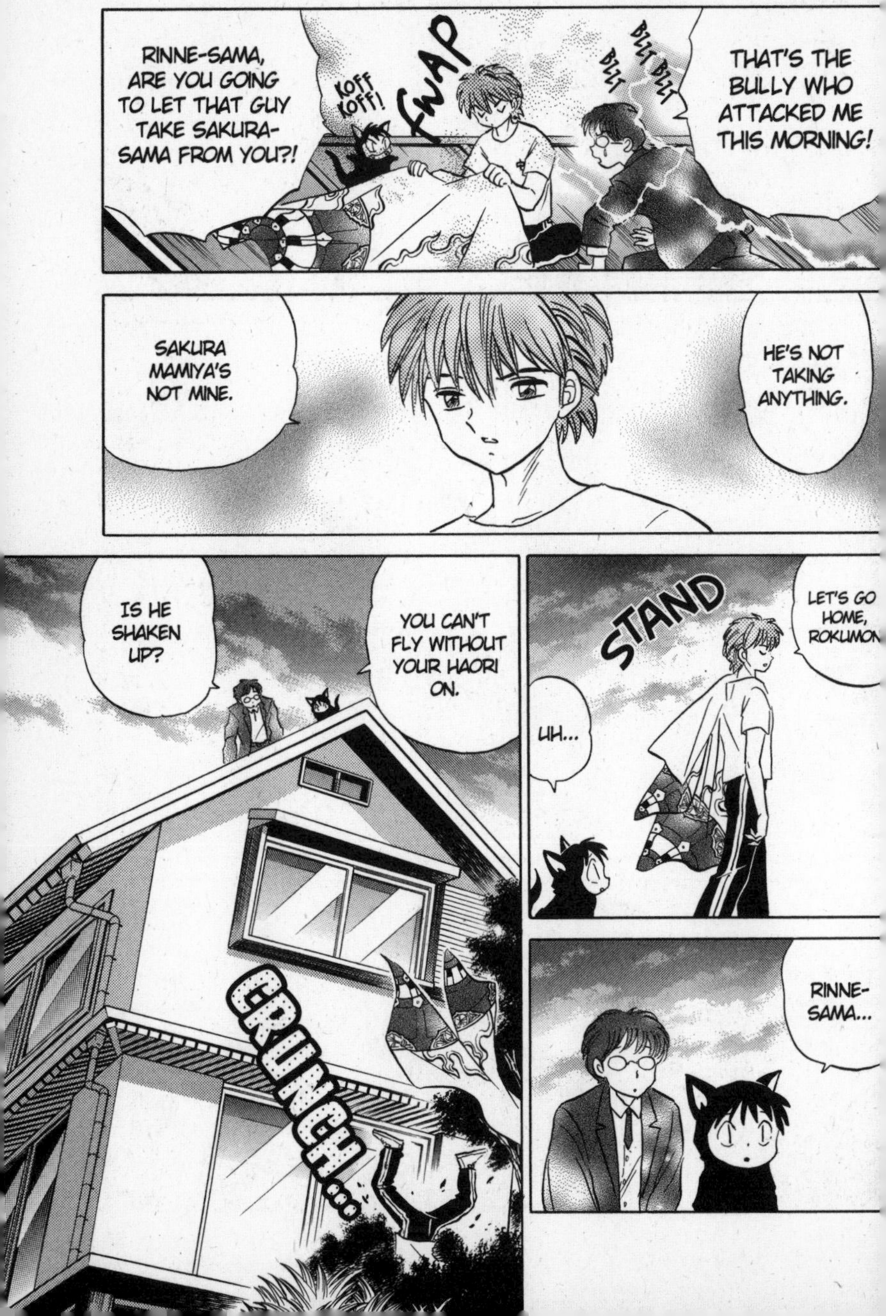
THAT'S THE BULLY WHO ATTACKED ME THIS MORNING!
BZZT BZZT BZZT
FWAP
KOFF KOFF!
RINNE-SAMA, ARE YOU GOING TO LET THAT GUY TAKE SAKURA-SAMA FROM YOU?!
HE'S NOT TAKING ANYTHING.
SAKURA MAMIYA'S NOT MINE.
LET'S GO HOME, ROKUMON
STAND
UH...
RINNE-SAMA...
YOU CAN'T FLY WITHOUT YOUR HAORI ON.
IS HE SHAKEN UP?
CRUNCH...

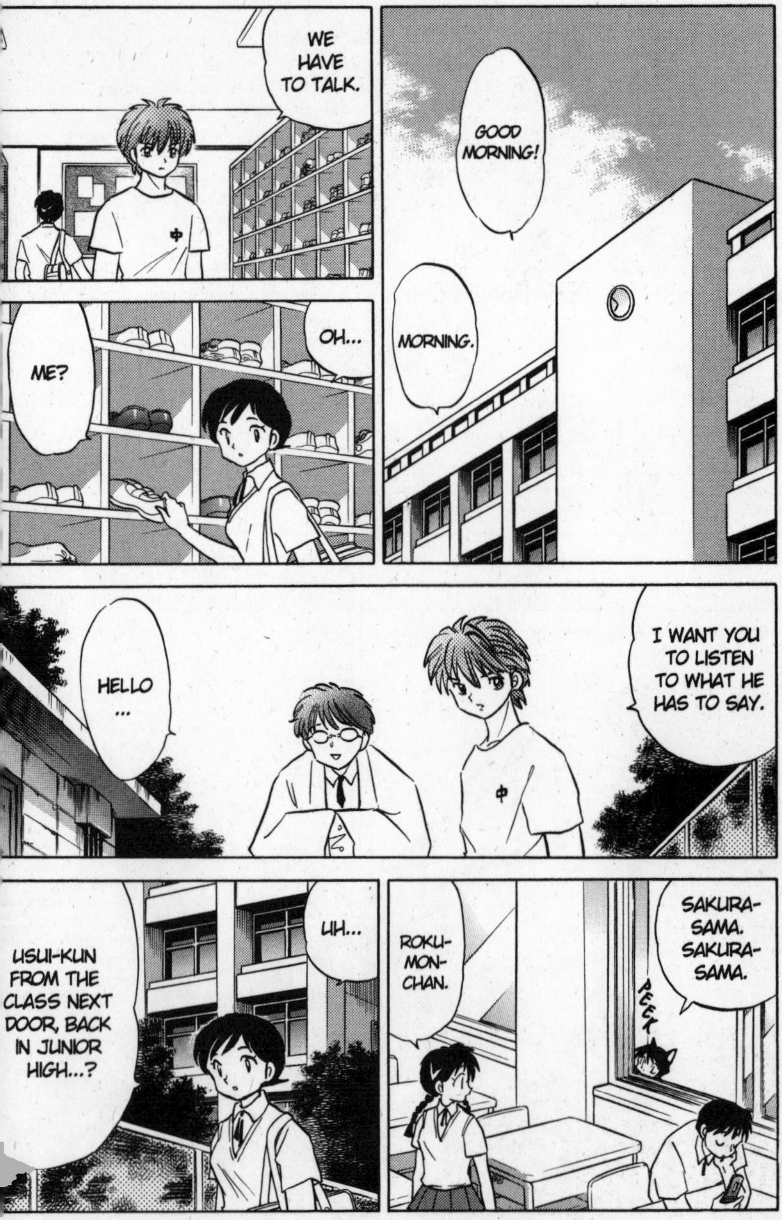
GOOD MORNING!
MORNING.
WE HAVE TO TALK.
OH...
ME?
I WANT YOU TO LISTEN TO WHAT HE HAS TO SAY.
HELLO ...
SAKURA-SAMA. SAKURA-SAMA.
PEEK
ROKU-MON-CHAN.
UH...
USUI-KUN FROM THE CLASS NEXT DOOR, BACK IN JUNIOR HIGH...?

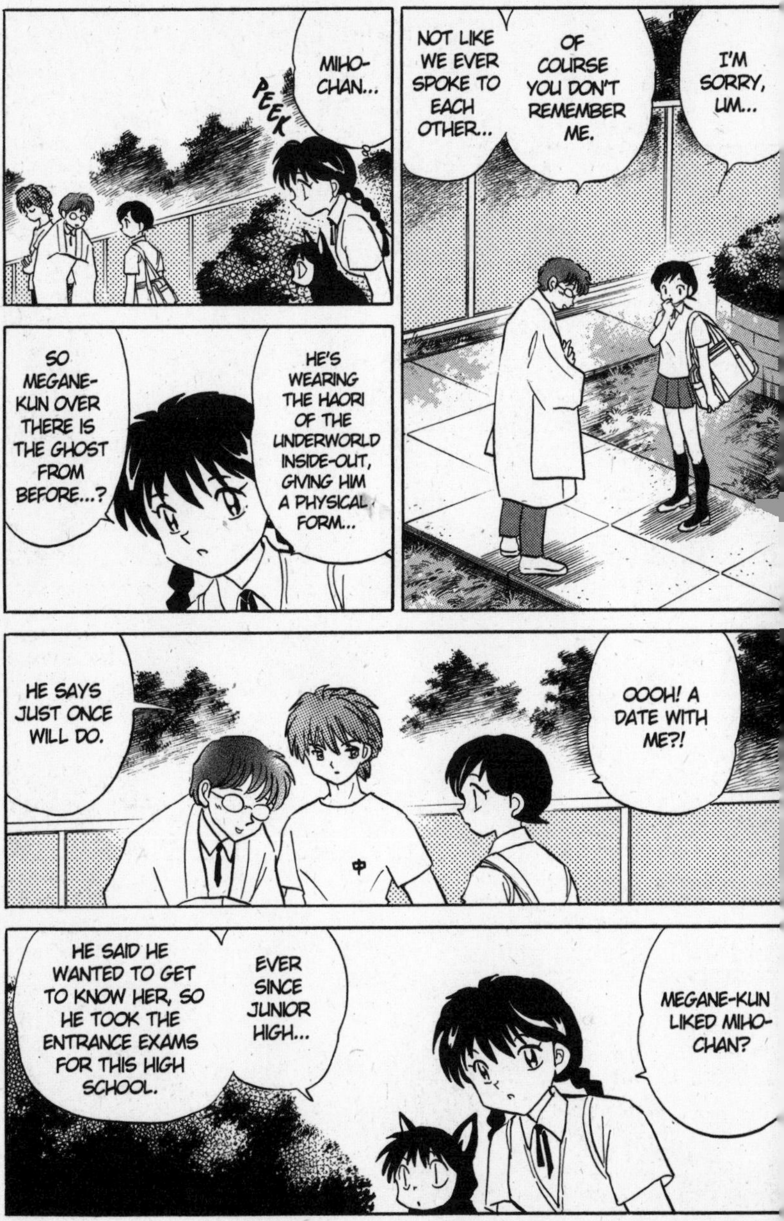
I'M SORRY, UM...
OF COURSE YOU DON'T REMEMBER ME.
NOT LIKE WE EVER SPOKE TO EACH OTHER...
MIHO-CHAN...
PEEK
HE'S WEARING THE HAORI OF THE UNDERWORLD INSIDE-OUT, GIVING HIM A PHYSICAL FORM...
SO MEGANE-KUN OVER THERE IS THE GHOST FROM BEFORE...?
OOOH! A DATE WITH ME?!
HE SAYS JUST ONCE WILL DO.
MEGANE-KUN LIKED MIHO-CHAN?
EVER SINCE JUNIOR HIGH...
HE SAID HE WANTED TO GET TO KNOW HER, SO HE TOOK THE ENTRANCE EXAMS FOR THIS HIGH SCHOOL.

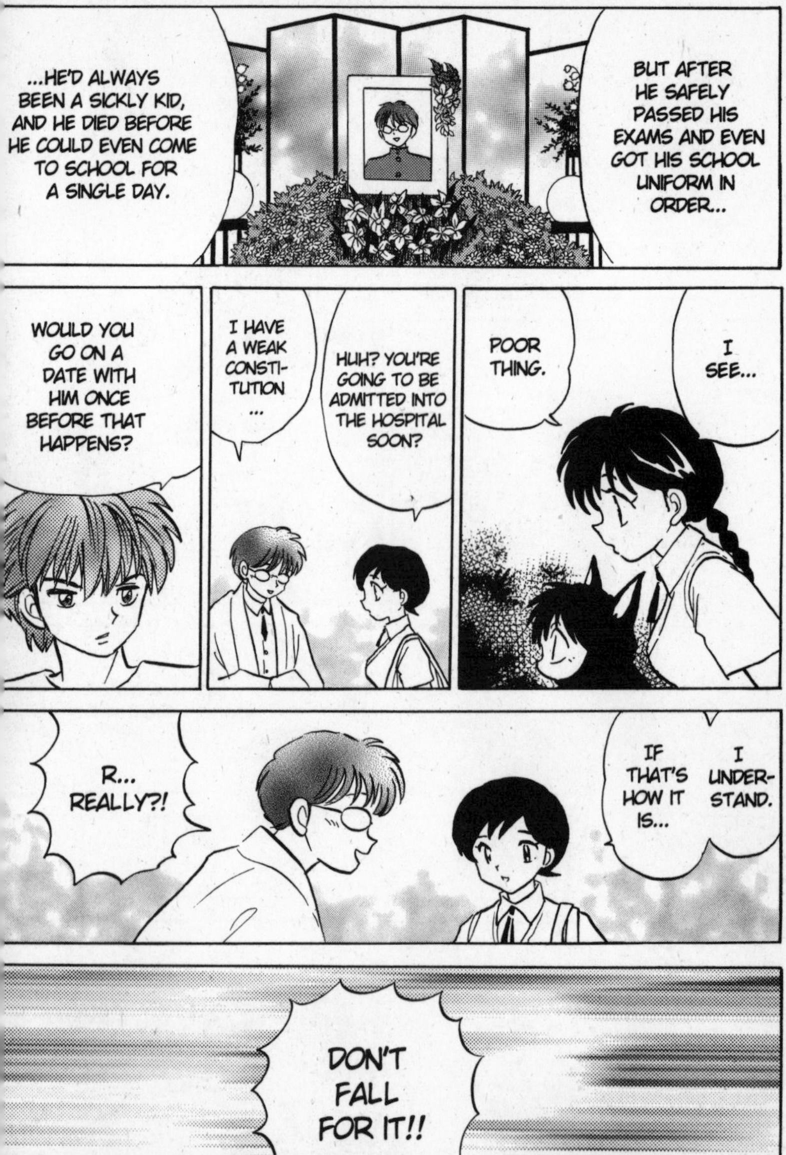

BUT AFTER HE SAFELY PASSED HIS EXAMS AND EVEN GOT HIS SCHOOL UNIFORM IN ORDER...
...HE'D ALWAYS BEEN A SICKLY KID, AND HE DIED BEFORE HE COULD EVEN COME TO SCHOOL FOR A SINGLE DAY.
I SEE...
POOR THING.
HUH? YOU'RE GOING TO BE ADMITTED INTO THE HOSPITAL SOON?
I HAVE A WEAK CONSTI-TUTION...
WOULD YOU GO ON A DATE WITH HIM ONCE BEFORE THAT HAPPENS?
I UNDER-STAND.
IF THAT'S HOW IT IS...
R... REALLY?!
DON'T FALL FOR IT!!

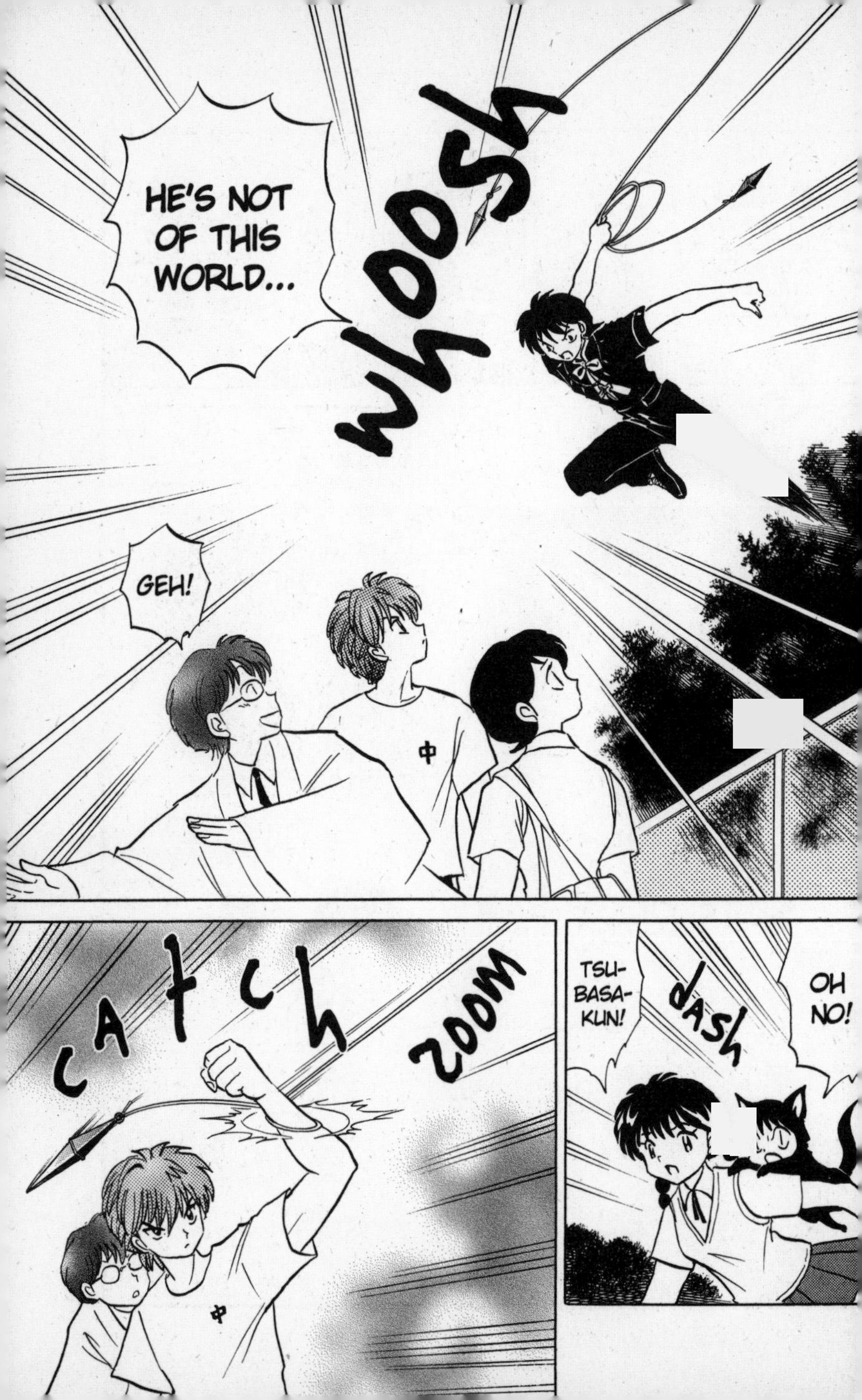

HE'S NOT OF THIS WORLD...
whoosh
GEH!
OH NO!
dash
TSU-BASA-KUN!
catch
zoom

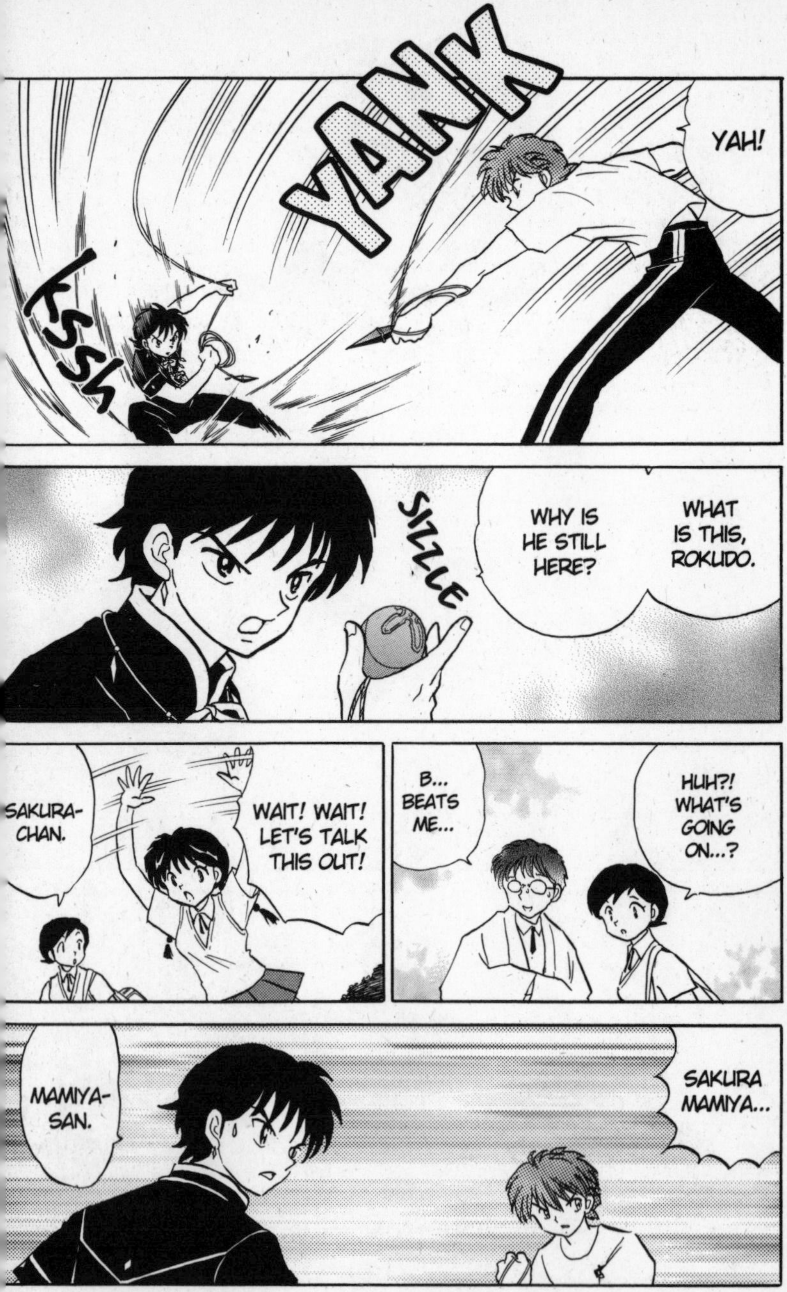
YAH!
YANK
KSSH
WHAT IS THIS, ROKUDO.
WHY IS HE STILL HERE?
SIZZLE
HUH?! WHAT'S GOING ON...?
B... BEATS ME...
WAIT! WAIT! LET'S TALK THIS OUT!
SAKURA-CHAN.
SAKURA MAMIYA...
MAMIYA-SAN.

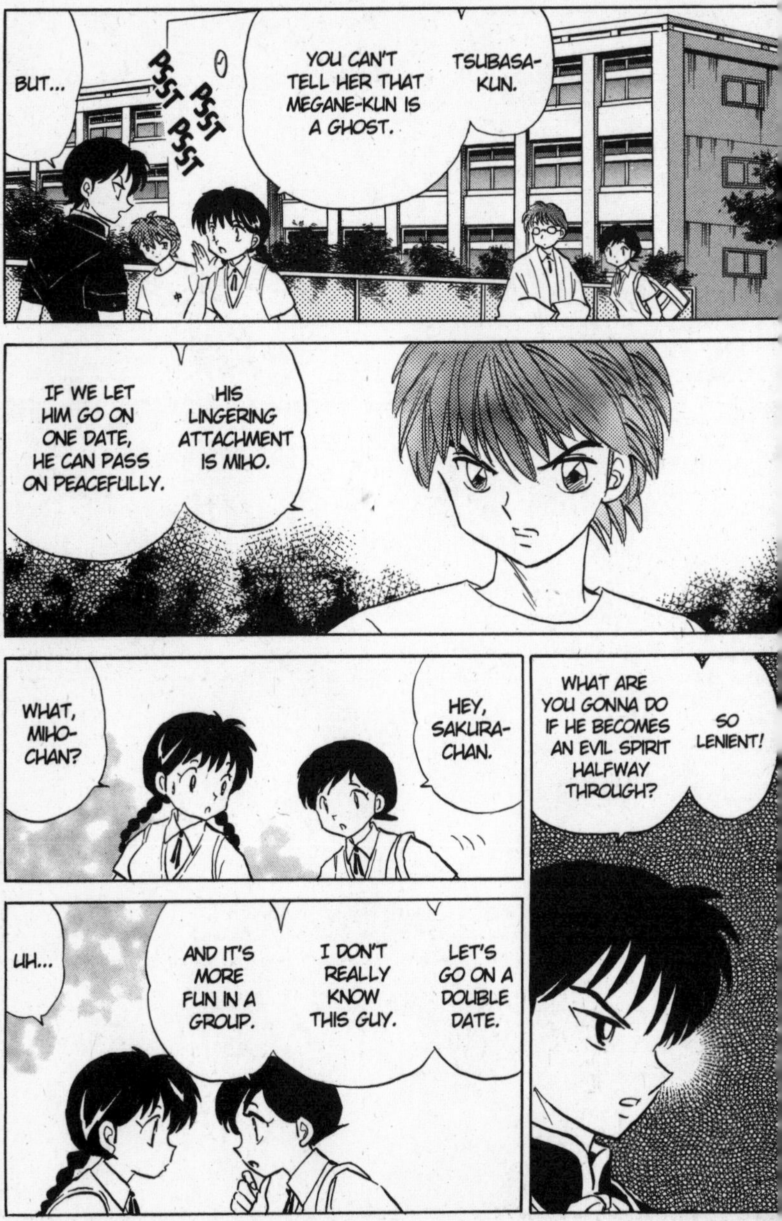
TSUBASA-KUN.
YOU CAN'T TELL HER THAT MEGANE-KUN IS A GHOST.
PSST PSST PSST PSST
BUT...
HIS LINGERING ATTACHMENT IS MIHO.
IF WE LET HIM GO ON ONE DATE, HE CAN PASS ON PEACEFULLY.
SO LENIENT!
WHAT ARE YOU GONNA DO IF HE BECOMES AN EVIL SPIRIT HALFWAY THROUGH?
HEY, SAKURA-CHAN.
WHAT, MIHO-CHAN?
LET'S GO ON A DOUBLE DATE.
I DON'T REALLY KNOW THIS GUY.
AND IT'S MORE FUN IN A GROUP.
UH...

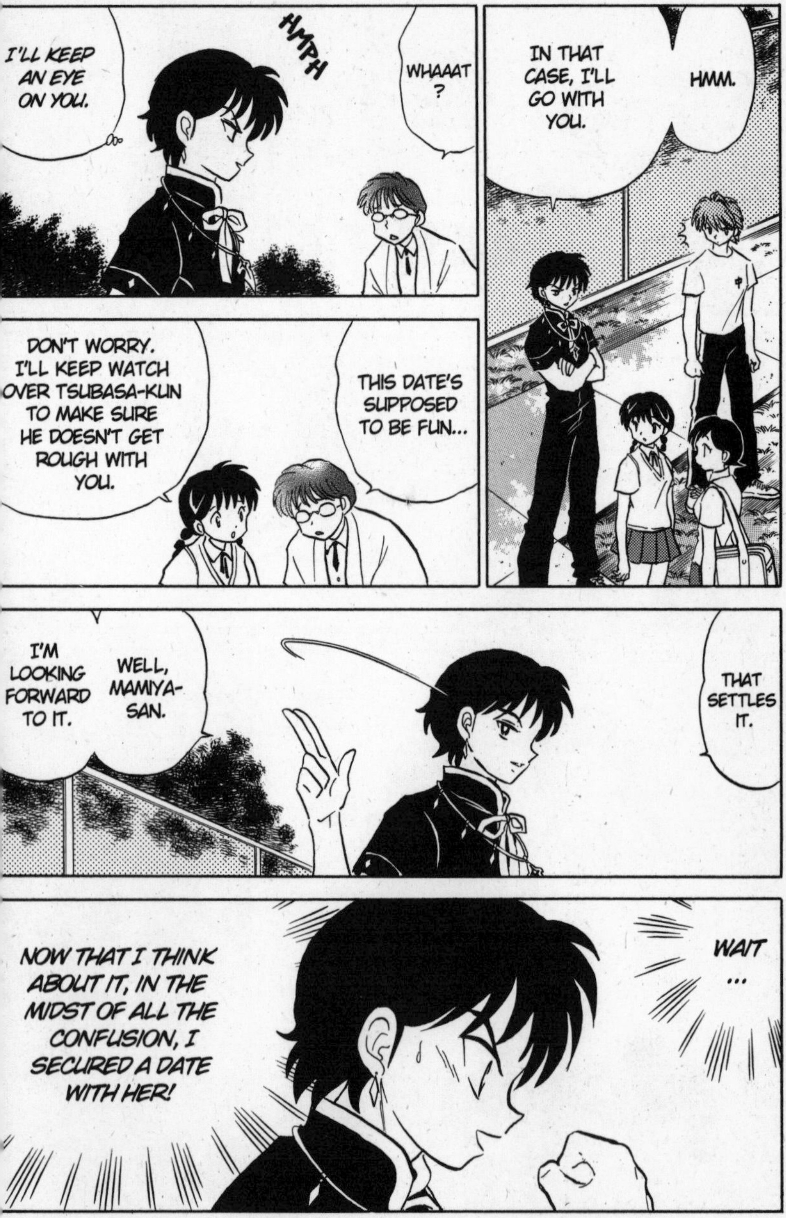
HMM.
IN THAT CASE, I'LL GO WITH YOU.
WHAAAT?
HMPH
I'LL KEEP AN EYE ON YOU.
THIS DATE'S SUPPOSED TO BE FUN...
DON'T WORRY. I'LL KEEP WATCH OVER TSUBASA-KUN TO MAKE SURE HE DOESN'T GET ROUGH WITH YOU.
THAT SETTLES IT.
WELL, MAMIYA-SAN.
I'M LOOKING FORWARD TO IT.
WAIT...
NOW THAT I THINK ABOUT IT, IN THE MIDST OF ALL THE CONFUSION, I SECURED A DATE WITH HER!

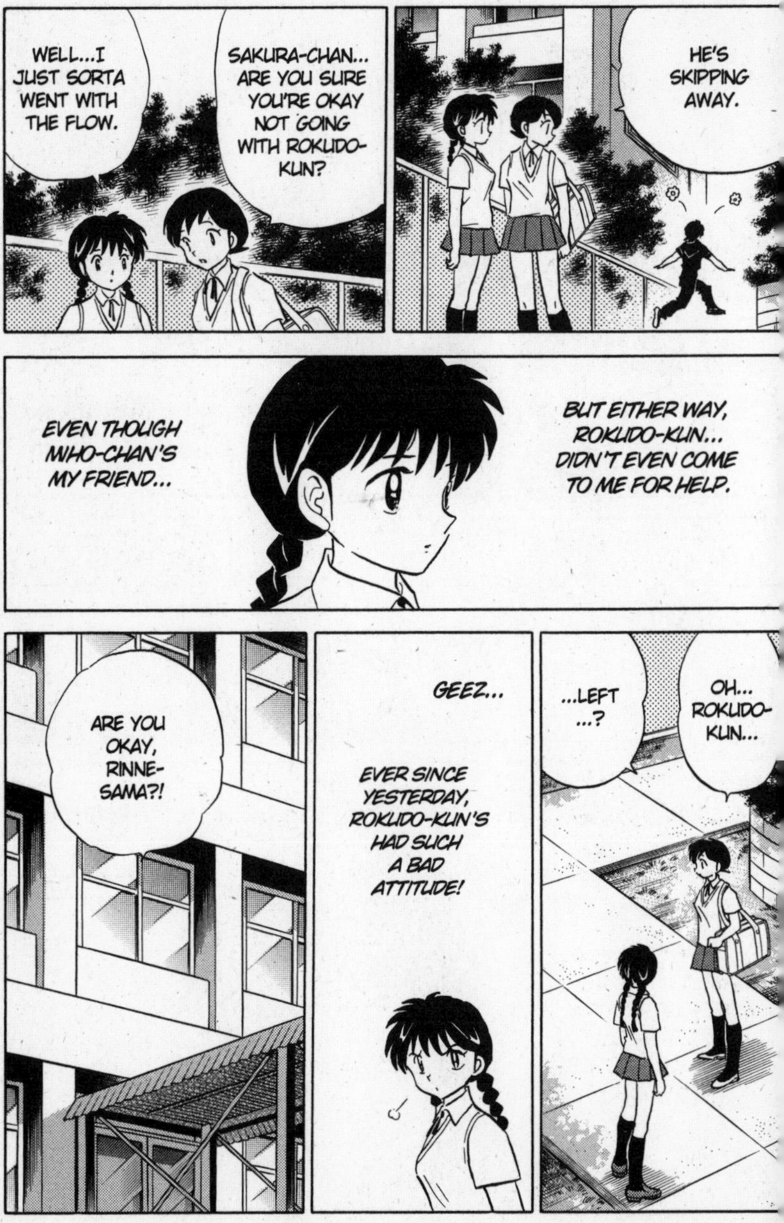
HE'S SKIPPING AWAY.
SAKURA-CHAN... ARE YOU SURE YOU'RE OKAY NOT GOING WITH ROKUDO-KUN?
WELL...I JUST SORTA WENT WITH THE FLOW.
BUT EITHER WAY, ROKUDO-KUN... DIDN'T EVEN COME TO ME FOR HELP.
EVEN THOUGH MIHO-CHAN'S MY FRIEND...
OH... ROKUDO-KUN...
...LEFT ...?
GEEZ...
EVER SINCE YESTERDAY, ROKUDO-KUN'S HAD SUCH A BAD ATTITUDE!
ARE YOU OKAY, RINNE-SAMA?!

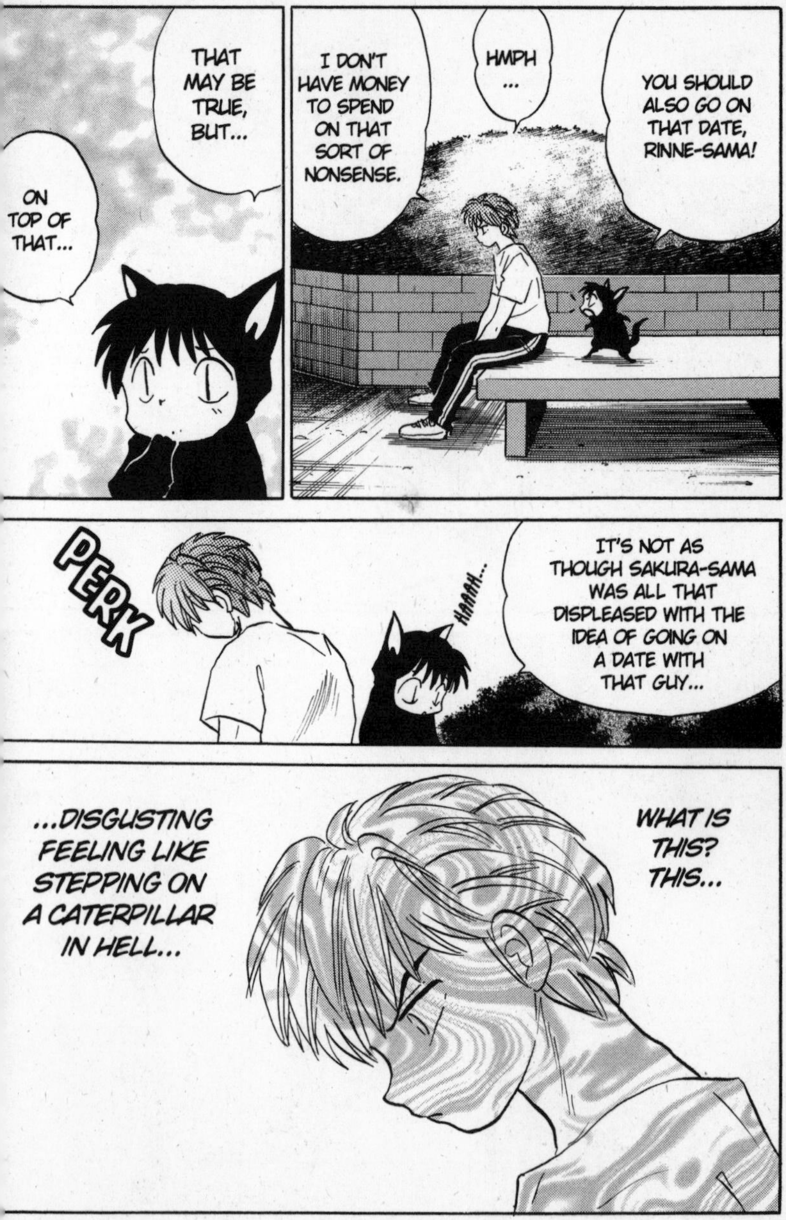
YOU SHOULD ALSO GO ON THAT DATE, RINNE-SAMA!
HMPH ...
I DON'T HAVE MONEY TO SPEND ON THAT SORT OF NONSENSE.
THAT MAY BE TRUE, BUT...
ON TOP OF THAT...
IT'S NOT AS THOUGH SAKURA-SAMA WAS ALL THAT DISPLEASED WITH THE IDEA OF GOING ON A DATE WITH THAT GUY...
HAAAH...
PERK
WHAT IS THIS? THIS...
...DISGUSTING FEELING LIKE STEPPING ON A CATERPILLAR IN HELL...

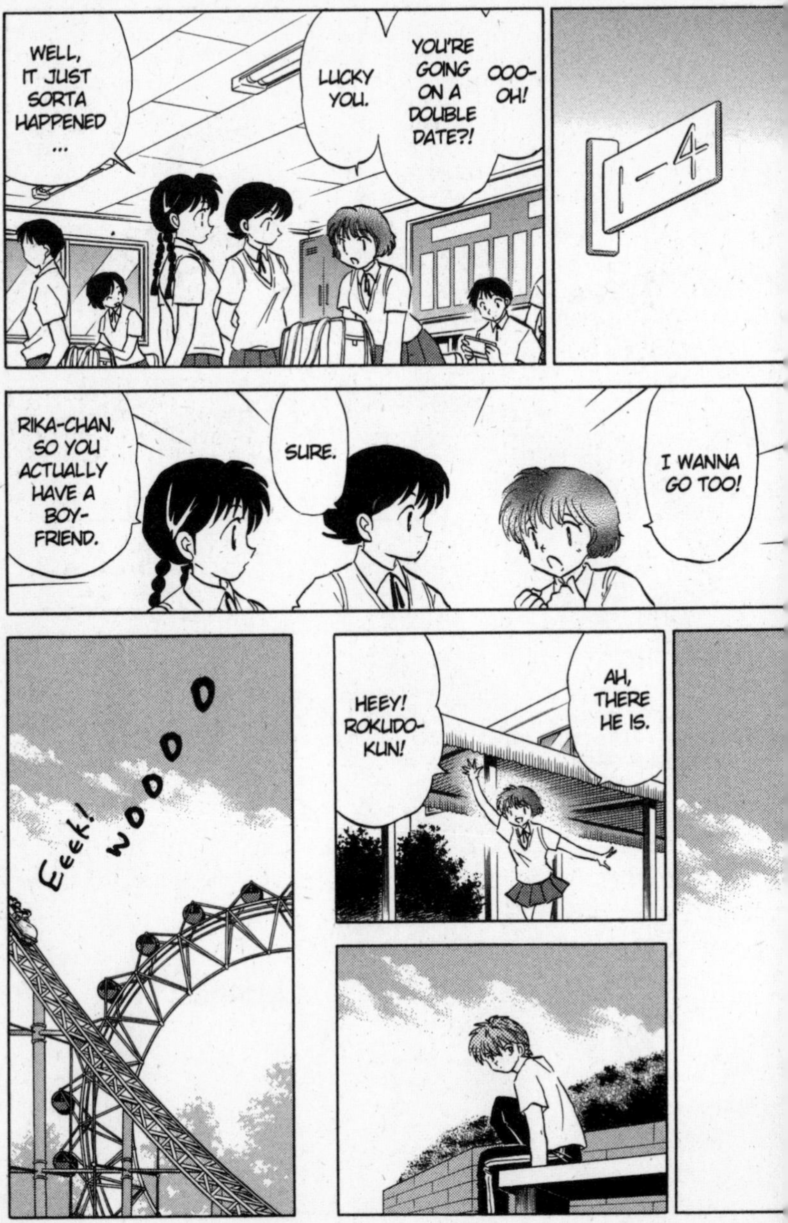
1-4
OOO-OH!
YOU'RE GOING ON A DOUBLE DATE?!
LUCKY YOU.
WELL, IT JUST SORTA HAPPENED ...
I WANNA GO TOO!
SURE.
RIKA-CHAN, SO YOU ACTUALLY HAVE A BOY-FRIEND.
AH, THERE HE IS.
HEEY! ROKUDO-KUN!
WOOOOO
Eeeek!

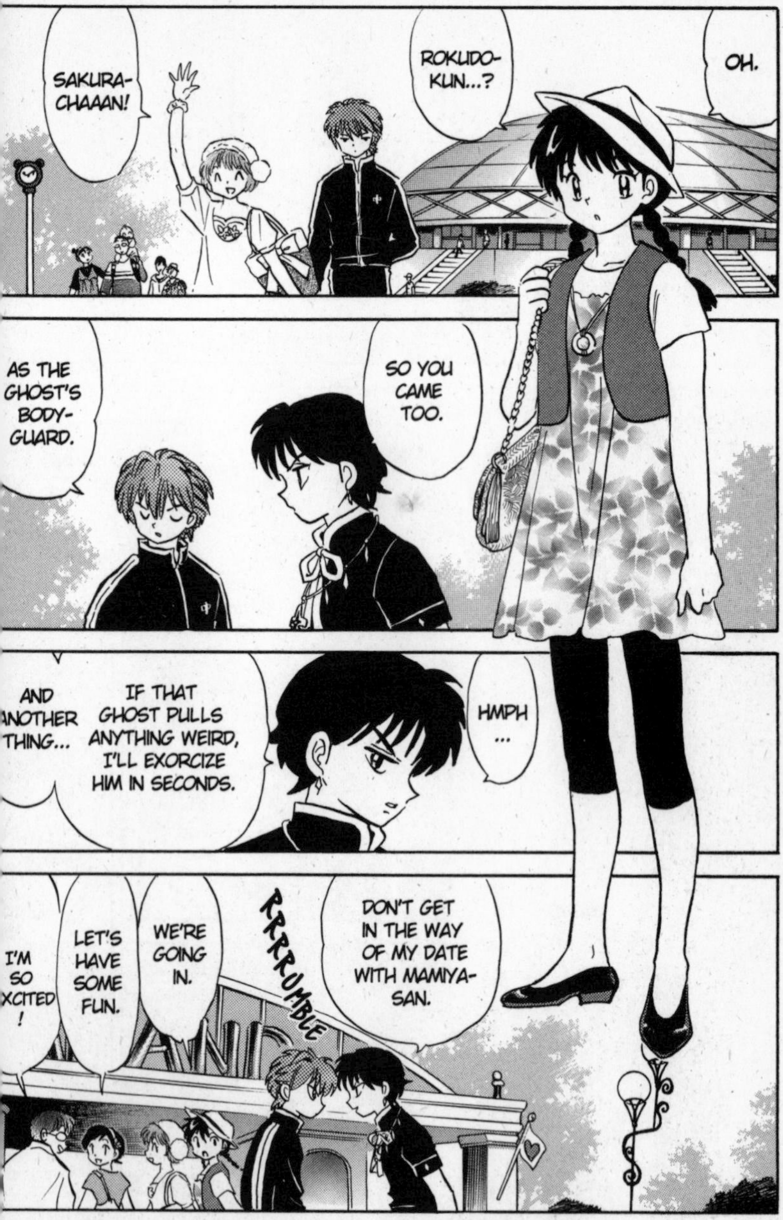
OH.
ROKUDO-KUN...?
SAKURA-CHAAAN!
SO YOU CAME TOO.
AS THE GHOST'S BODY-GUARD.
HMPH ...
IF THAT GHOST PULLS ANYTHING WEIRD, I'LL EXORCIZE HIM IN SECONDS.
AND ANOTHER THING...
DON'T GET IN THE WAY OF MY DATE WITH MAMIYA-SAN.
RRRRUMBLE
WE'RE GOING IN.
LET'S HAVE SOME FUN.
I'M SO EXCITED!

CHAPTER 21: A FUN DATE

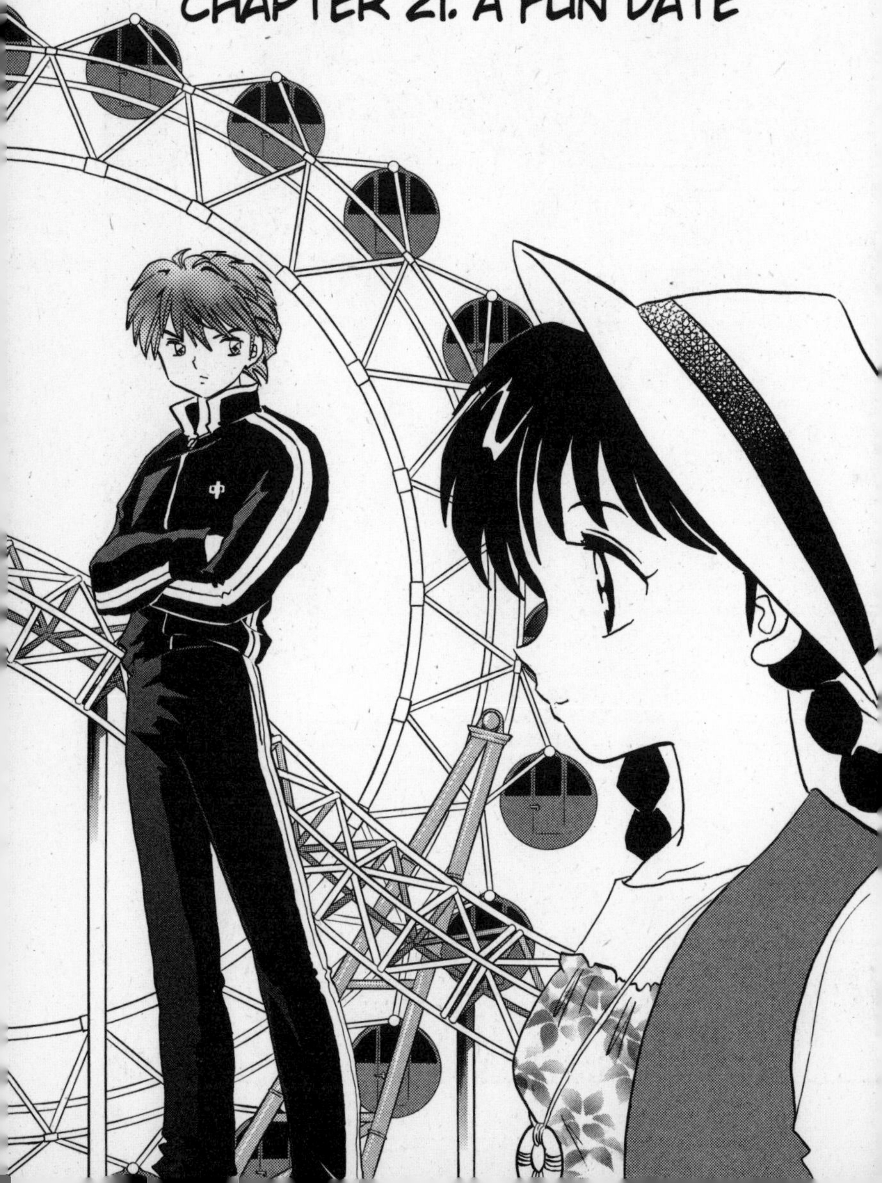

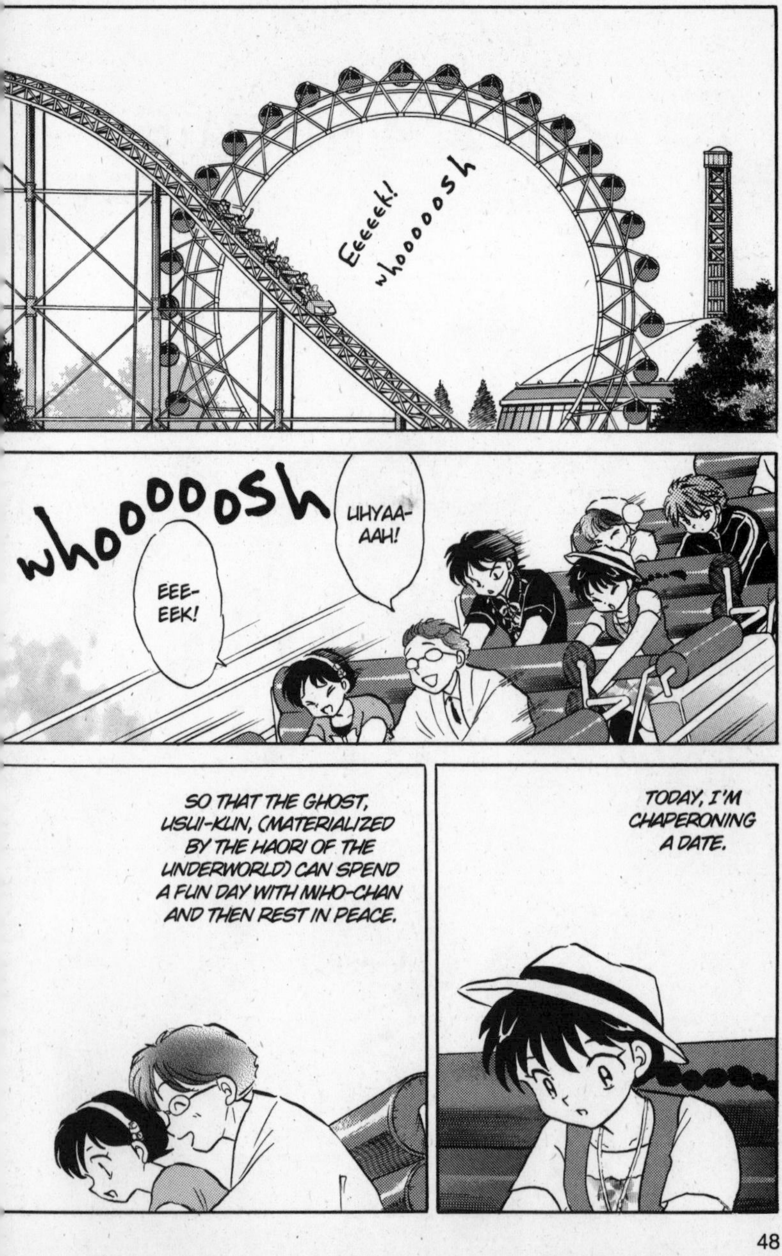
Eeeeek!
whoooosh
whooooosh
UHYAA-AAH!
EEE-EEK!
TODAY, I'M CHAPERONING A DATE.
SO THAT THE GHOST, USUI-KUN, (MATERIALIZED BY THE HAORI OF THE UNDERWORLD) CAN SPEND A FUN DAY WITH MIHO-CHAN AND THEN REST IN PEACE.

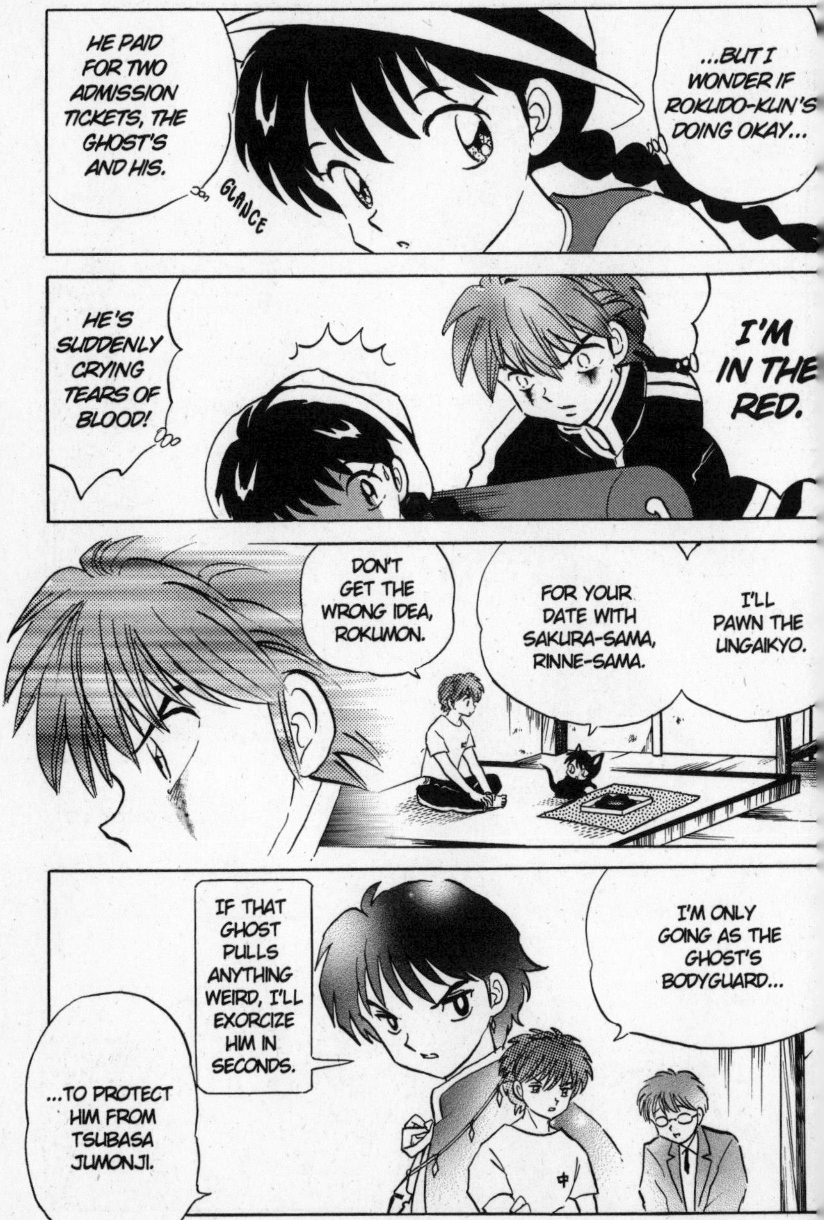
...BUT I WONDER IF ROKUDO-KUN'S DOING OKAY...
GLANCE
HE PAID FOR TWO ADMISSION TICKETS, THE GHOST'S AND HIS.
I'M IN THE RED.
HE'S SUDDENLY CRYING TEARS OF BLOOD!
I'LL PAWN THE UNGAIKYO.
FOR YOUR DATE WITH SAKURA-SAMA, RINNE-SAMA.
DON'T GET THE WRONG IDEA, ROKUMON.
I'M ONLY GOING AS THE GHOST'S BODYGUARD...
IF THAT GHOST PULLS ANYTHING WEIRD, I'LL EXORCIZE HIM IN SECONDS.
...TO PROTECT HIM FROM TSUBASA JUMONJI.

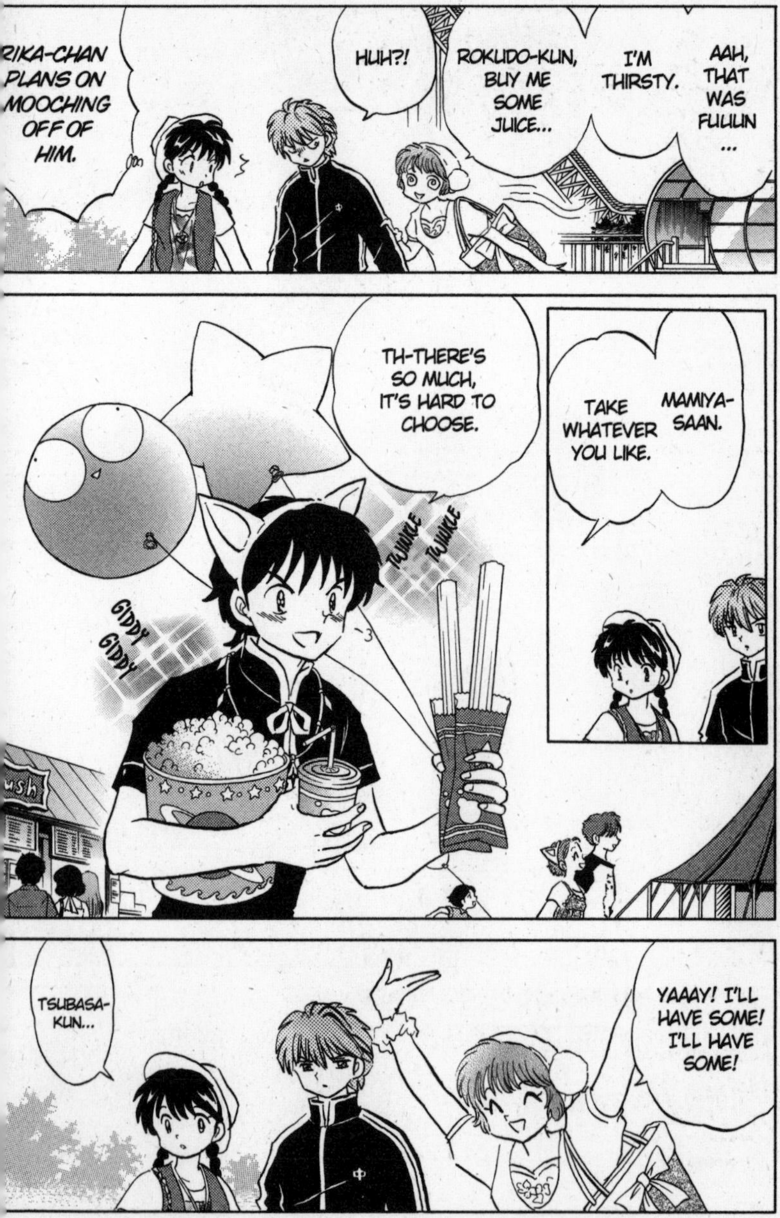
AAH, THAT WAS FUUUN ...
I'M THIRSTY.
ROKUDO-KUN, BUY ME SOME JUICE...
HUH?!
RIKA-CHAN PLANS ON MOOCHING OFF OF HIM.
MAMIYA-SAAN.
TAKE WHATEVER YOU LIKE.
TH-THERE'S SO MUCH, IT'S HARD TO CHOOSE.
TWINKLE TWINKLE
GIDDY GIDDY
YAAAY! I'LL HAVE SOME! I'LL HAVE SOME!
TSUBASA-KUN...

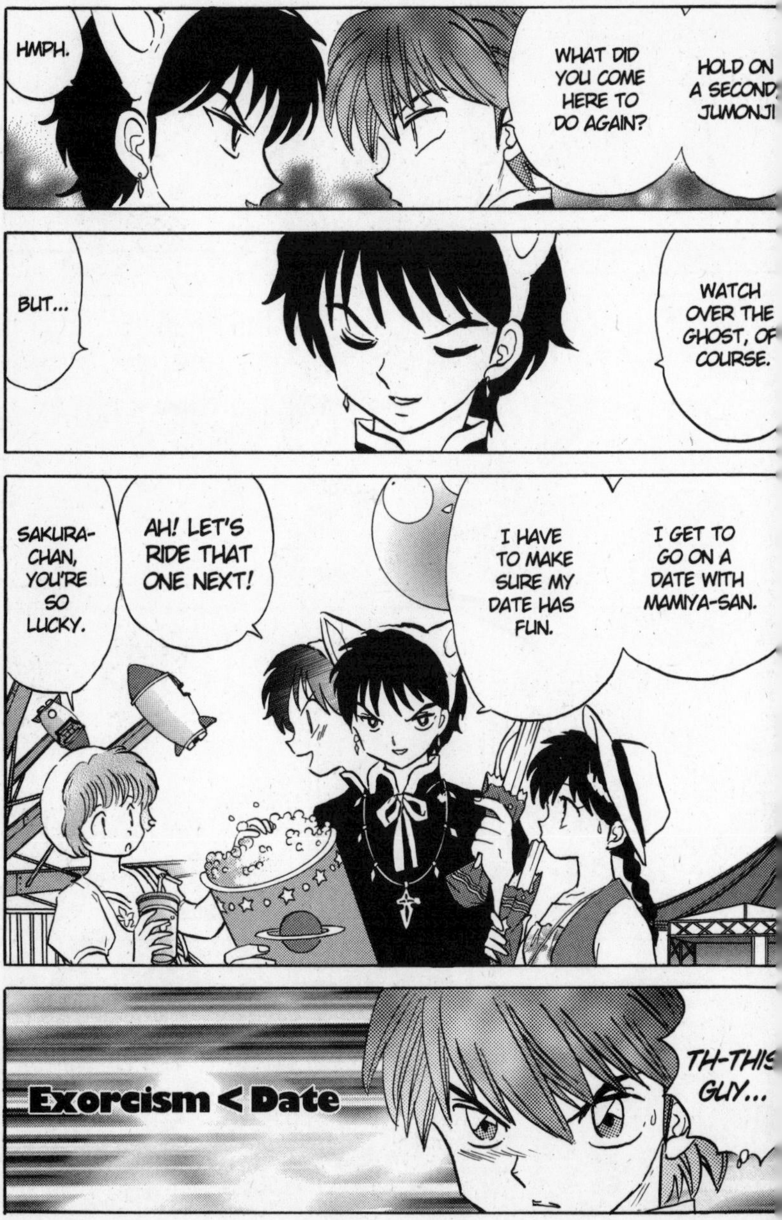
HOLD ON A SECOND, JUMONJI
WHAT DID YOU COME HERE TO DO AGAIN?
HMPH.
WATCH OVER THE GHOST, OF COURSE.
BUT...
I GET TO GO ON A DATE WITH MAMIYA-SAN.
I HAVE TO MAKE SURE MY DATE HAS FUN.
AH! LET'S RIDE THAT ONE NEXT!
SAKURA-CHAN, YOU'RE SO LUCKY.
TH-THIS GUY...
Exorcism < Date

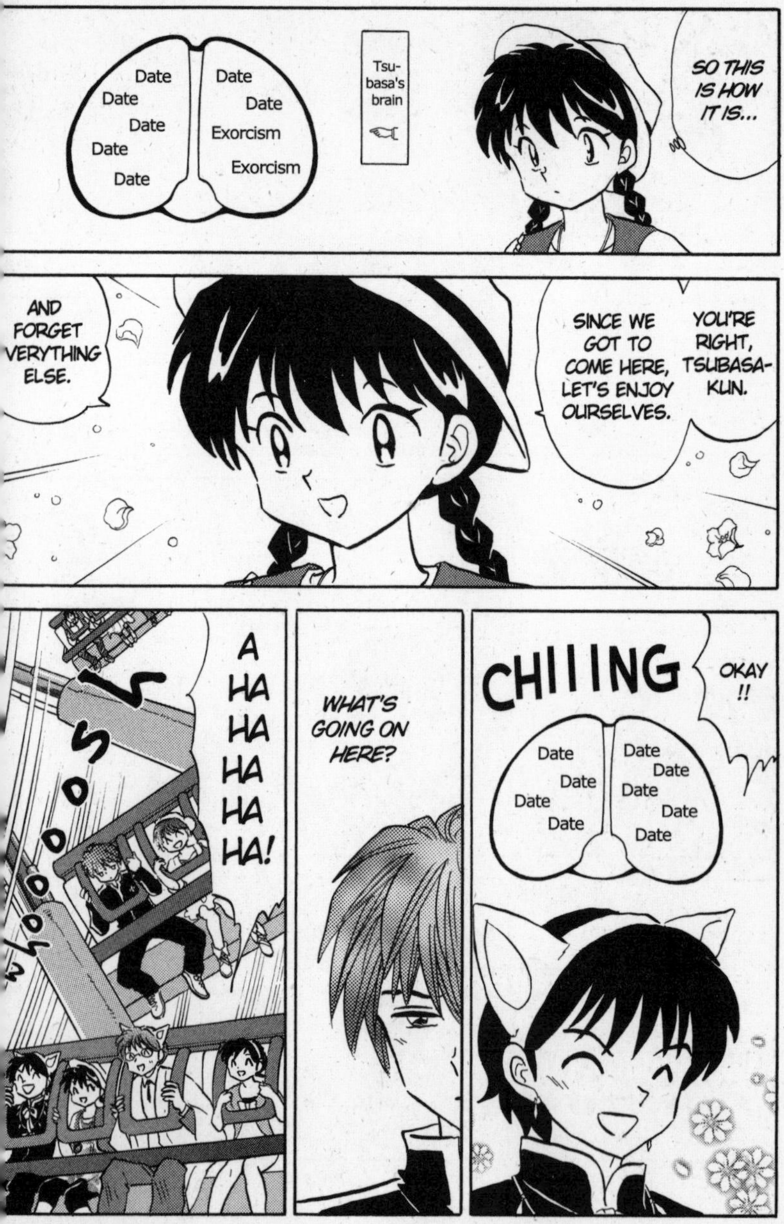
SO THIS IS HOW IT IS...
Tsu-basa's brain
Date
Date
Date
Date
Date
Date
Date
Exorcism
Exorcism
YOU'RE RIGHT, TSUBASA-KUN.
SINCE WE GOT TO COME HERE, LET'S ENJOY OURSELVES.
AND FORGET VERYTHING ELSE.
OKAY!!
CHIIING
Date
Date
Date
Date
Date
Date
Date
Date
Date
Date
WHAT'S GOING ON HERE?
A HA HA HA HA HA!

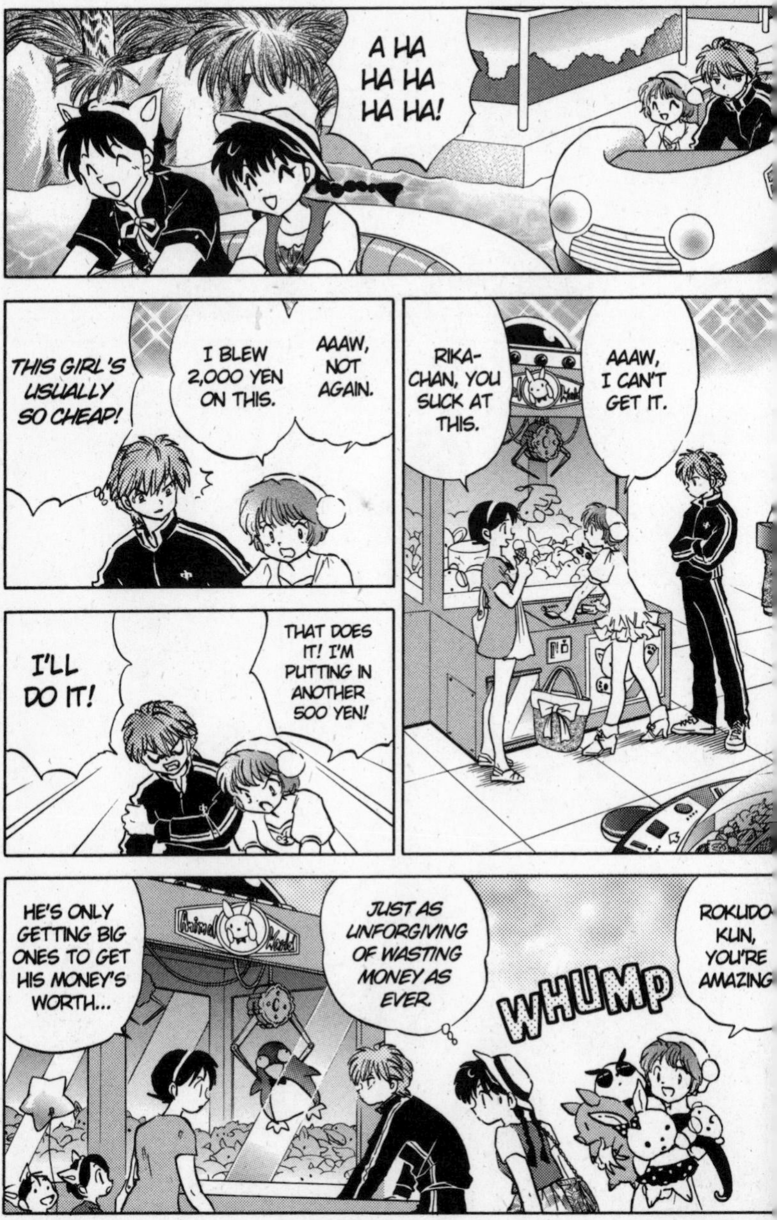
A HA HA HA HA HA!
AAAW, I CAN'T GET IT.
RIKA-CHAN, YOU SUCK AT THIS.
AAAW, NOT AGAIN.
I BLEW 2,000 YEN ON THIS.
THIS GIRL'S USUALLY SO CHEAP!
THAT DOES IT! I'M PUTTING IN ANOTHER 500 YEN!
I'LL DO IT!
ROKUDO-KUN, YOU'RE AMAZING
WHUMP
JUST AS UNFORGIVING OF WASTING MONEY AS EVER.
HE'S ONLY GETTING BIG ONES TO GET HIS MONEY'S WORTH...

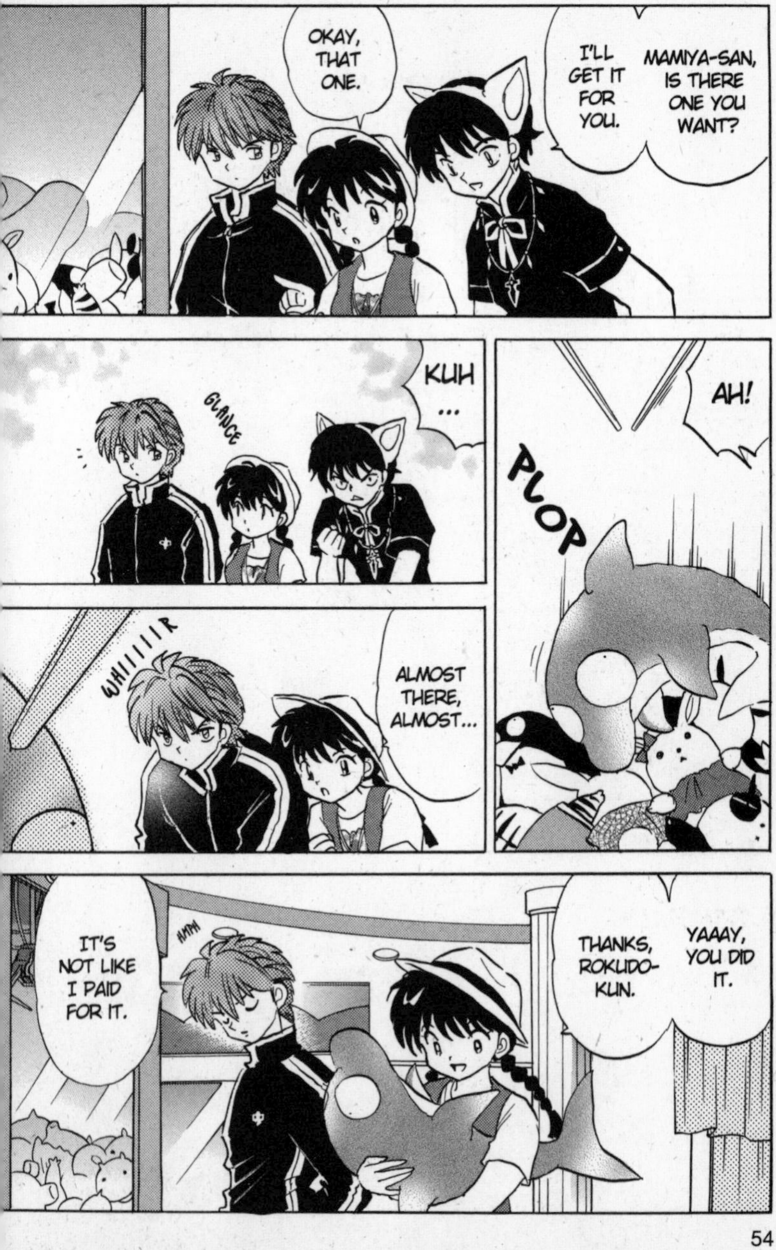
MAMIYA-SAN, IS THERE ONE YOU WANT?
I'LL GET IT FOR YOU.
OKAY, THAT ONE.
KUH ...
GLANCE
WHIIIIIR
ALMOST THERE, ALMOST...
AH!
PLOP
YAAAY, YOU DID IT.
THANKS, ROKUDO-KUN.
HMPH
IT'S NOT LIKE I PAID FOR IT.

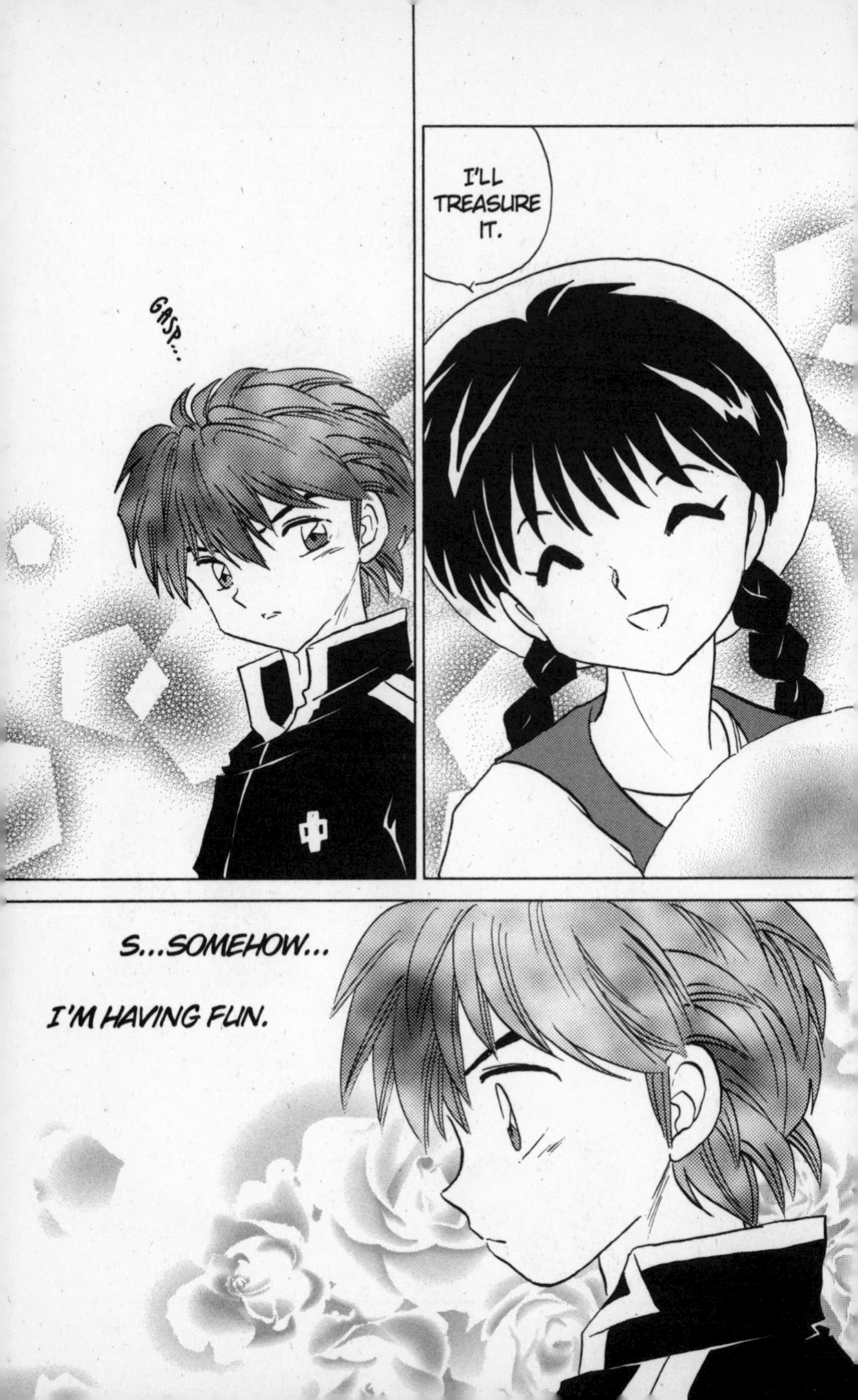
I'LL TREASURE IT.
GASP...
S...SOMEHOW...
I'M HAVING FUN.

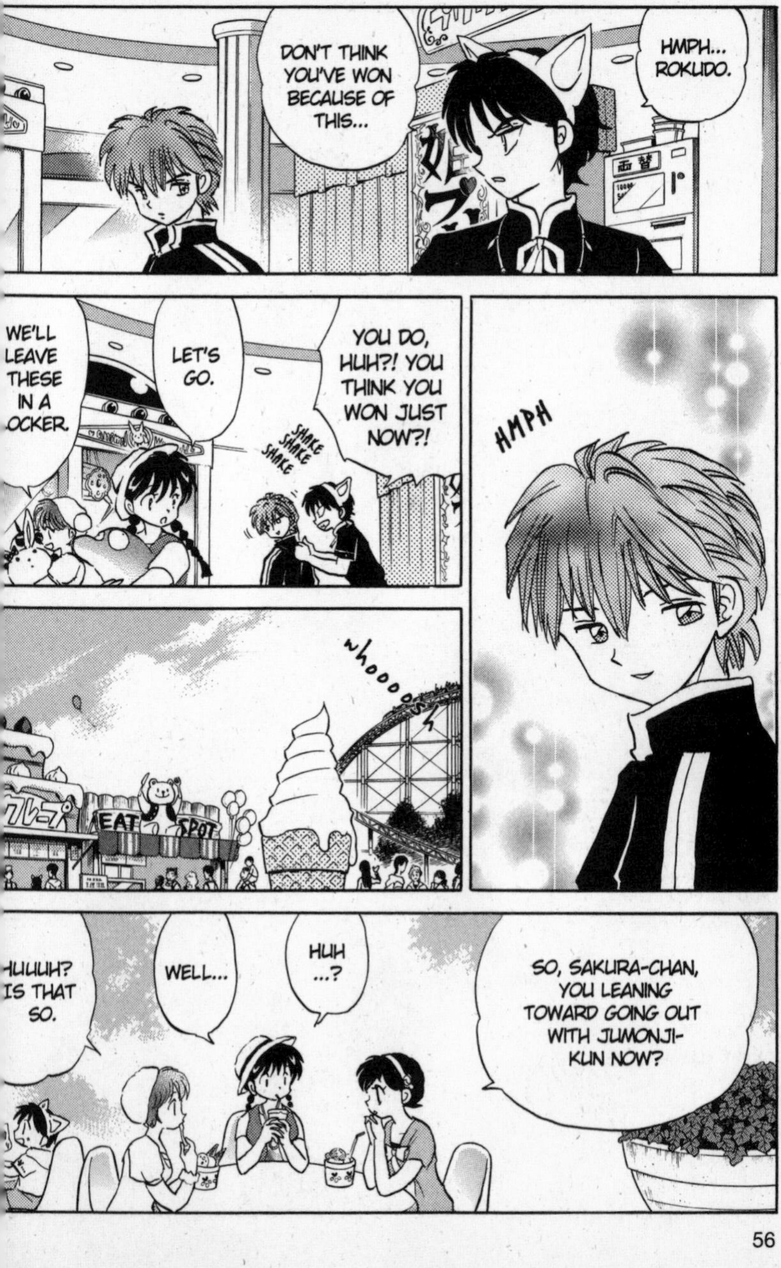
HMPH... ROKUDO.
DON'T THINK YOU'VE WON BECAUSE OF THIS...
HMPH
YOU DO, HUH?! YOU THINK YOU WON JUST NOW?!
SHAKE SHAKE SHAKE
LET'S GO.
WE'LL LEAVE THESE IN A OCKER.
whooooosh
SO, SAKURA-CHAN, YOU LEANING TOWARD GOING OUT WITH JUMONJI-KUN NOW?
HUH ...?
WELL...
HUUUH? IS THAT SO.

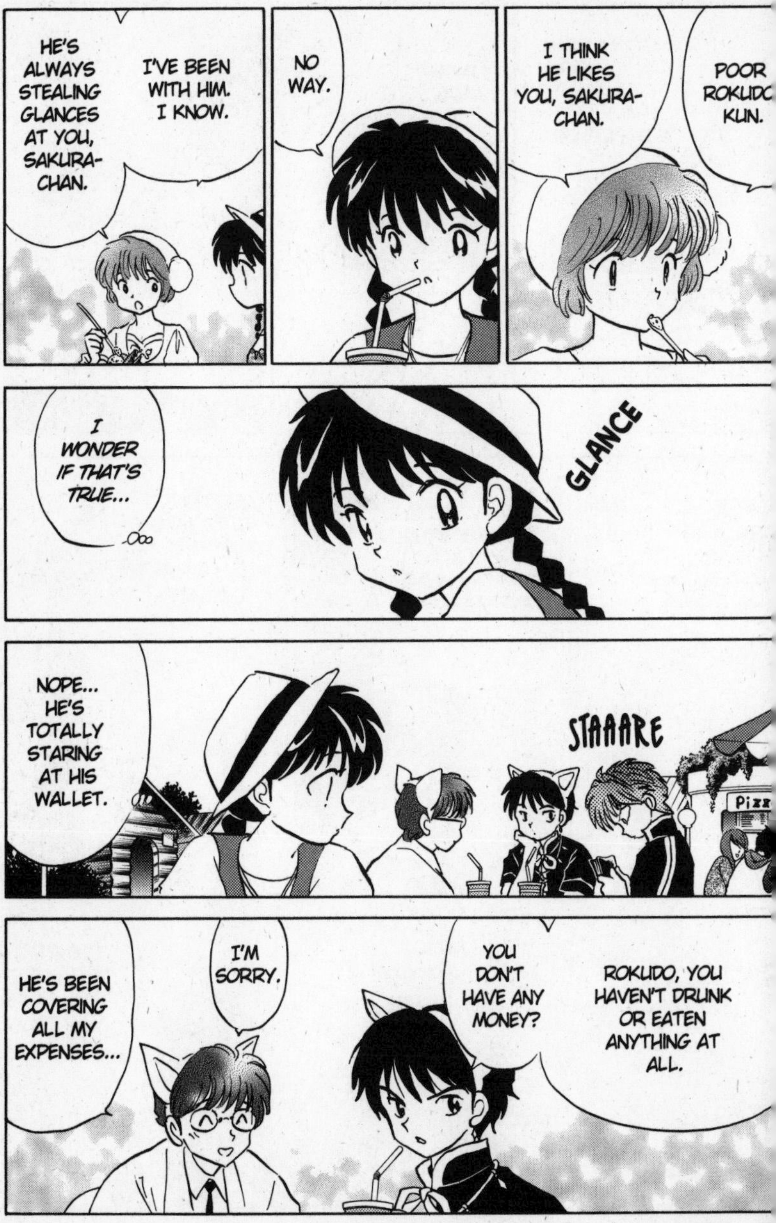
POOR ROKUDO KUN.
I THINK HE LIKES YOU, SAKURA-CHAN.
NO WAY.
HE'S ALWAYS STEALING GLANCES AT YOU, SAKURA-CHAN.
I'VE BEEN WITH HIM. I KNOW.
GLANCE
I WONDER IF THAT'S TRUE...
STAAARE
NOPE... HE'S TOTALLY STARING AT HIS WALLET.
ROKUDO, YOU HAVEN'T DRUNK OR EATEN ANYTHING AT ALL.
YOU DON'T HAVE ANY MONEY?
I'M SORRY.
HE'S BEEN COVERING ALL MY EXPENSES...

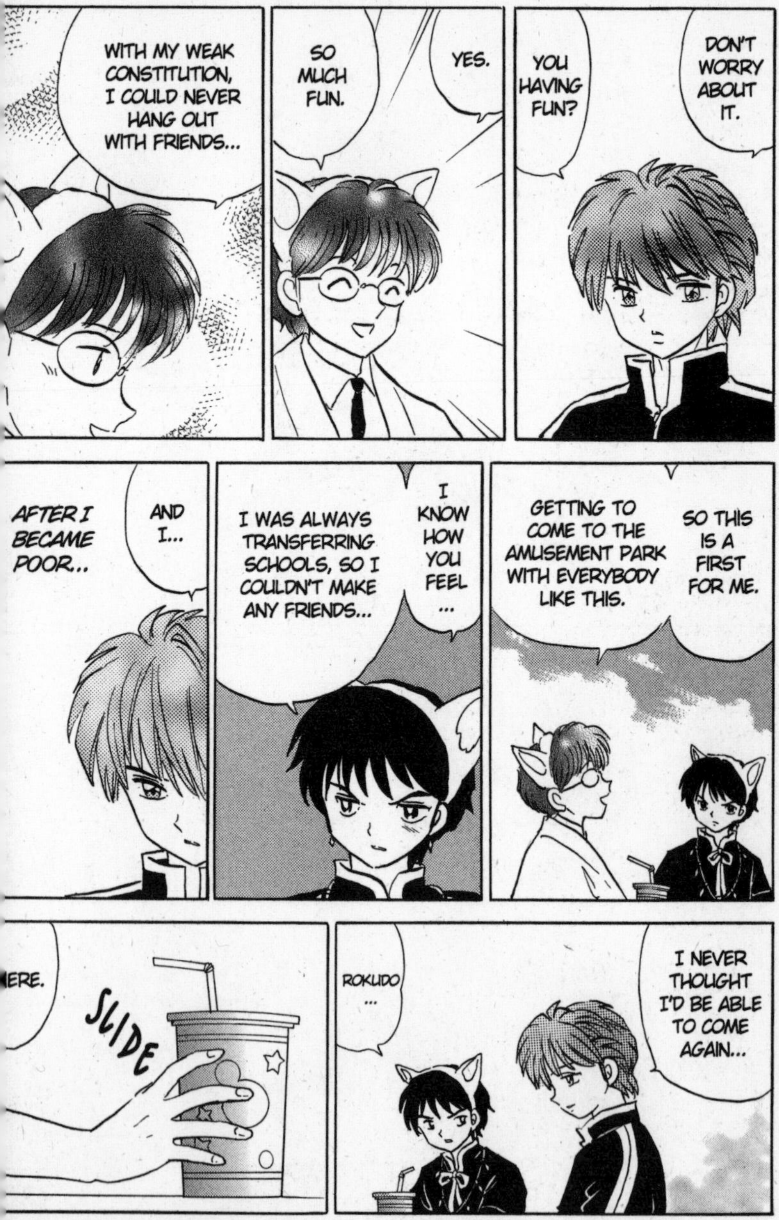
DON'T WORRY ABOUT IT.
YOU HAVING FUN?
YES.
SO MUCH FUN.
WITH MY WEAK CONSTITUTION, I COULD NEVER HANG OUT WITH FRIENDS...
SO THIS IS A FIRST FOR ME.
GETTING TO COME TO THE AMUSEMENT PARK WITH EVERYBODY LIKE THIS.
I KNOW HOW YOU FEEL ...
I WAS ALWAYS TRANSFERRING SCHOOLS, SO I COULDN'T MAKE ANY FRIENDS...
AND I...
AFTER I BECAME POOR...
I NEVER THOUGHT I'D BE ABLE TO COME AGAIN...
ROKUDO ...
ERE.
SLIDE

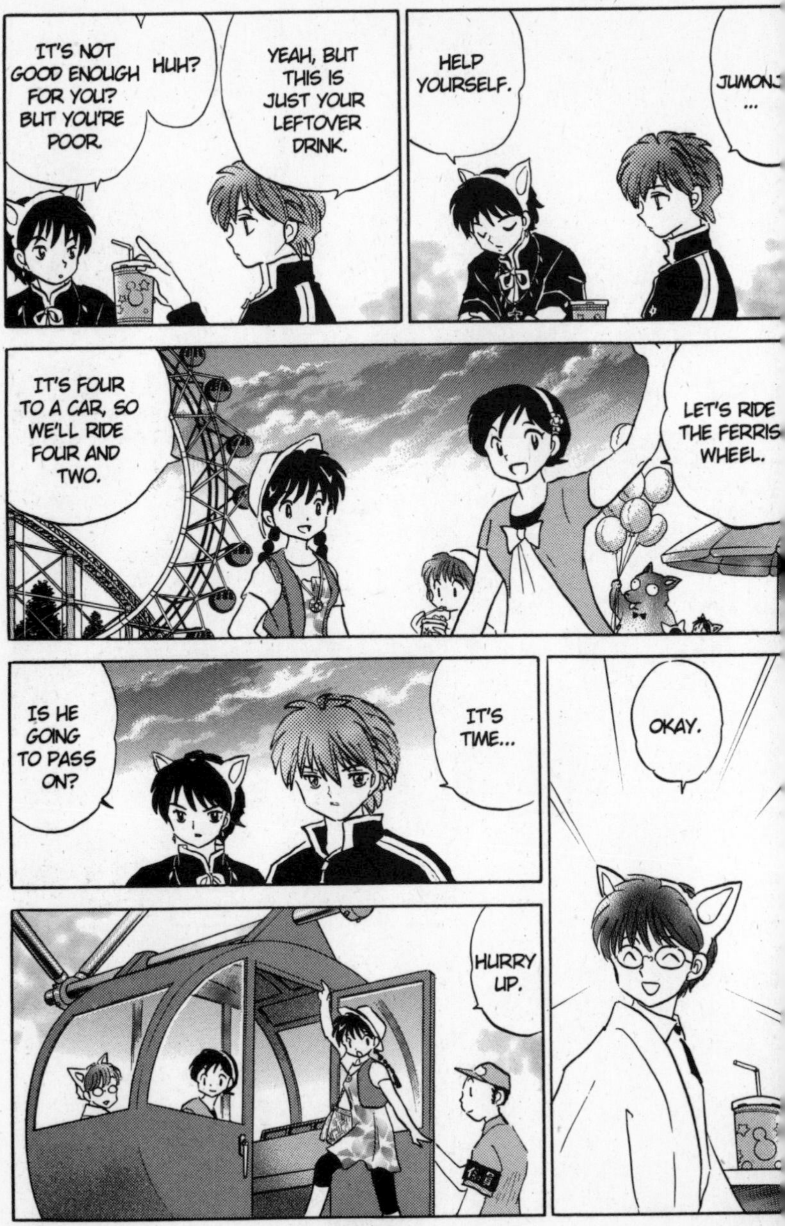
JUMONJ ...
HELP YOURSELF.
YEAH, BUT THIS IS JUST YOUR LEFTOVER DRINK.
HUH?
IT'S NOT GOOD ENOUGH FOR YOU? BUT YOU'RE POOR.
LET'S RIDE THE FERRIS WHEEL.
IT'S FOUR TO A CAR, SO WE'LL RIDE FOUR AND TWO.
OKAY.
IT'S TIME...
IS HE GOING TO PASS ON?
HURRY UP.

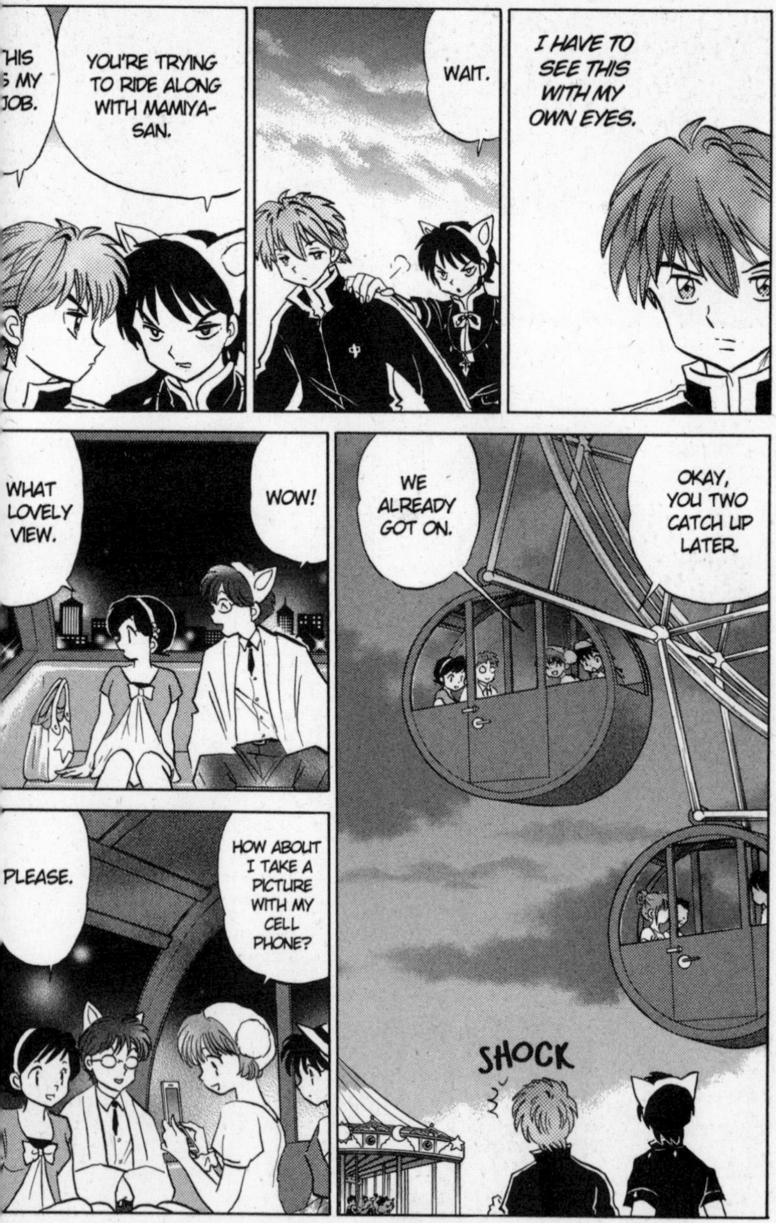
I HAVE TO SEE THIS WITH MY OWN EYES.
WAIT.
YOU'RE TRYING TO RIDE ALONG WITH MAMIYA-SAN.
MY JOB.
OKAY, YOU TWO CATCH UP LATER.
WE ALREADY GOT ON.
SHOCK
WOW!
WHAT LOVELY VIEW.
HOW ABOUT I TAKE A PICTURE WITH MY CELL PHONE?
PLEASE.

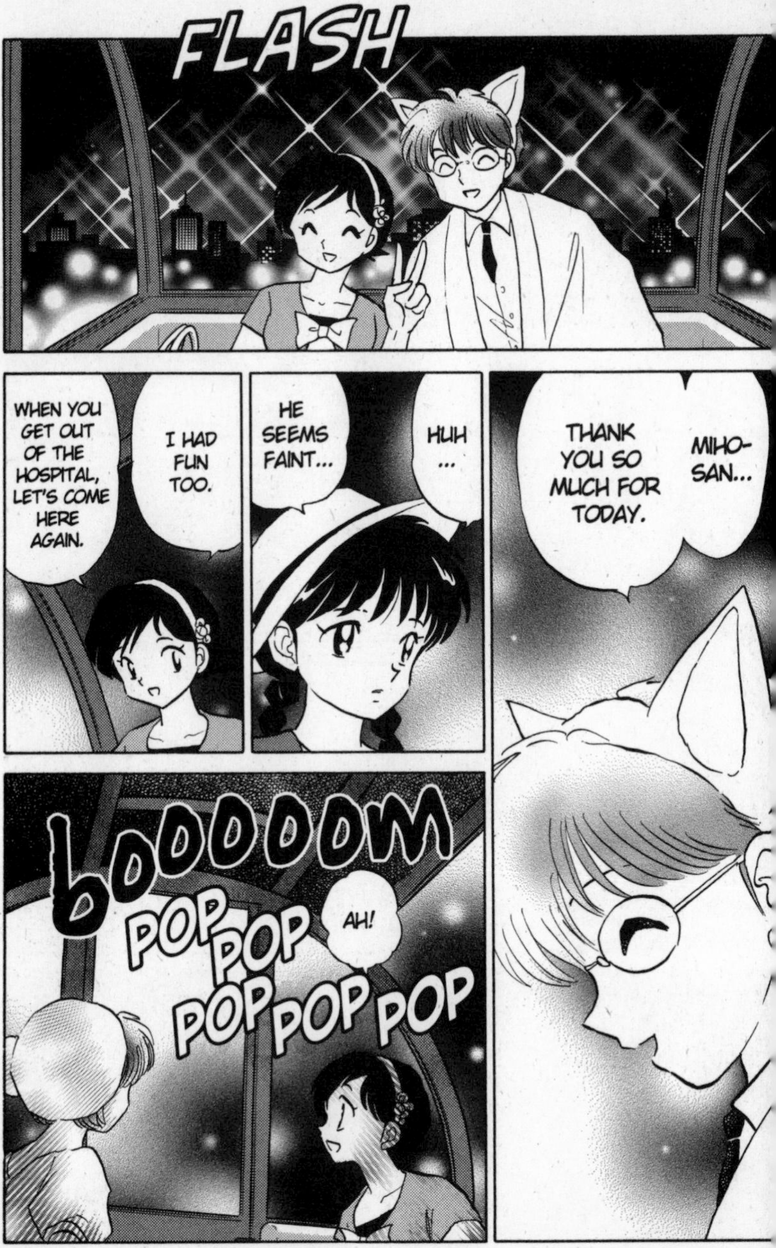
FLASH
MIHO-SAN...
THANK YOU SO MUCH FOR TODAY.
HUH ...
HE SEEMS FAINT...
I HAD FUN TOO.
WHEN YOU GET OUT OF THE HOSPITAL, LET'S COME HERE AGAIN.
BOOOOOM
POP POP POP POP POP
AH!

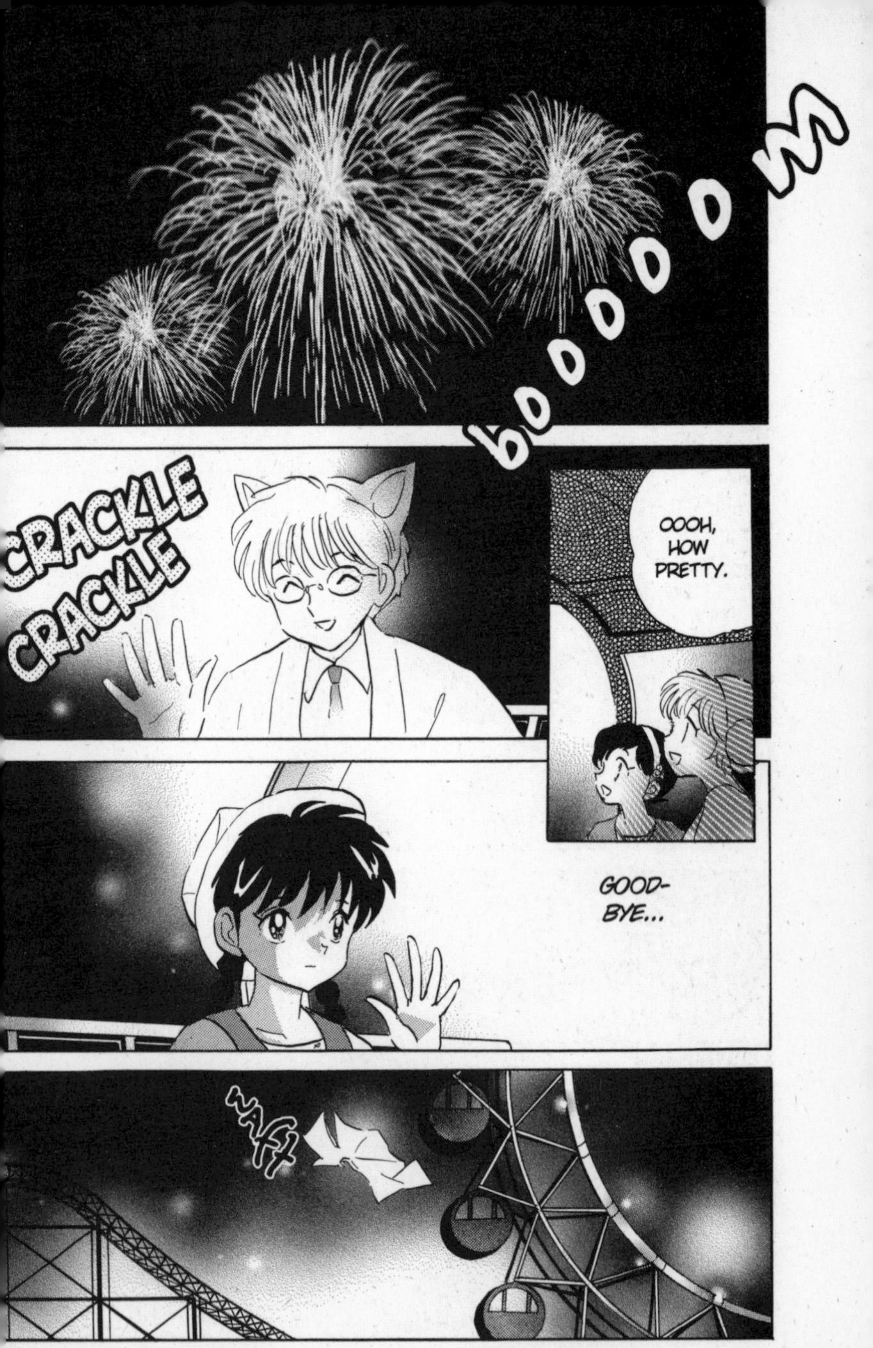
BOOOOOOM
OOOH, HOW PRETTY.
CRACKLE CRACKLE
GOOD-BYE...
waft

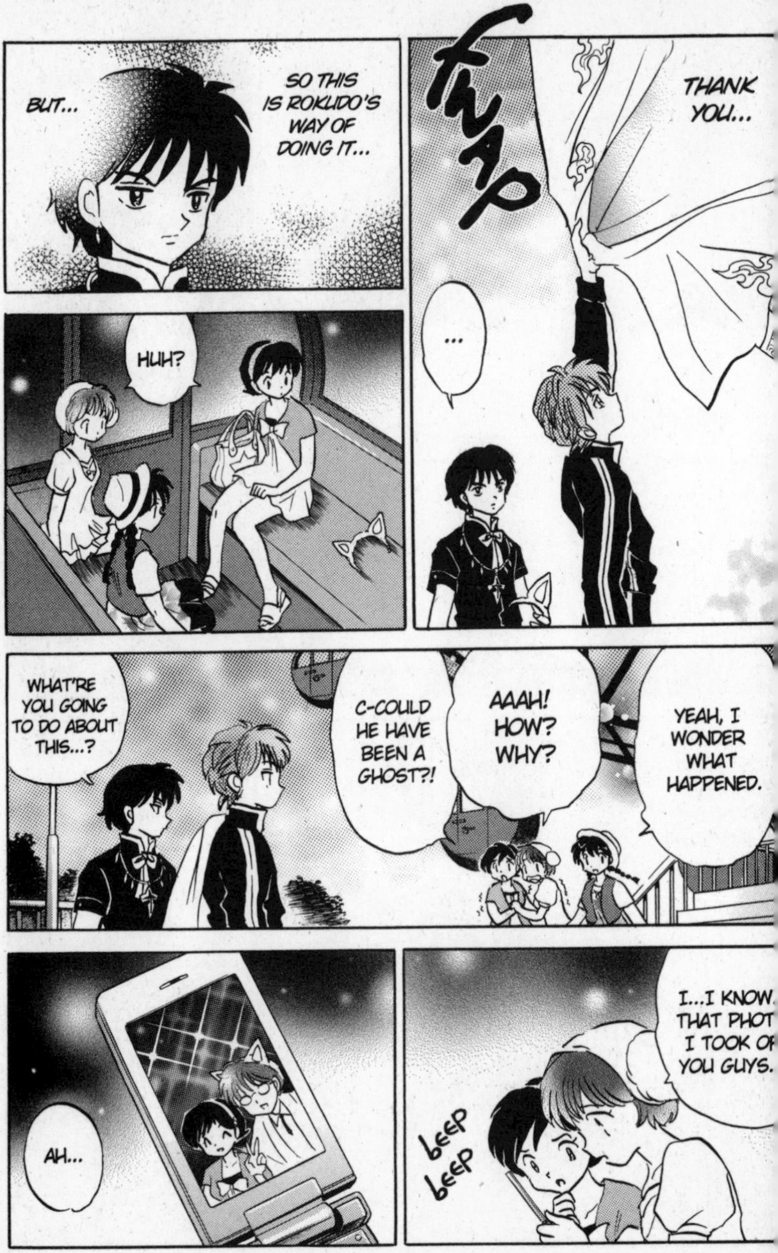
FWAP
THANK YOU...
SO THIS IS ROKUDO'S WAY OF DOING IT...
BUT...
...
HUH?
YEAH, I WONDER WHAT HAPPENED.
AAAH! HOW? WHY?
C-COULD HE HAVE BEEN A GHOST?!
WHAT'RE YOU GOING TO DO ABOUT THIS...?
I...I KNOW. THAT PHOT I TOOK OF YOU GUYS.
beep beep
AH...

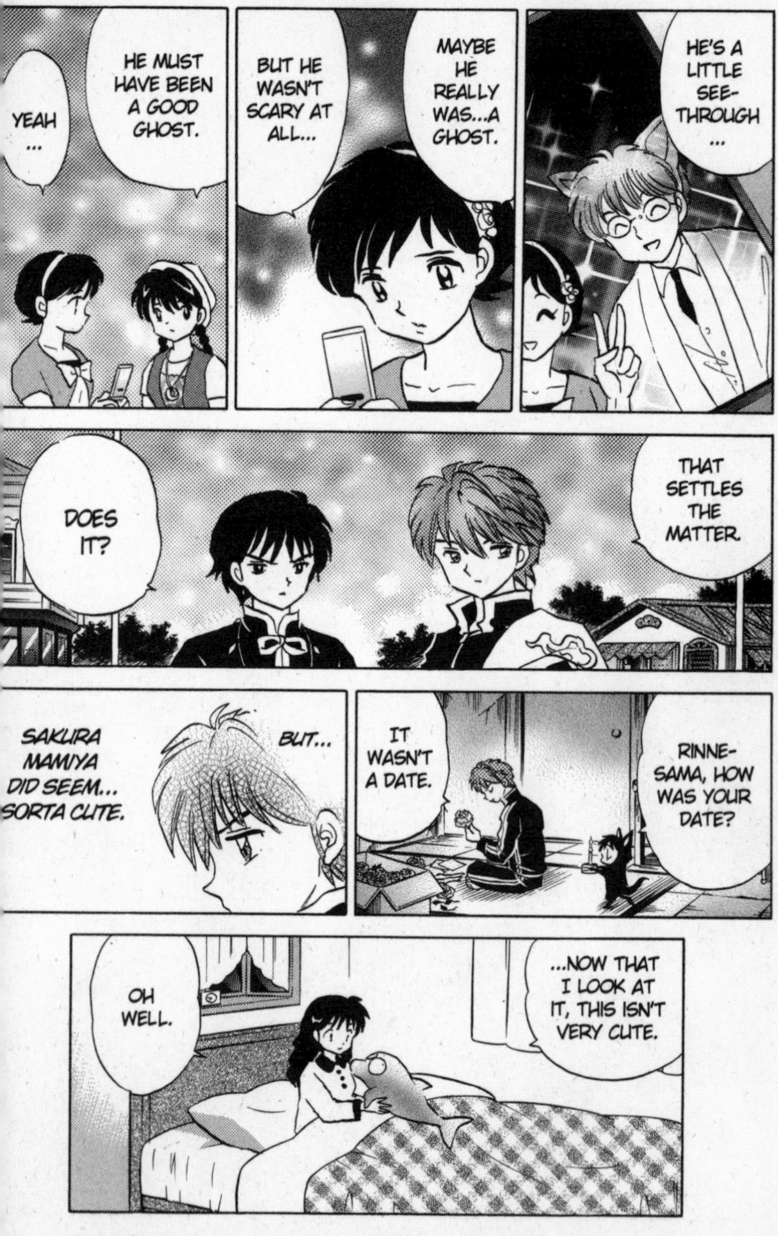
HE'S A LITTLE SEE-THROUGH ...
MAYBE HE REALLY WAS...A GHOST.
BUT HE WASN'T SCARY AT ALL...
HE MUST HAVE BEEN A GOOD GHOST.
YEAH ...
THAT SETTLES THE MATTER.
DOES IT?
RINNE-SAMA, HOW WAS YOUR DATE?
IT WASN'T A DATE.
BUT...
SAKURA MAMIYA DID SEEM... SORTA CUTE.
...NOW THAT I LOOK AT IT, THIS ISN'T VERY CUTE.
OH WELL.

CHAPTER 22: ONE HUNDRED THOUSAND YEN

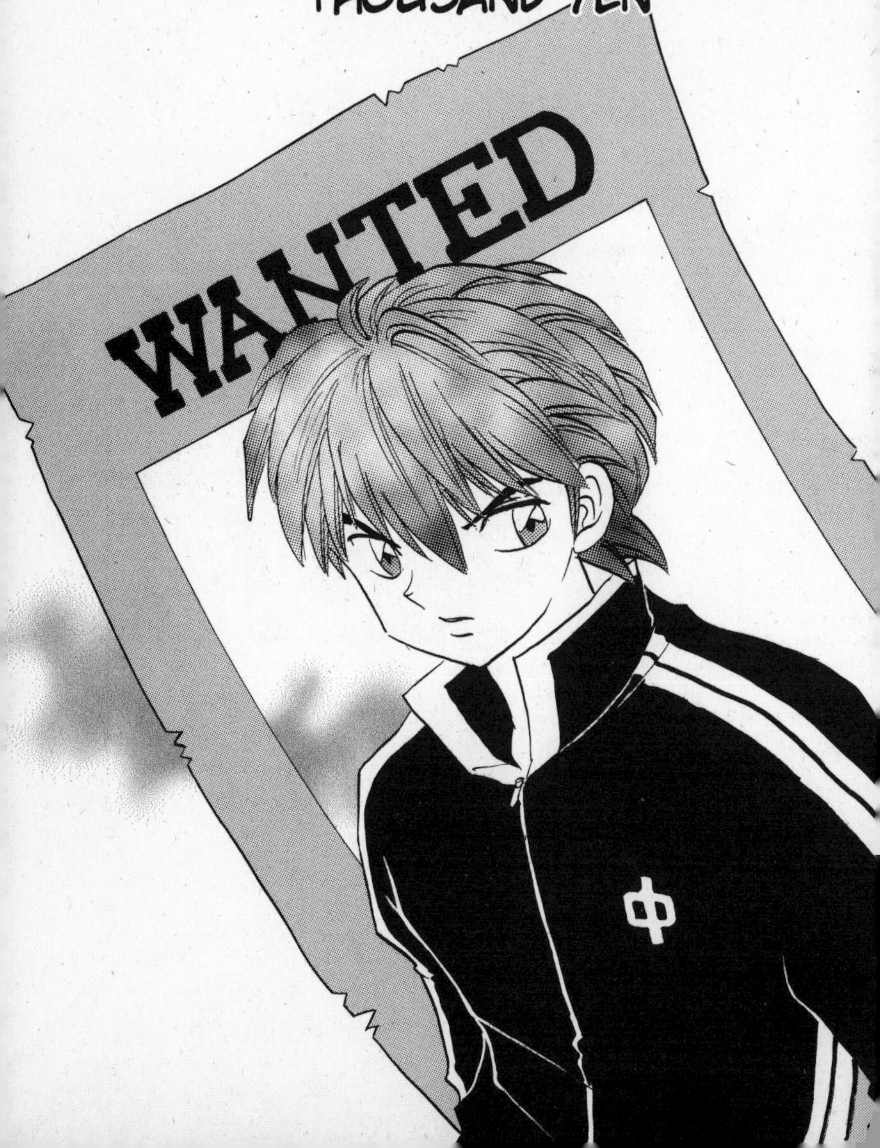
WANTED

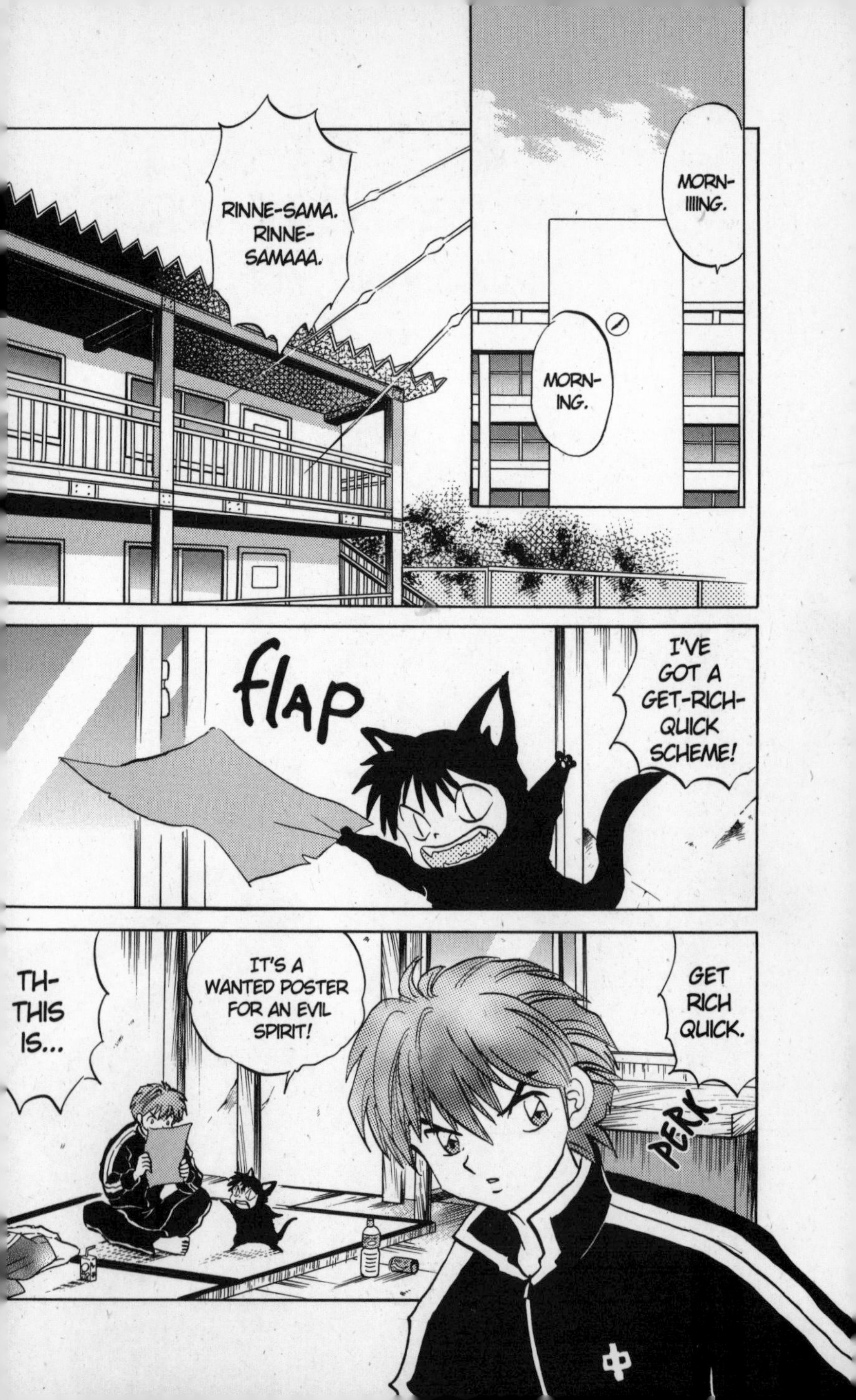
MORN-
IIIING.
MORN-
ING.
RINNE-SAMA. RINNE-SAMAAA.
I'VE GOT A GET-RICH-QUICK SCHEME!
flap
GET RICH QUICK.
PERK
IT'S A WANTED POSTER FOR AN EVIL SPIRIT!
TH-THIS IS...

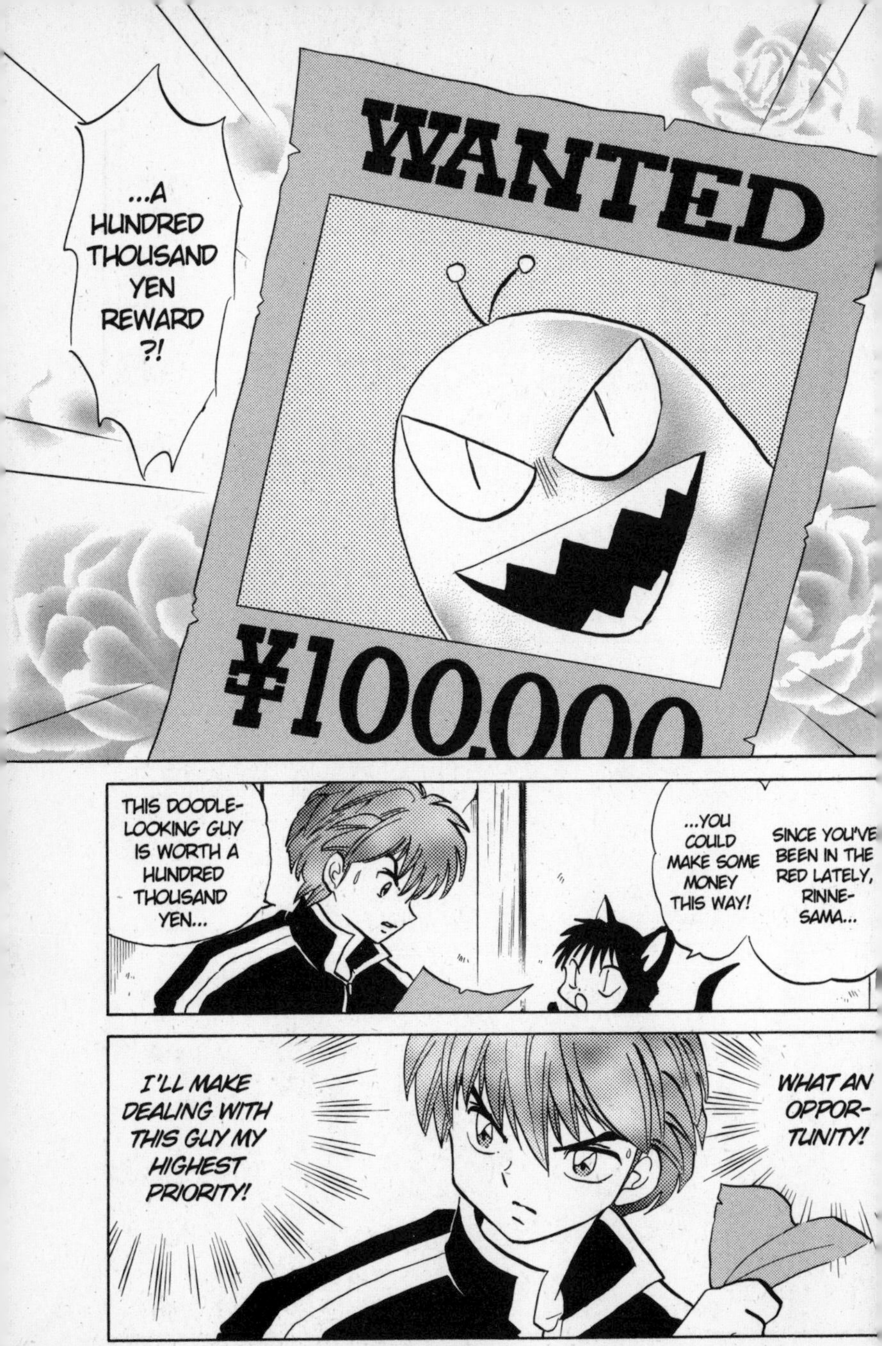
WANTED
¥100,000
...A HUNDRED THOUSAND YEN REWARD ?!
SINCE YOU'VE BEEN IN THE RED LATELY, RINNE-SAMA...
...YOU COULD MAKE SOME MONEY THIS WAY!
THIS DOODLE-LOOKING GUY IS WORTH A HUNDRED THOUSAND YEN...
WHAT AN OPPORTUNITY!
I'LL MAKE DEALING WITH THIS GUY MY HIGHEST PRIORITY!

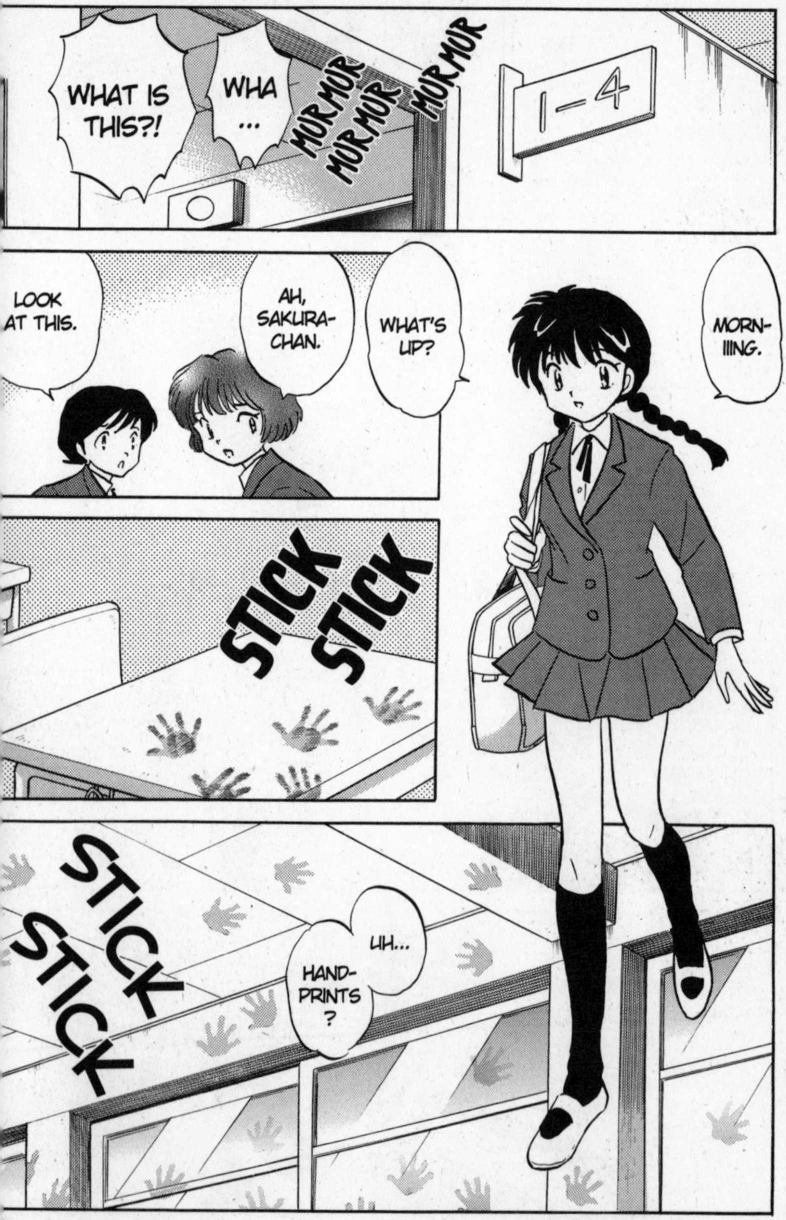
1-4
MUR MUR
MUR MUR
MUR MUR
WHA ...
WHAT IS THIS?!
MORN-IIING.
WHAT'S UP?
AH, SAKURA-CHAN.
LOOK AT THIS.
STICK STICK
UH...
HAND-PRINTS?
STICK STICK

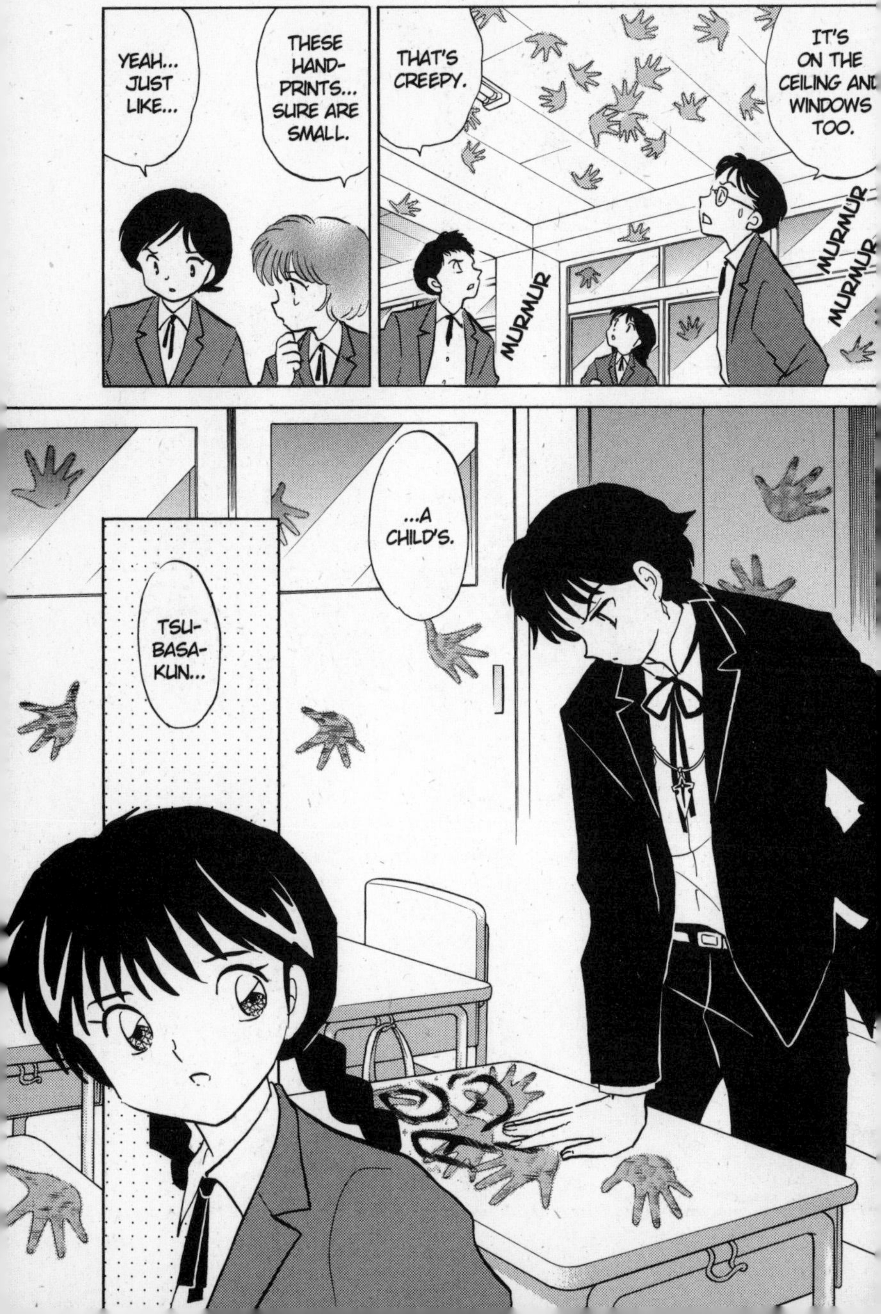
IT'S ON THE CEILING AN WINDOWS TOO.
MURMUR MURMUR
THAT'S CREEPY.
MURMUR
THESE HAND-PRINTS... SURE ARE SMALL.
YEAH... JUST LIKE...
...A CHILD'S.
TSU-BASA-KUN...

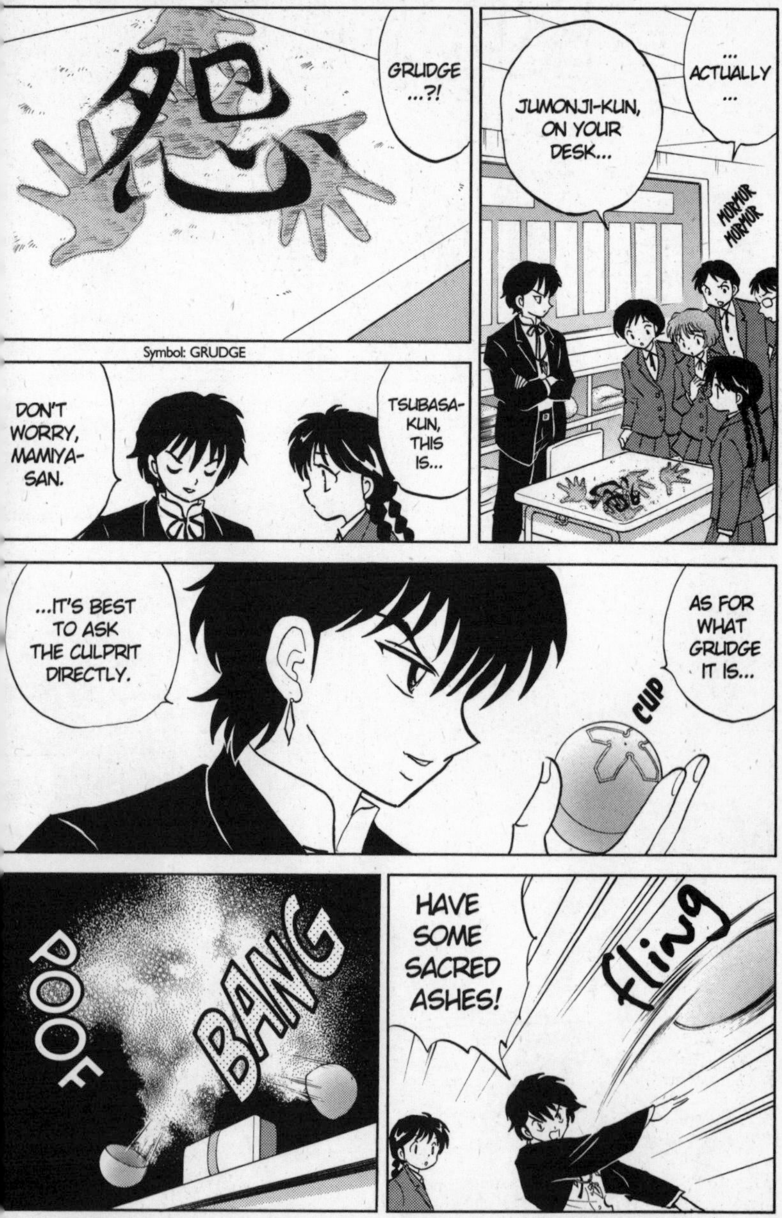
...
ACTUALLY
...
JUMONJI-KUN, ON YOUR DESK...
MORMOR MORMOR
GRUDGE ...?!
怨
Symbol: GRUDGE
TSUBASA-KUN, THIS IS...
DON'T WORRY, MAMIYA-SAN.
AS FOR WHAT GRUDGE IT IS...
CUP
...IT'S BEST TO ASK THE CULPRIT DIRECTLY.
HAVE SOME SACRED ASHES!
fling
BANG
POOF

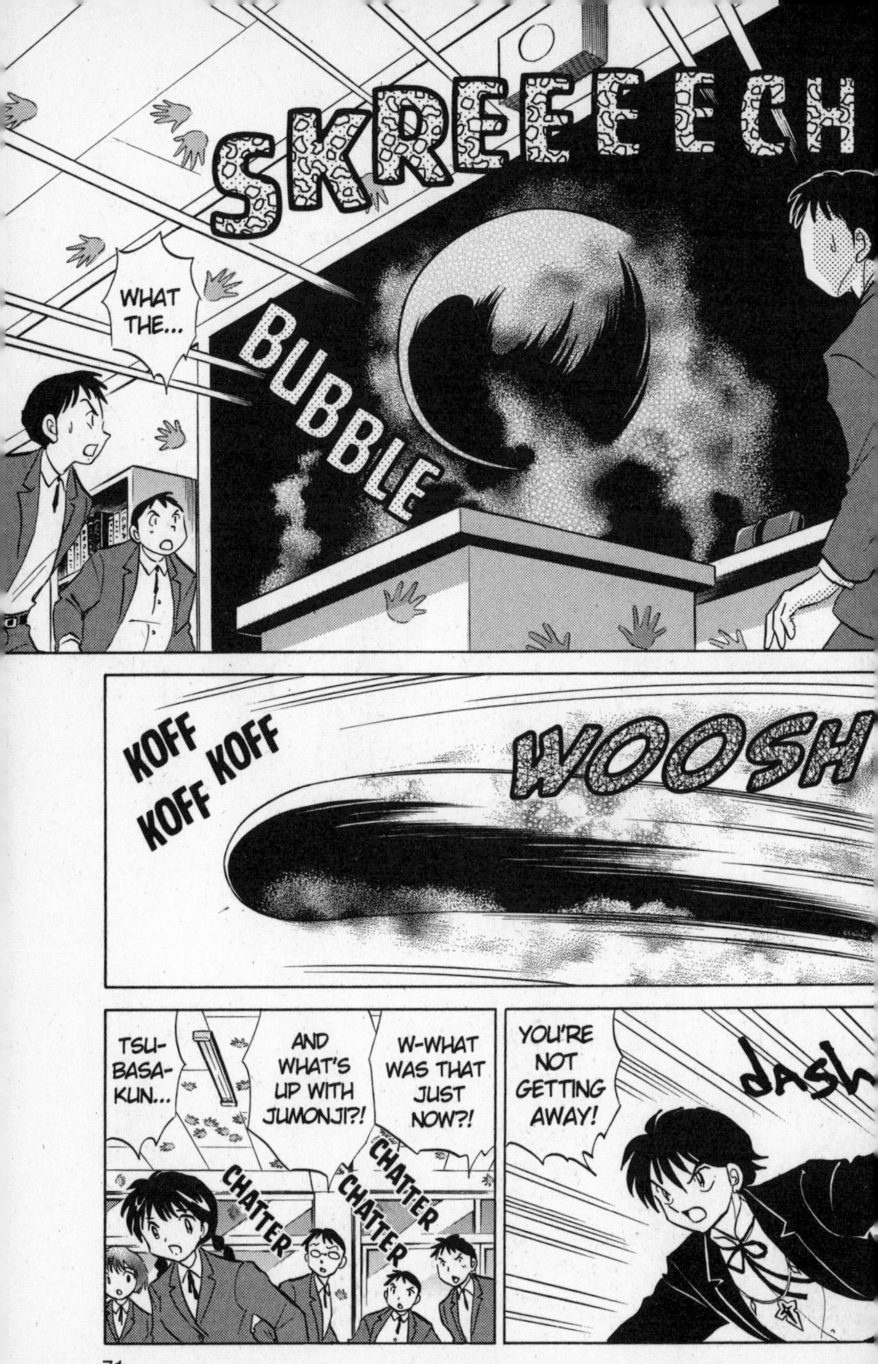
SKREEECH
BUBBLE
WHAT THE...
WOOSH
KOFF KOFF KOFF
dash
YOU'RE NOT GETTING AWAY!
W-WHAT WAS THAT JUST NOW?!
AND WHAT'S UP WITH JUMONJI?!
TSU-BASA-KUN...
CHATTER
CHATTER
CHATTER

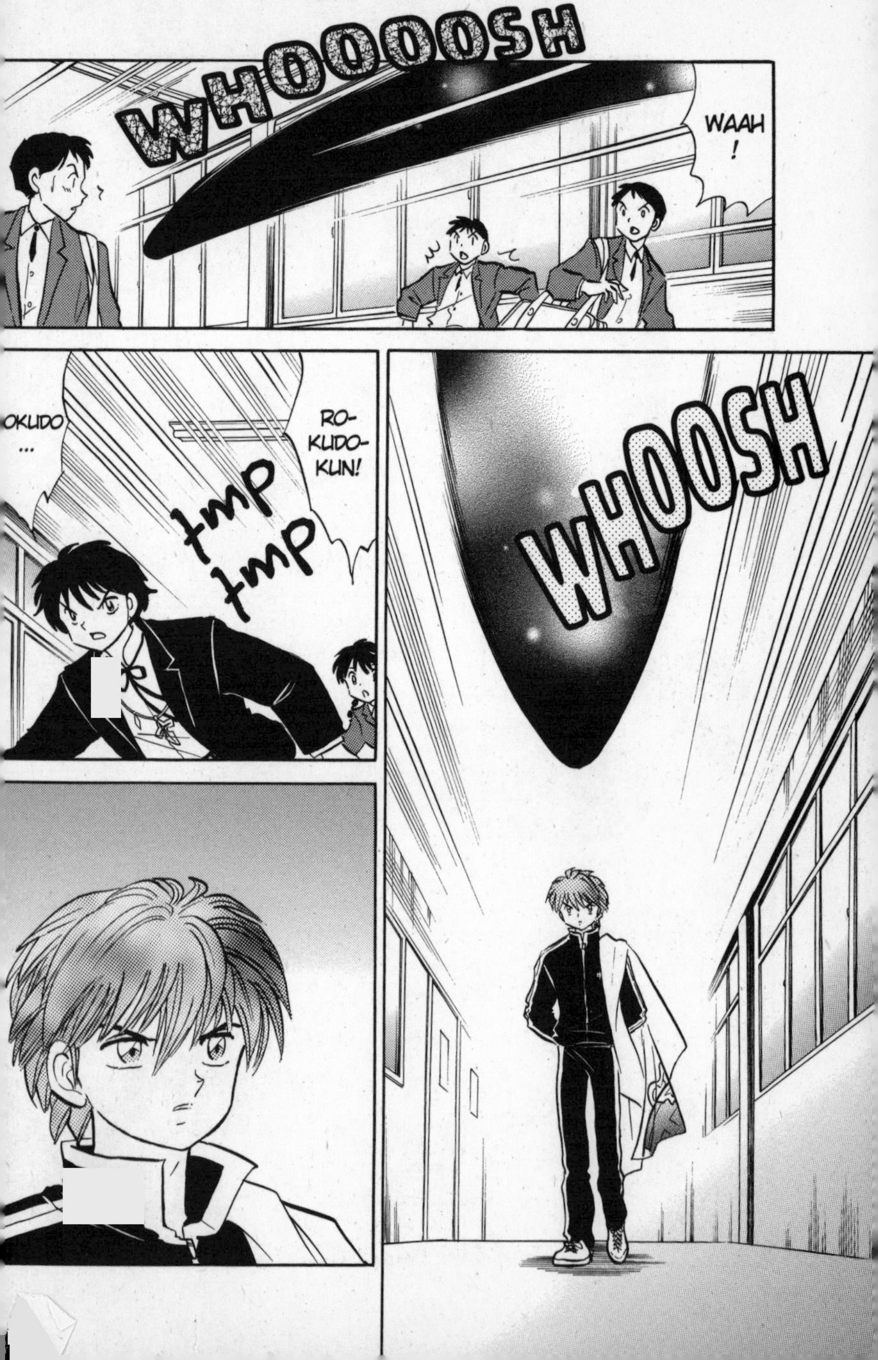
WHOOOOOSH
WAAH!
WHOOSH
RO-KUDO-KUN!
tmp tmp
OKUDO...

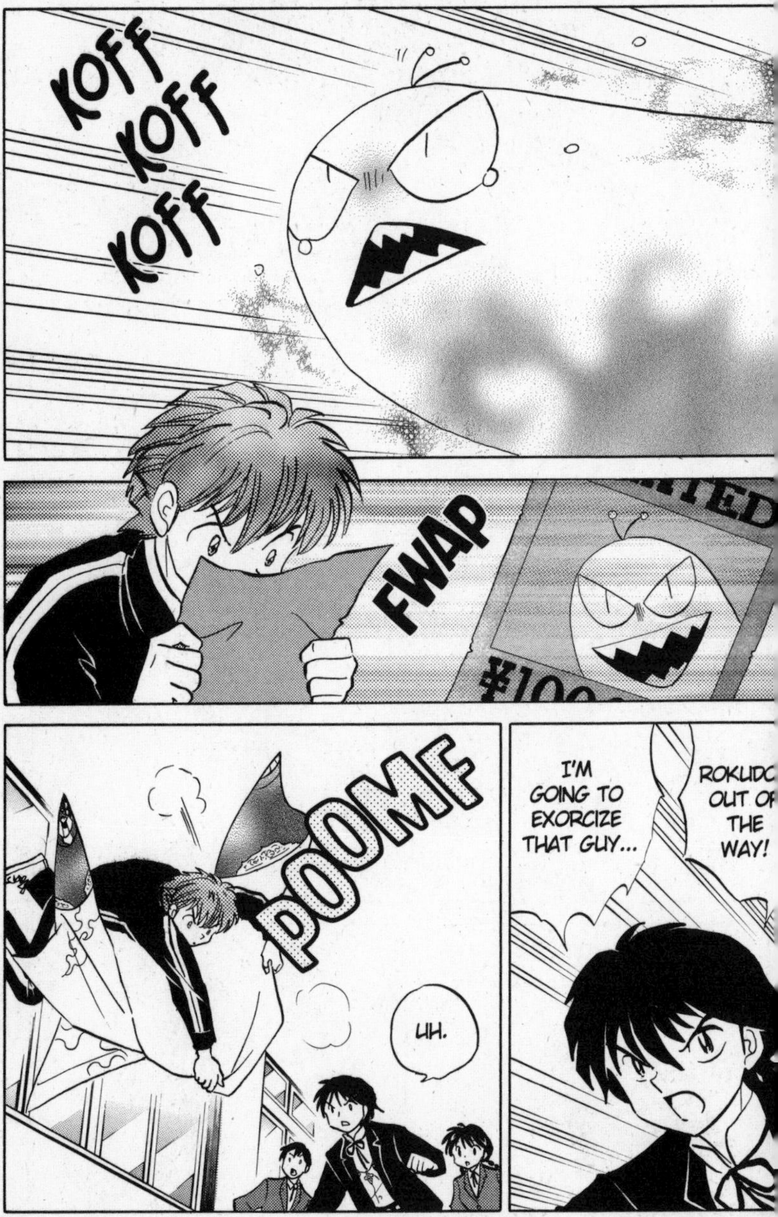
KOFF KOFF KOFF
FWAP
THE WAY!
I'M GOING TO EXORCIZE THAT GUY...
POOMF
UH.

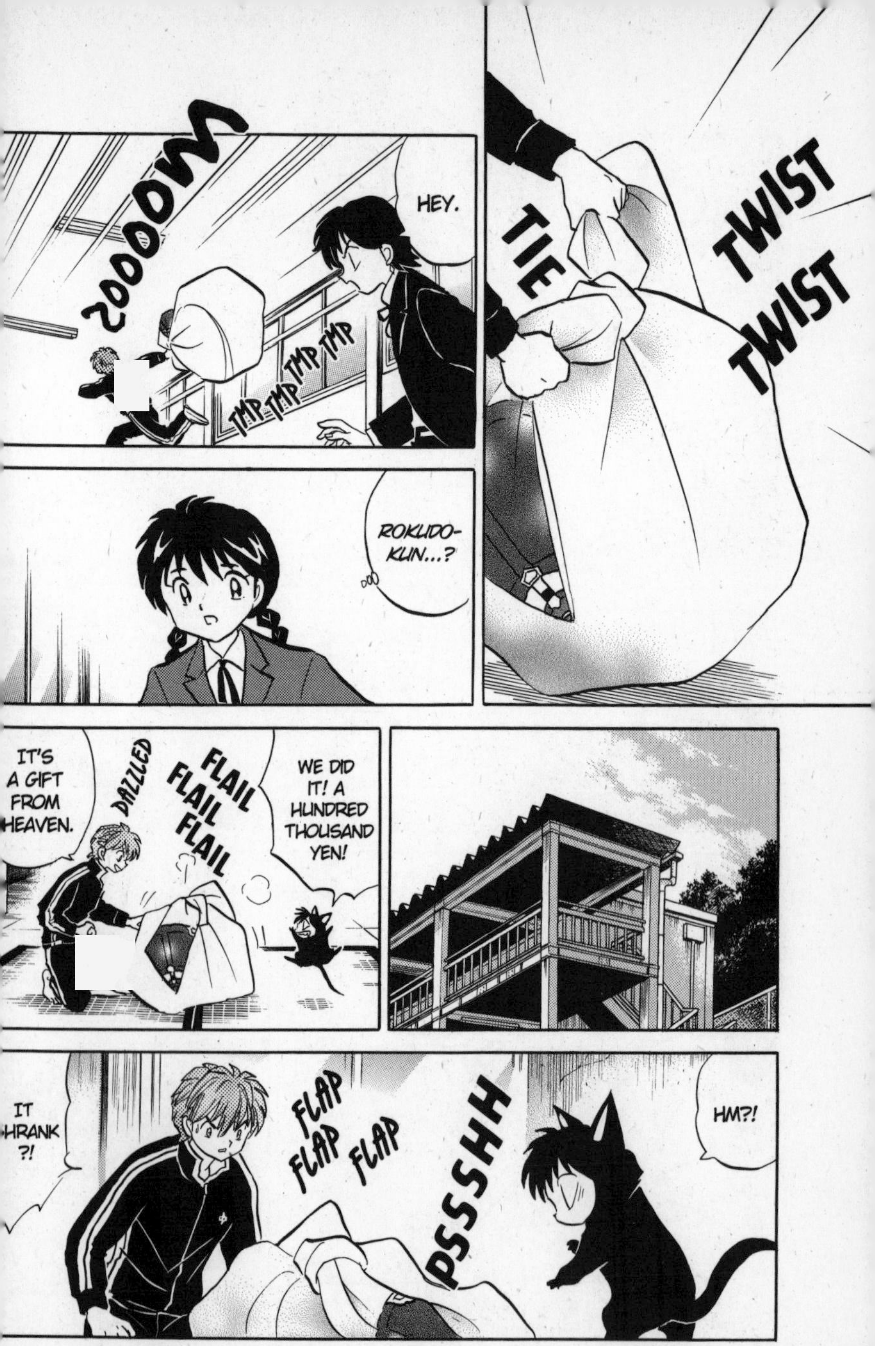
TIE
TWIST TWIST
ZOOOOM
HEY.
TMP TMP TMP TMP
ROKUDO-KUN...?
WE DID IT! A HUNDRED THOUSAND YEN!
FLAIL FLAIL FLAIL
DAZZLED
IT'S A GIFT FROM HEAVEN.
HM?!
PSSSHH
FLAP FLAP FLAP
IT SHRANK?!

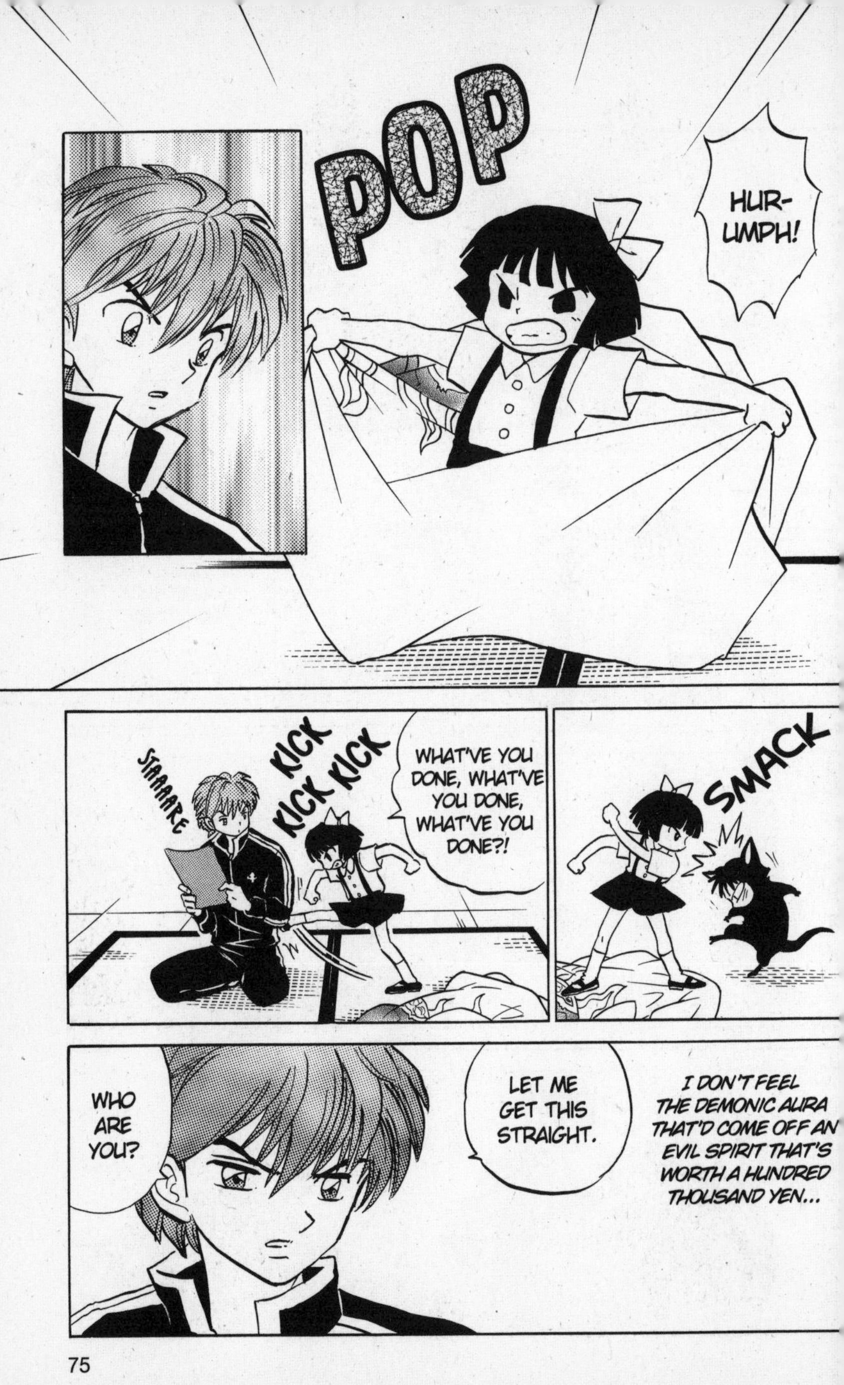
POP
HUR-UMPH!
SMACK
KICK KICK KICK
WHAT'VE YOU DONE, WHAT'VE YOU DONE, WHAT'VE YOU DONE?!
STAAAARE
I DON'T FEEL THE DEMONIC AURA THAT'D COME OFF AN EVIL SPIRIT THAT'S WORTH A HUNDRED THOUSAND YEN...
LET ME GET THIS STRAIGHT.
WHO ARE YOU?

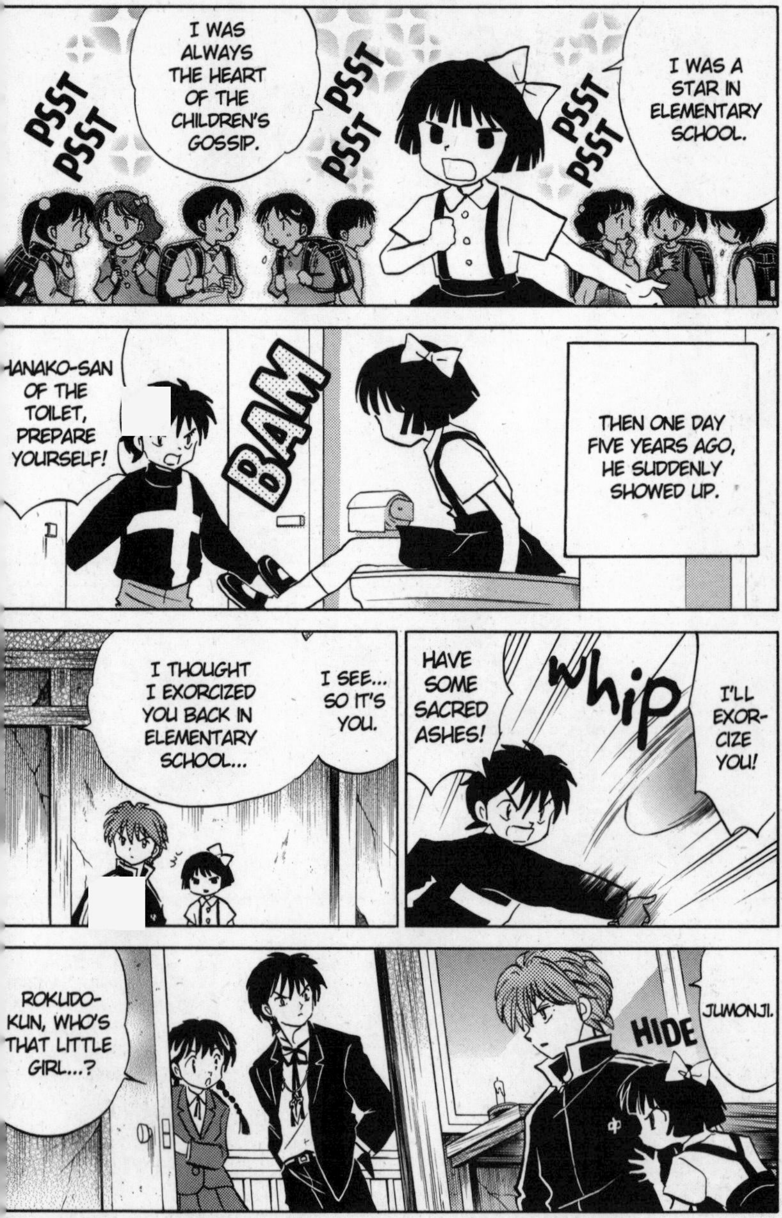
I WAS A STAR IN ELEMENTARY SCHOOL.
PSST PSST
PSST PSST
PSST PSST
I WAS ALWAYS THE HEART OF THE CHILDREN'S GOSSIP.
THEN ONE DAY FIVE YEARS AGO, HE SUDDENLY SHOWED UP.
BAM
HANAKO-SAN OF THE TOILET, PREPARE YOURSELF!
I'LL EXOR-CIZE YOU!
whip
HAVE SOME SACRED ASHES!
I SEE... SO IT'S YOU.
I THOUGHT I EXORCIZED YOU BACK IN ELEMENTARY SCHOOL...
JUMONJI.
HIDE
ROKUDO-KUN, WHO'S THAT LITTLE GIRL...?

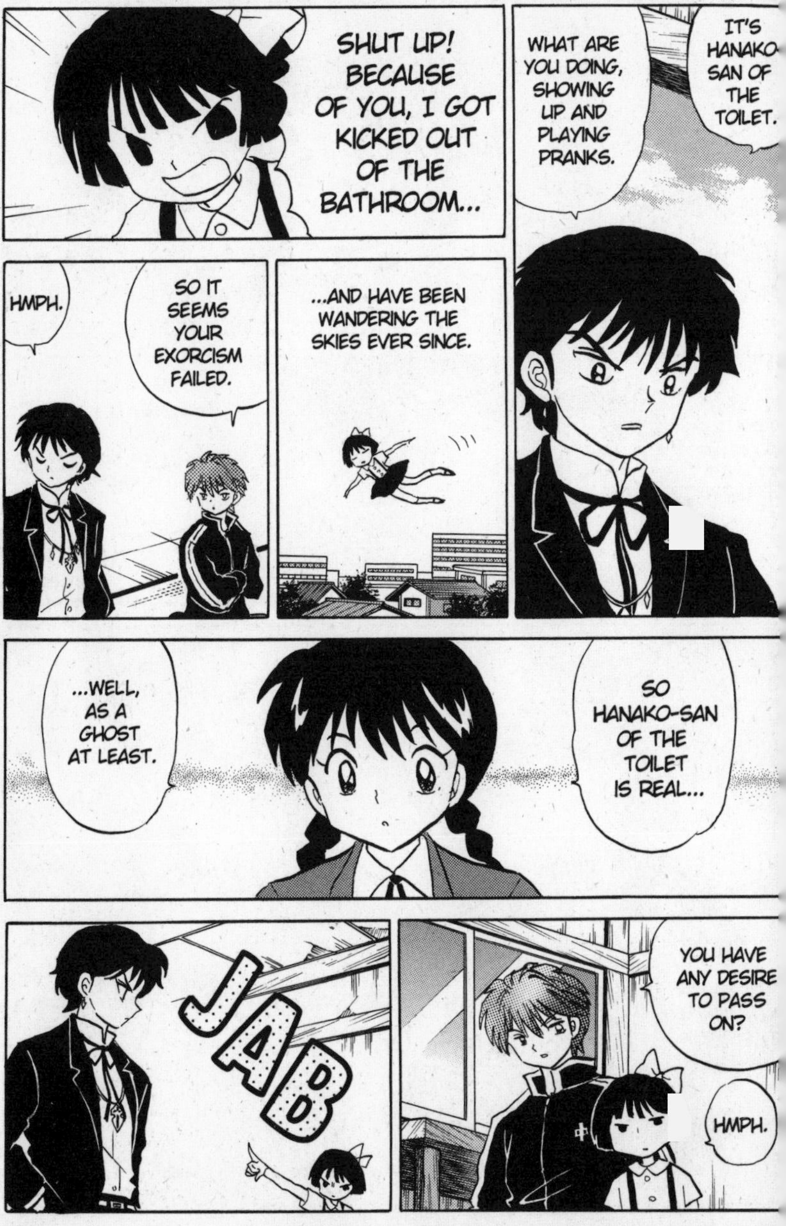
IT'S HANAKO-SAN OF THE TOILET.
WHAT ARE YOU DOING, SHOWING UP AND PLAYING PRANKS.
SHUT UP! BECAUSE OF YOU, I GOT KICKED OUT OF THE BATHROOM...
...AND HAVE BEEN WANDERING THE SKIES EVER SINCE.
SO IT SEEMS YOUR EXORCISM FAILED.
HMPH.
SO HANAKO-SAN OF THE TOILET IS REAL...
...WELL, AS A GHOST AT LEAST.
YOU HAVE ANY DESIRE TO PASS ON?
HMPH.
JAB

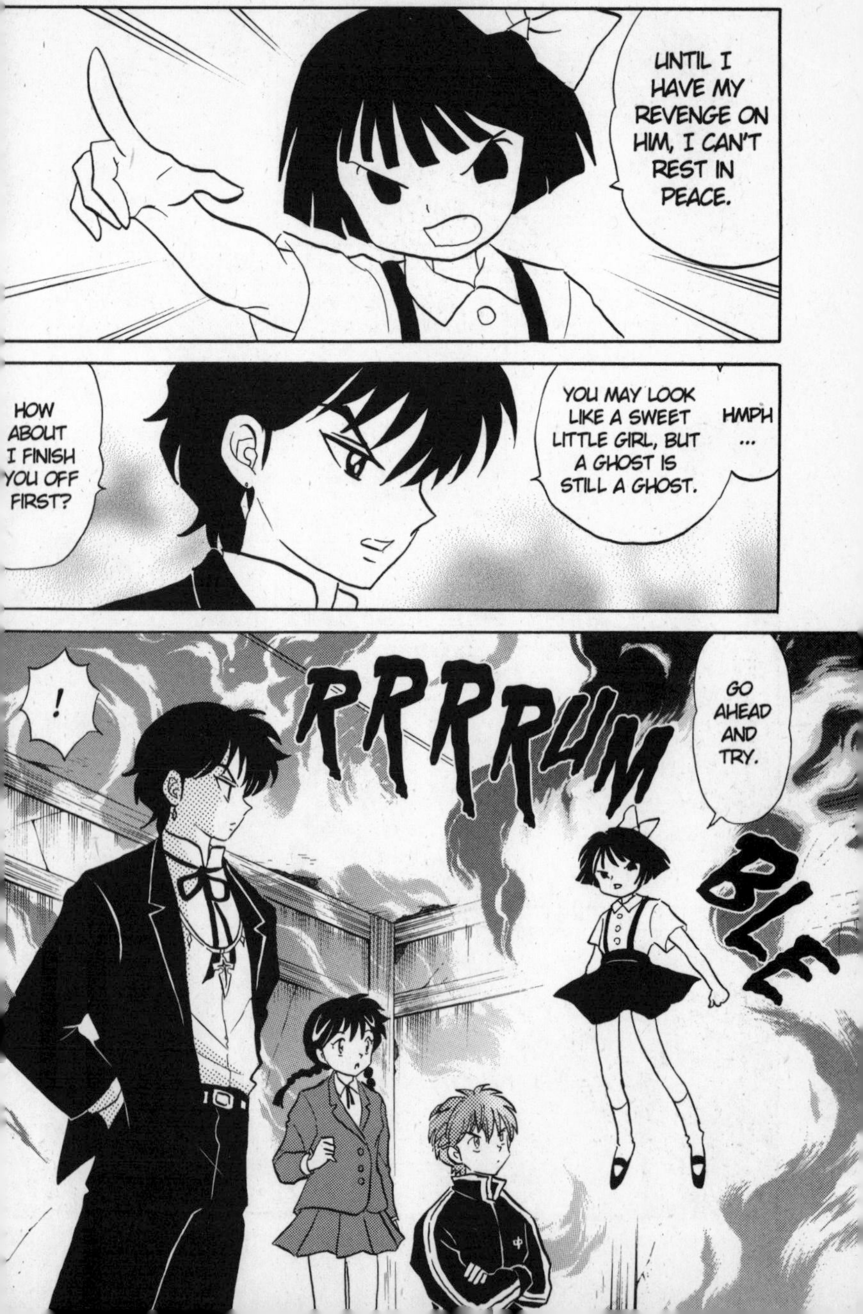
UNTIL I HAVE MY REVENGE ON HIM, I CAN'T REST IN PEACE.
HMPH ...
YOU MAY LOOK LIKE A SWEET LITTLE GIRL, BUT A GHOST IS STILL A GHOST.
HOW ABOUT I FINISH YOU OFF FIRST?
GO AHEAD AND TRY.
RRRRUM
BLE
!

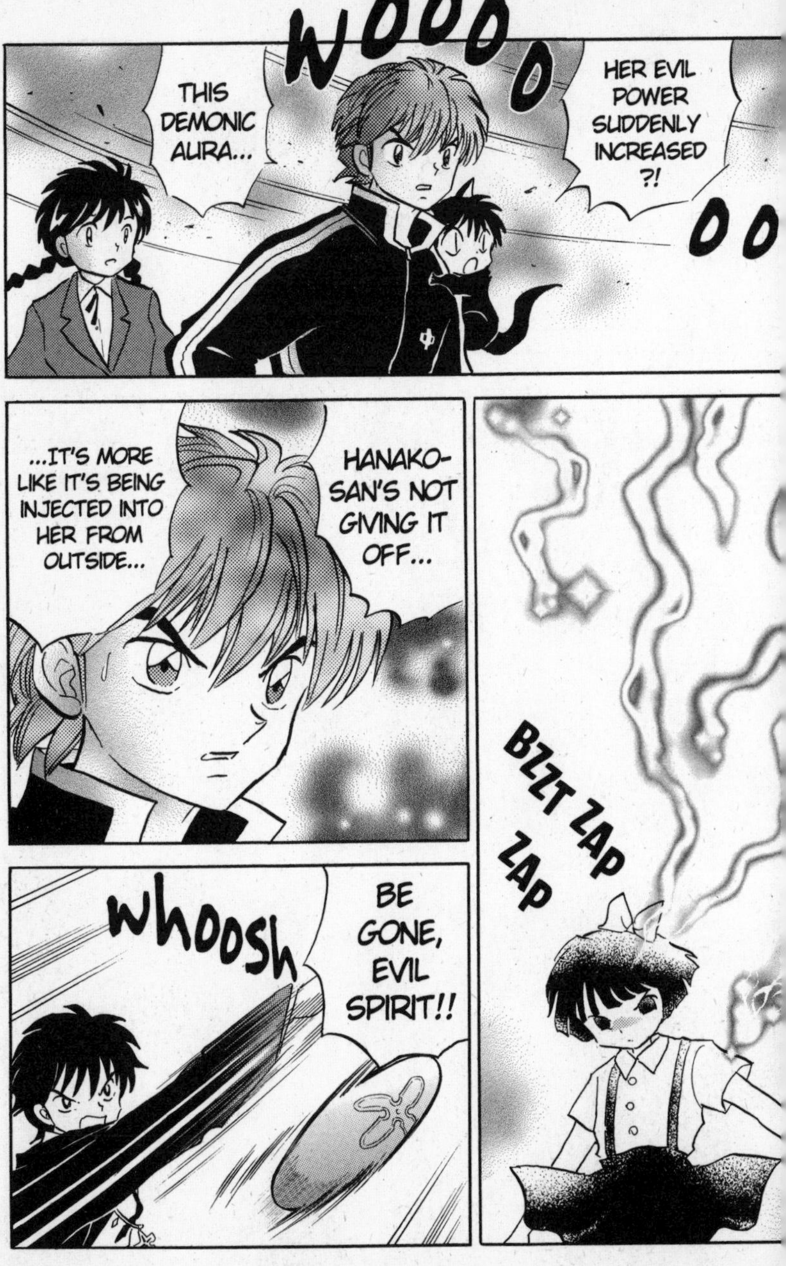
WOOOOOOO
HER EVIL POWER SUDDENLY INCREASED ?!
THIS DEMONIC AURA...
HANAKO-SAN'S NOT GIVING IT OFF...
...IT'S MORE LIKE IT'S BEING INJECTED INTO HER FROM OUTSIDE...
BZZT ZAP ZAP
BE GONE, EVIL SPIRIT!!
whoosh

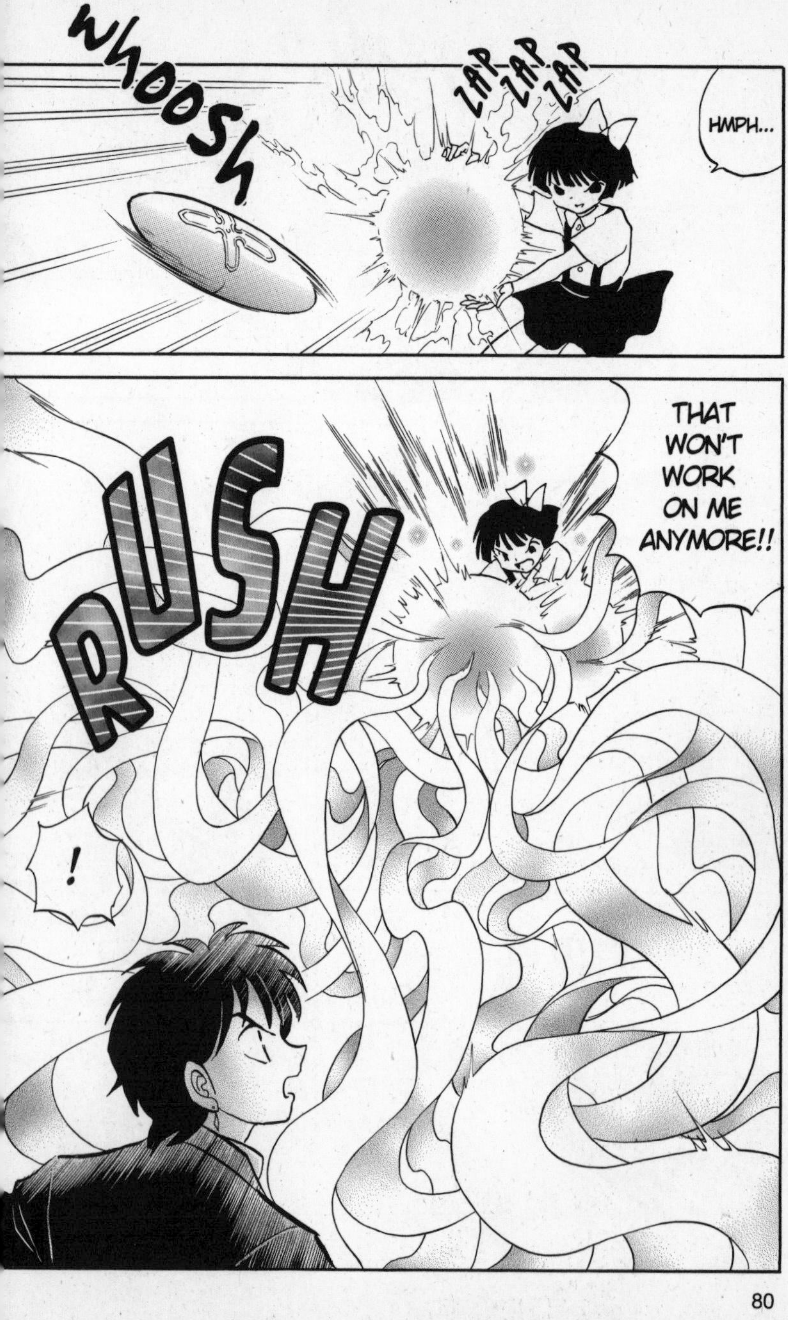
HMPH...
ZAP ZAP ZAP
WHOOSH
THAT WON'T WORK ON ME ANYMORE!!
RUSH
!

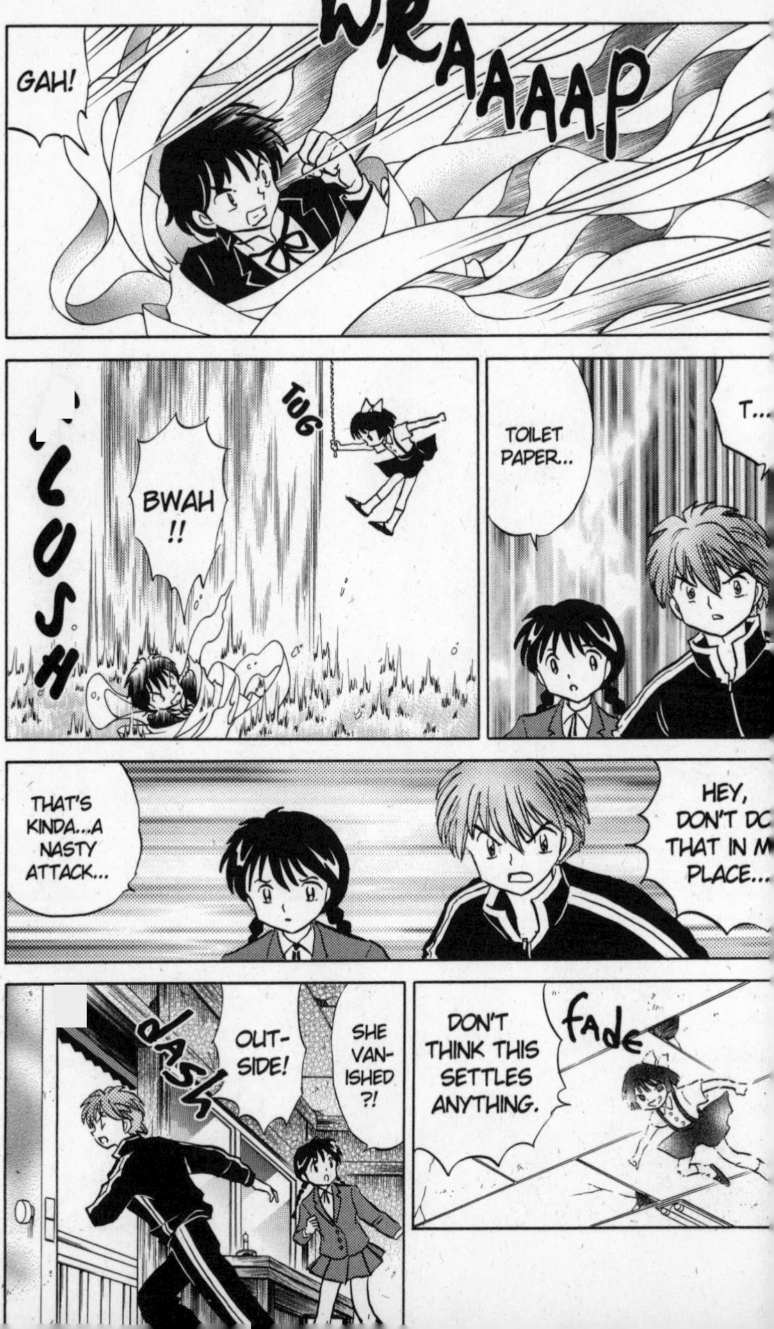
WRAAAAP
GAH!
T...
TOILET PAPER...
TUG
BWAH !!
LUSH
HEY, DON'T DO THAT IN M PLACE...
THAT'S KINDA...A NASTY ATTACK...
fade
DON'T THINK THIS SETTLES ANYTHING.
SHE VAN-ISHED ?!
OUT-SIDE!
dash

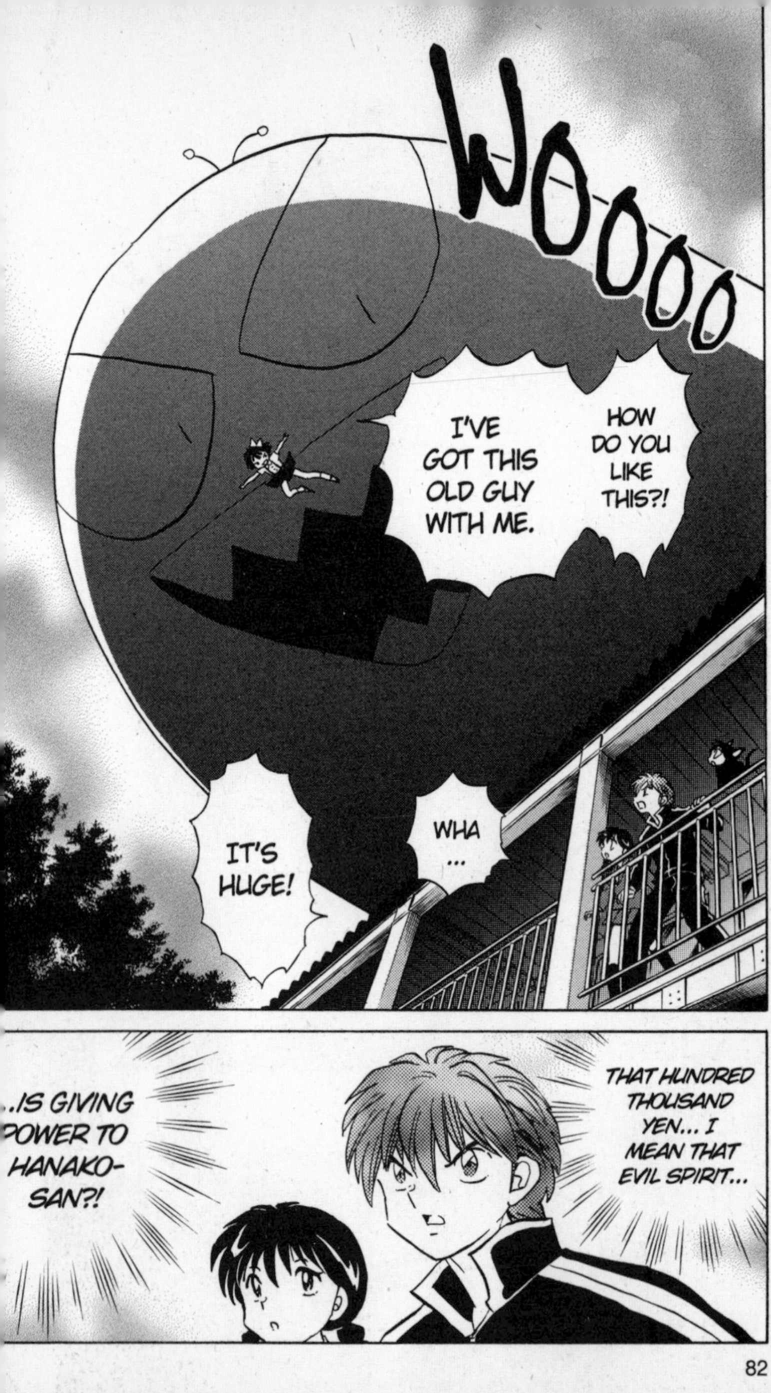
WOOOOO
HOW DO YOU LIKE THIS?!
I'VE GOT THIS OLD GUY WITH ME.
WHA ...
IT'S HUGE!
THAT HUNDRED THOUSAND YEN... I MEAN THAT EVIL SPIRIT...
..IS GIVING POWER TO HANAKO-SAN?!

CHAPTER 23: THE PRICE OF POWER

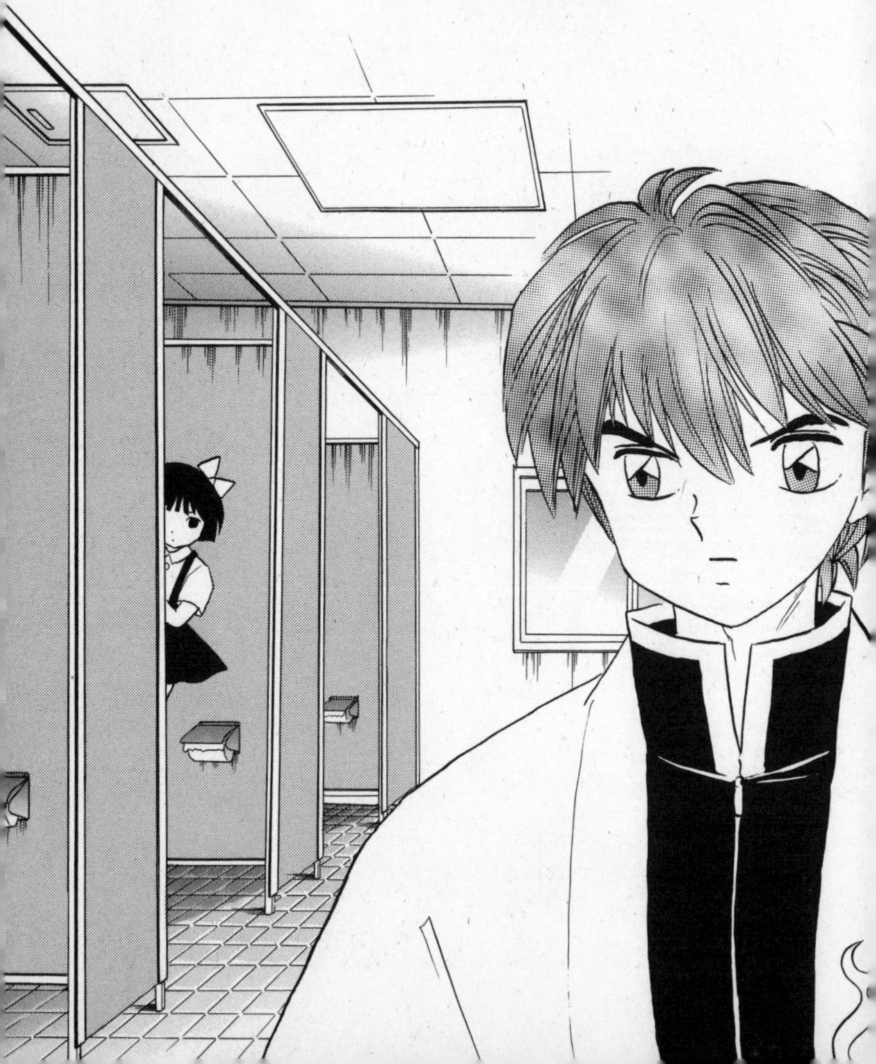

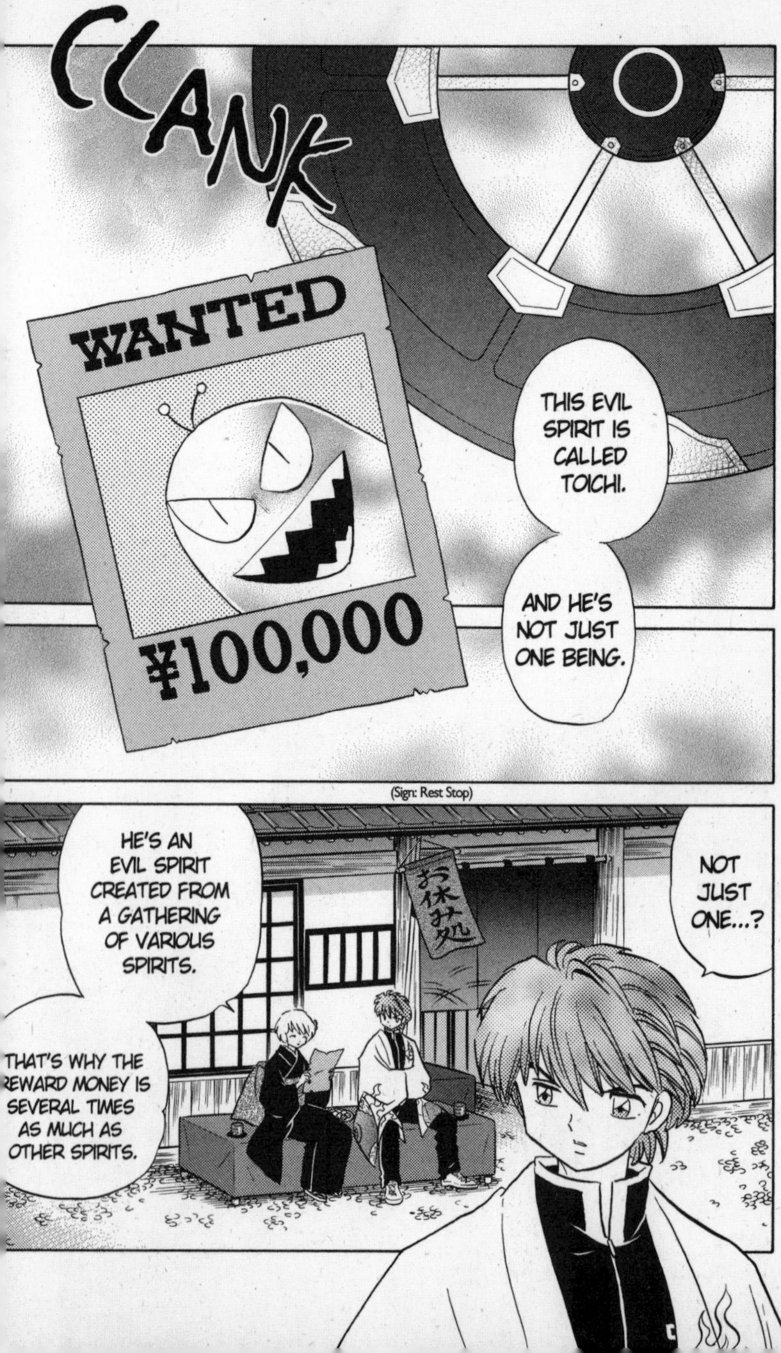
CLANK
WANTED
¥100,000
THIS EVIL SPIRIT IS CALLED TOICHI.
AND HE'S NOT JUST ONE BEING.
(Sign: Rest Stop)
NOT JUST ONE...?
HE'S AN EVIL SPIRIT CREATED FROM A GATHERING OF VARIOUS SPIRITS.
THAT'S WHY THE REWARD MONEY IS SEVERAL TIMES AS MUCH AS OTHER SPIRITS.

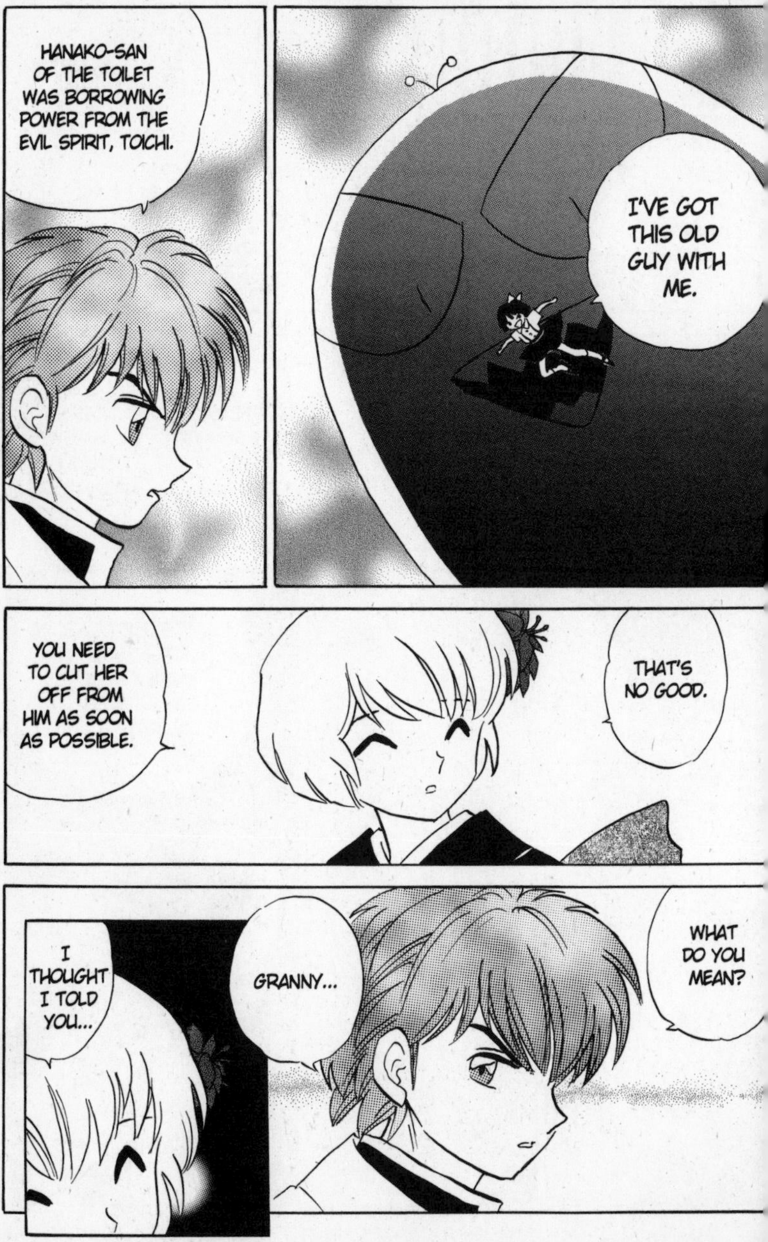
I'VE GOT THIS OLD GUY WITH ME.
HANAKO-SAN OF THE TOILET WAS BORROWING POWER FROM THE EVIL SPIRIT, TOICHI.
THAT'S NO GOOD.
YOU NEED TO CUT HER OFF FROM HIM AS SOON AS POSSIBLE.
WHAT DO YOU MEAN?
GRANNY...
I THOUGHT I TOLD YOU...

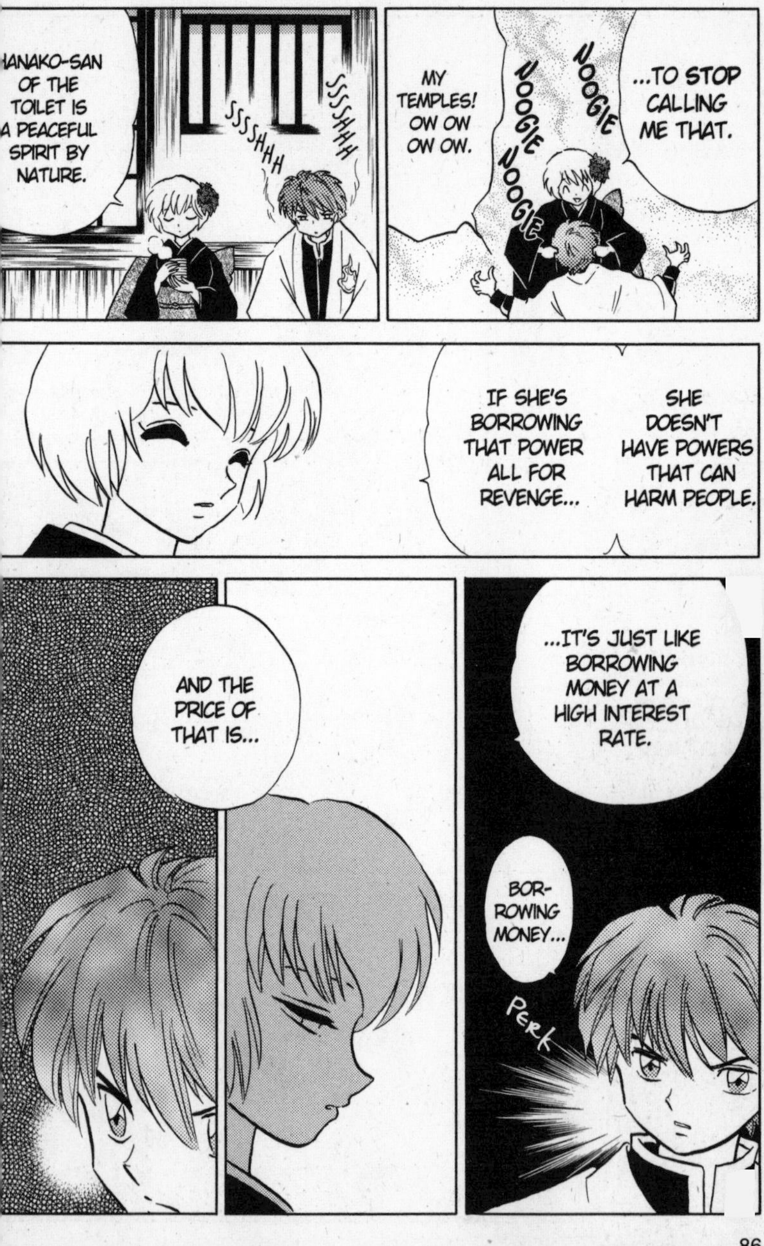
...TO STOP CALLING ME THAT.
NOOGIE NOOGIE NOOGIE
MY TEMPLES! OW OW OW OW.
HANAKO-SAN OF THE TOILET IS A PEACEFUL SPIRIT BY NATURE.
SSSSHHH
SSSSHHH
SHE DOESN'T HAVE POWERS THAT CAN HARM PEOPLE.
IF SHE'S BORROWING THAT POWER ALL FOR REVENGE...
...IT'S JUST LIKE BORROWING MONEY AT A HIGH INTEREST RATE.
BOR-ROWING MONEY...
PERK
AND THE PRICE OF THAT IS...

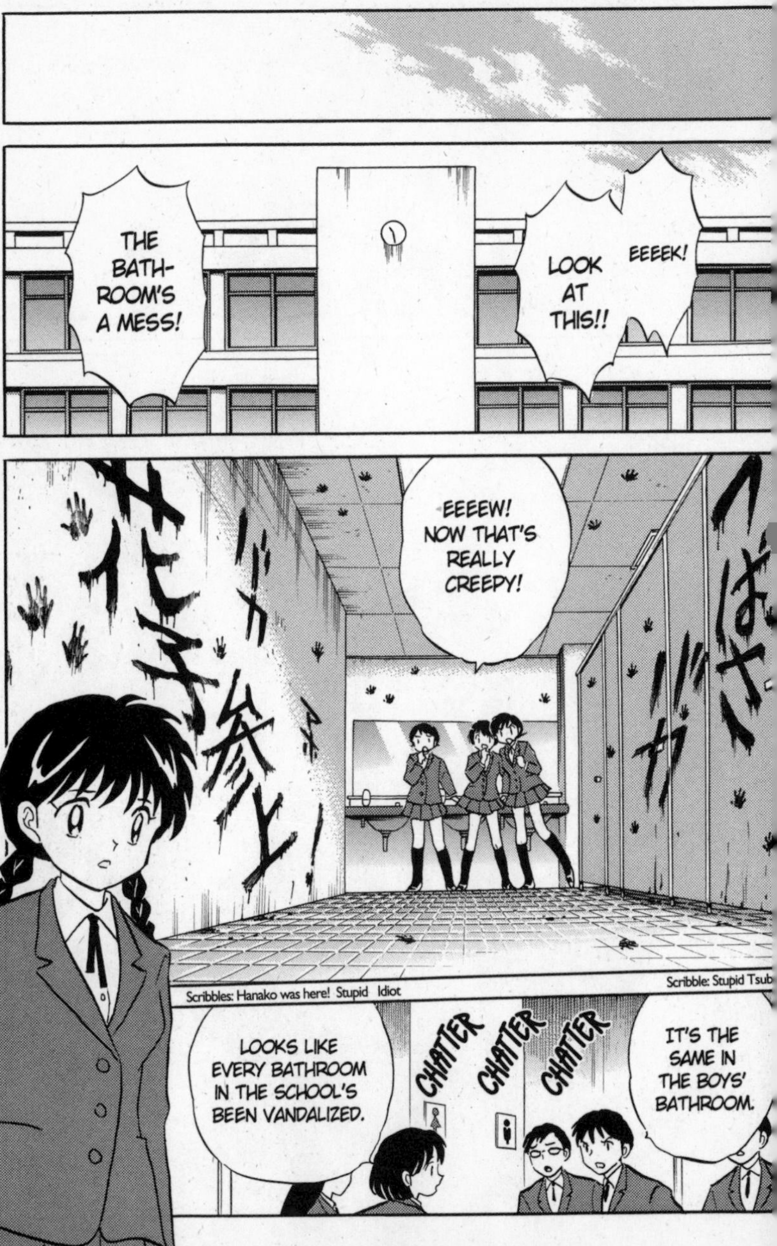
EEEEK!
LOOK AT THIS!!
THE BATH-ROOM'S A MESS!
EEEEW! NOW THAT'S REALLY CREEPY!
Scribble: Stupid Tsub
Scribbles: Hanako was here! Stupid Idiot
IT'S THE SAME IN THE BOYS' BATHROOM.
CHATTER
CHATTER
CHATTER
LOOKS LIKE EVERY BATHROOM IN THE SCHOOL'S BEEN VANDALIZED.

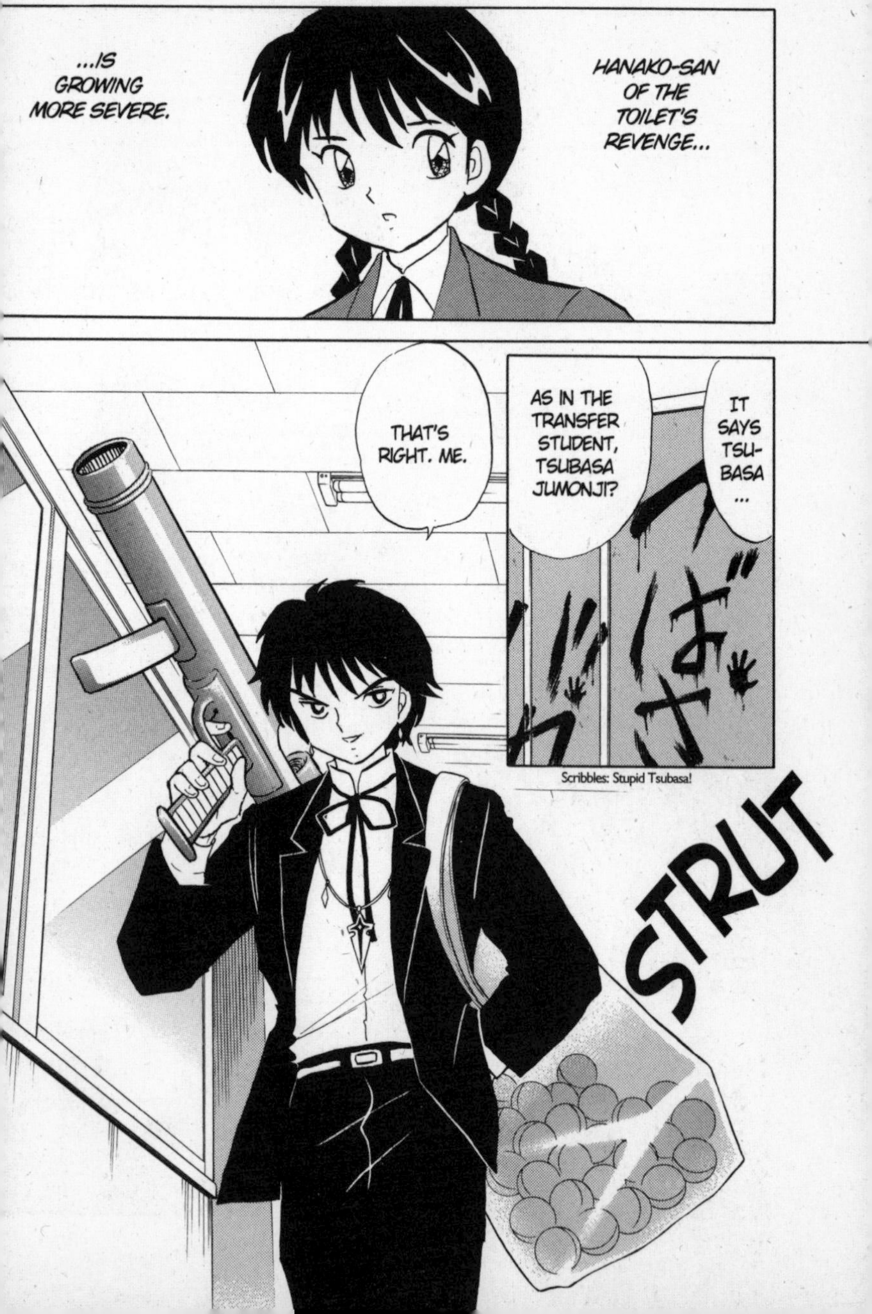
HANAKO-SAN OF THE TOILET'S REVENGE...
...IS GROWING MORE SEVERE.
IT SAYS TSU-BASA ...
AS IN THE TRANSFER STUDENT, TSUBASA JUMONJI?
Scribbles: Stupid Tsubasa!
THAT'S RIGHT. ME.
STRUT

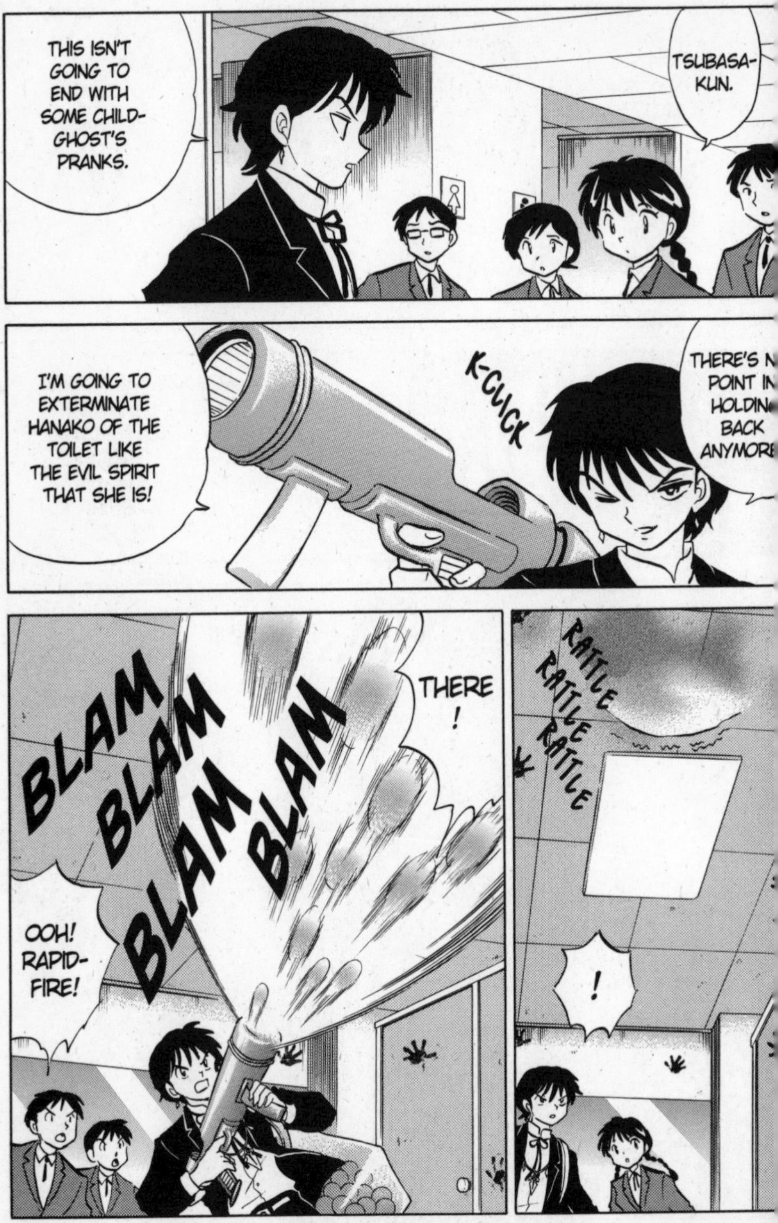
TSUBASA-KUN.
THIS ISN'T GOING TO END WITH SOME CHILD-GHOST'S PRANKS.
THERE'S N POINT IN HOLDIN BACK ANYMORE
K-CLICK
I'M GOING TO EXTERMINATE HANAKO OF THE TOILET LIKE THE EVIL SPIRIT THAT SHE IS!
RATTLE RATTLE RATTLE
!
THERE!
BLAM BLAM BLAM BLAM
OOH! RAPID-FIRE!

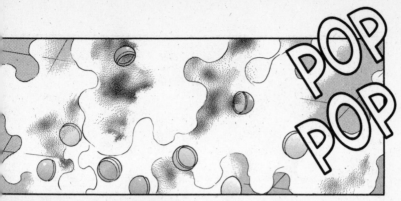

POP POP

THAT'S NOT ALL. THESE SACRED ASH BOMBS ARE A SPECIAL BLEND WITH TEN TIMES THE POTENCY OF THE USUAL ANTI-EVIL SPIRIT KIND I USE!

KOFF KOFF!

FAZE

ZAP ZAP

HMPH.

HANAKO-SAN!

KOFF KOFF!

KOFF KOFF!

90

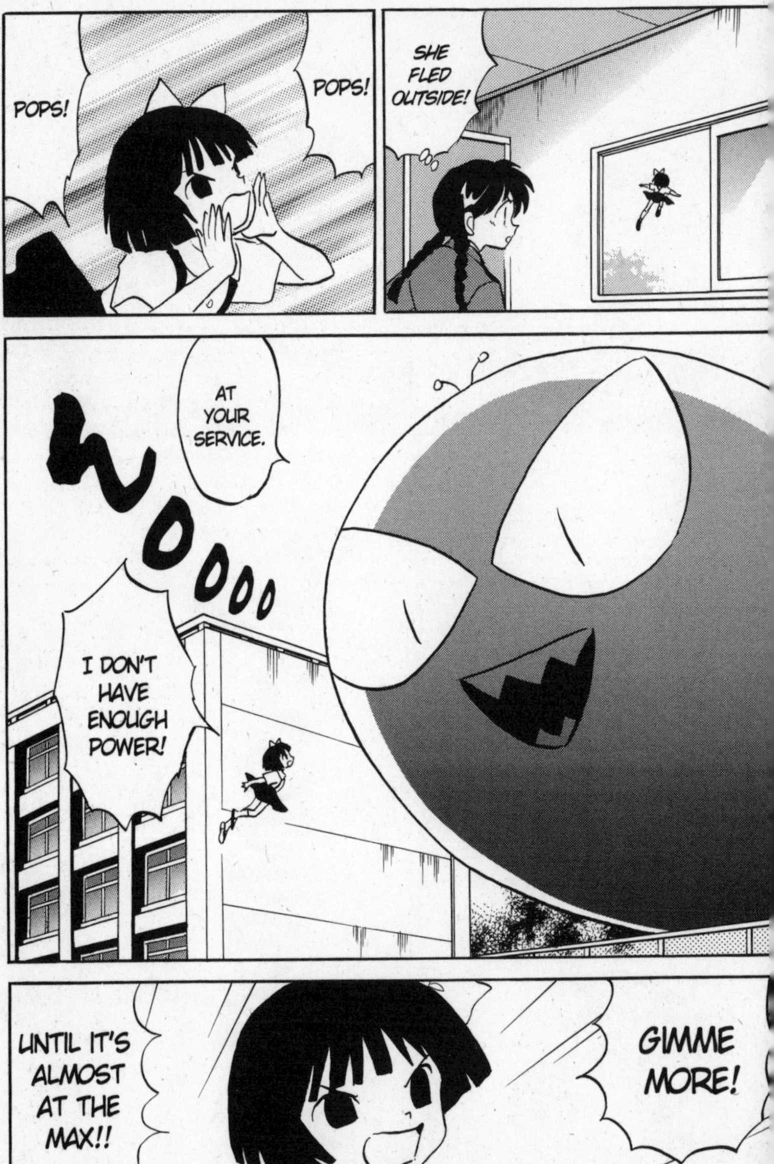
SHE FLED OUTSIDE!
POPS!
POPS!
AT YOUR SERVICE.
WOOOOO
I DON'T HAVE ENOUGH POWER!
GIMME MORE!
UNTIL IT'S ALMOST AT THE MAX!!

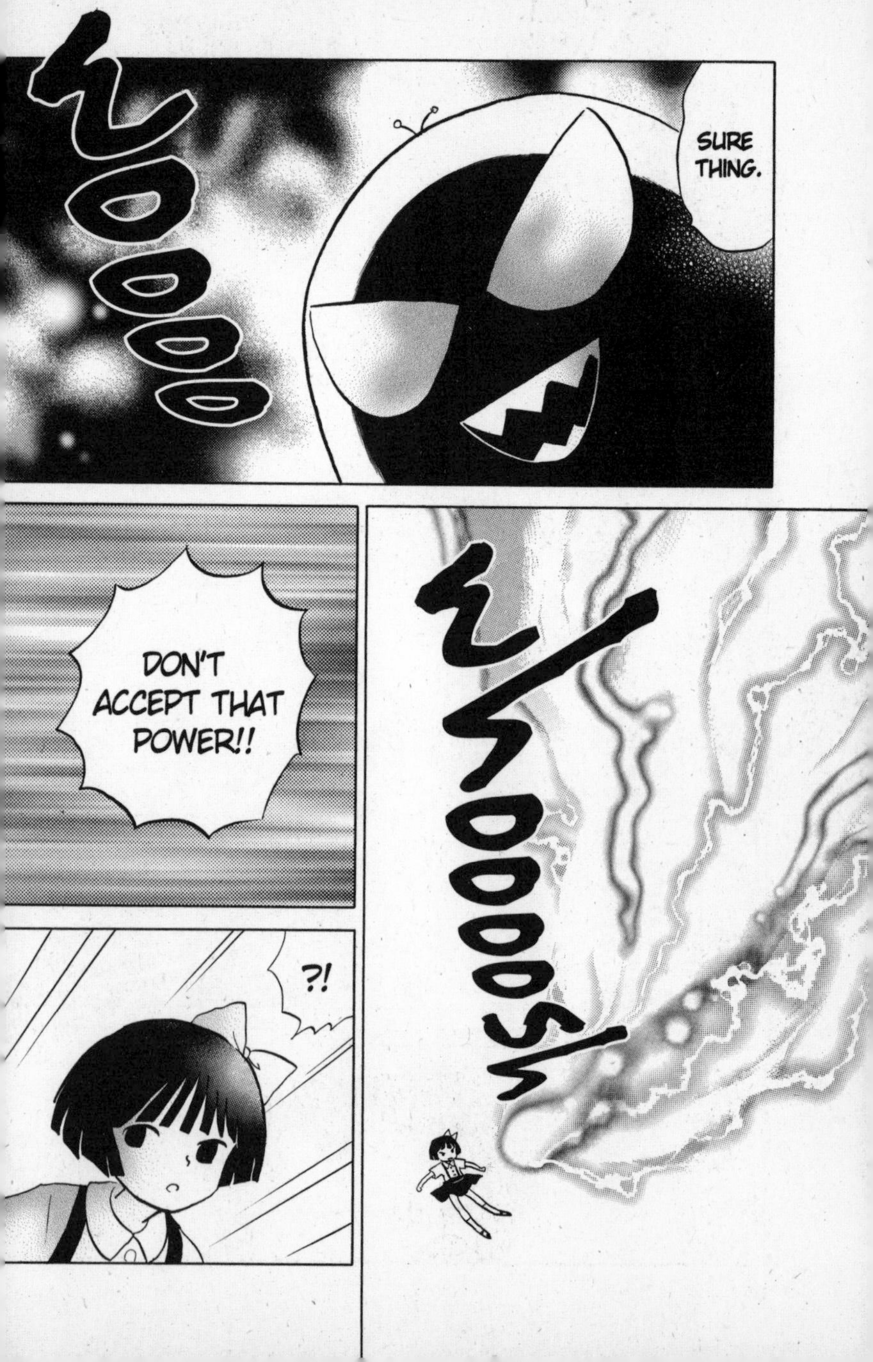
SURE THING.
DON'T ACCEPT THAT POWER!!
?!

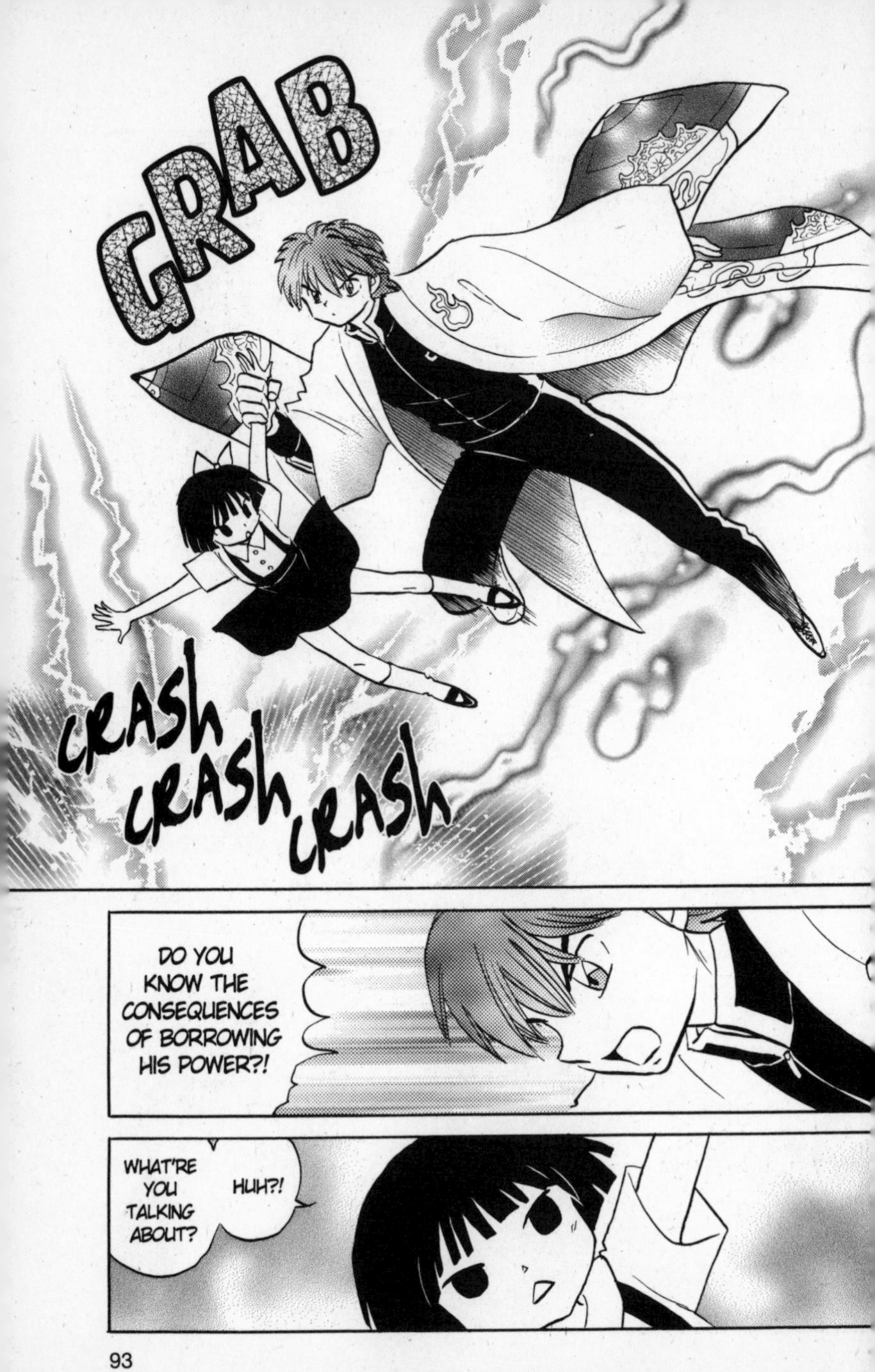
GRAB
CRASH CRASH CRASH
DO YOU KNOW THE CONSEQUENCES OF BORROWING HIS POWER?!
HUH?!
WHAT'RE YOU TALKING ABOUT?

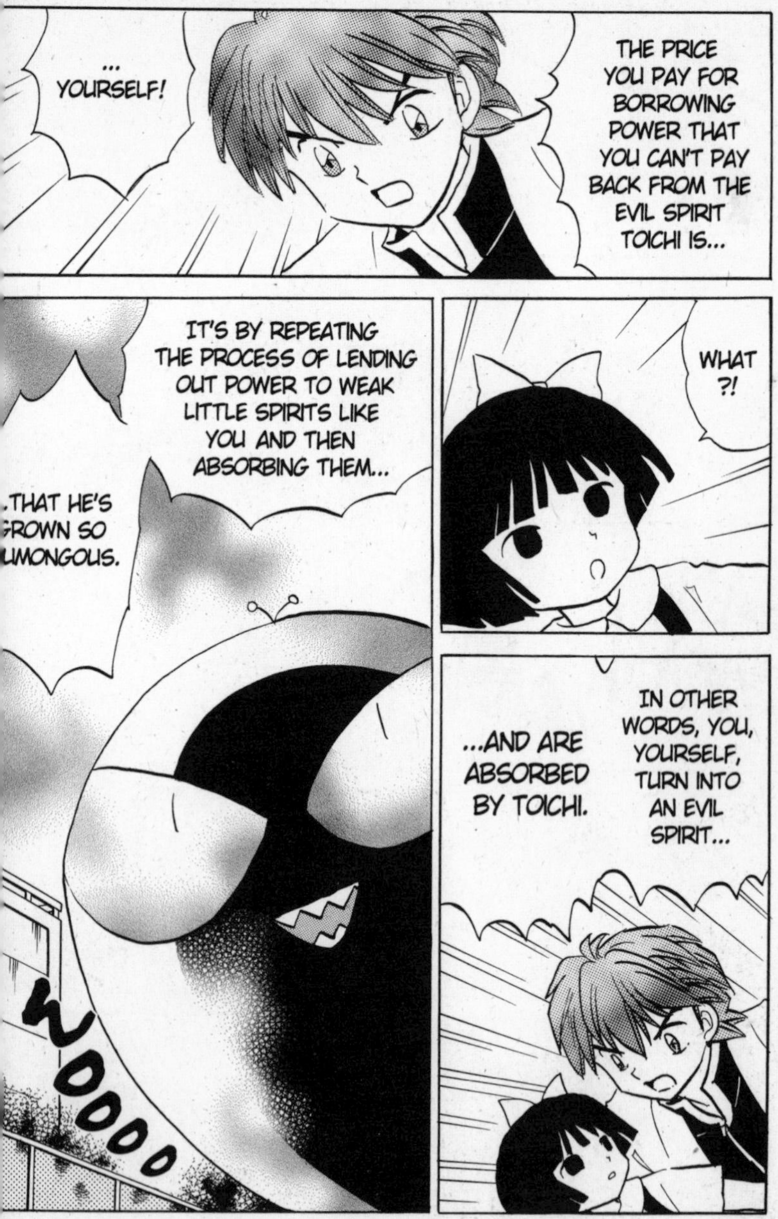
THE PRICE YOU PAY FOR BORROWING POWER THAT YOU CAN'T PAY BACK FROM THE EVIL SPIRIT TOICHI IS...
... YOURSELF!
WHAT ?!
IT'S BY REPEATING THE PROCESS OF LENDING OUT POWER TO WEAK LITTLE SPIRITS LIKE YOU AND THEN ABSORBING THEM...
.THAT HE'S GROWN SO UMONGOUS.
WOOOOO
IN OTHER WORDS, YOU, YOURSELF, TURN INTO AN EVIL SPIRIT...
...AND ARE ABSORBED BY TOICHI.

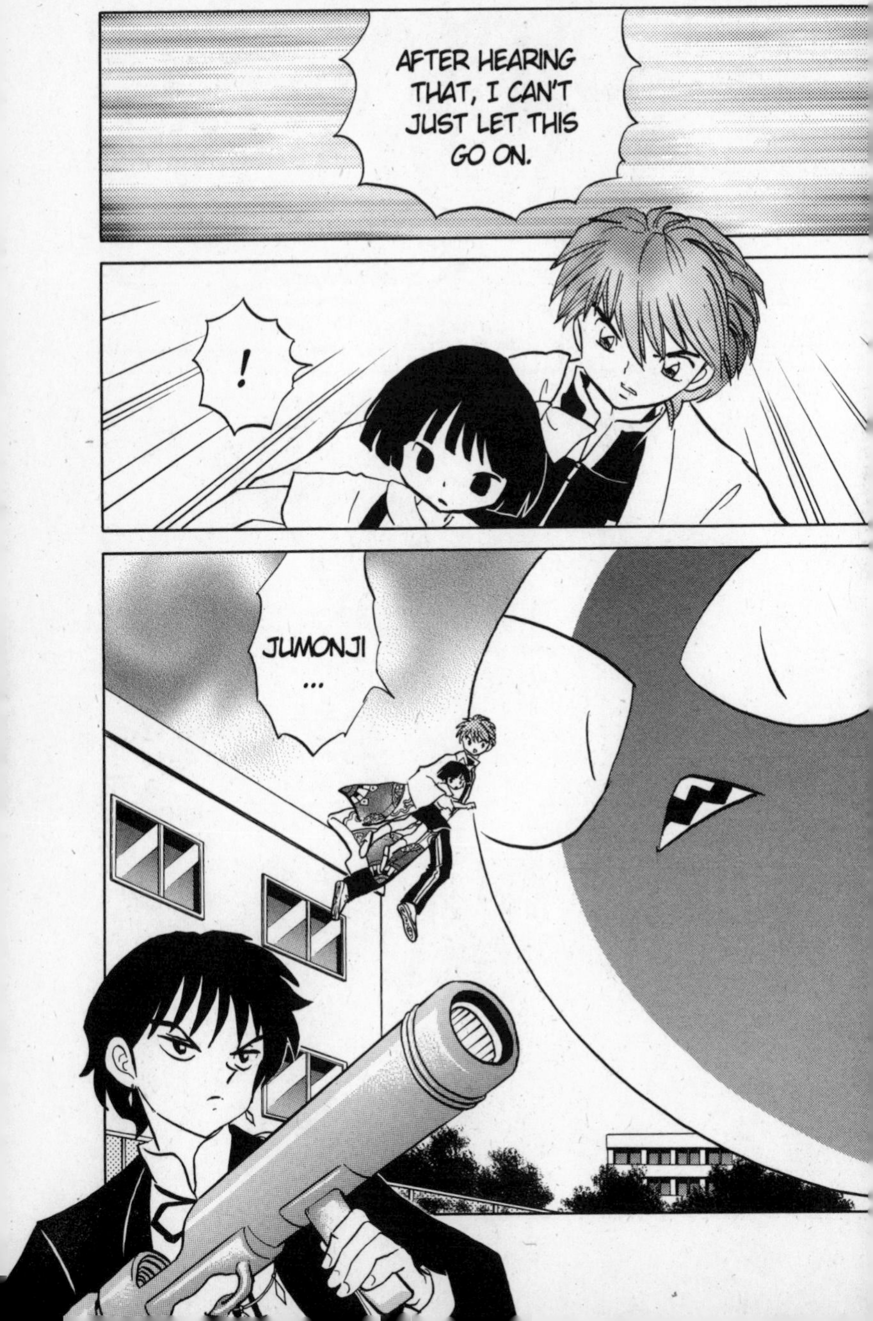
AFTER HEARING THAT, I CAN'T JUST LET THIS GO ON.
!
JUMONJI ...

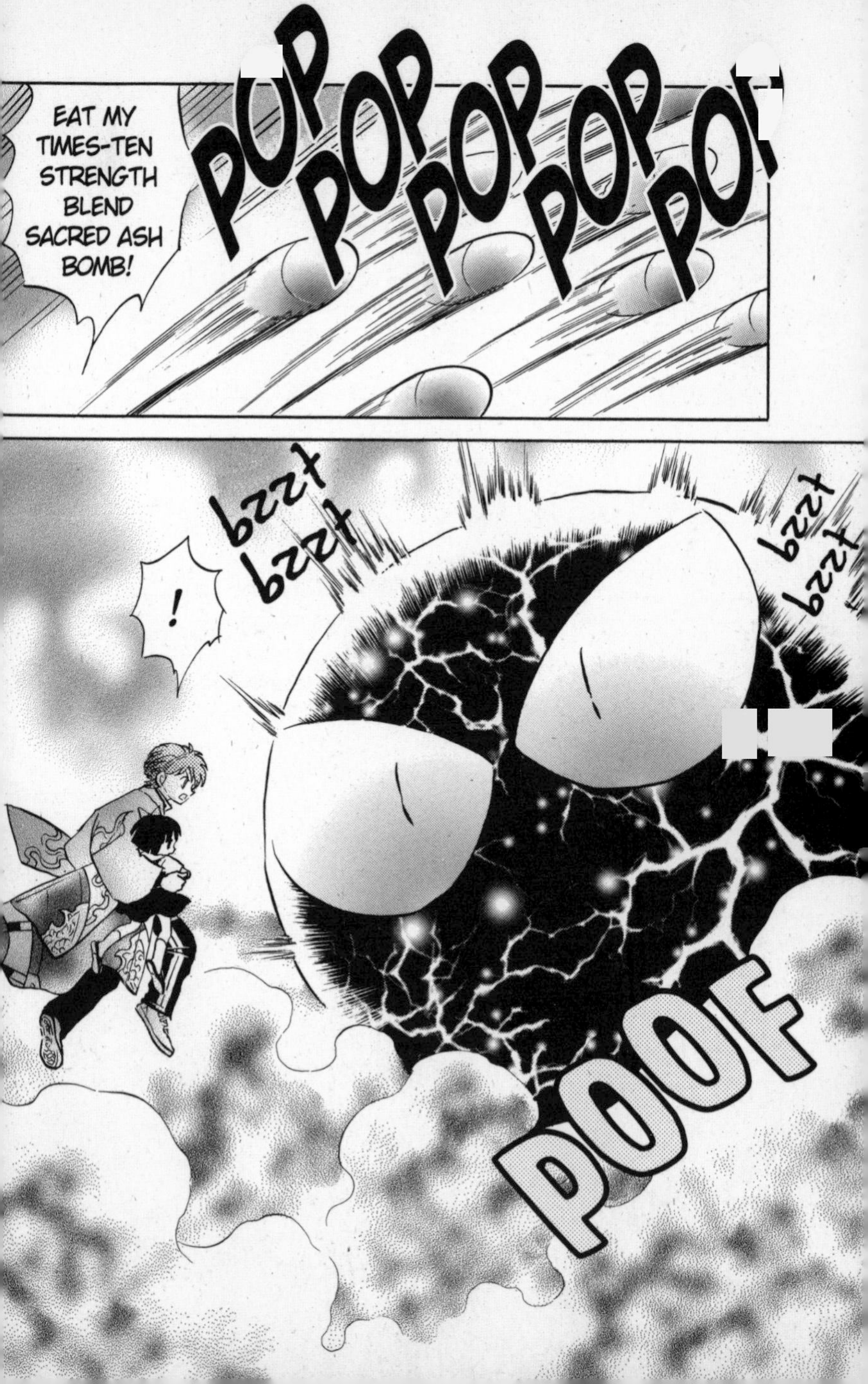
POP POP POP POP POP
EAT MY TIMES-TEN STRENGTH BLEND SACRED ASH BOMB!
bzzt bzzt
bzzt bzzt
!
POOF

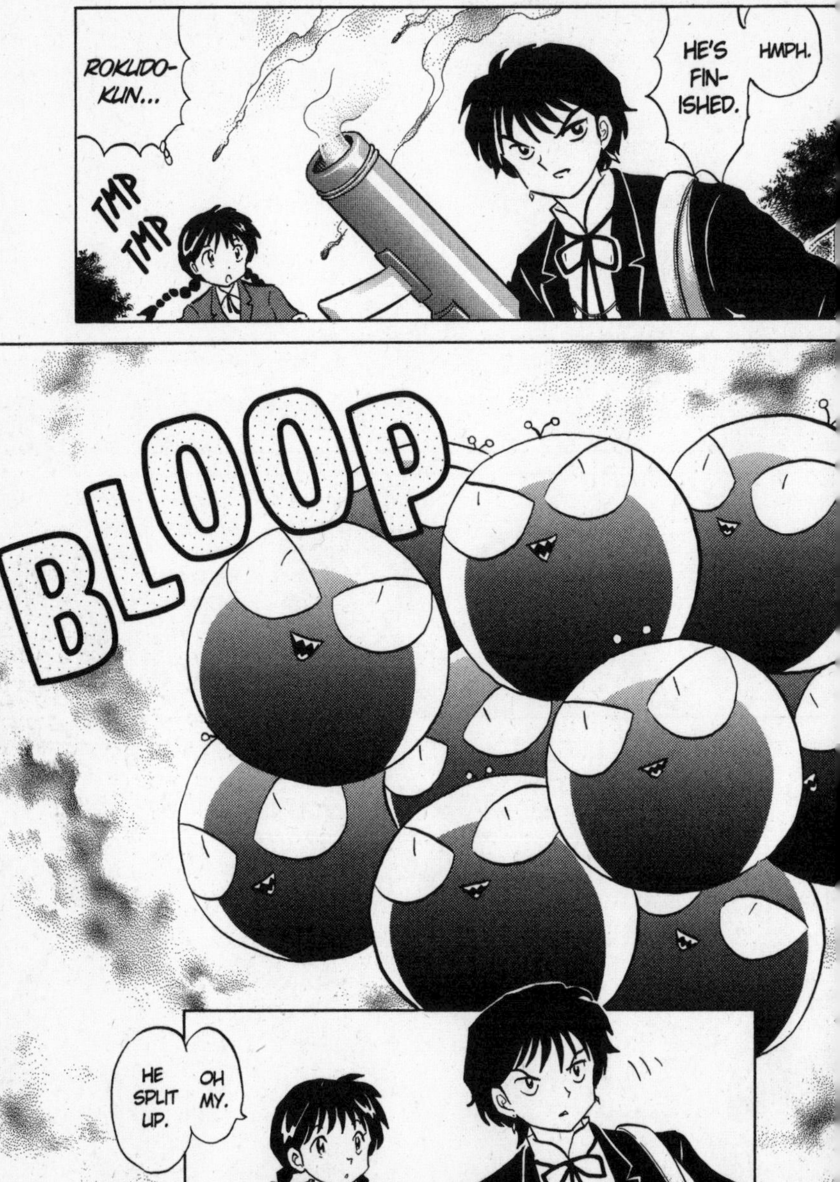
HMPH.
HE'S FIN-ISHED.
ROKUDO-KUN...
TMP TMP
BLOOP
OH MY.
HE SPLIT UP.

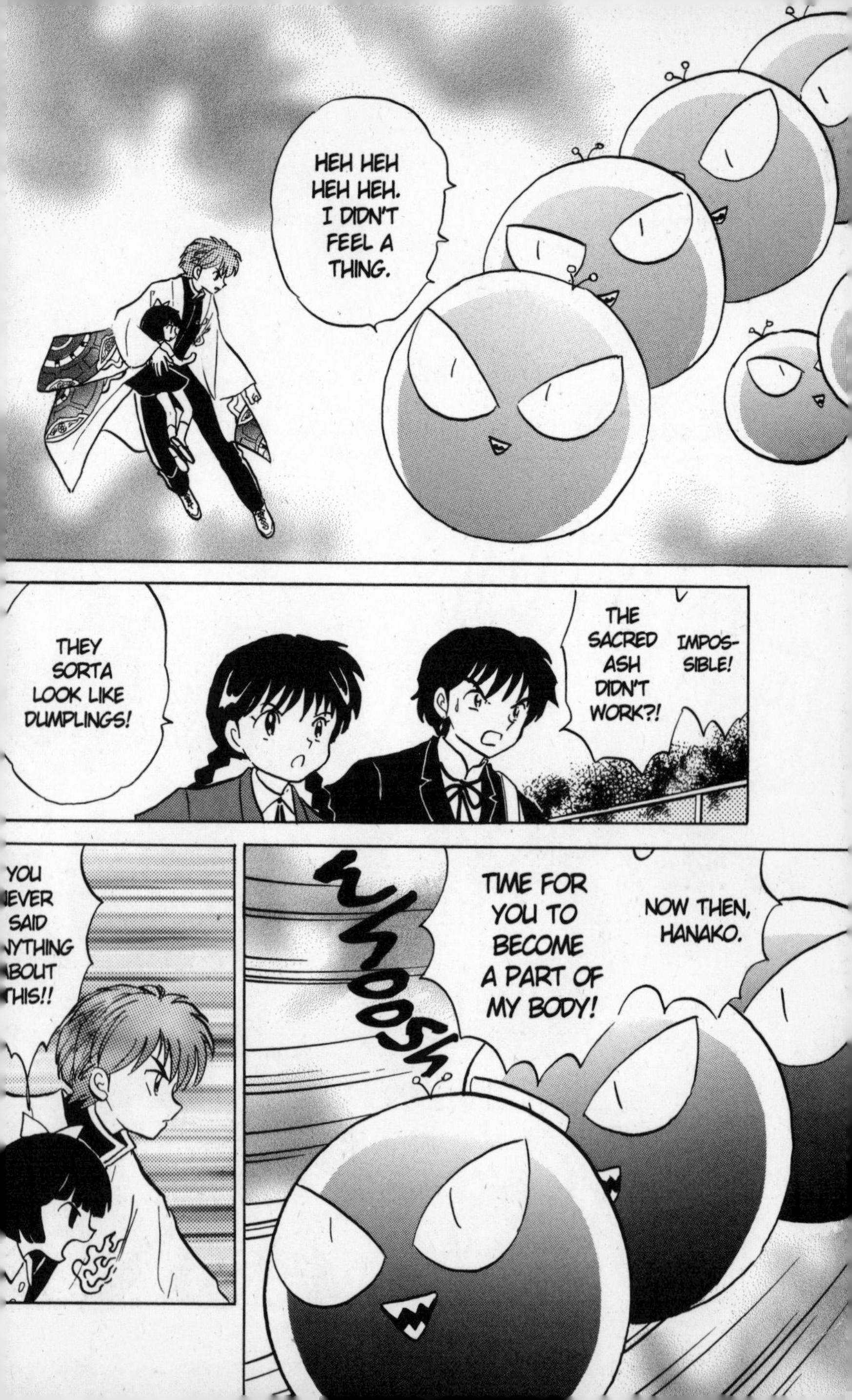
HEH HEH HEH HEH. I DIDN'T FEEL A THING.
IMPOS-SIBLE!
THE SACRED ASH DIDN'T WORK?!
THEY SORTA LOOK LIKE DUMPLINGS!
NOW THEN, HANAKO.
TIME FOR YOU TO BECOME A PART OF MY BODY!
WHOOSH
YOU NEVER SAID NYTHING BOUT THIS!!

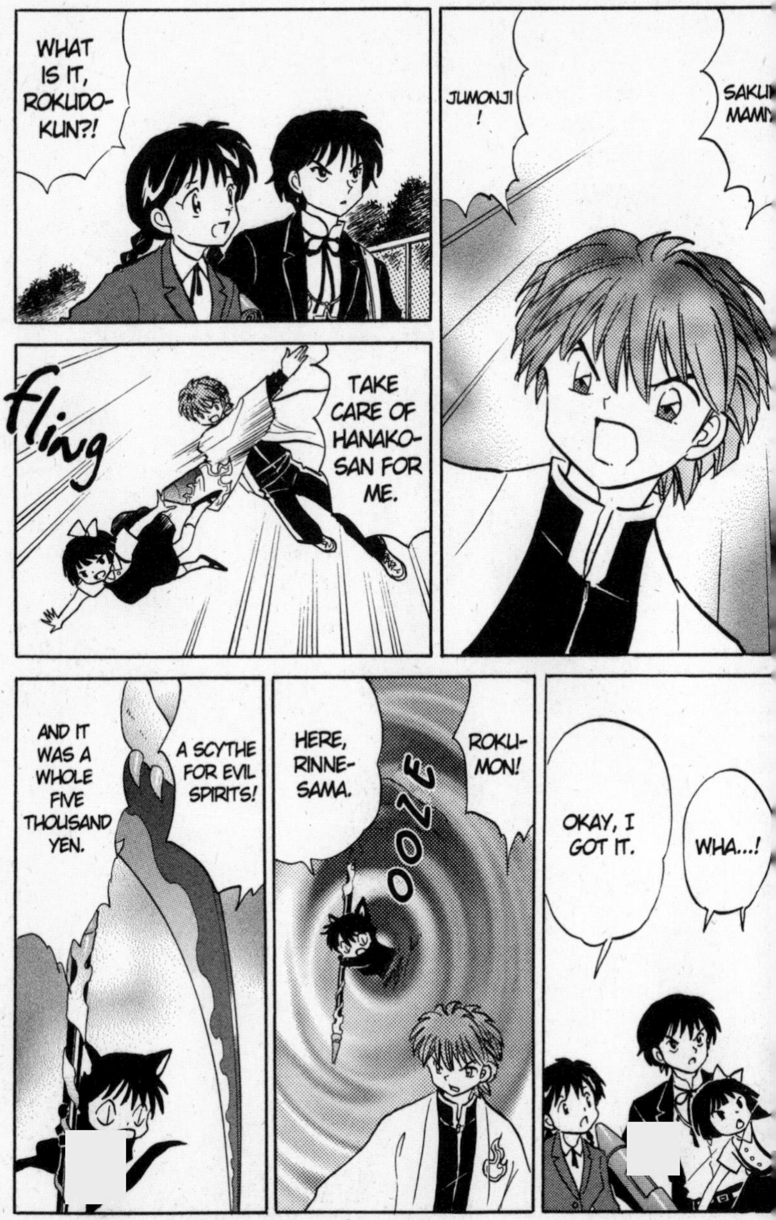
JUMONJI!
WHAT IS IT, ROKUDO-KUN?!
TAKE CARE OF HANAKO-SAN FOR ME.
fling
WHA...!
OKAY, I GOT IT.
ROKU-MON!
OOZE
HERE, RINNE-SAMA.
A SCYTHE FOR EVIL SPIRITS!
AND IT WAS A WHOLE FIVE THOUSAND YEN.

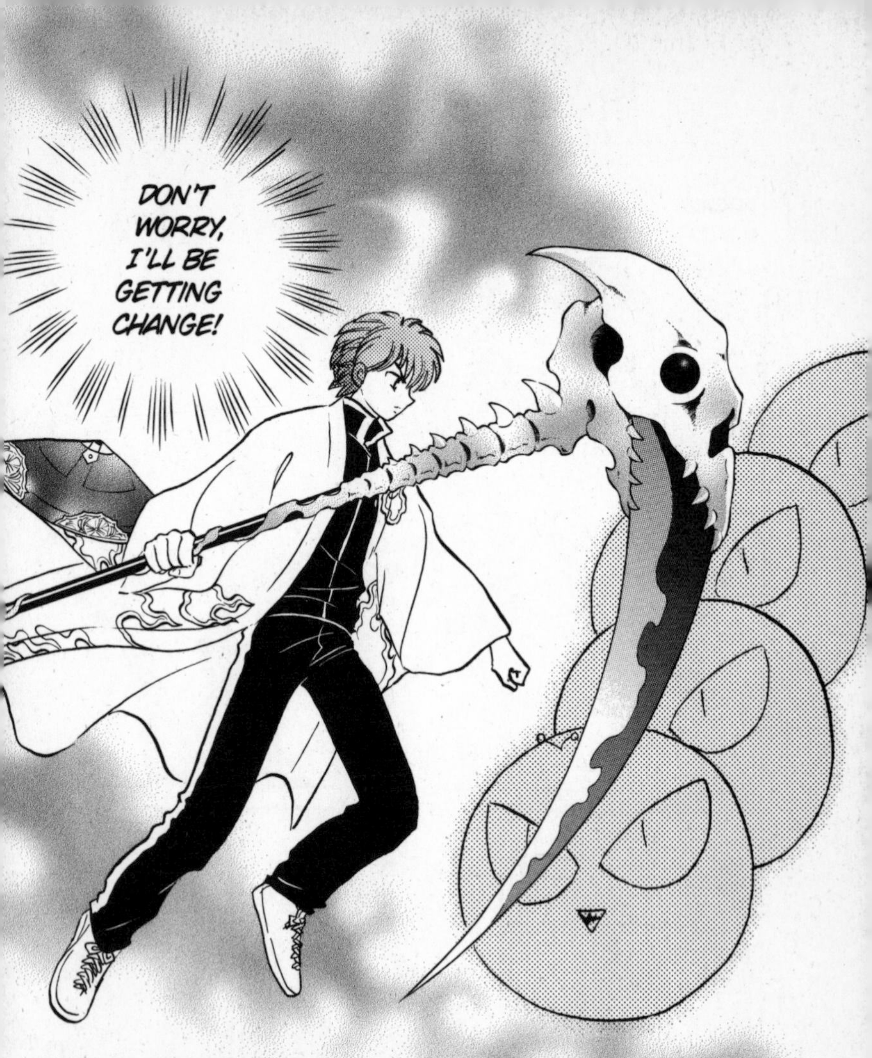
DON'T WORRY, I'LL BE GETTING CHANGE!

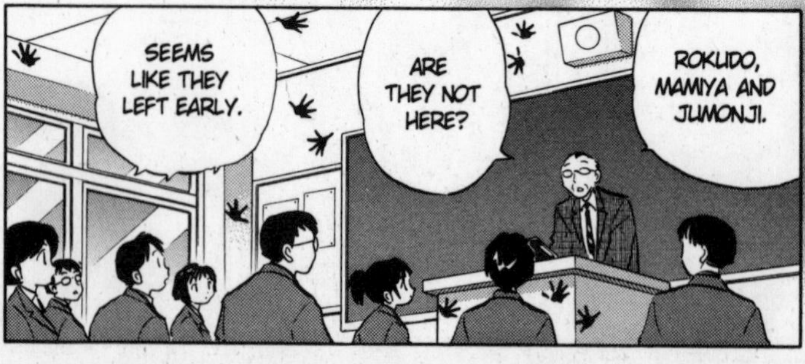
ROKUDO, MAMIYA AND JUMONJI.
ARE THEY NOT HERE?
SEEMS LIKE THEY LEFT EARLY.

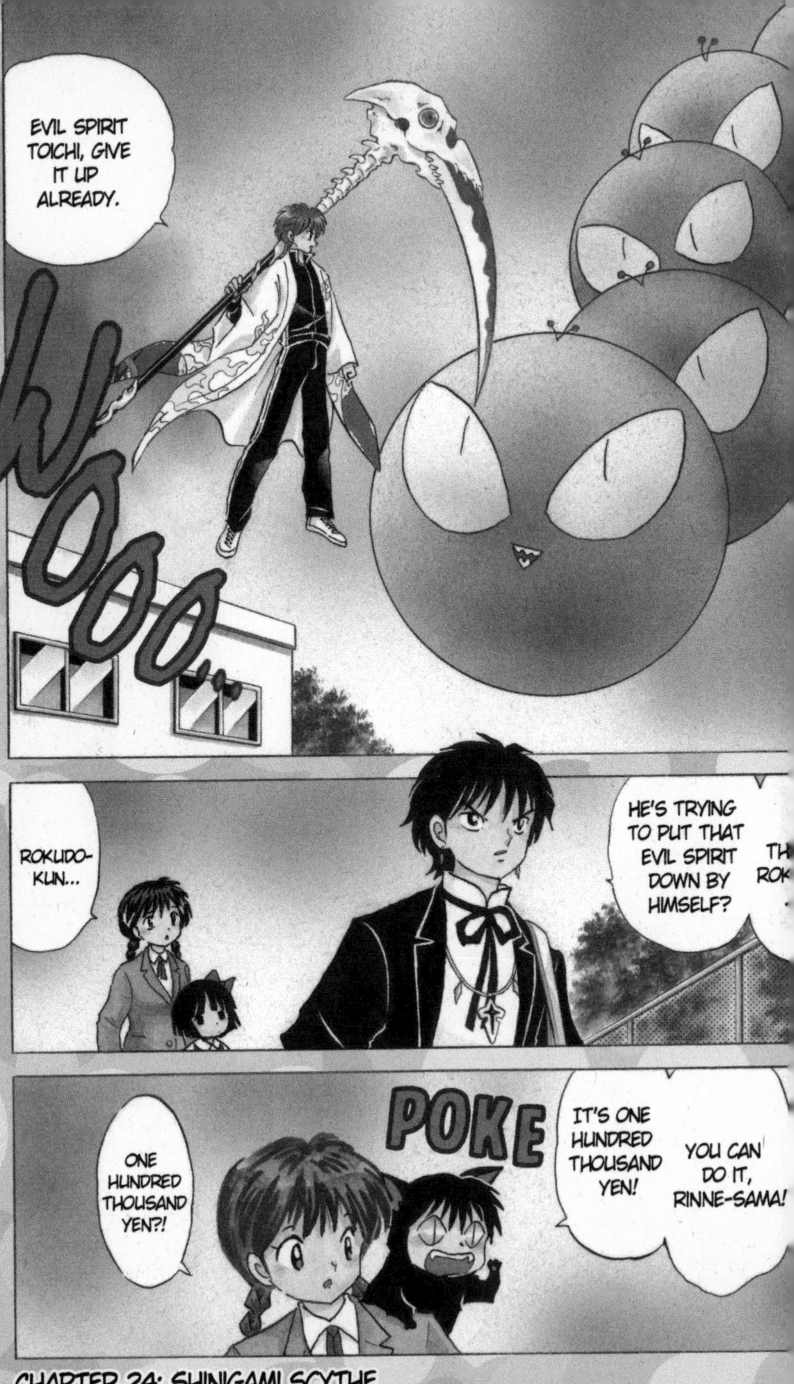
EVIL SPIRIT TOICHI, GIVE IT UP ALREADY.
WOOOO...
HE'S TRYING TO PUT THAT EVIL SPIRIT DOWN BY HIMSELF?
ROKUDO-KUN...
YOU CAN DO IT, RINNE-SAMA!
IT'S ONE HUNDRED THOUSAND YEN!
POKE
ONE HUNDRED THOUSAND YEN?!

CHAPTER 24: SHINIGAMI SCYTHE

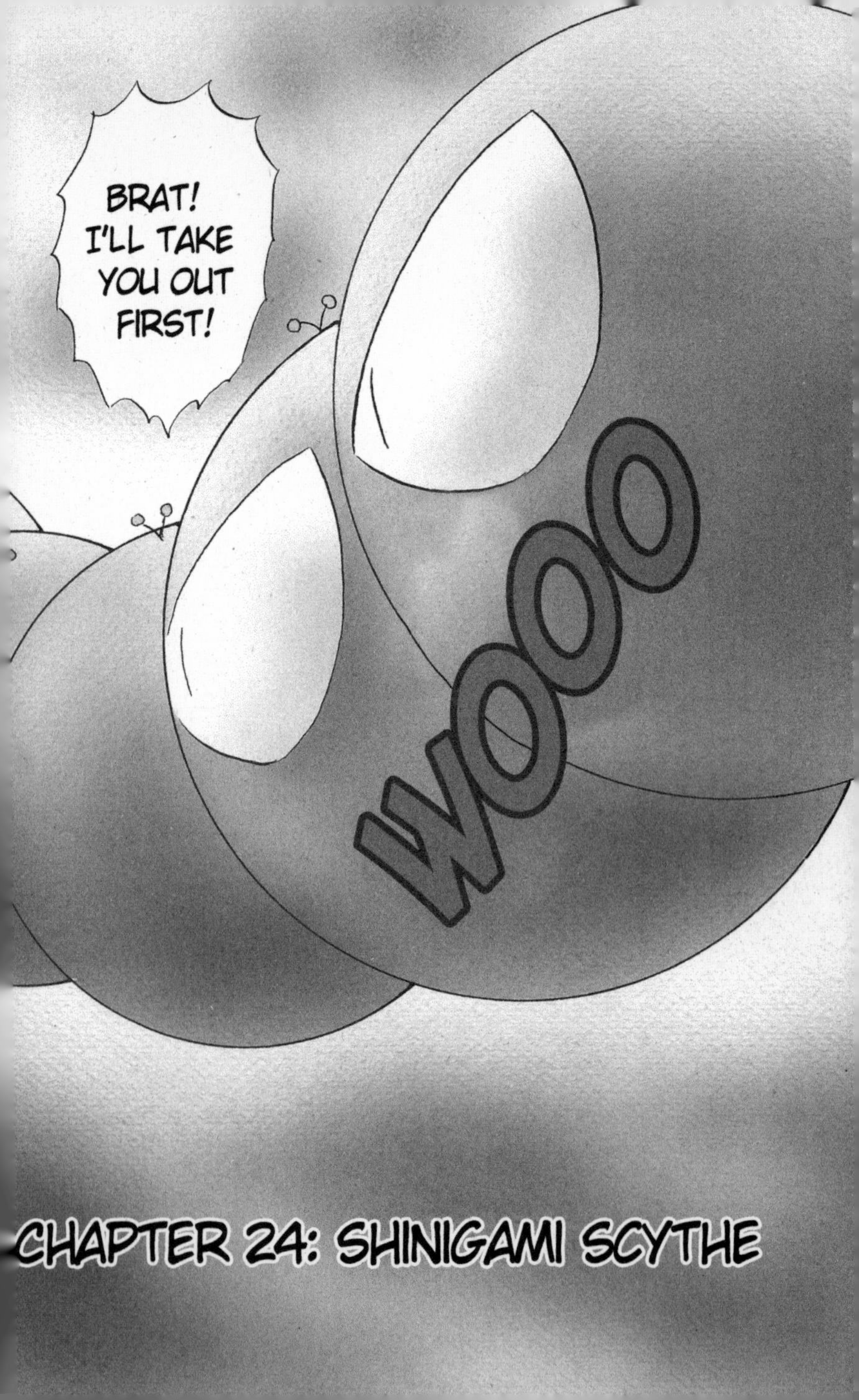
BRAT! I'LL TAKE YOU OUT FIRST!
WOOO

CHAPTER 24: SHINIGAMI SCYTHE

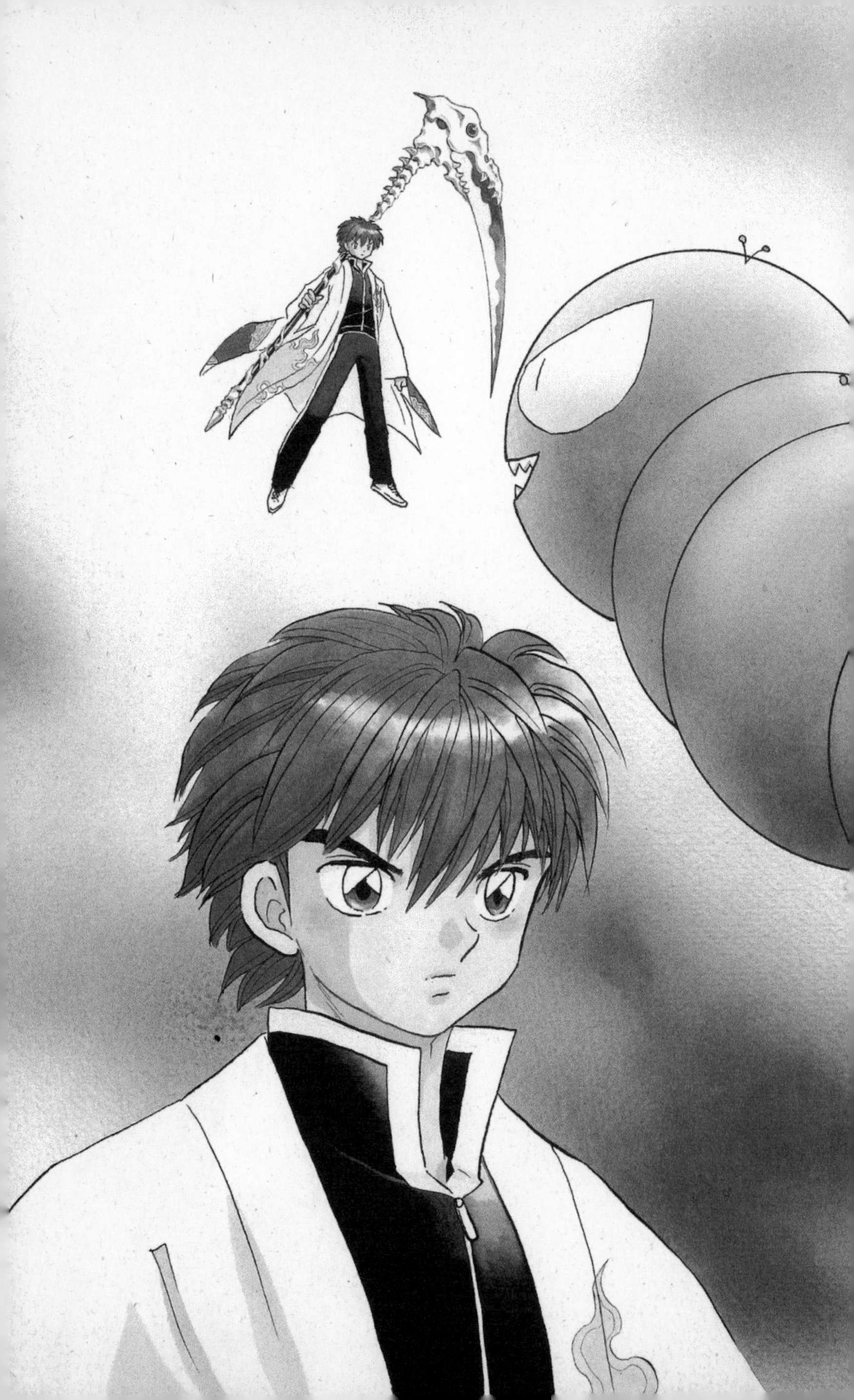

RIN-NE

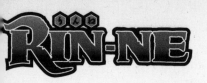

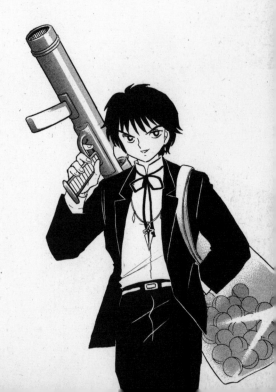

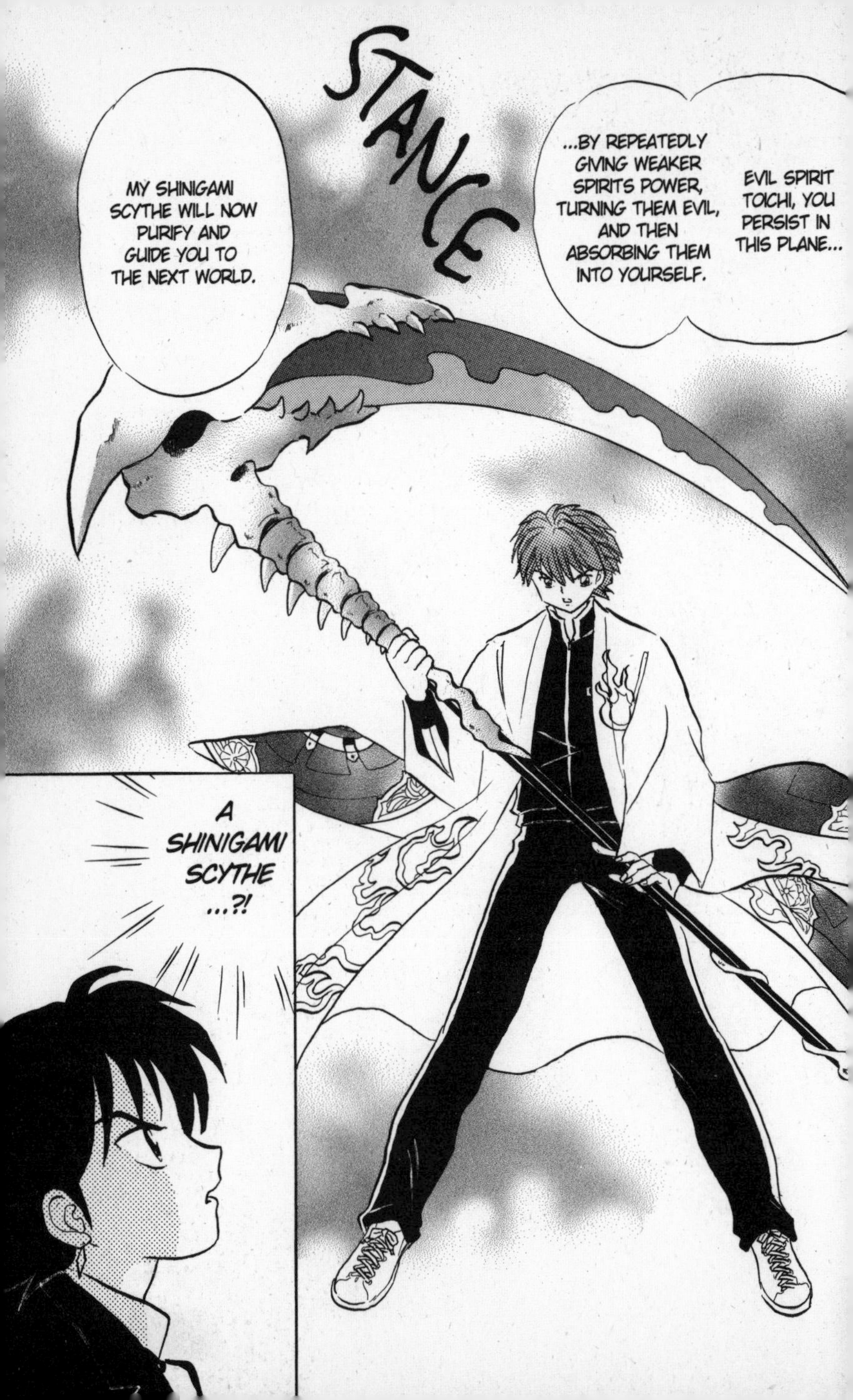
EVIL SPIRIT TOICHI, YOU PERSIST IN THIS PLANE...
...BY REPEATEDLY GIVING WEAKER SPIRITS POWER, TURNING THEM EVIL, AND THEN ABSORBING THEM INTO YOURSELF.
STANCE
MY SHINIGAMI SCYTHE WILL NOW PURIFY AND GUIDE YOU TO THE NEXT WORLD.
A SHINIGAMI SCYTHE ...?!

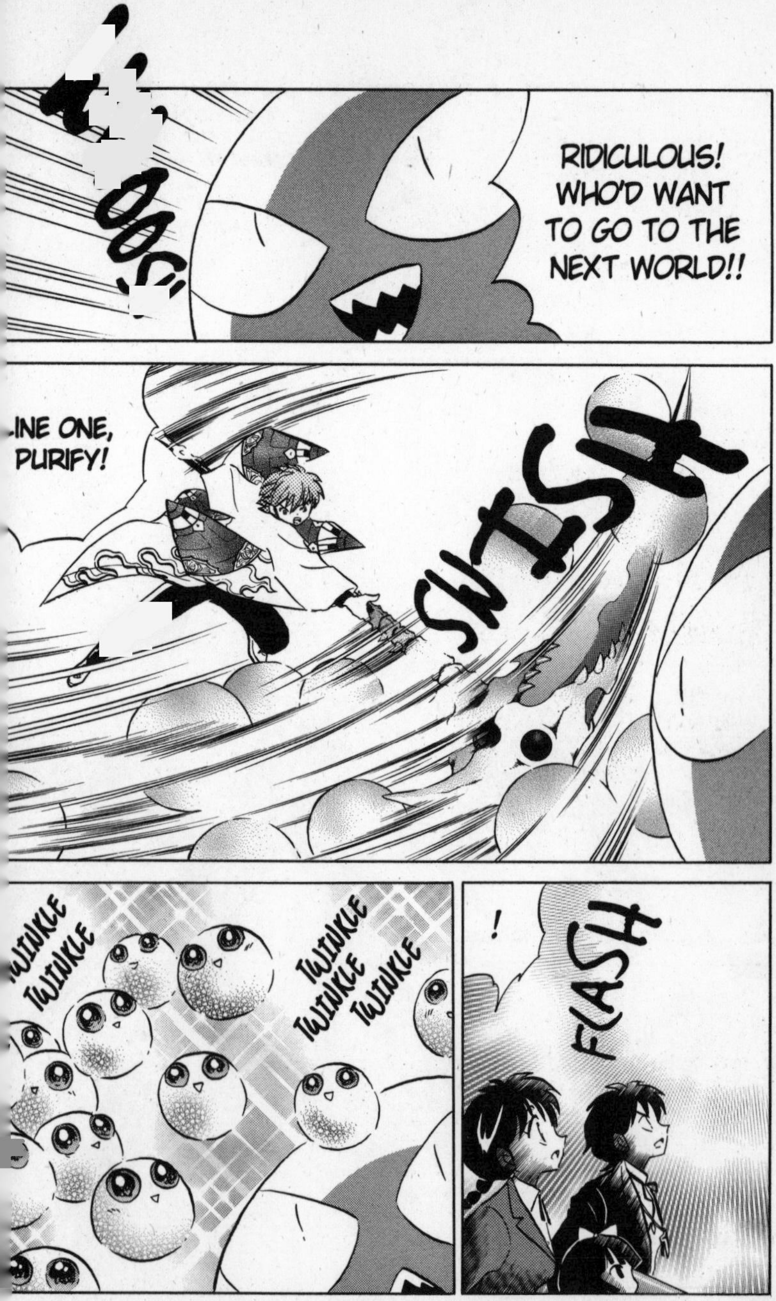
RIDICULOUS! WHO'D WANT TO GO TO THE NEXT WORLD!!
SWISH
LINE ONE, PURIFY!
FLASH
!
TWINKLE TWINKLE TWINKLE
TWINKLE TWINKLE

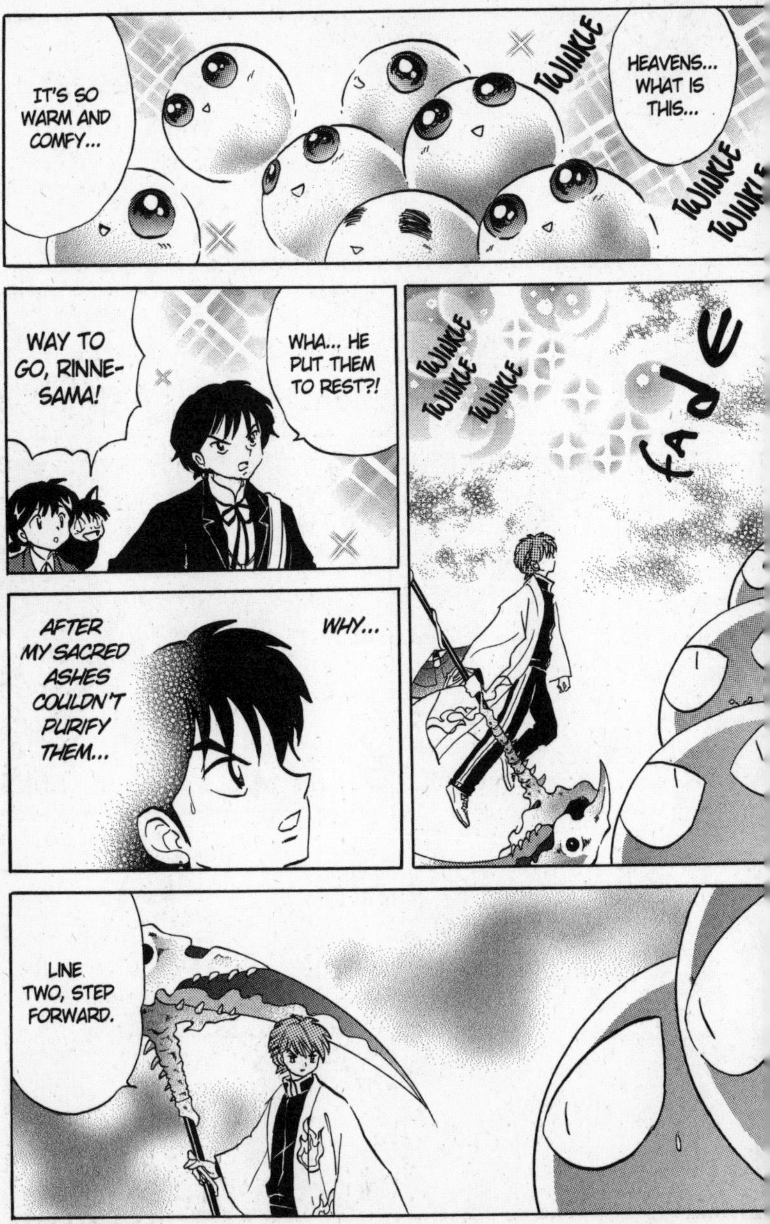
HEAVENS... WHAT IS THIS...
TWINKLE
TWINKLE
TWINKLE
IT'S SO WARM AND COMFY...
FADE
TWINKLE
TWINKLE
TWINKLE
WHA... HE PUT THEM TO REST?!
WAY TO GO, RINNE-SAMA!
WHY...
AFTER MY SACRED ASHES COULDN'T PURIFY THEM...
LINE TWO, STEP FORWARD.

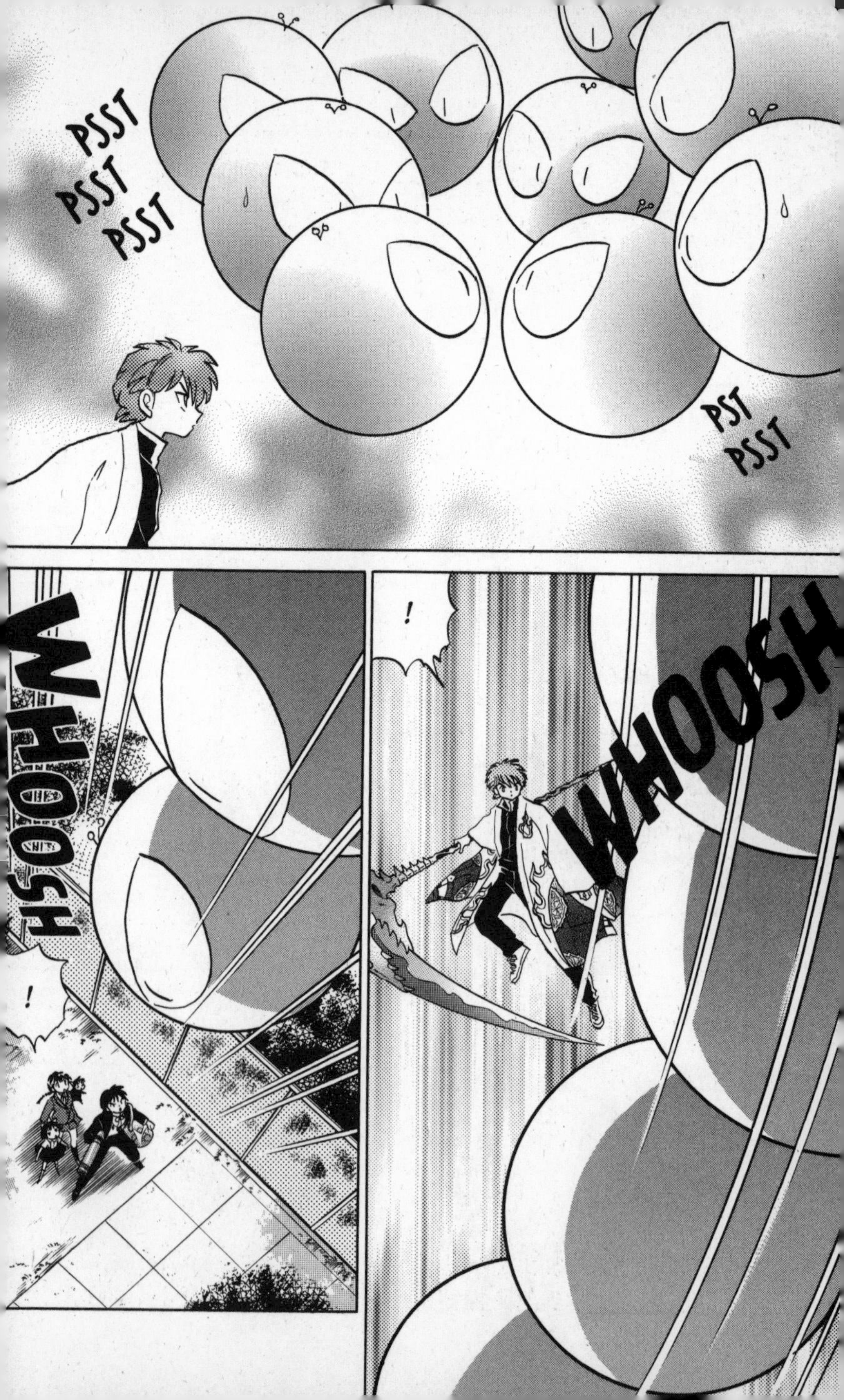
PSST
PSST
PSST
PSST
PST
PSST
!
WHOOSH
WHOOSH
!

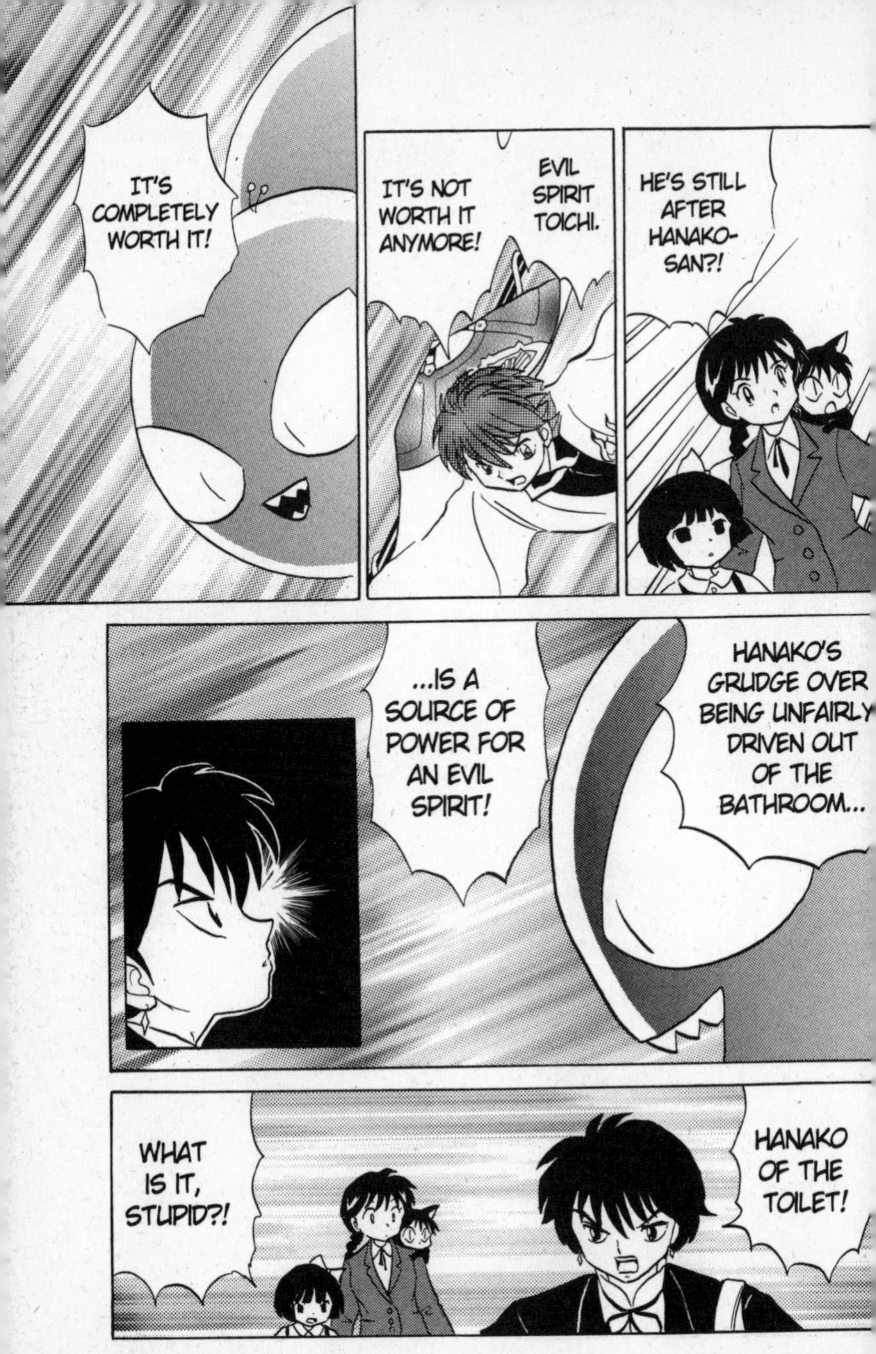
HE'S STILL AFTER HANAKO-SAN?!
EVIL SPIRIT TOICHI.
IT'S NOT WORTH IT ANYMORE!
IT'S COMPLETELY WORTH IT!
HANAKO'S GRUDGE OVER BEING UNFAIRLY DRIVEN OUT OF THE BATHROOM...
...IS A SOURCE OF POWER FOR AN EVIL SPIRIT!
HANAKO OF THE TOILET!
WHAT IS IT, STUPID?!

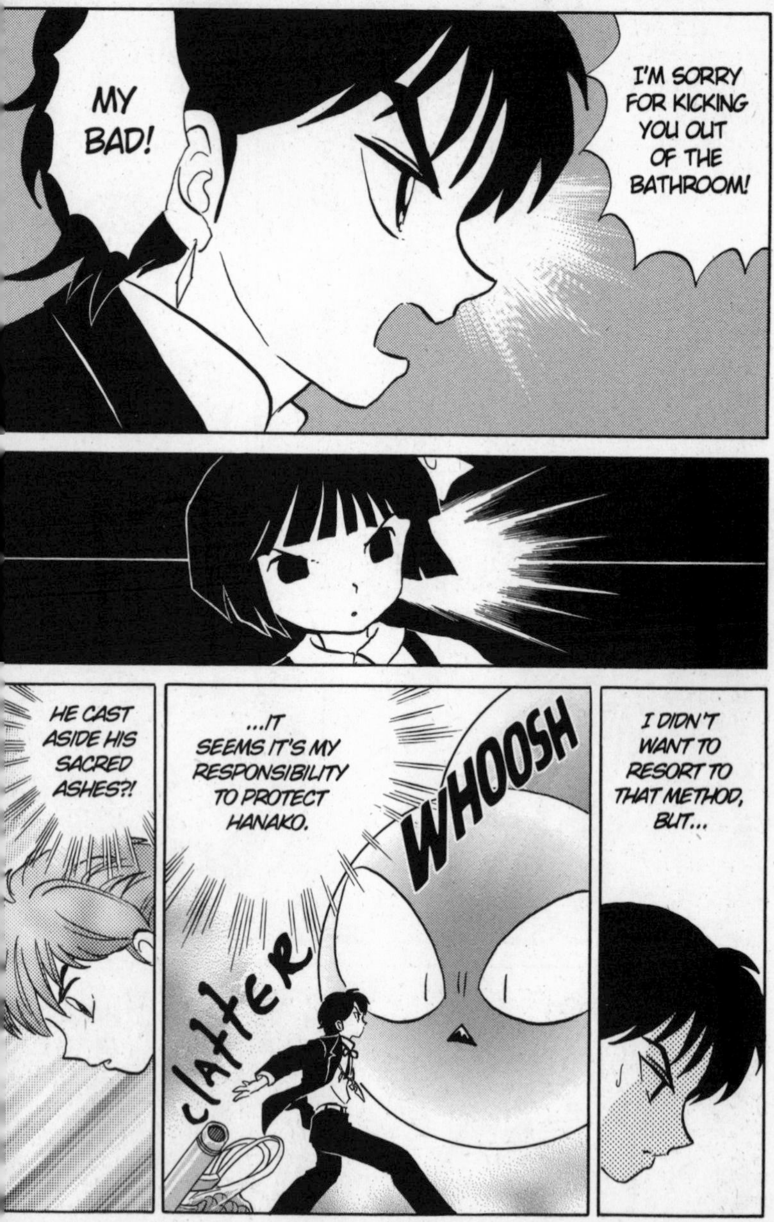
I'M SORRY FOR KICKING YOU OUT OF THE BATHROOM!
MY BAD!
I DIDN'T WANT TO RESORT TO THAT METHOD, BUT...
...IT SEEMS IT'S MY RESPONSIBILITY TO PROTECT HANAKO.
WHOOSH
clatter
HE CAST ASIDE HIS SACRED ASHES?!

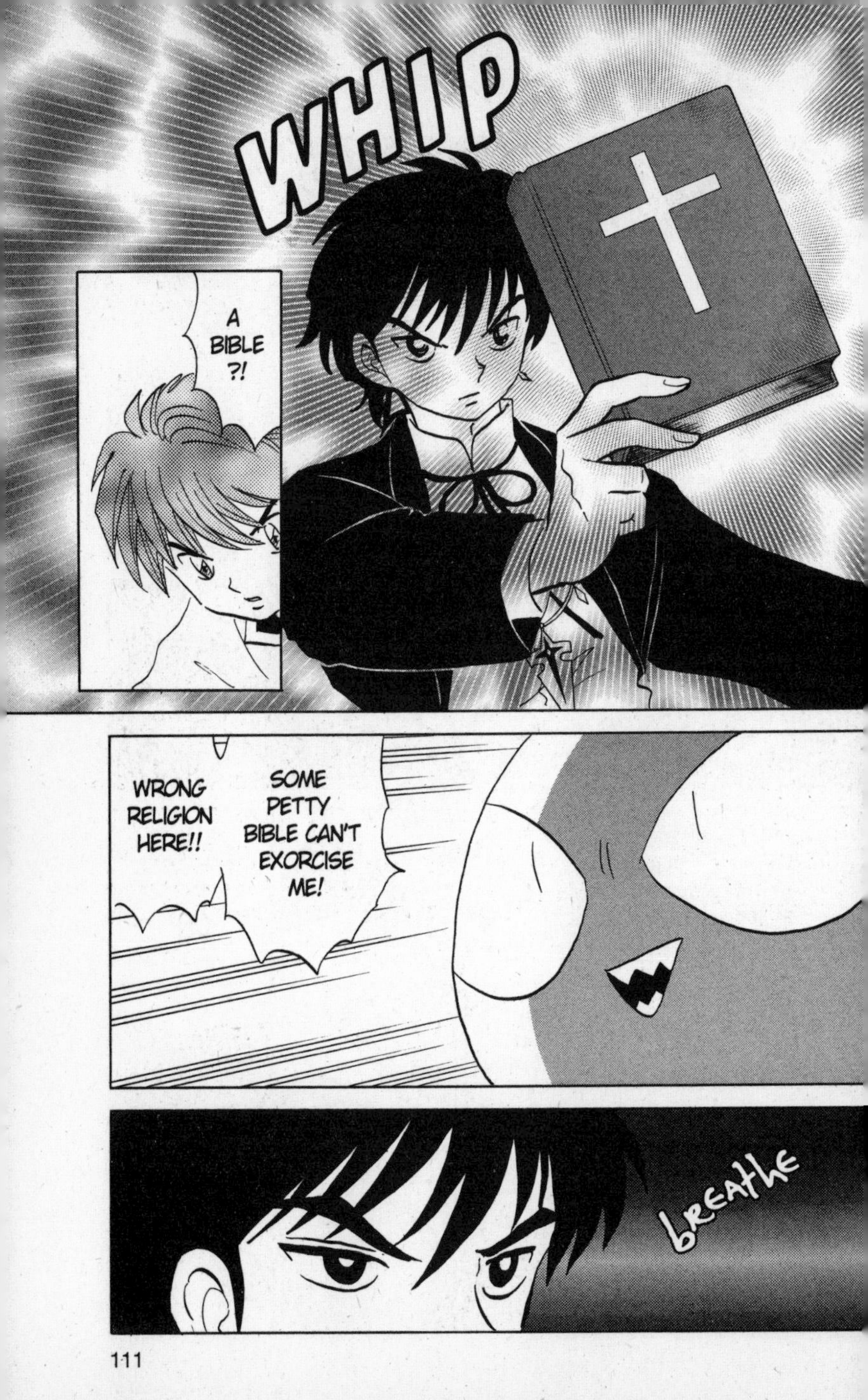
WHIP
A BIBLE ?!
SOME PETTY BIBLE CAN'T EXORCISE ME!
WRONG RELIGION HERE!!
breathe

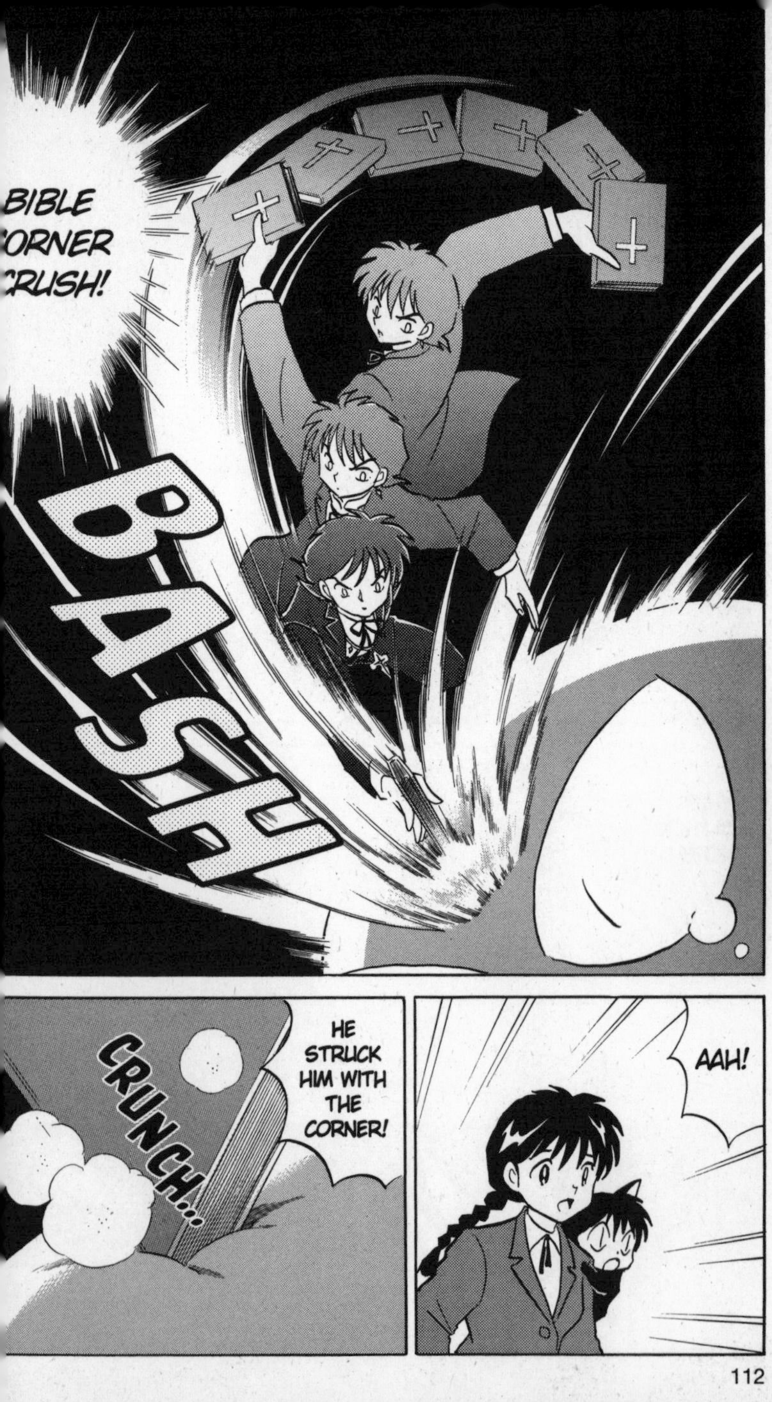
BIBLE
CORNER
CRUSH!
BASH
AAH!
HE STRUCK HIM WITH THE CORNER!
CRUNCH...

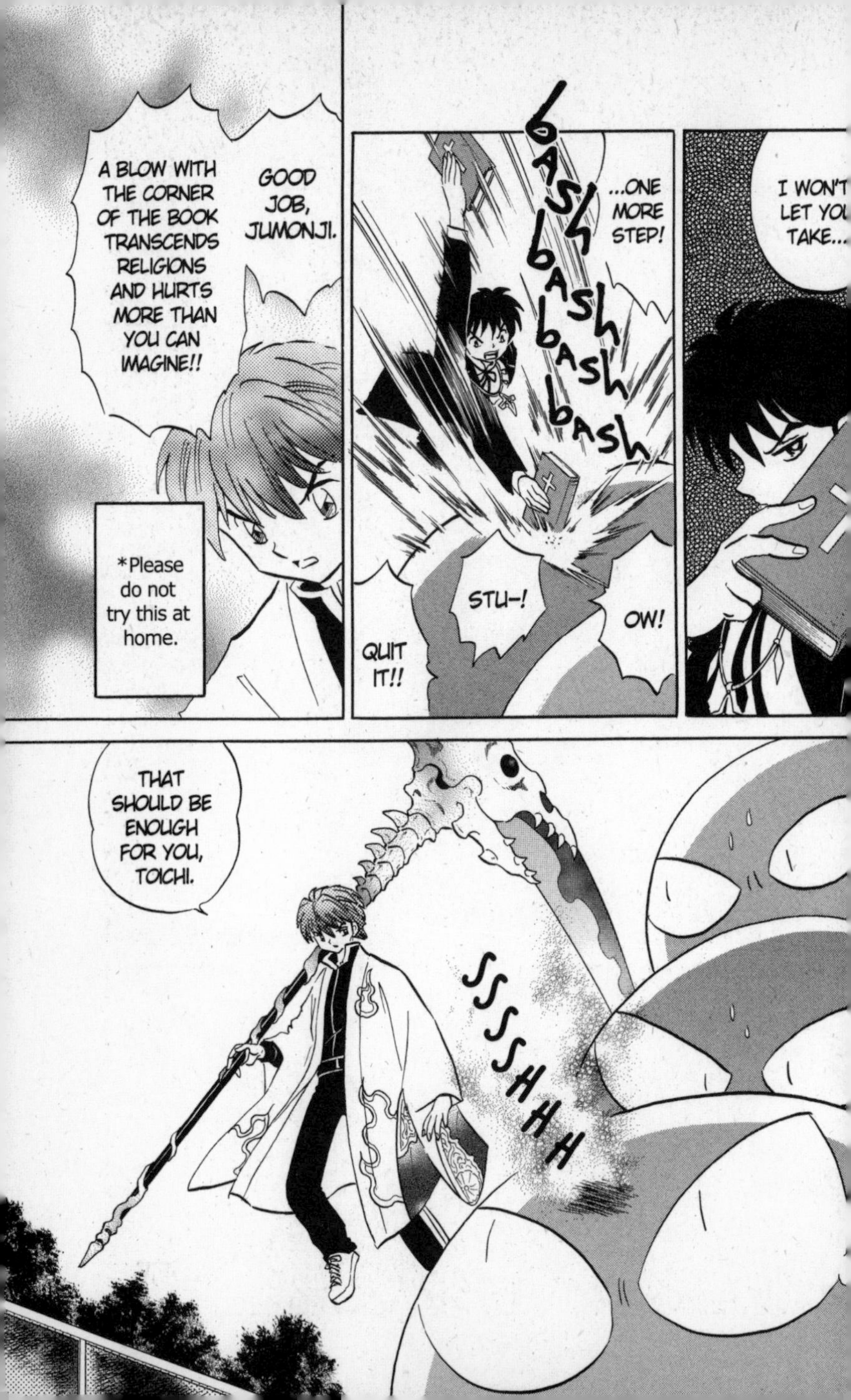
I WON'T LET YOU TAKE...
...ONE MORE STEP!
bash bash bash bash
OW!
STU-!
QUIT IT!!
GOOD JOB, JUMONJI.
A BLOW WITH THE CORNER OF THE BOOK TRANSCENDS RELIGIONS AND HURTS MORE THAN YOU CAN IMAGINE!!
*Please do not try this at home.
THAT SHOULD BE ENOUGH FOR YOU, TOICHI.
SSSSHHH

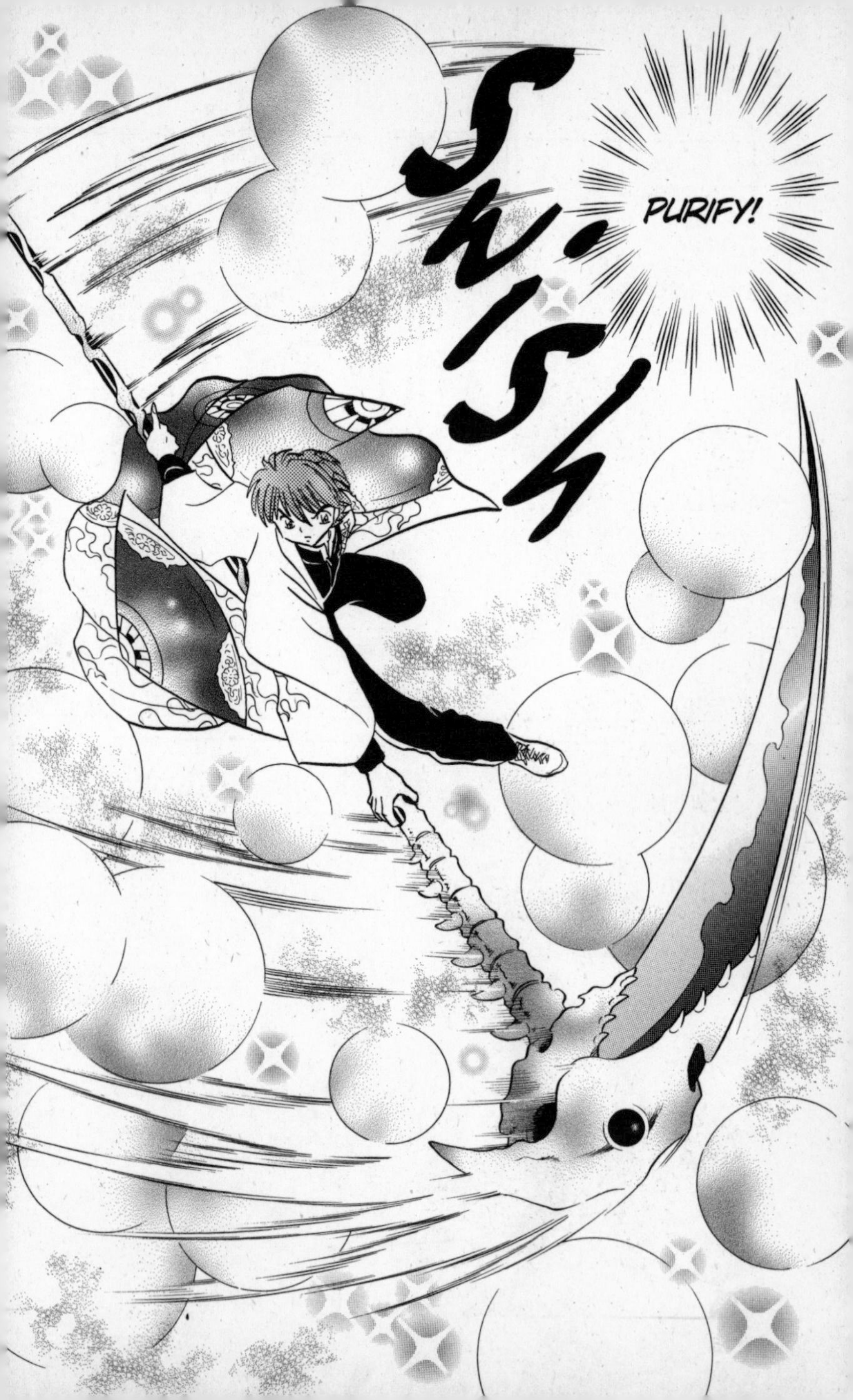
SWISH
PURIFY!

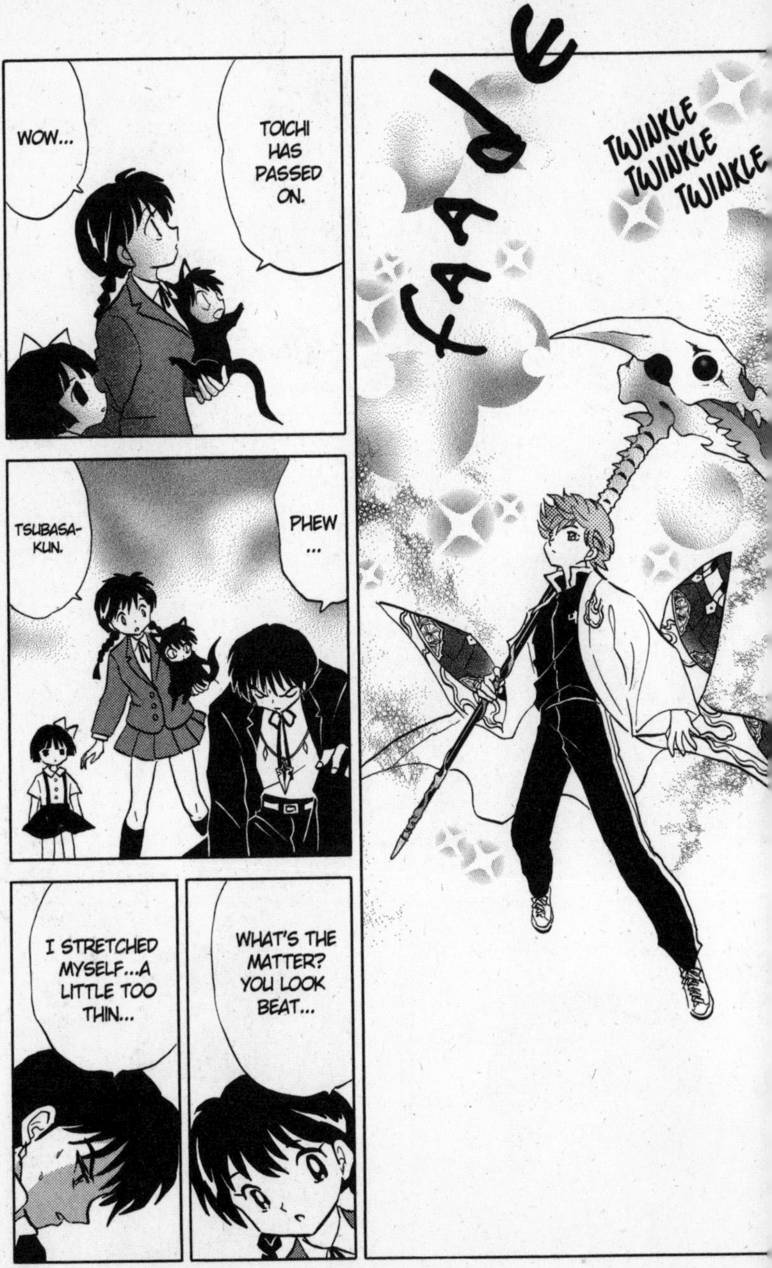
FADE
TWINKLE TWINKLE TWINKLE
TOICHI HAS PASSED ON.
WOW...
PHEW ...
TSUBASA-KUN.
WHAT'S THE MATTER? YOU LOOK BEAT...
I STRETCHED MYSELF...A LITTLE TOO THIN...

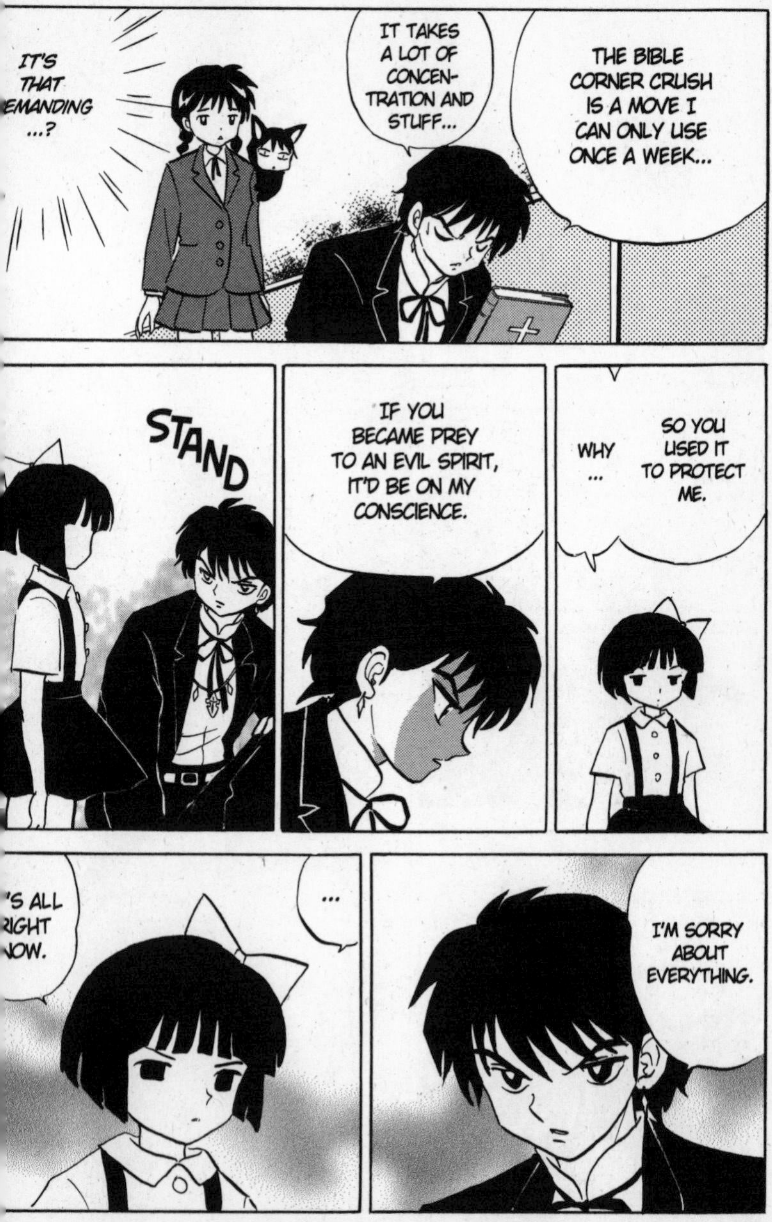
THE BIBLE CORNER CRUSH IS A MOVE I CAN ONLY USE ONCE A WEEK...
IT TAKES A LOT OF CONCEN-TRATION AND STUFF...
IT'S THAT EMANDING ...?
SO YOU USED IT TO PROTECT ME.
WHY ...
IF YOU BECAME PREY TO AN EVIL SPIRIT, IT'D BE ON MY CONSCIENCE.
STAND
I'M SORRY ABOUT EVERYTHING.
...
'S ALL RIGHT NOW.

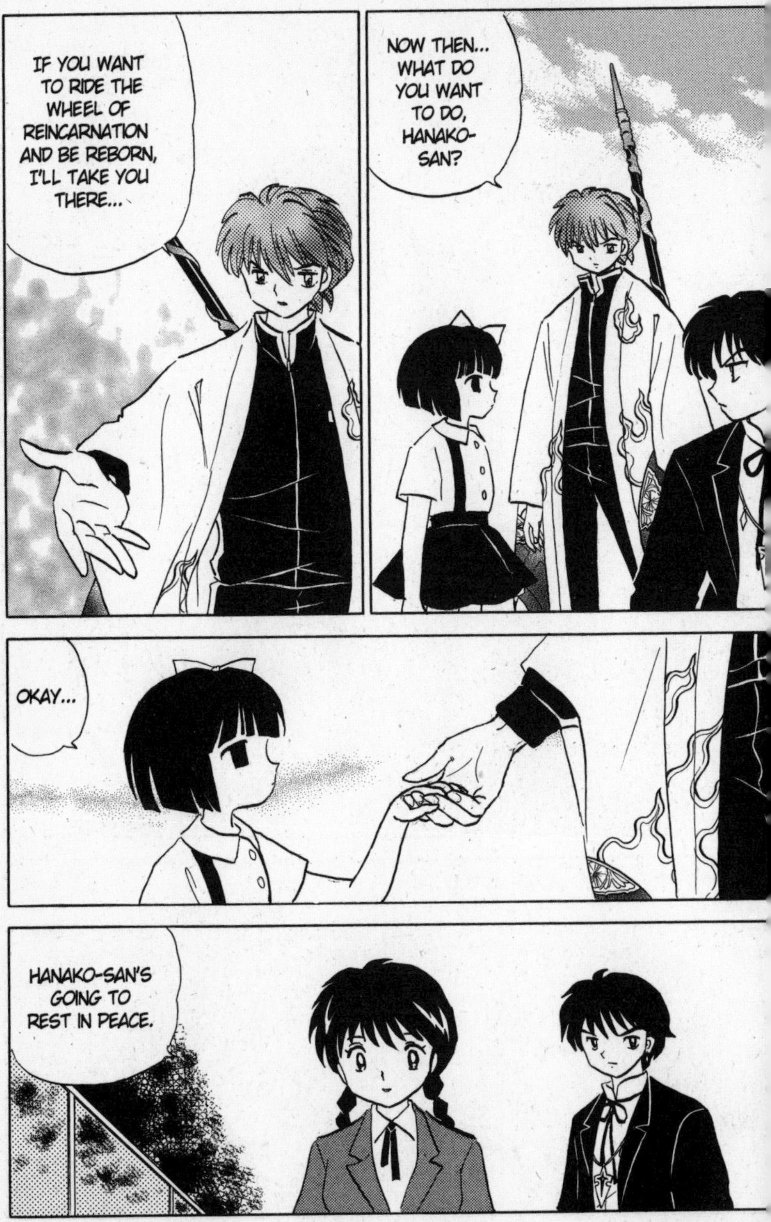
NOW THEN... WHAT DO YOU WANT TO DO, HANAKO-SAN?
IF YOU WANT TO RIDE THE WHEEL OF REINCARNATION AND BE REBORN, I'LL TAKE YOU THERE...
OKAY...
HANAKO-SAN'S GOING TO REST IN PEACE.

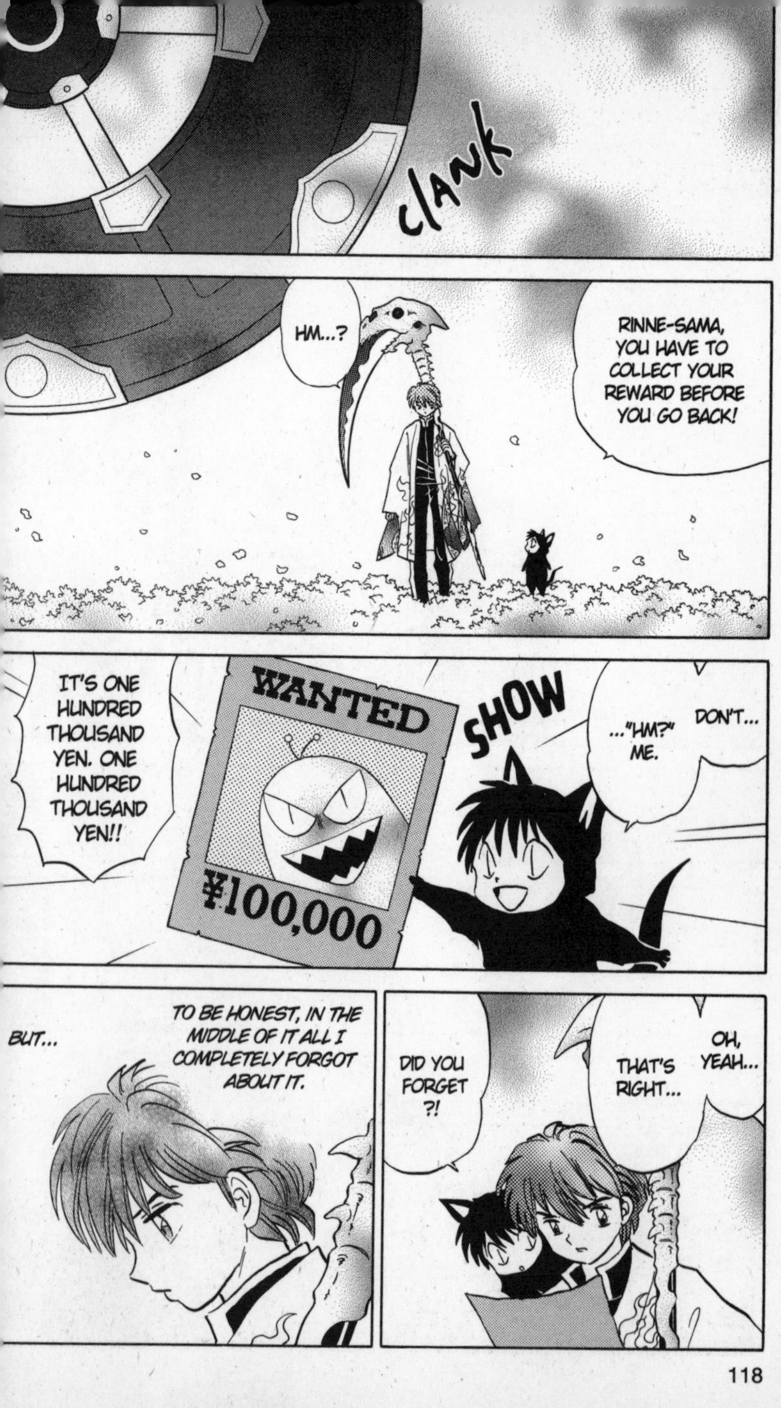
CLANK
RINNE-SAMA, YOU HAVE TO COLLECT YOUR REWARD BEFORE YOU GO BACK!
HM...?
DON'T...
..."HM?" ME.
SHOW
WANTED
¥100,000
IT'S ONE HUNDRED THOUSAND YEN. ONE HUNDRED THOUSAND YEN!!
OH, YEAH...
THAT'S RIGHT...
DID YOU FORGET?!
TO BE HONEST, IN THE MIDDLE OF IT ALL I COMPLETELY FORGOT ABOUT IT.
BUT...

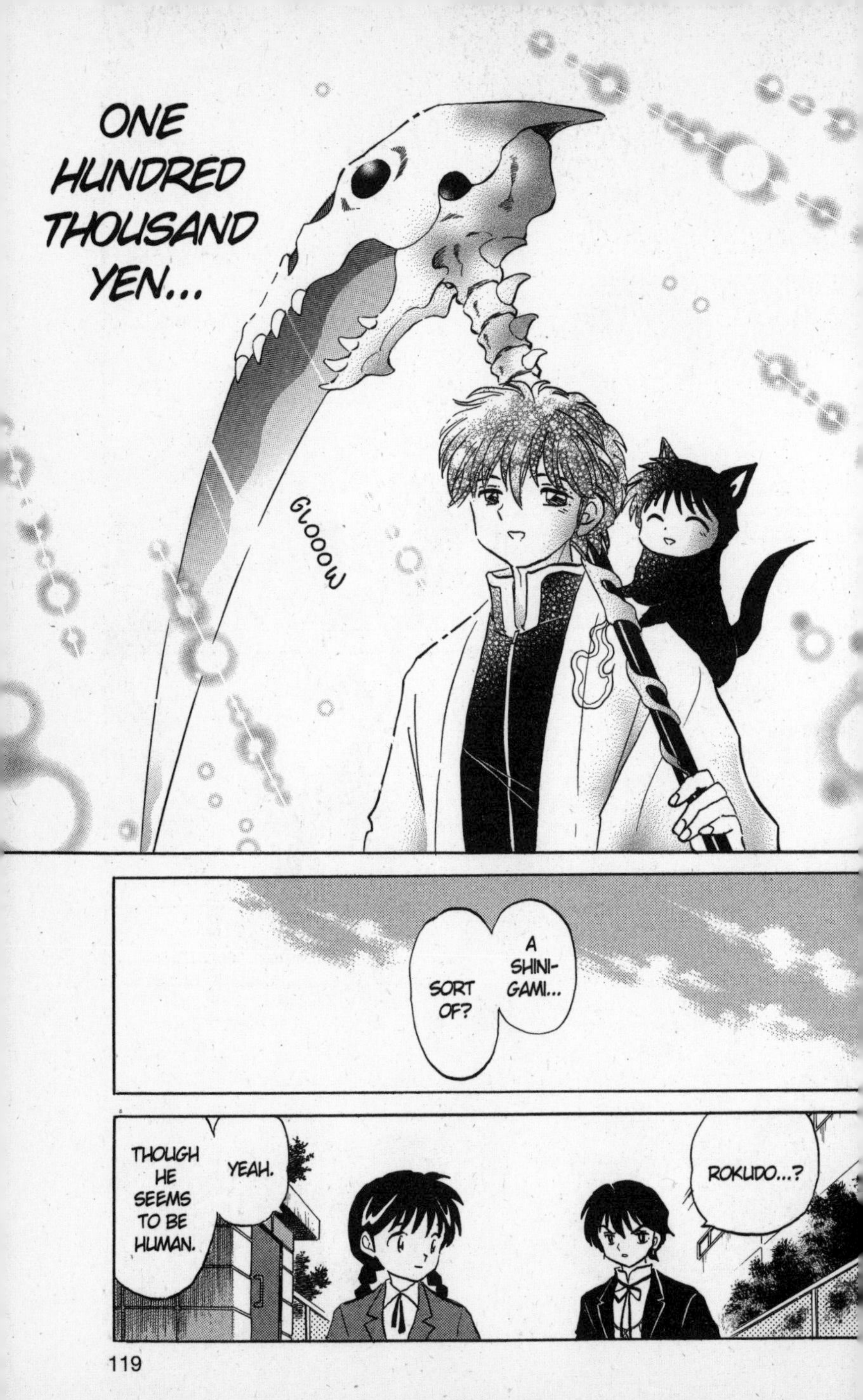
ONE HUNDRED THOUSAND YEN...
GLOOOW
A SHINI-GAMI... SORT OF?
ROKUDO...?
YEAH.
THOUGH HE SEEMS TO BE HUMAN.

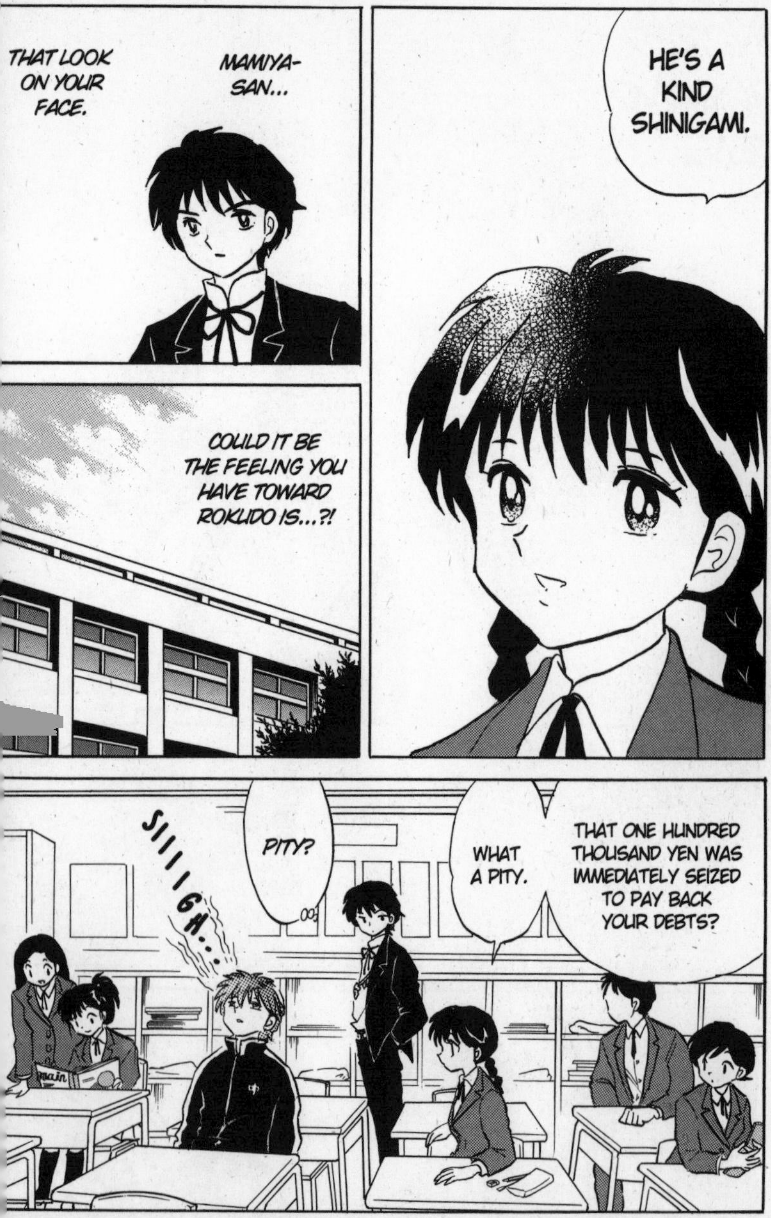
HE'S A KIND SHINIGAMI.
MAMIYA-SAN...
THAT LOOK ON YOUR FACE.
COULD IT BE THE FEELING YOU HAVE TOWARD ROKUDO IS...?!
THAT ONE HUNDRED THOUSAND YEN WAS IMMEDIATELY SEIZED TO PAY BACK YOUR DEBTS?
WHAT A PITY.
PITY?
SIIIIGH...

CHAPTER 25: LURE OF THE PUMPKINHEAD

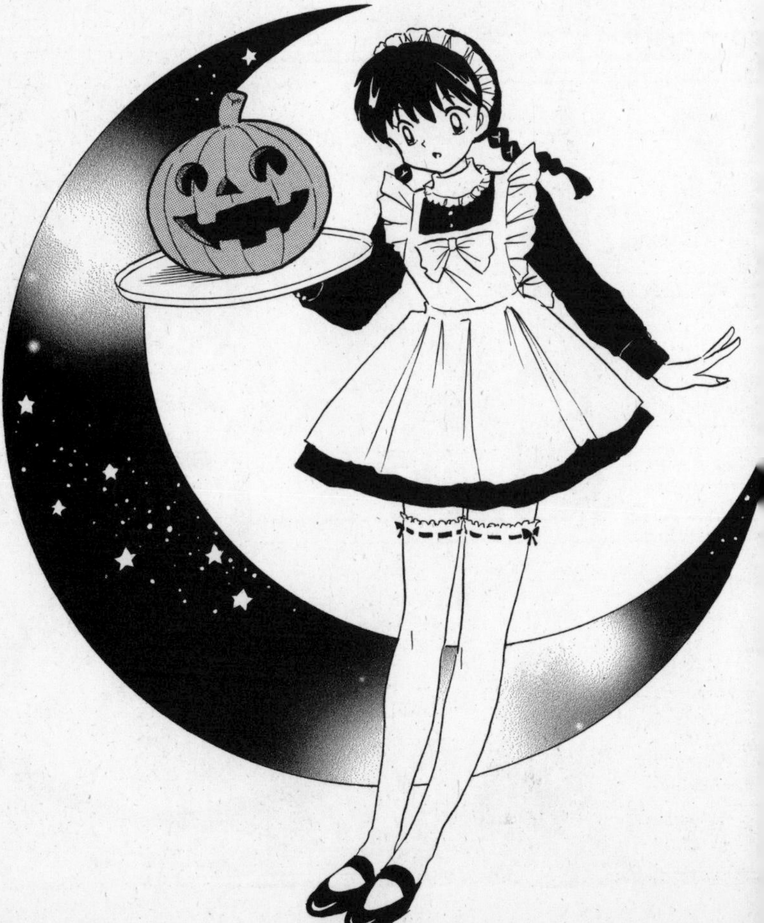

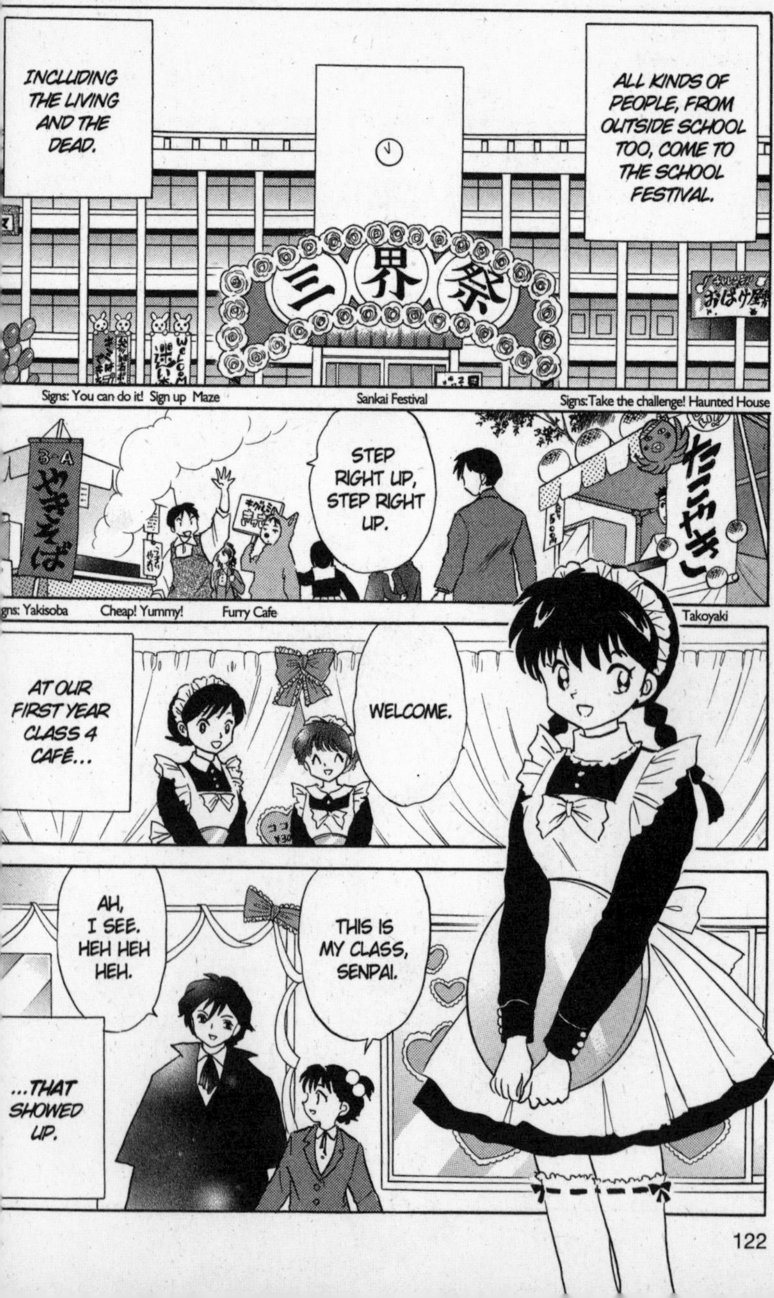
ALL KINDS OF PEOPLE, FROM OUTSIDE SCHOOL TOO, COME TO THE SCHOOL FESTIVAL.
INCLUDING THE LIVING AND THE DEAD.
Signs: You can do it! Sign up Maze
Sankai Festival
Signs:Take the challenge! Haunted House
STEP RIGHT UP, STEP RIGHT UP.
Signs: Yakisoba
Cheap! Yummy!
Furry Cafe
Takoyaki
WELCOME.
AT OUR FIRST YEAR CLASS 4 CAFÉ...
THIS IS MY CLASS, SENPAI.
AH, I SEE. HEH HEH HEH.
...THAT SHOWED UP.

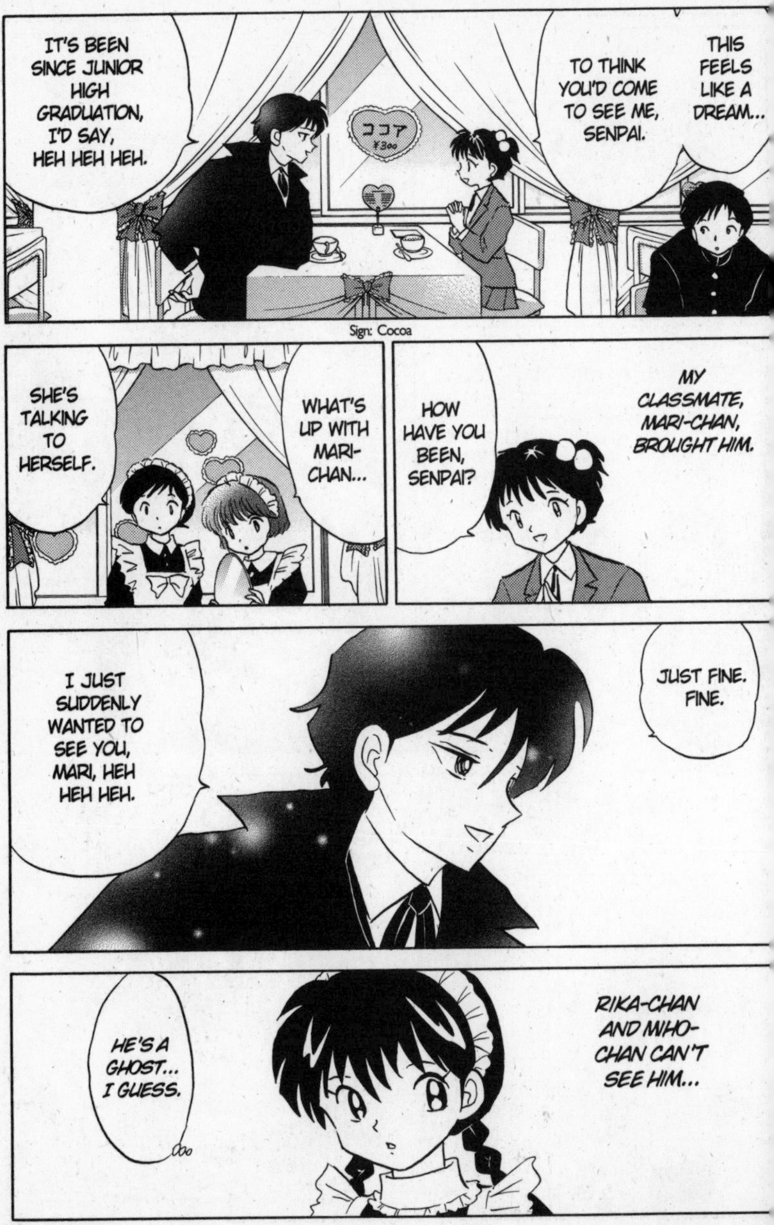
THIS FEELS LIKE A DREAM...
TO THINK YOU'D COME TO SEE ME, SENPAI.
IT'S BEEN SINCE JUNIOR HIGH GRADUATION, I'D SAY, HEH HEH HEH.
MY CLASSMATE, MARI-CHAN, BROUGHT HIM.
HOW HAVE YOU BEEN, SENPAI?
WHAT'S UP WITH MARI-CHAN...
SHE'S TALKING TO HERSELF.
JUST FINE. FINE.
I JUST SUDDENLY WANTED TO SEE YOU, MARI, HEH HEH HEH.
RIKA-CHAN AND MIHO-CHAN CAN'T SEE HIM...
HE'S A GHOST... I GUESS.

Sign: Cocoa

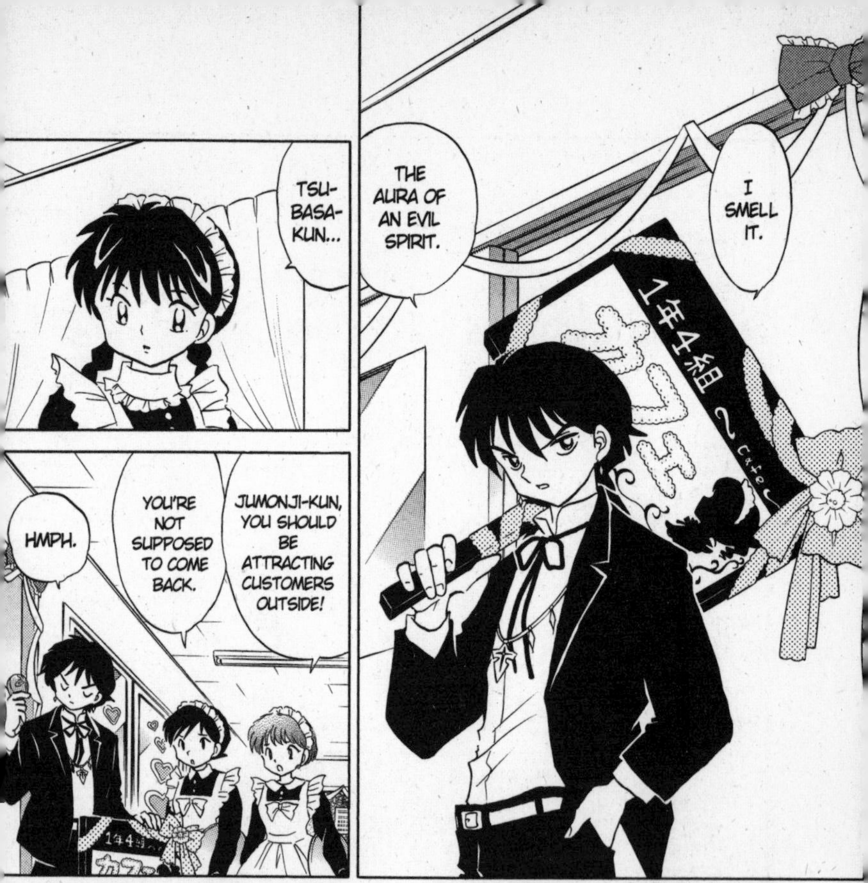
I SMELL IT.
THE AURA OF AN EVIL SPIRIT.
1年4組 ~Cafe~
TSU-BASA-KUN...
JUMONJI-KUN, YOU SHOULD BE ATTRACTING CUSTOMERS OUTSIDE!
YOU'RE NOT SUPPOSED TO COME BACK.
HMPH.

Sign: First Year Class 4 Café

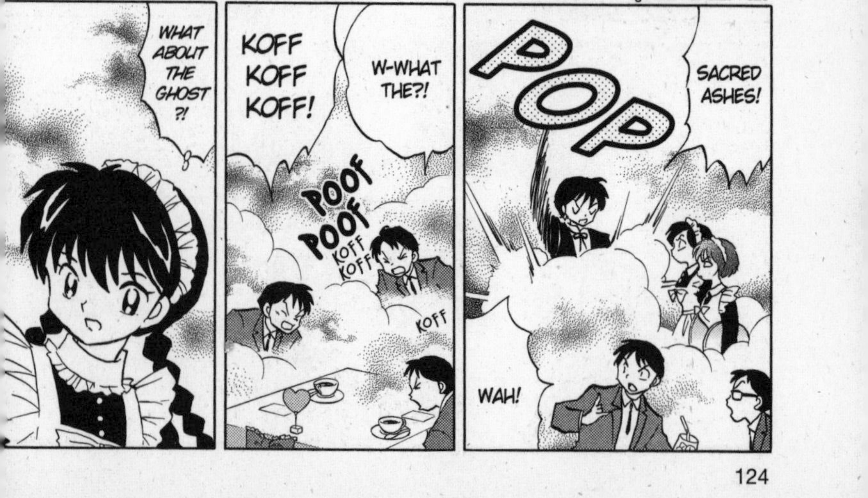
SACRED ASHES!
POP
WAH!
W-WHAT THE?!
KOFF KOFF KOFF!
POOF POOF
KOFF KOFF
KOFF
WHAT ABOUT THE GHOST?!

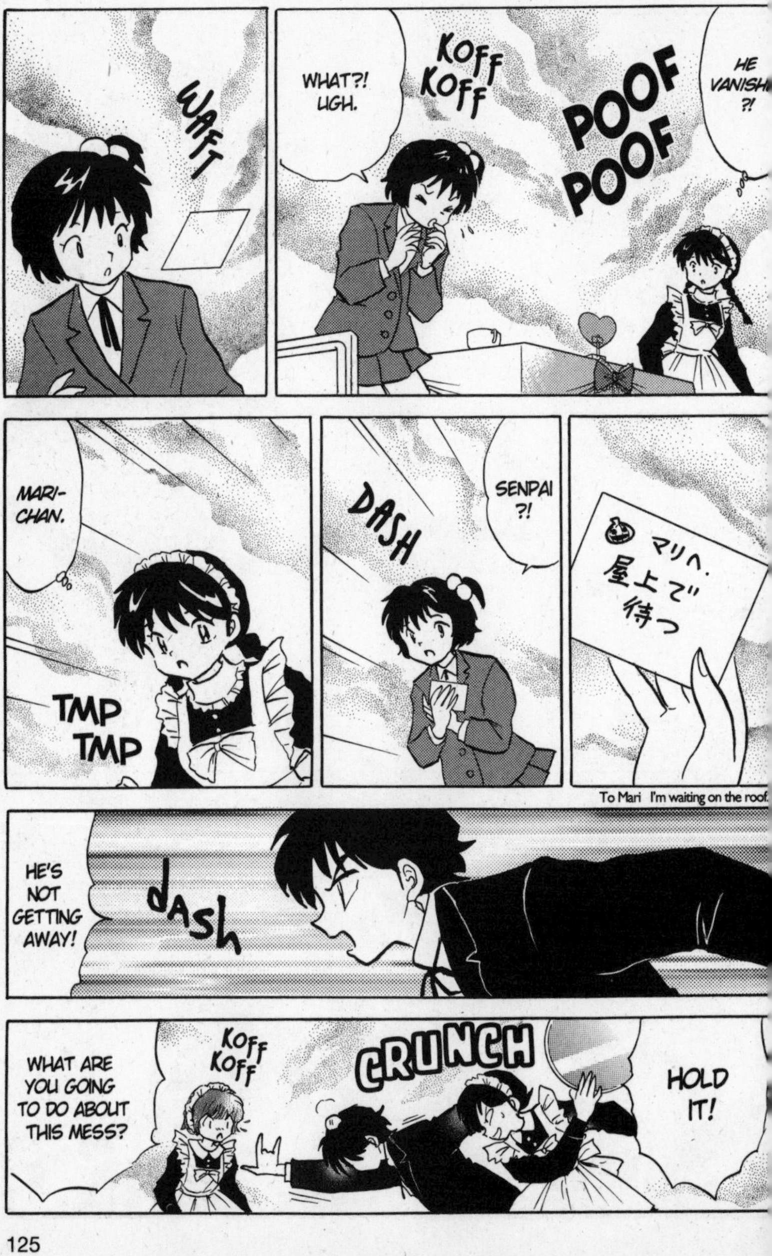
HE VANISH ?!
POOF POOF
KOFF KOFF
WHAT?! UGH.
WAFT
マリへ 屋上で待つ
SENPAI ?!
DASH
MARI-CHAN.
TMP TMP
To Mari I'm waiting on the roof.
HE'S NOT GETTING AWAY!
dash
HOLD IT!
CRUNCH
KOFF KOFF
WHAT ARE YOU GOING TO DO ABOUT THIS MESS?

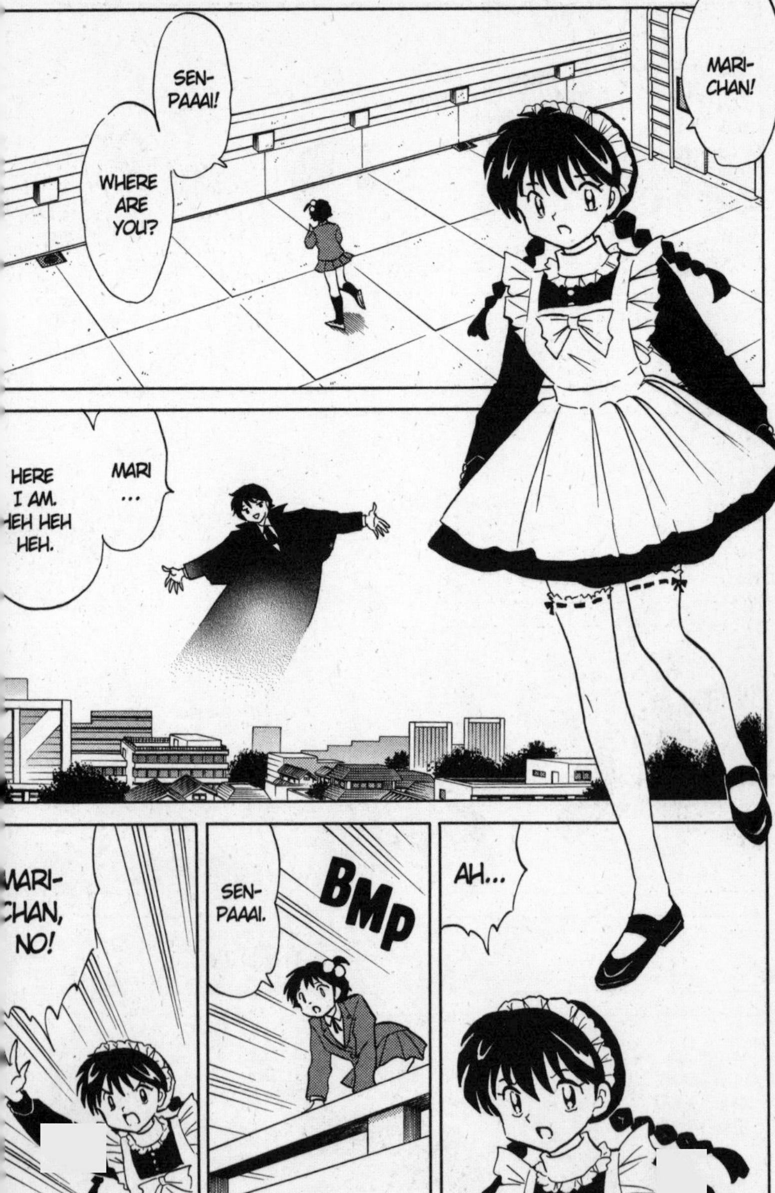
MARI-CHAN!
SEN-PAAAI!
WHERE ARE YOU?
MARI ...
HERE I AM. HEH HEH HEH.
AH...
BMP
SEN-PAAAI.
MARI-CHAN, NO!

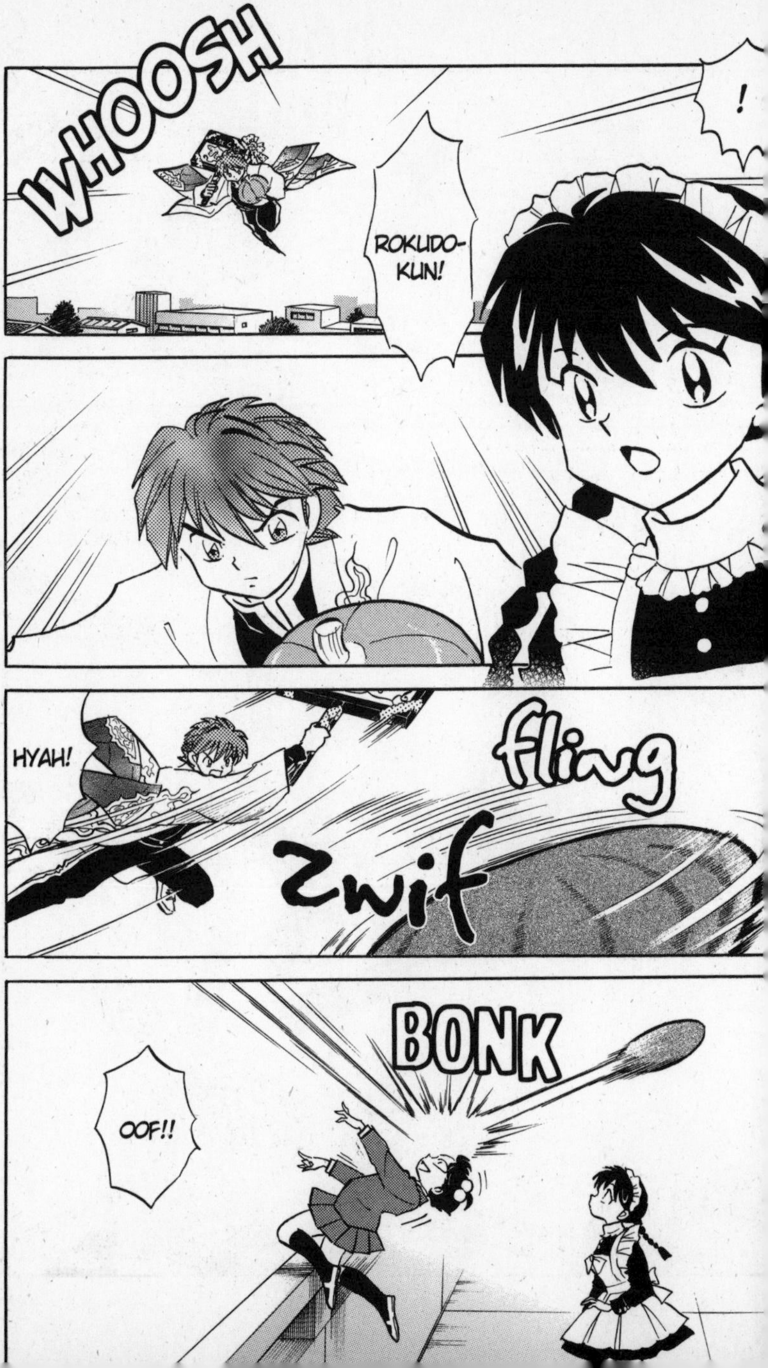

!
ROKUDO-KUN!
WHOOSH
fling
HYAH!
Zwif
BONK
OOF!!

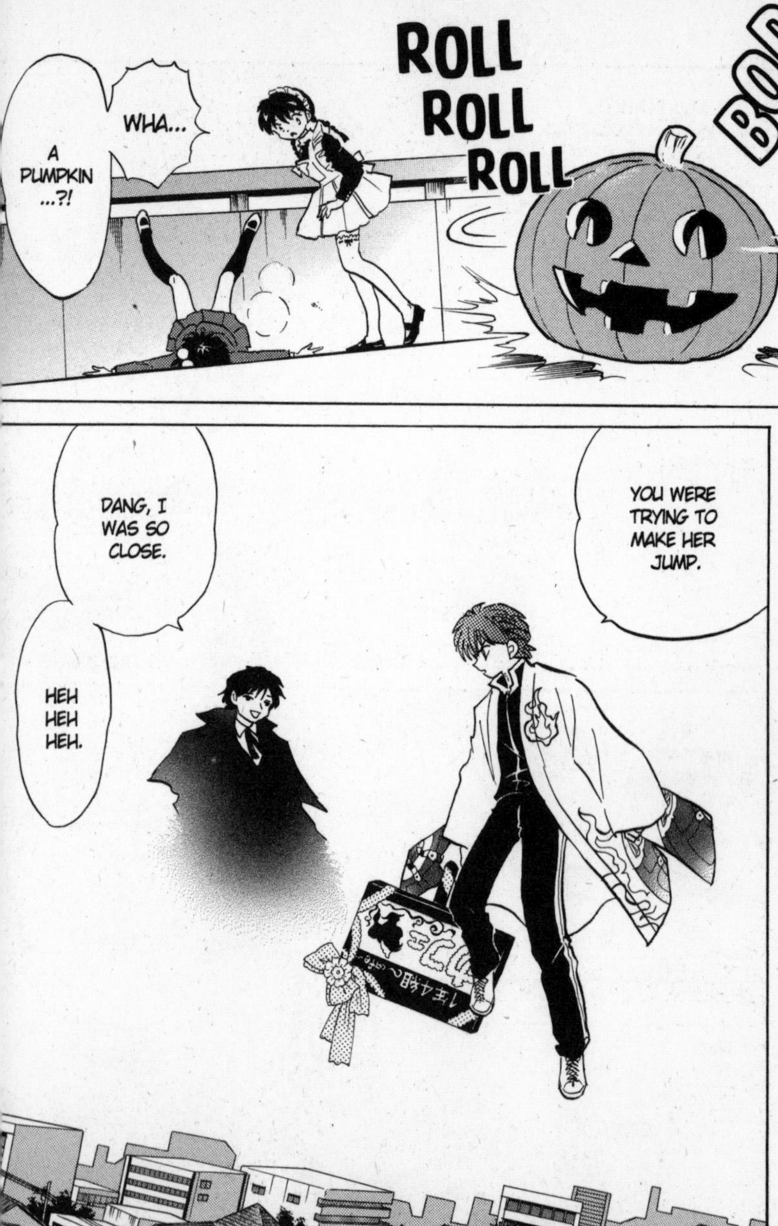
BOP
ROLL ROLL ROLL
WHA...
A PUMPKIN ...?!
YOU WERE TRYING TO MAKE HER JUMP.
DANG, I WAS SO CLOSE.
HEH HEH HEH.

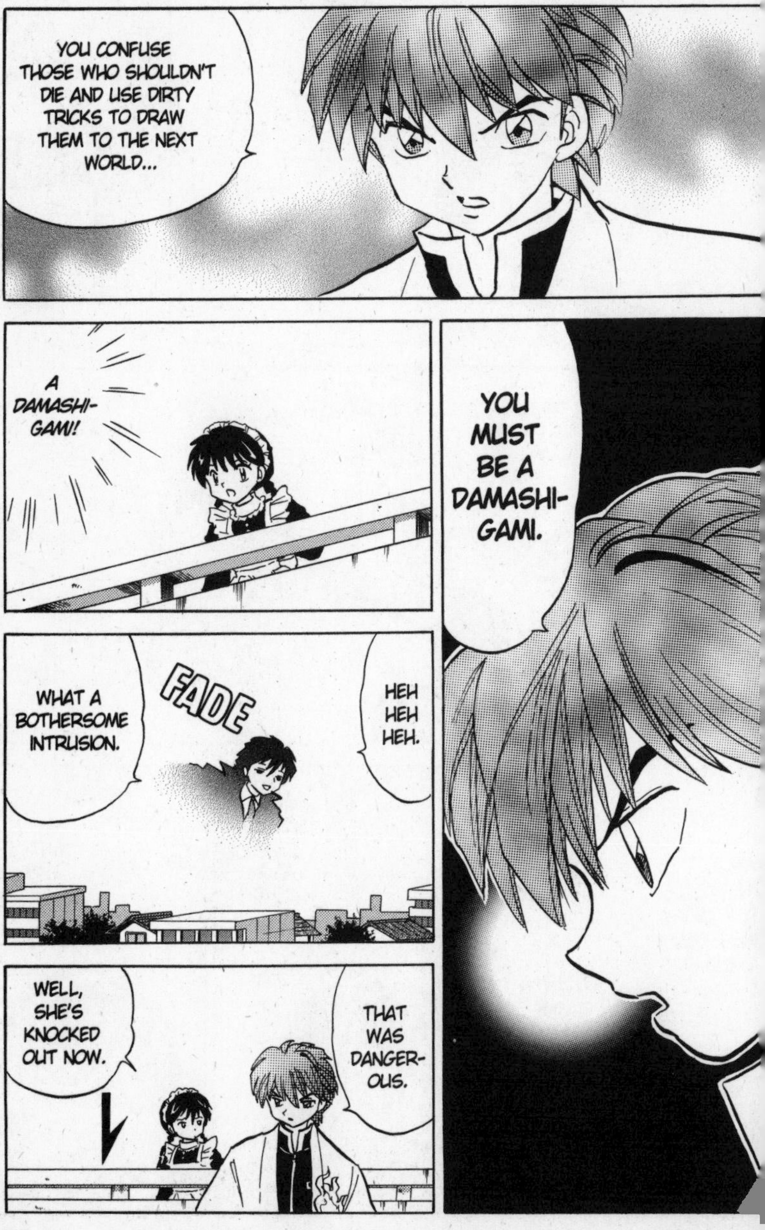
YOU CONFUSE THOSE WHO SHOULDN'T DIE AND USE DIRTY TRICKS TO DRAW THEM TO THE NEXT WORLD...
YOU MUST BE A DAMASHI-GAMI.
A DAMASHI-GAMI!
HEH HEH HEH.
FADE
WHAT A BOTHERSOME INTRUSION.
THAT WAS DANGER-OUS.
WELL, SHE'S KNOCKED OUT NOW.

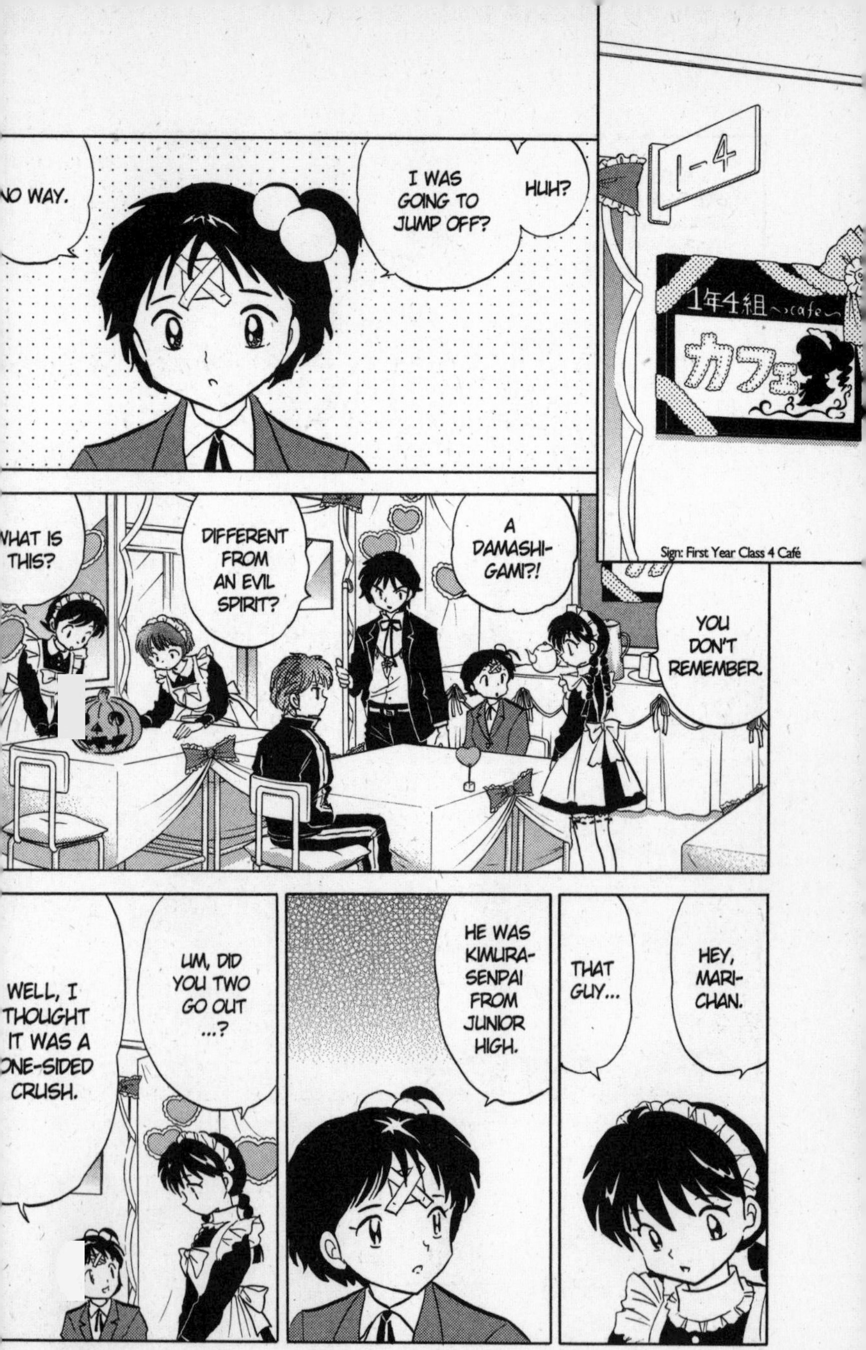
1-4
1年4組 ~cafe~
カフェ
Sign: First Year Class 4 Café
HUH?
I WAS GOING TO JUMP OFF?
NO WAY.
YOU DON'T REMEMBER.
A DAMASHI-GAMI?!
DIFFERENT FROM AN EVIL SPIRIT?
WHAT IS THIS?
HEY, MARI-CHAN.
THAT GUY...
HE WAS KIMURA-SENPAI FROM JUNIOR HIGH.
UM, DID YOU TWO GO OUT ...?
WELL, I THOUGHT IT WAS A ONE-SIDED CRUSH.

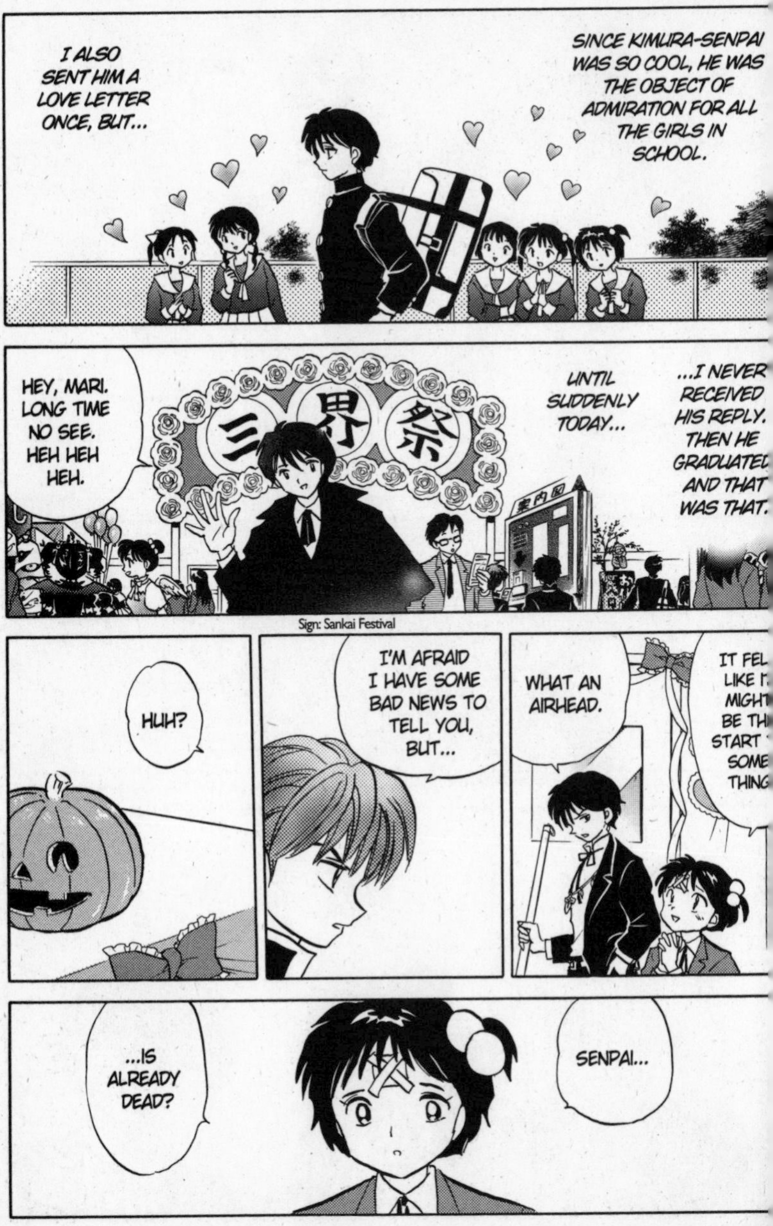
SINCE KIMURA-SENPAI WAS SO COOL, HE WAS THE OBJECT OF ADMIRATION FOR ALL THE GIRLS IN SCHOOL.
I ALSO SENT HIM A LOVE LETTER ONCE, BUT...
...I NEVER RECEIVED HIS REPLY. THEN HE GRADUATED AND THAT WAS THAT.
UNTIL SUDDENLY TODAY...
HEY, MARI. LONG TIME NO SEE. HEH HEH HEH.
IT FEL LIKE I MIGH BE TH START SOME THING
WHAT AN AIRHEAD.
I'M AFRAID I HAVE SOME BAD NEWS TO TELL YOU, BUT...
HUH?
SENPAI...
...IS ALREADY DEAD?
Sign: Sankai Festival

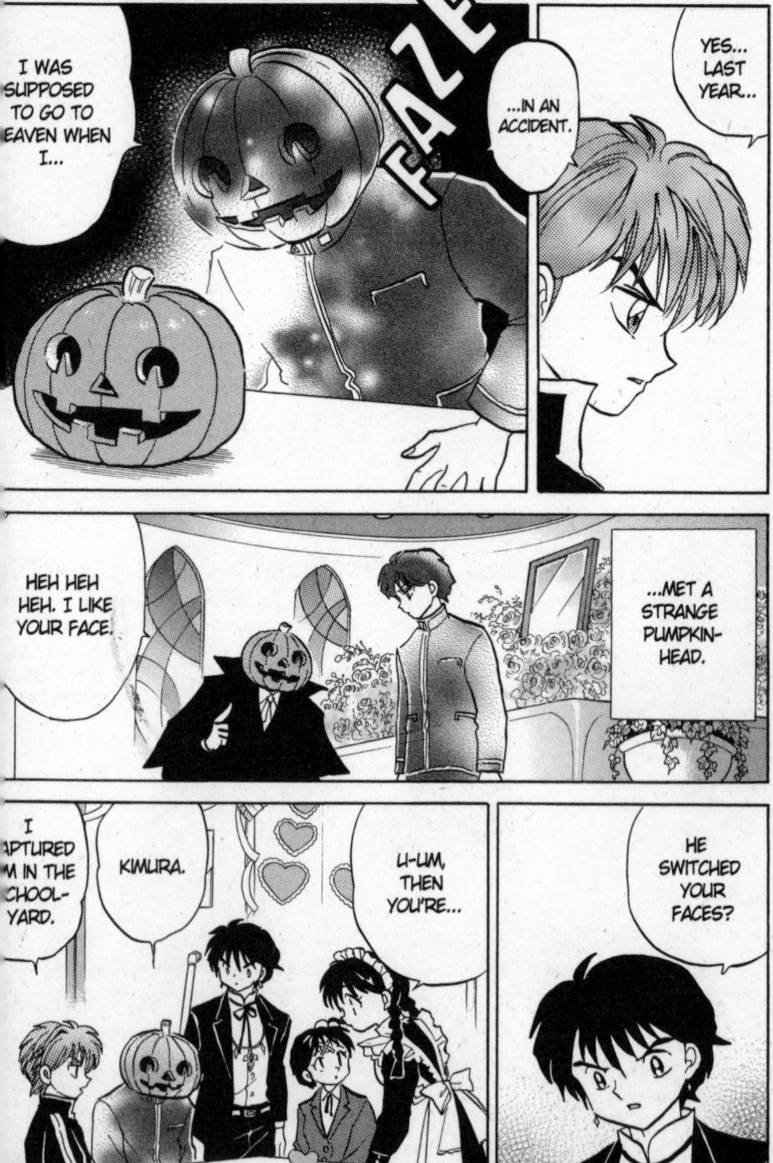
YES... LAST YEAR...
...IN AN ACCIDENT.
FAZE
I WAS SUPPOSED TO GO TO EAVEN WHEN I...
...MET A STRANGE PUMPKIN-HEAD.
HEH HEH HEH. I LIKE YOUR FACE.
HE SWITCHED YOUR FACES?
U-UM, THEN YOU'RE...
KIMURA.
I APTURED M IN THE CHOOL-YARD.

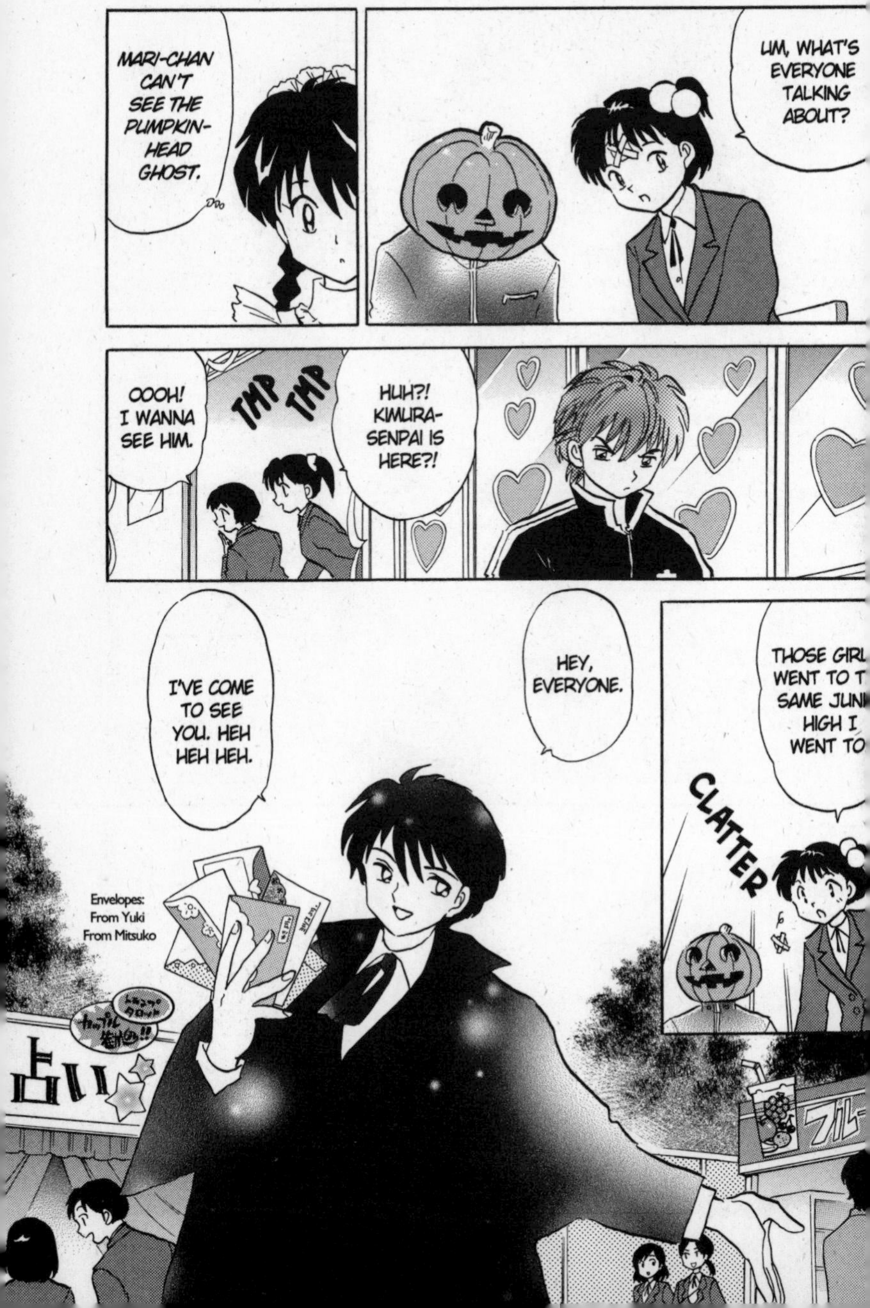
UM, WHAT'S EVERYONE TALKING ABOUT?
MARI-CHAN CAN'T SEE THE PUMPKIN-HEAD GHOST.
HUH?! KIMURA-SENPAI IS HERE?!
TMP TMP
OOOH! I WANNA SEE HIM.
THOSE GIRL WENT TO T SAME JUN HIGH I WENT TO
CLATTER
HEY, EVERYONE.
I'VE COME TO SEE YOU. HEH HEH HEH.
Envelopes: From Yuki From Mitsuko

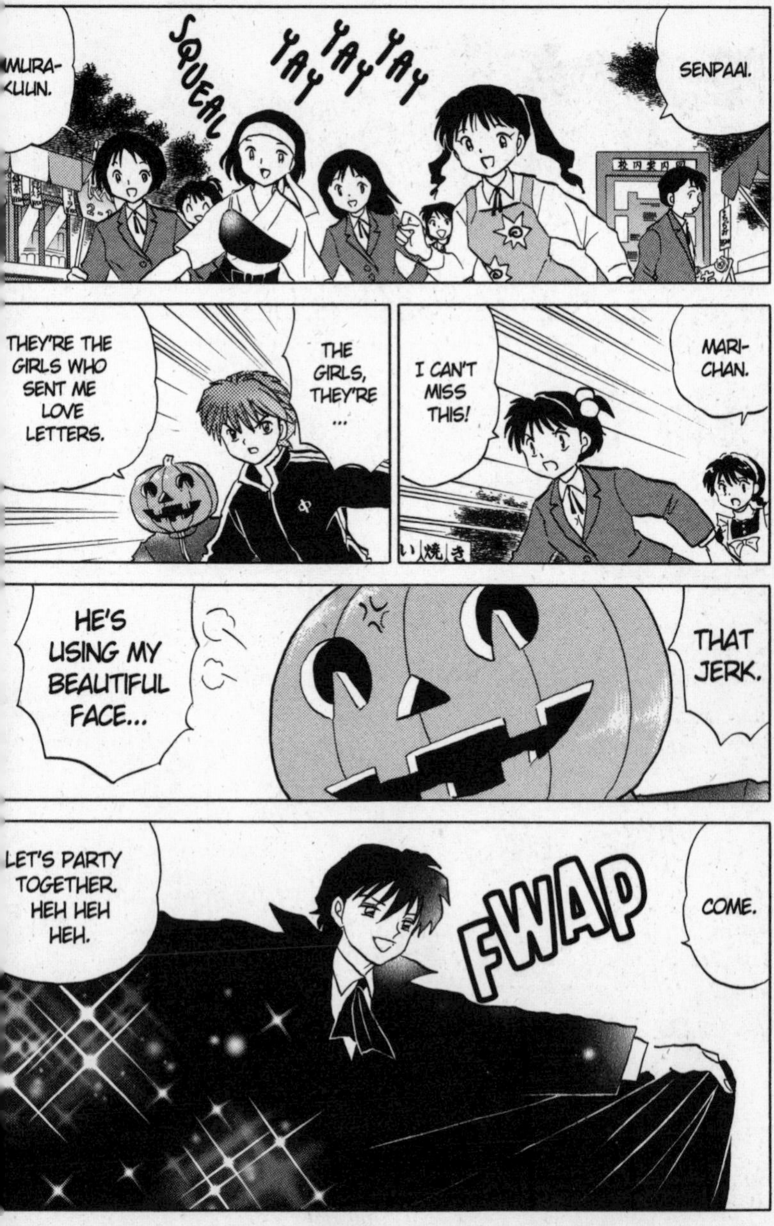
SENPAAI.
YAY YAY YAY
SQUEAL
MURA-KUUN.
MARI-CHAN.
I CAN'T MISS THIS!
THE GIRLS, THEY'RE ...
THEY'RE THE GIRLS WHO SENT ME LOVE LETTERS.
THAT JERK.
HE'S USING MY BEAUTIFUL FACE...
COME.
FWAP
LET'S PARTY TOGETHER. HEH HEH HEH.

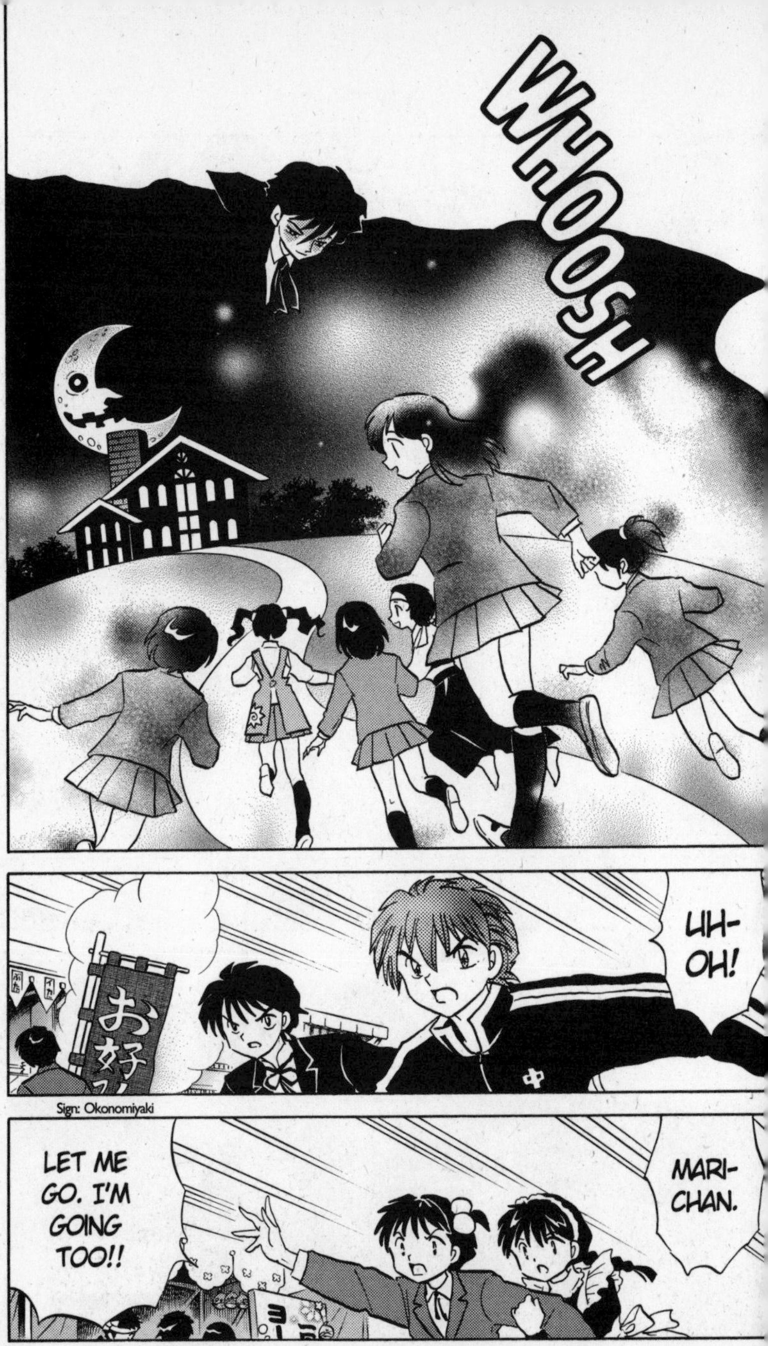
WHOOSH
UH-OH!
MARI-CHAN.
LET ME GO. I'M GOING TOO!!
Sign: Okonomiyaki

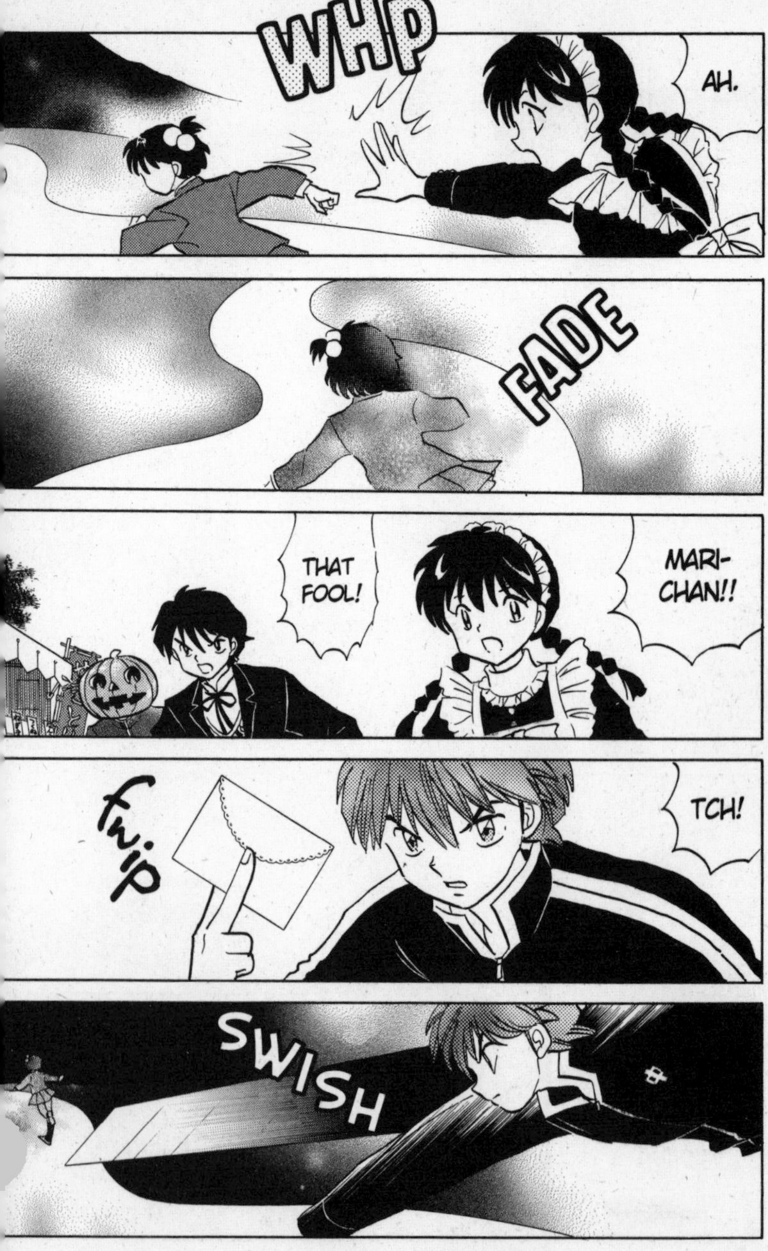
AH.
WHP
FADE
MARI-
CHAN!!
THAT
FOOL!
TCH!
fwip
SWISH

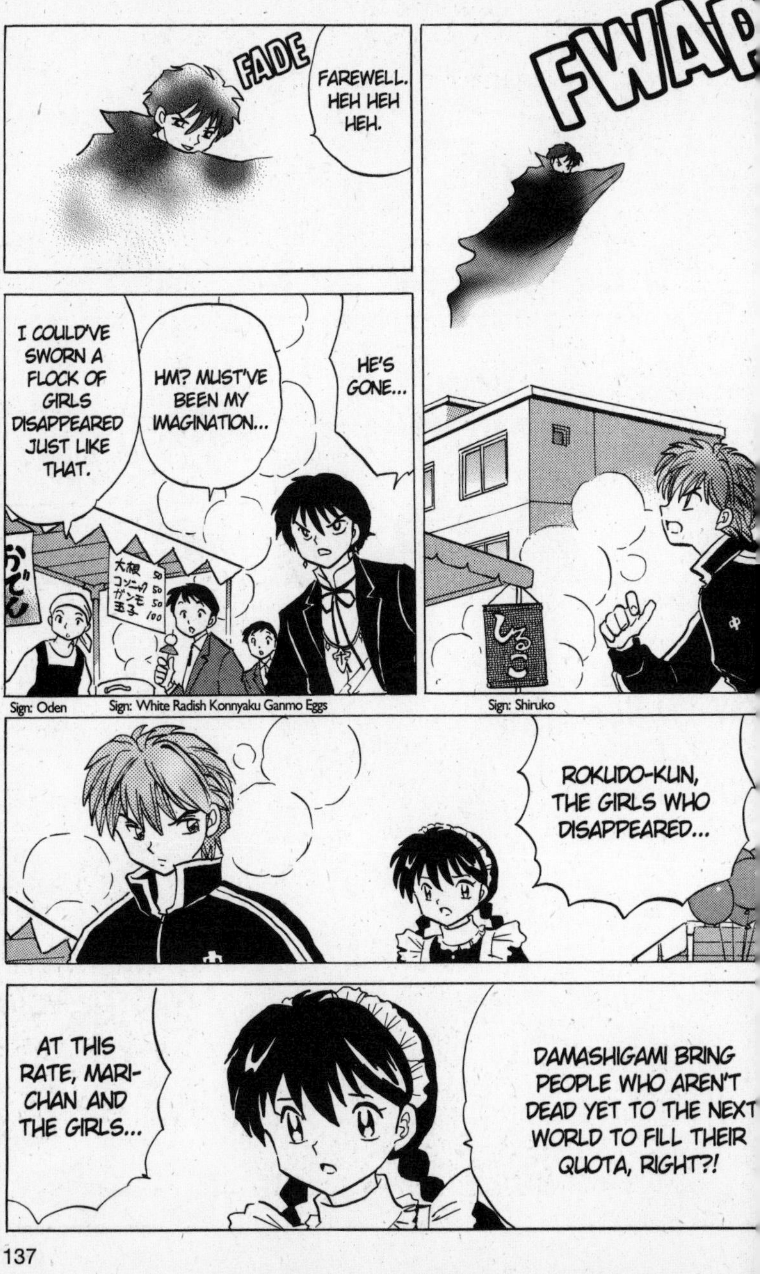
FWAP
FADE
FAREWELL. HEH HEH HEH.
HE'S GONE...
HM? MUST'VE BEEN MY IMAGINATION...
I COULD'VE SWORN A FLOCK OF GIRLS DISAPPEARED JUST LIKE THAT.
おでん
大根 50
コンニャク 50
ガンモ 50
玉子 100
しるこ
ROKUDO-KUN, THE GIRLS WHO DISAPPEARED...
DAMASHIGAMI BRING PEOPLE WHO AREN'T DEAD YET TO THE NEXT WORLD TO FILL THEIR QUOTA, RIGHT?!
AT THIS RATE, MARI-CHAN AND THE GIRLS...

Sign: Oden Sign: White Radish Konnyaku Ganmo Eggs Sign: Shiruko

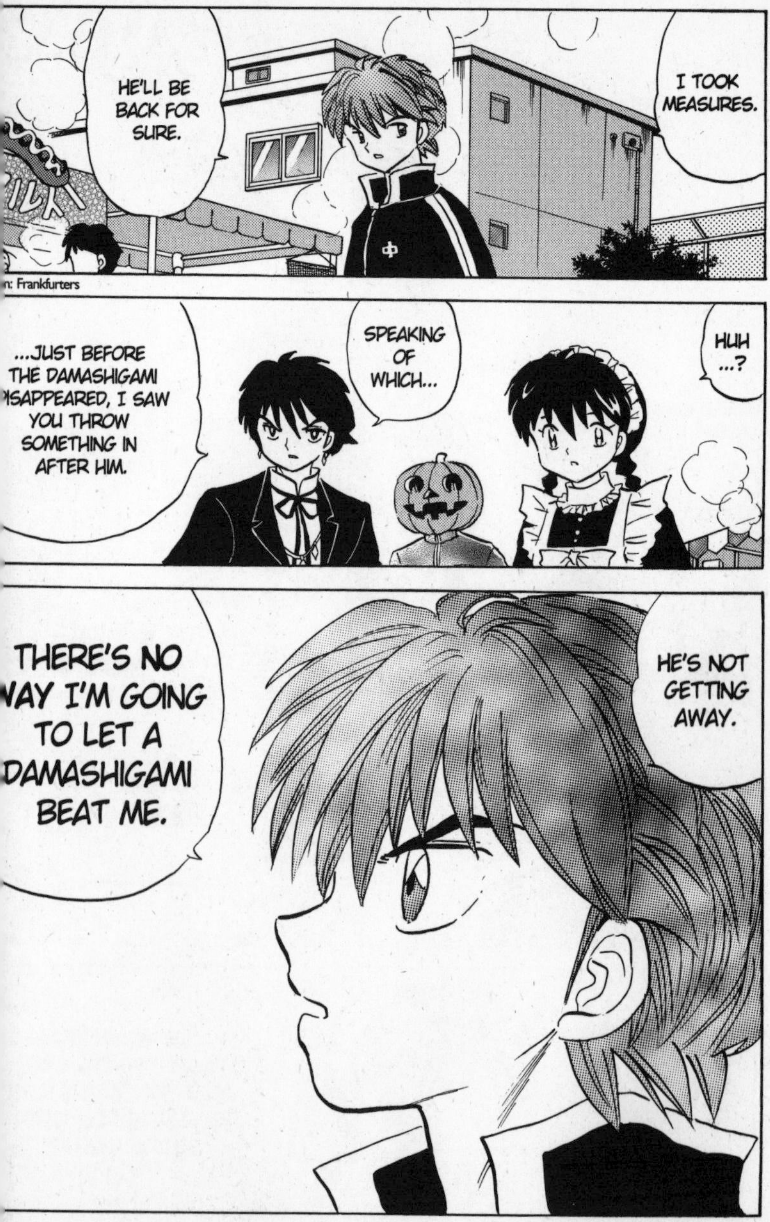

I TOOK MEASURES.
HE'LL BE BACK FOR SURE.
n: Frankfurters
HUH ...?
SPEAKING OF WHICH...
...JUST BEFORE THE DAMASHIGAMI ISAPPEARED, I SAW YOU THROW SOMETHING IN AFTER HIM.
HE'S NOT GETTING AWAY.
THERE'S NO VAY I'M GOING TO LET A DAMASHIGAMI BEAT ME.

CHAPTER 26: HALL OF THE DAMASHIGAMI

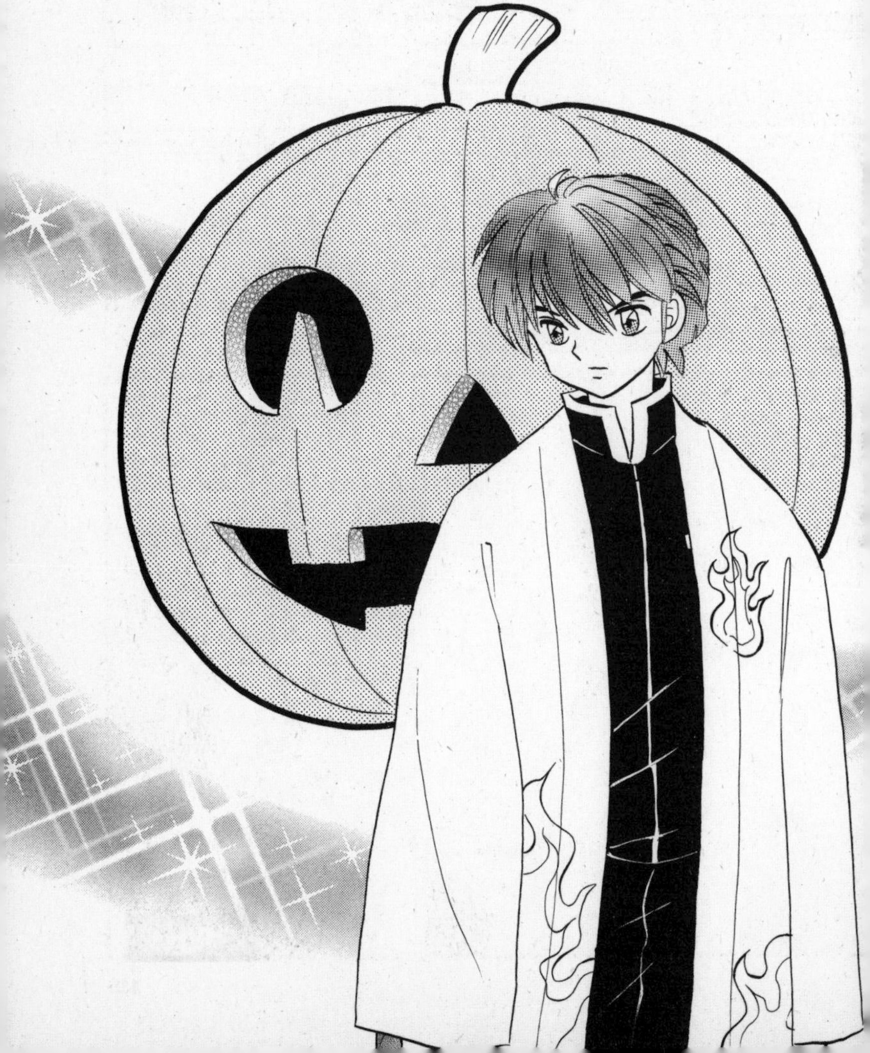

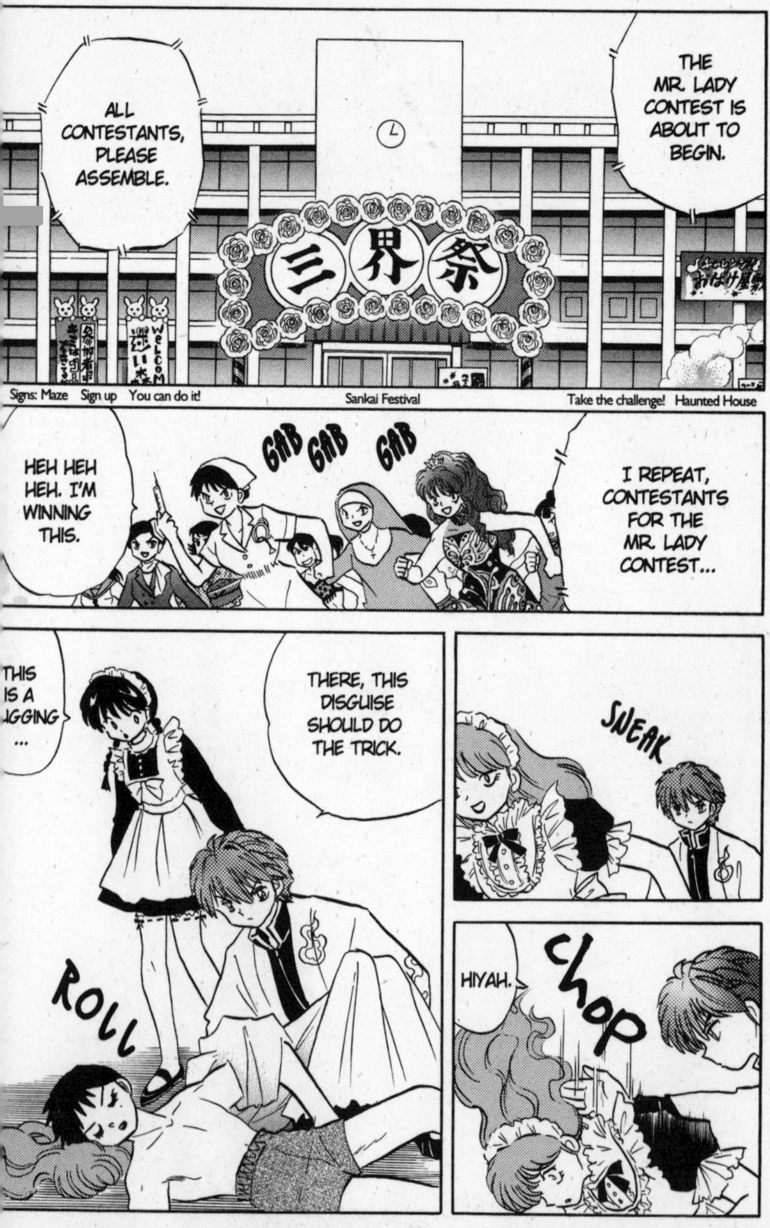
THE MR. LADY CONTEST IS ABOUT TO BEGIN.
ALL CONTESTANTS, PLEASE ASSEMBLE.
Signs: Maze Sign up You can do it!
Sankai Festival
Take the challenge! Haunted House
I REPEAT, CONTESTANTS FOR THE MR. LADY CONTEST...
GAB GAB GAB
HEH HEH HEH. I'M WINNING THIS.
SNEAK
CHOP
HIYAH.
THERE, THIS DISGUISE SHOULD DO THE TRICK.
THIS IS A
...
ROLL

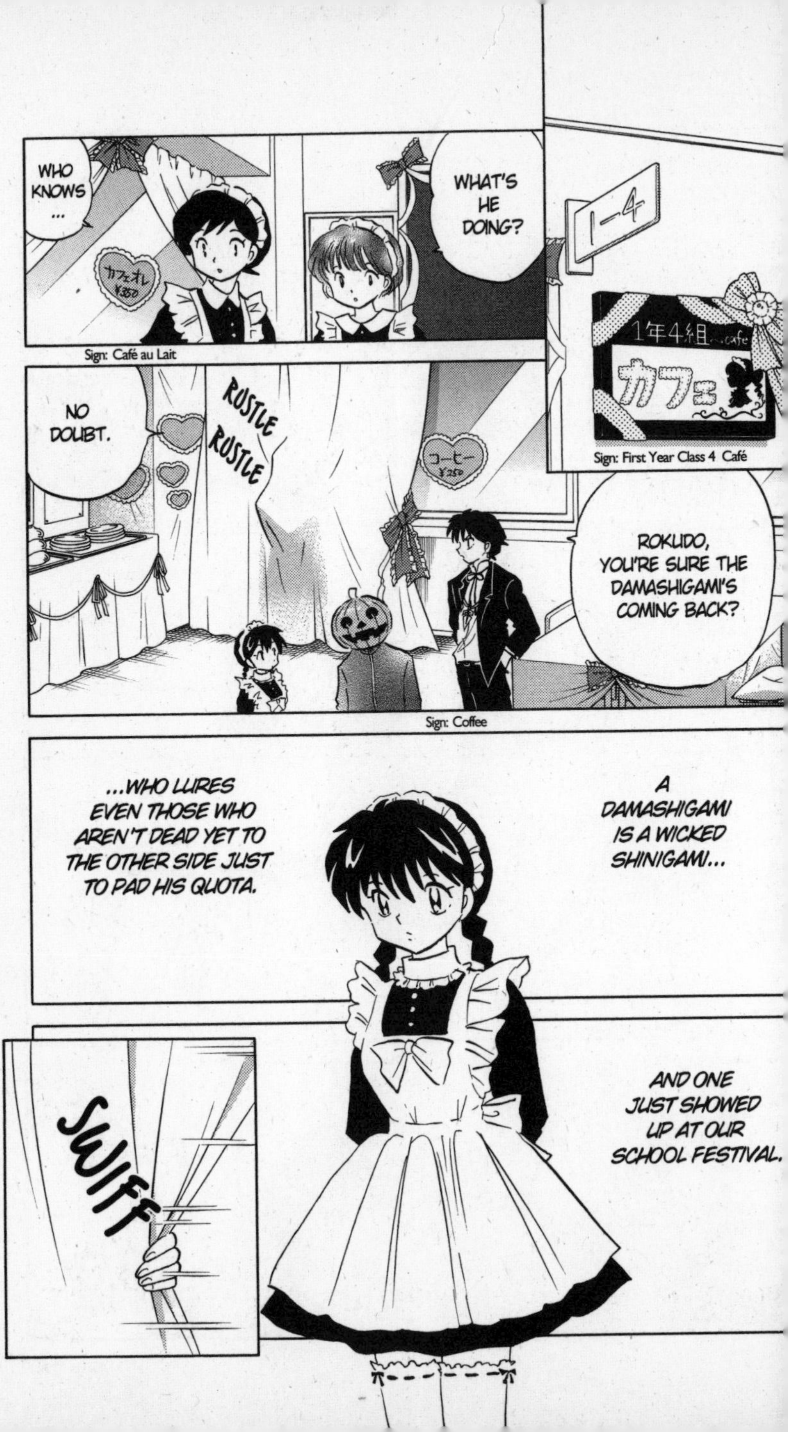
1-4
1年4組…cafe
カフェ
Sign: First Year Class 4 Café
WHAT'S HE DOING?
WHO KNOWS ...
カフェオレ ¥350
Sign: Café au Lait
ROKUDO, YOU'RE SURE THE DAMASHIGAMI'S COMING BACK?
RUSTLE RUSTLE
NO DOUBT.
コーヒー ¥350
Sign: Coffee
A DAMASHIGAMI IS A WICKED SHINIGAMI...
...WHO LURES EVEN THOSE WHO AREN'T DEAD YET TO THE OTHER SIDE JUST TO PAD HIS QUOTA.
AND ONE JUST SHOWED UP AT OUR SCHOOL FESTIVAL.
SWIFF

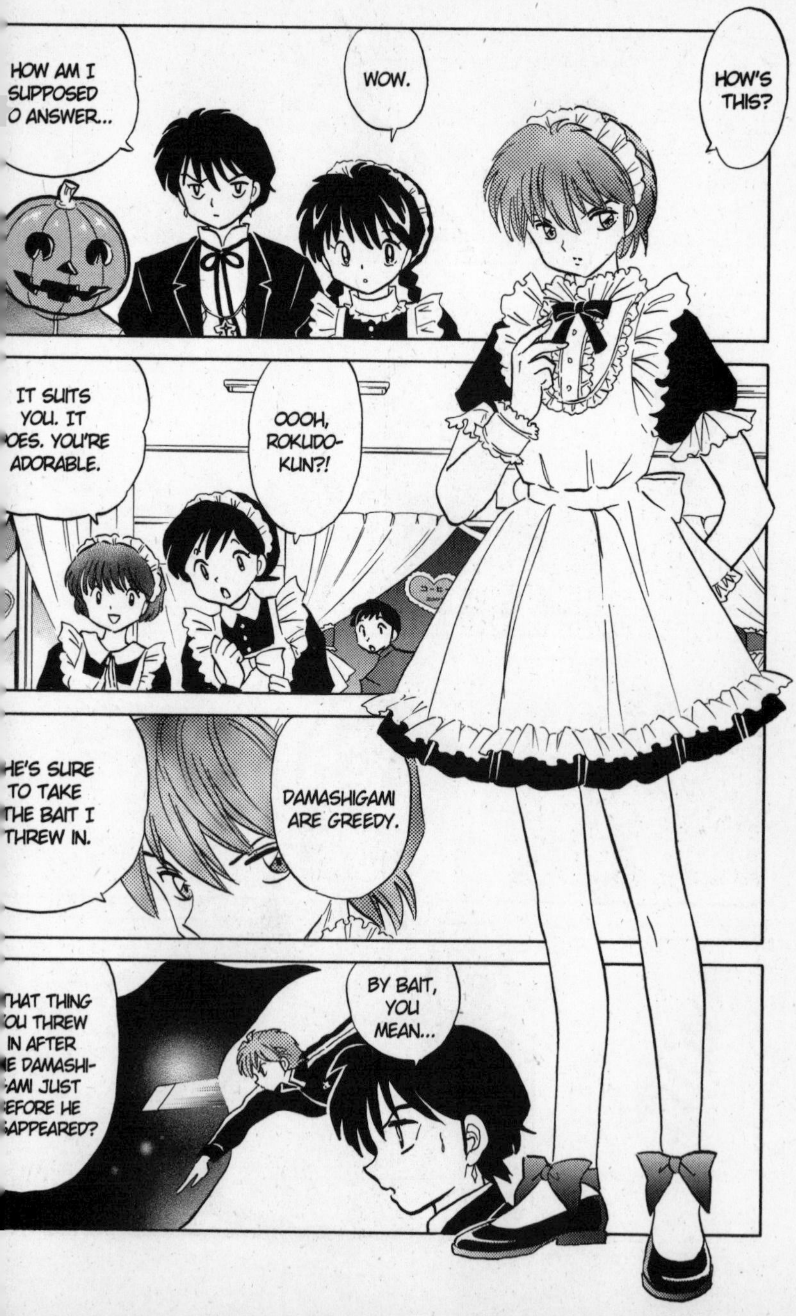
HOW'S THIS?
WOW.
HOW AM I SUPPOSED O ANSWER...
OOOH, ROKUDO-KUN?!
IT SUITS YOU. IT OES. YOU'RE ADORABLE.
DAMASHIGAMI ARE GREEDY.
HE'S SURE TO TAKE THE BAIT I THREW IN.
BY BAIT, YOU MEAN...
THAT THING OU THREW IN AFTER E DAMASHI-AMI JUST EFORE HE SAPPEARED?

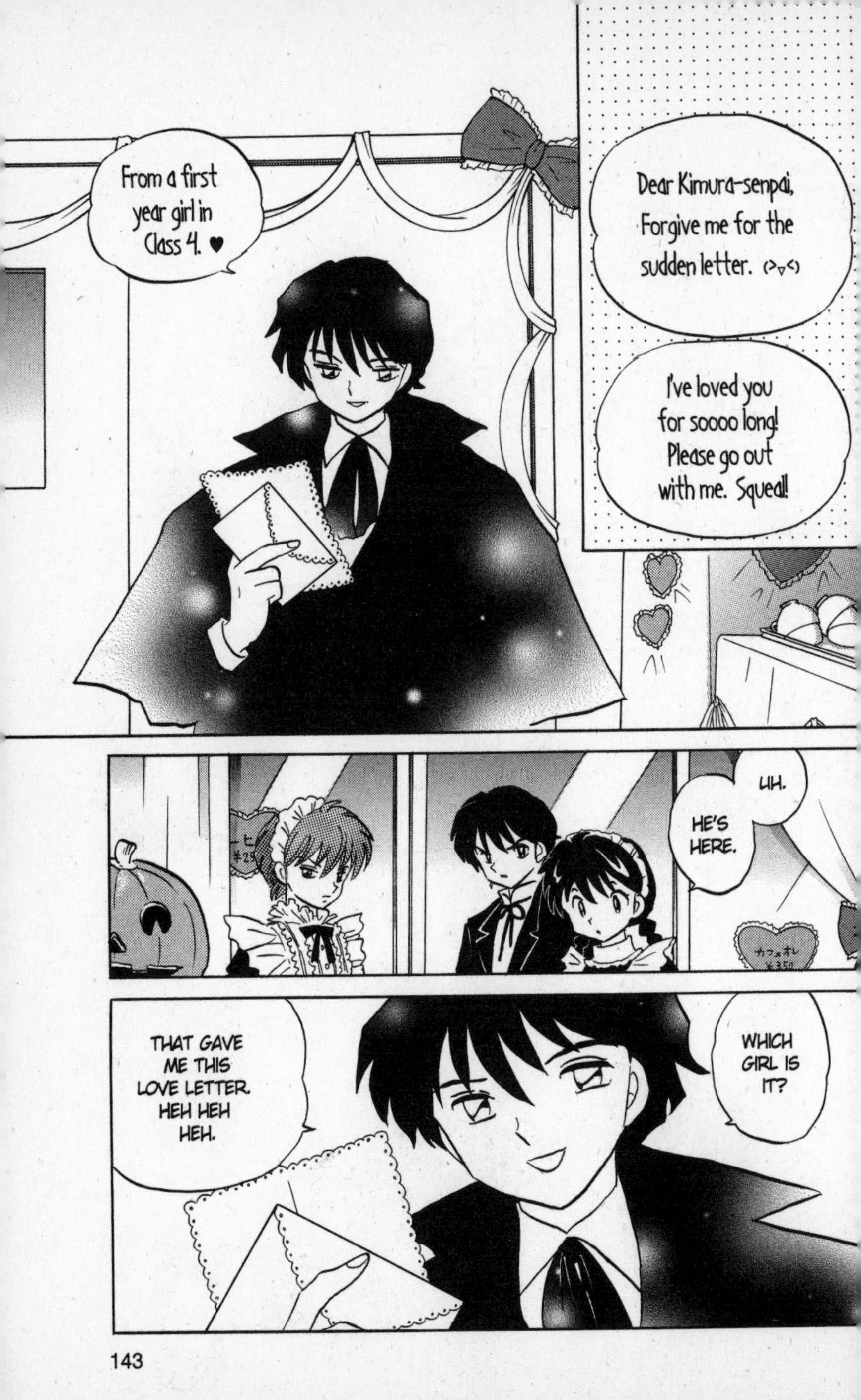
Dear Kimura-senpai, Forgive me for the sudden letter. (>▽<)
I've loved you for soooo long! Please go out with me. Squeal!
From a first year girl in Class 4. ♥
UH.
HE'S HERE.
WHICH GIRL IS IT?
THAT GAVE ME THIS LOVE LETTER. HEH HEH HEH.

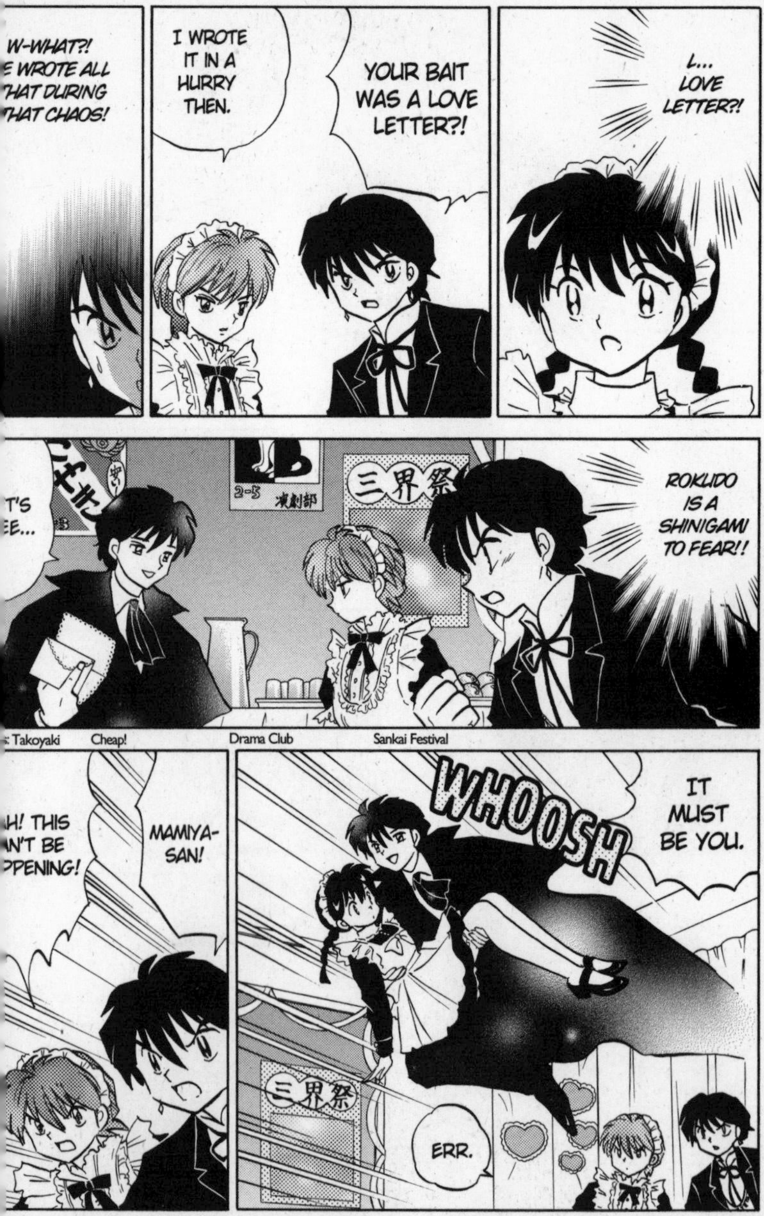
L... LOVE LETTER?!
YOUR BAIT WAS A LOVE LETTER?!
I WROTE IT IN A HURRY THEN.
W-WHAT?!
E WROTE ALL
HAT DURING
THAT CHAOS!
ROKUDO IS A SHINIGAMI TO FEAR!!
三界祭
演劇部
IT MUST BE YOU.
WHOOSH
ERR.
三界祭
MAMIYA-SAN!

s: Takoyaki Cheap! Drama Club Sankai Festival

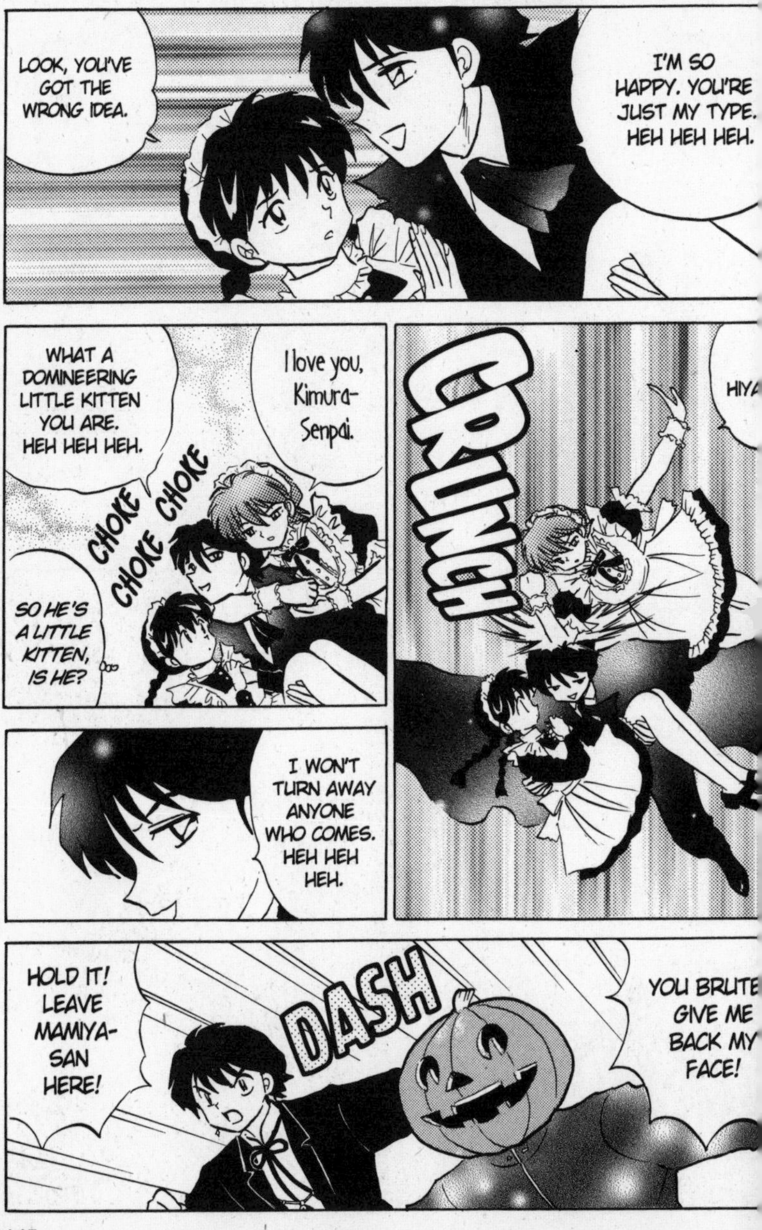
I'M SO HAPPY. YOU'RE JUST MY TYPE. HEH HEH HEH.
LOOK, YOU'VE GOT THE WRONG IDEA.
HIYA
CRUNCH
I love you, Kimura-Senpai.
WHAT A DOMINEERING LITTLE KITTEN YOU ARE. HEH HEH HEH.
CHOKE CHOKE CHOKE
SO HE'S A LITTLE KITTEN, IS HE?
I WON'T TURN AWAY ANYONE WHO COMES. HEH HEH HEH.
YOU BRUTE GIVE ME BACK MY FACE!
DASH
HOLD IT! LEAVE MAMIYA-SAN HERE!

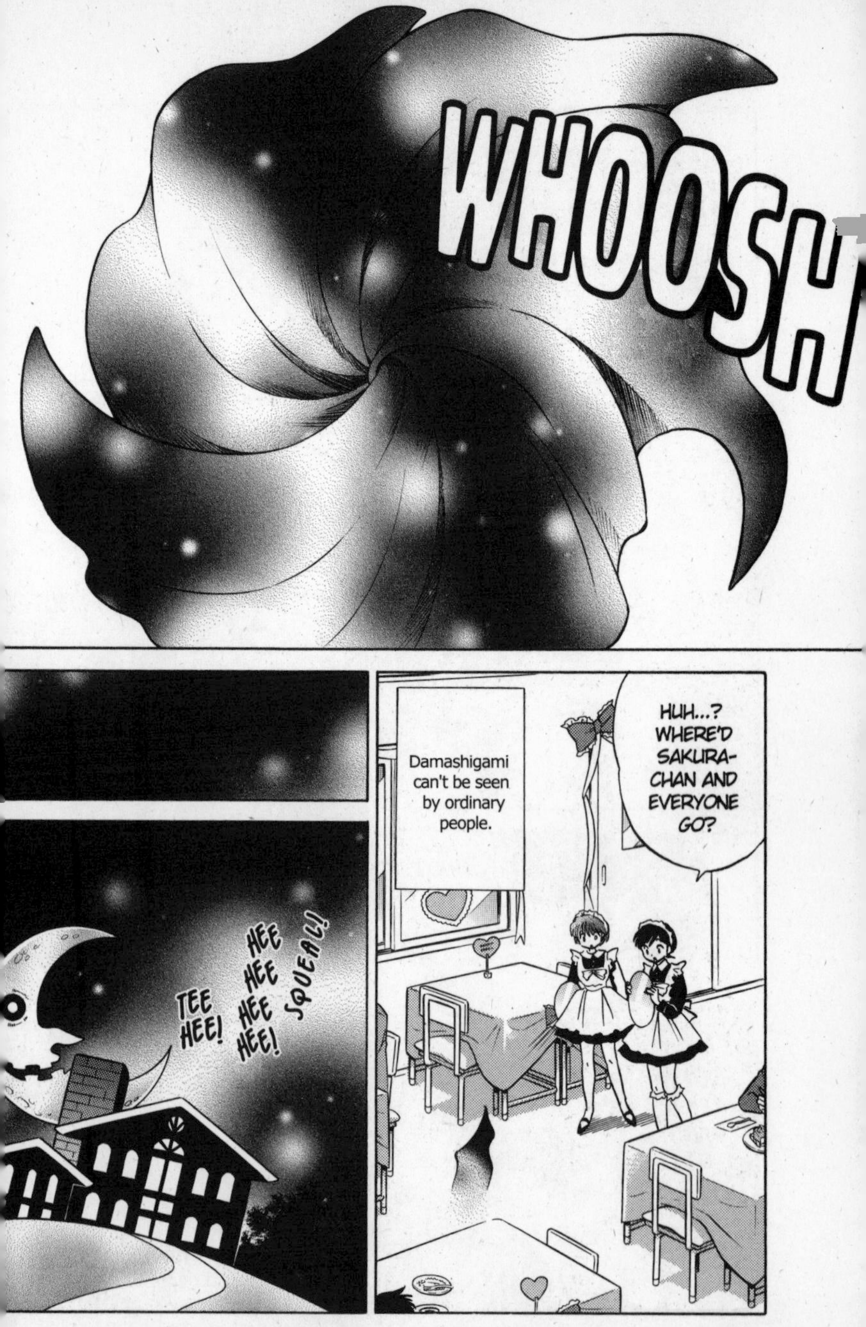
WHOOSH
Damashigami can't be seen by ordinary people.
HUH...? WHERE'D SAKURA-CHAN AND EVERYONE GO?
TEE HEE!
HEE HEE HEE HEE!
SQUEAL!

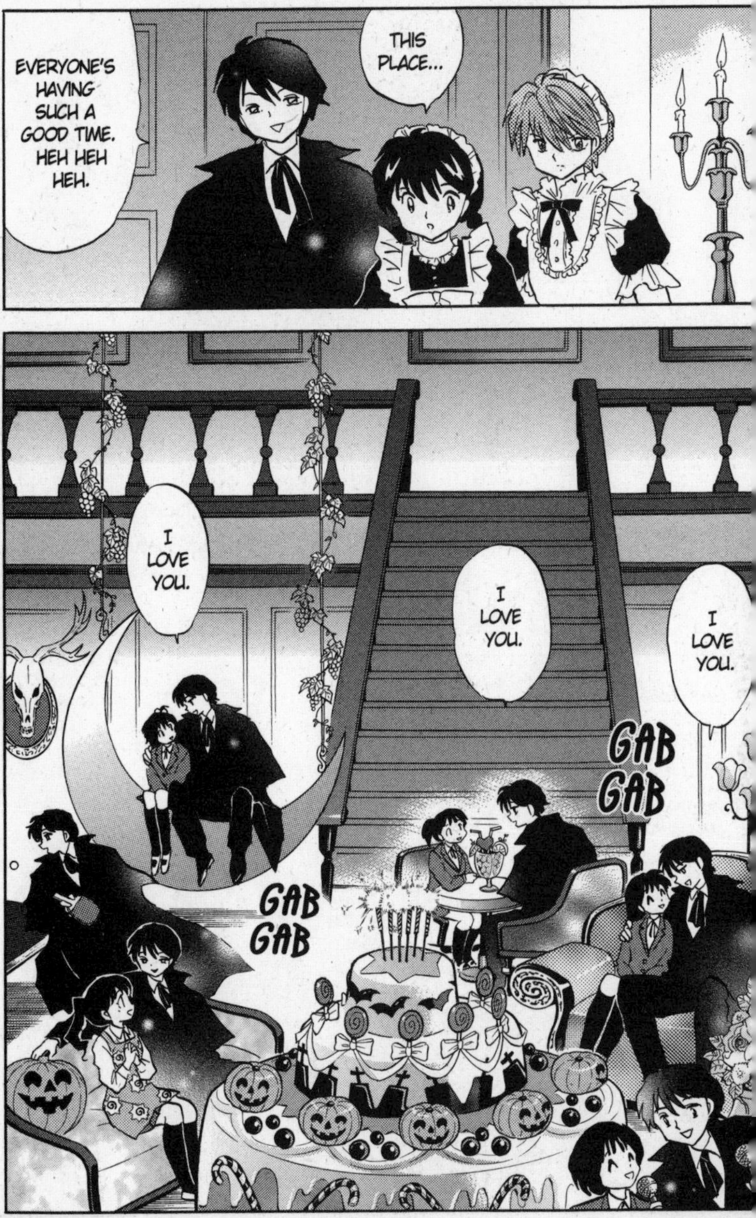
THIS PLACE...
EVERYONE'S HAVING SUCH A GOOD TIME. HEH HEH HEH.
I LOVE YOU.
I LOVE YOU.
I LOVE YOU.
GAB GAB
GAB GAB

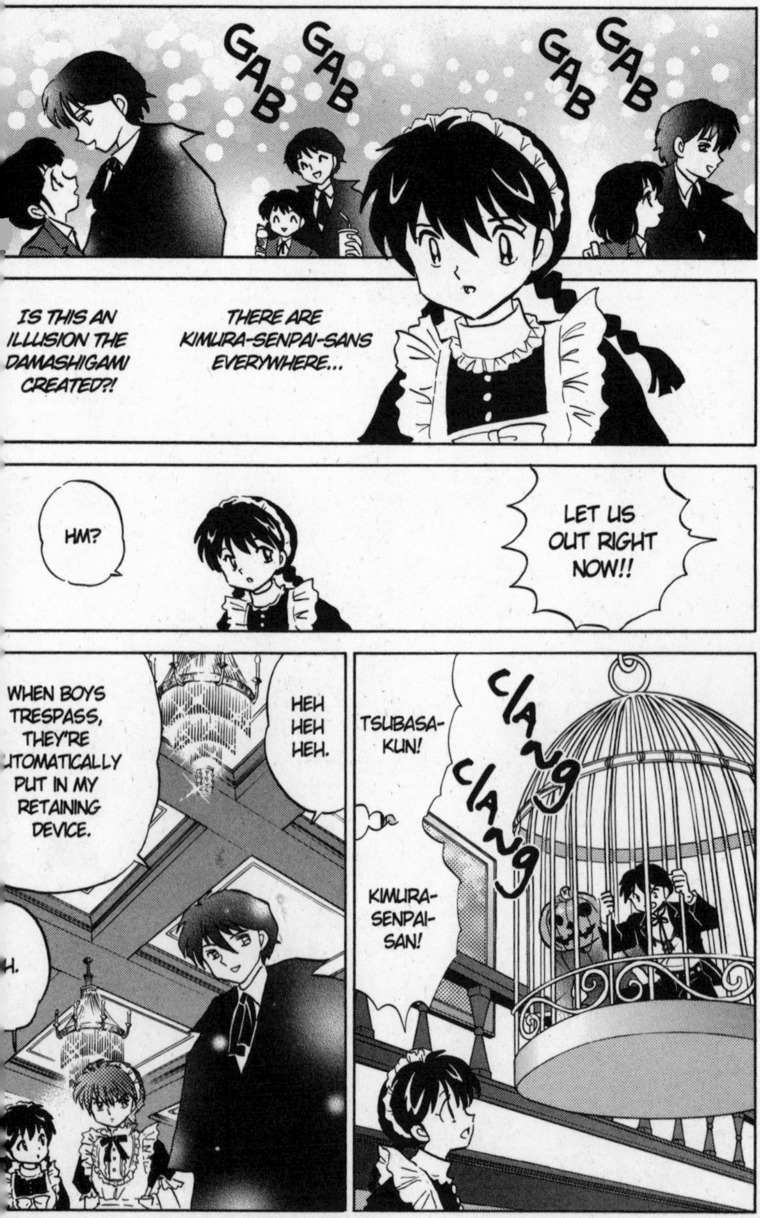
GAB GAB
GAB GAB
THERE ARE KIMURA-SENPAI-SANS EVERYWHERE...
IS THIS AN ILLUSION THE DAMASHIGAMI CREATED?!
LET US OUT RIGHT NOW!!
HM?
CLANG CLANG CLANG
TSUBASA-KUN!
KIMURA-SENPAI-SAN!
HEH HEH HEH.
WHEN BOYS TRESPASS, THEY'RE UTOMATICALLY PUT IN MY RETAINING DEVICE.

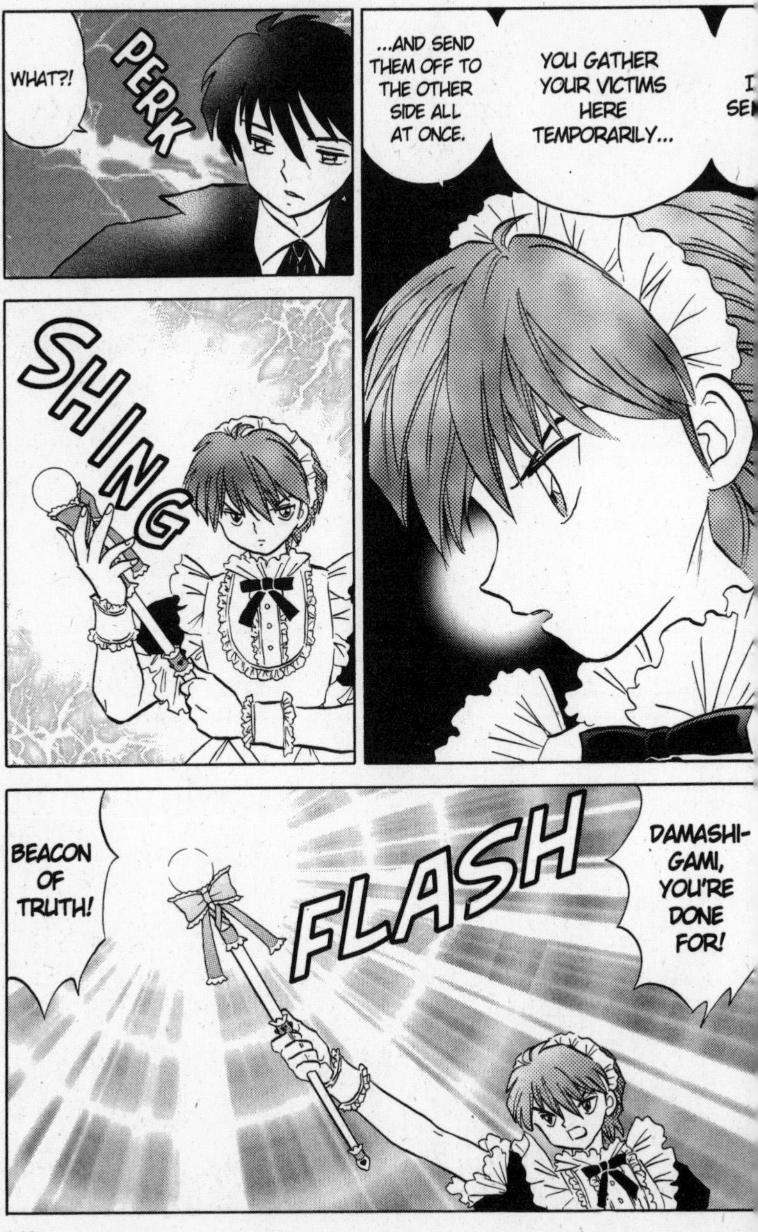
YOU GATHER YOUR VICTIMS HERE TEMPORARILY...
...AND SEND THEM OFF TO THE OTHER SIDE ALL AT ONCE.
PERK
WHAT?!
SHING
DAMASHI-GAMI, YOU'RE DONE FOR!
FLASH
BEACON OF TRUTH!

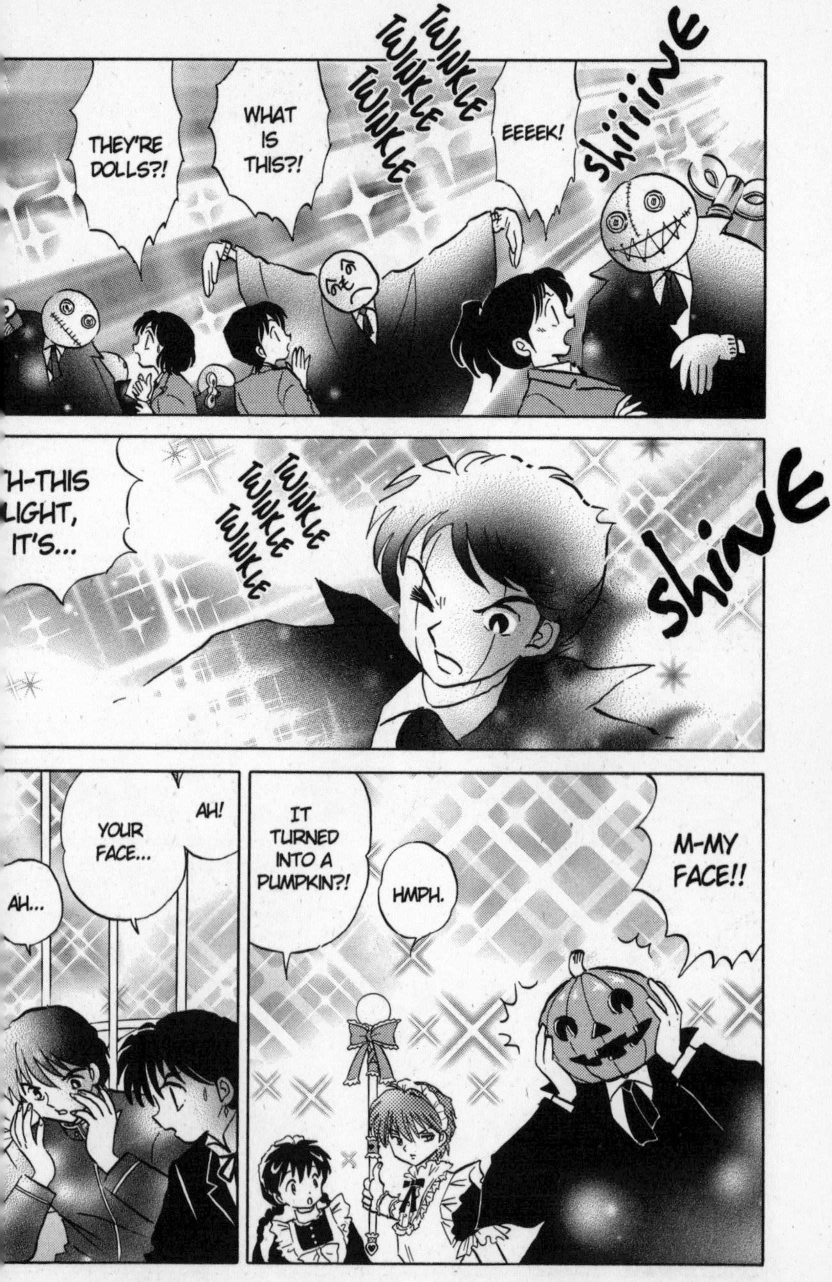
shiiiine
EEEEK!
TWINKLE TWINKLE TWINKLE
WHAT IS THIS?!
THEY'RE DOLLS?!
shine
TWINKLE TWINKLE TWINKLE
H-THIS LIGHT, IT'S...
M-MY FACE!!
HMPH.
IT TURNED INTO A PUMPKIN?!
AH!
YOUR FACE...
AH...

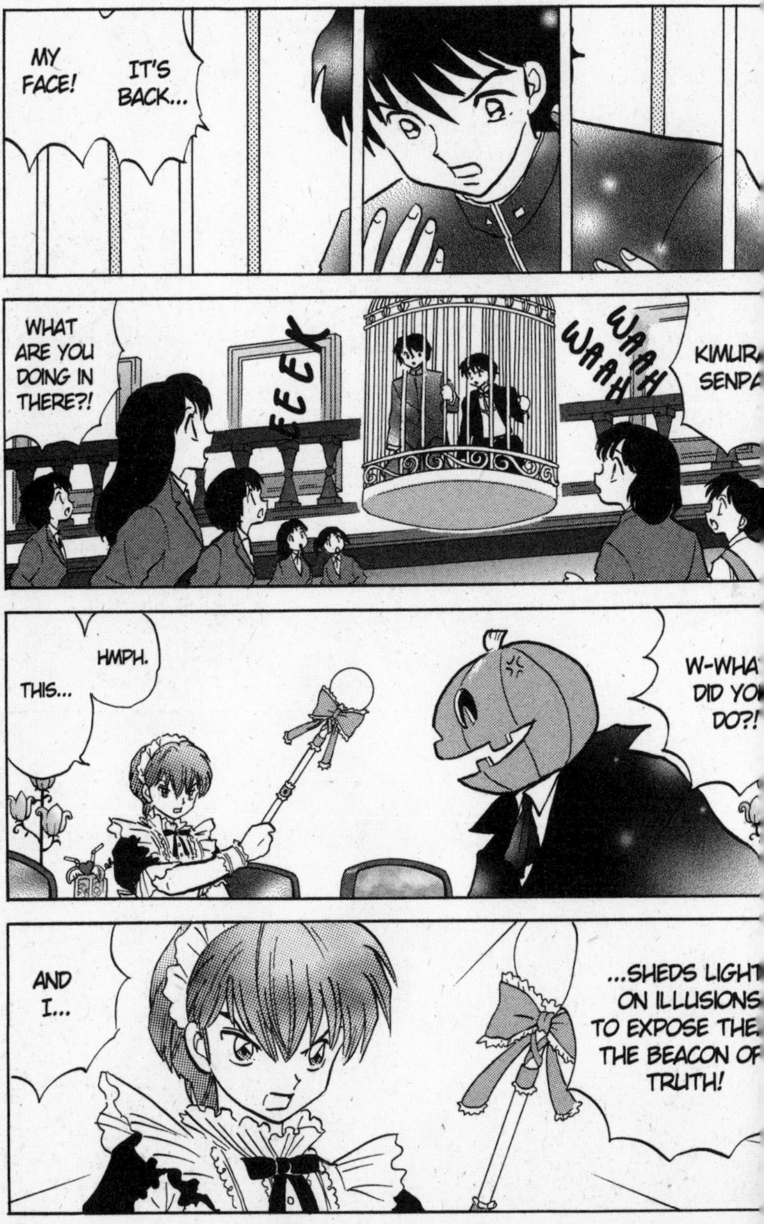

MY FACE!
IT'S BACK...
WHAT ARE YOU DOING IN THERE?!
EEEK
WAAAH WAAAH
KIMURA SENPA
THIS...
HMPH.
W-WHA DID YO DO?!
AND I...
...SHEDS LIGHT ON ILLUSIONS TO EXPOSE THE THE BEACON OF TRUTH!

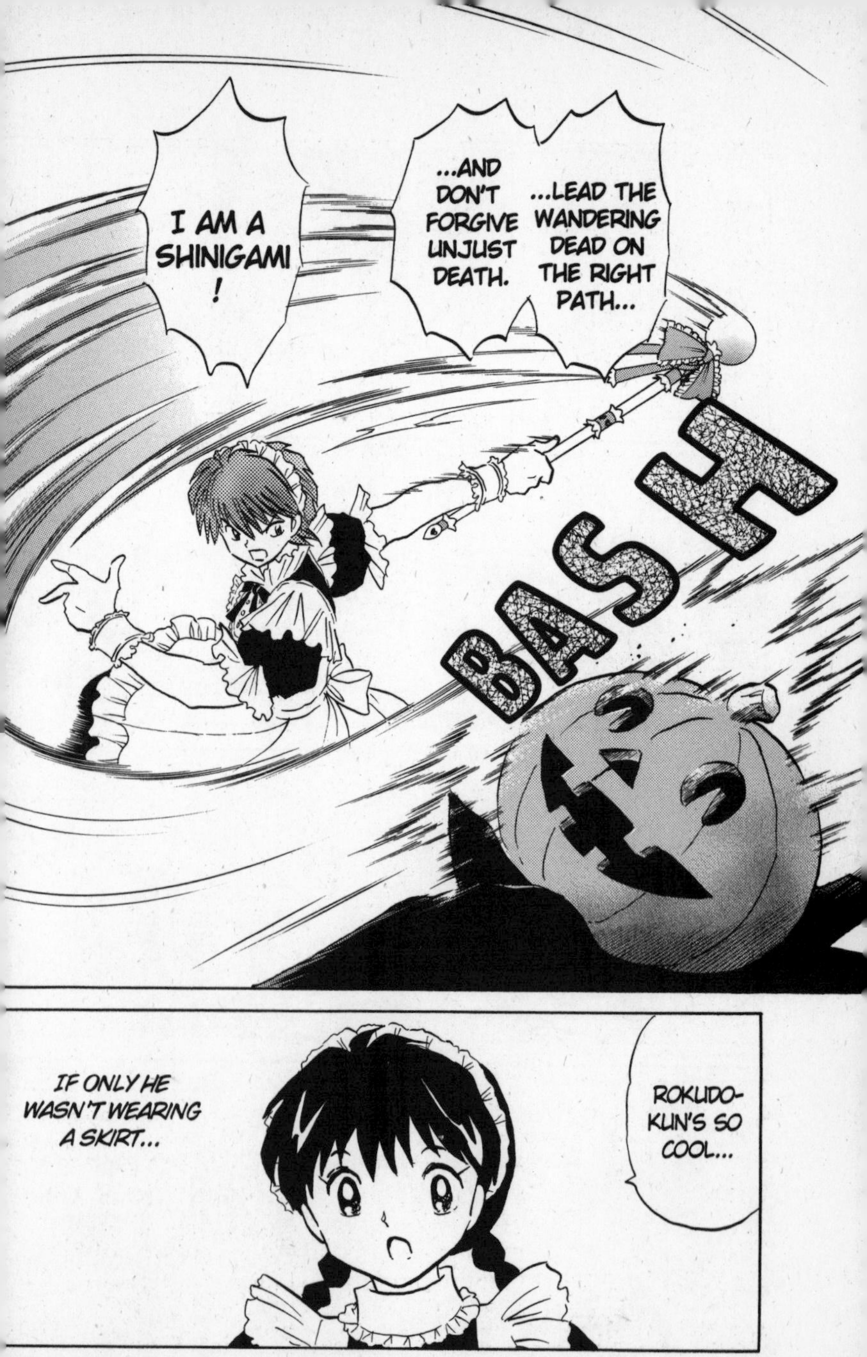
...LEAD THE WANDERING DEAD ON THE RIGHT PATH...
...AND DON'T FORGIVE UNJUST DEATH.
I AM A SHINIGAMI!
BASH
ROKUDO-KUN'S SO COOL...
IF ONLY HE WASN'T WEARING A SKIRT...

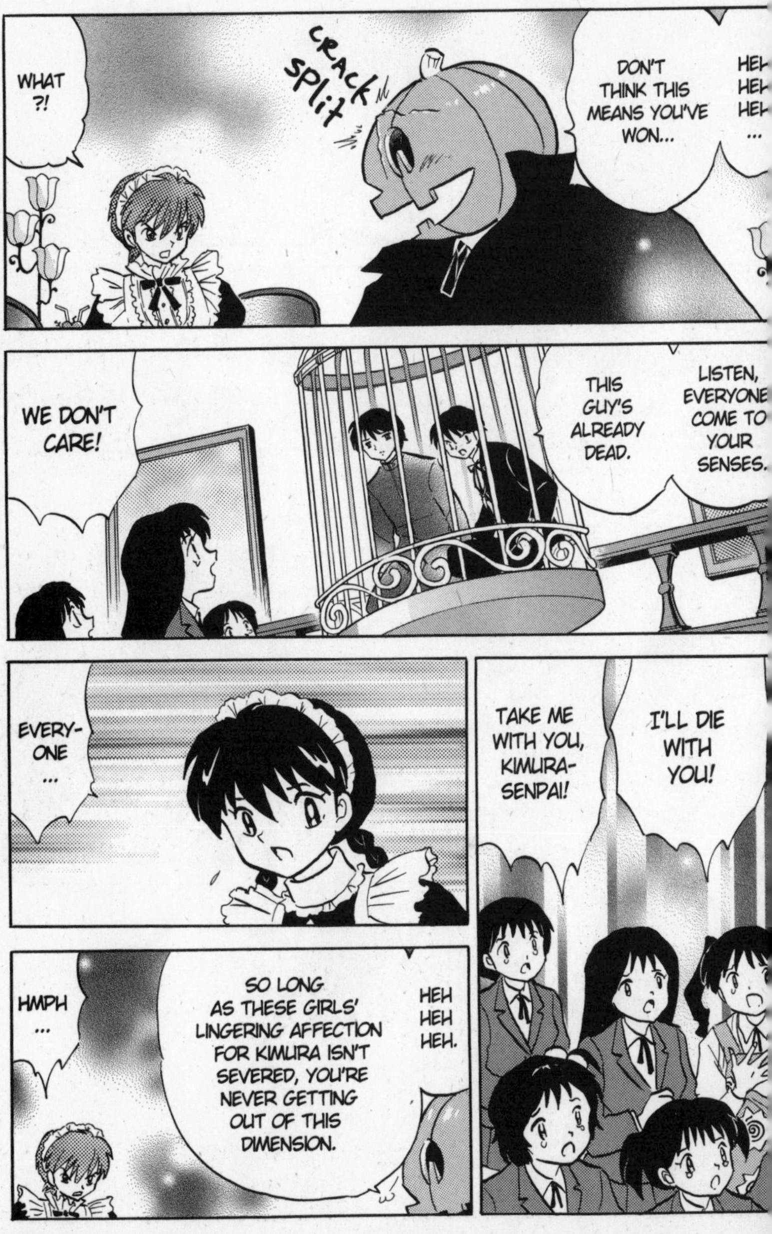
HEH HEH HEH ...
DON'T THINK THIS MEANS YOU'VE WON...
CRACK
SPLIT
WHAT ?!
LISTEN, EVERYONE COME TO YOUR SENSES.
THIS GUY'S ALREADY DEAD.
WE DON'T CARE!
I'LL DIE WITH YOU!
TAKE ME WITH YOU, KIMURA-SENPAI!
EVERY-ONE ...
HEH HEH HEH.
SO LONG AS THESE GIRLS' LINGERING AFFECTION FOR KIMURA ISN'T SEVERED, YOU'RE NEVER GETTING OUT OF THIS DIMENSION.
HMPH ...

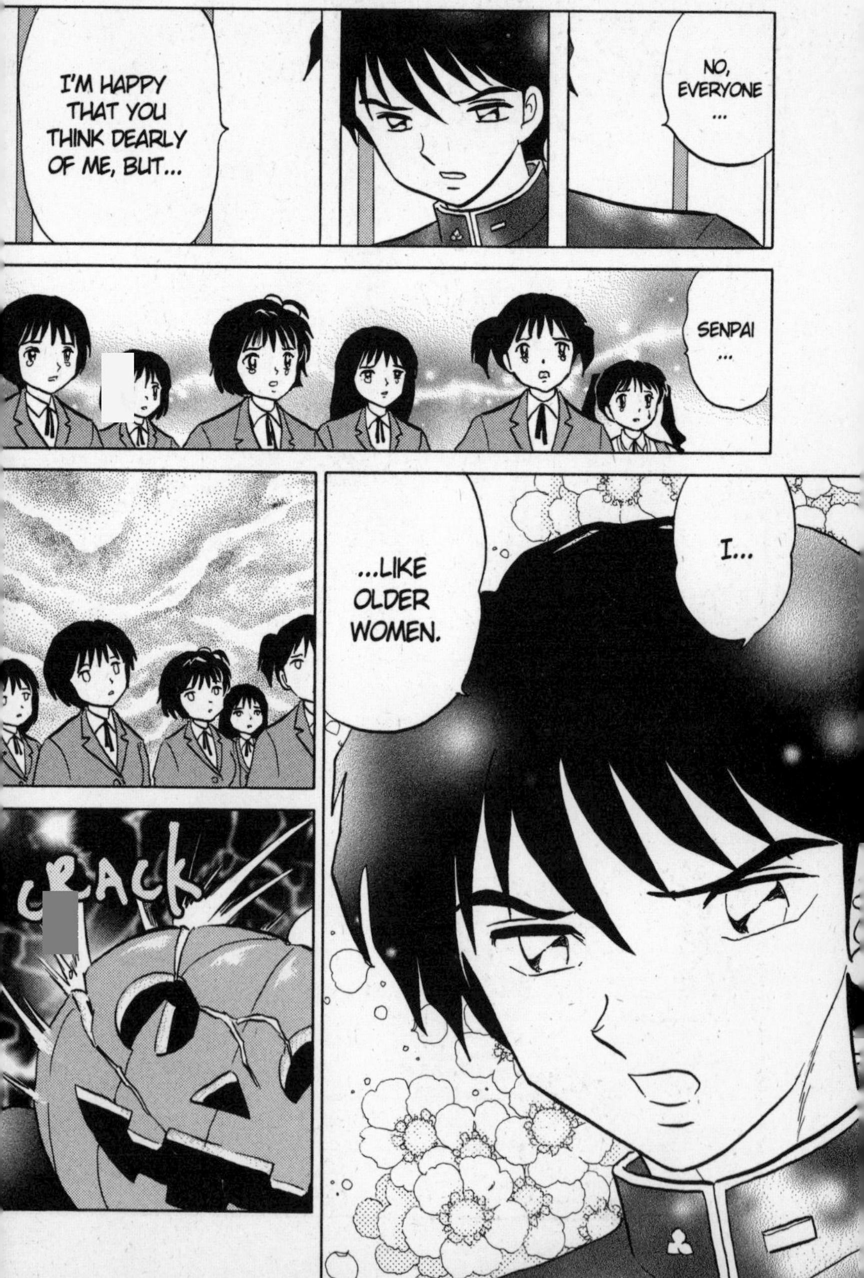
NO, EVERYONE ...
I'M HAPPY THAT YOU THINK DEARLY OF ME, BUT...
SENPAI ...
I...
...LIKE OLDER WOMEN.
CRACK

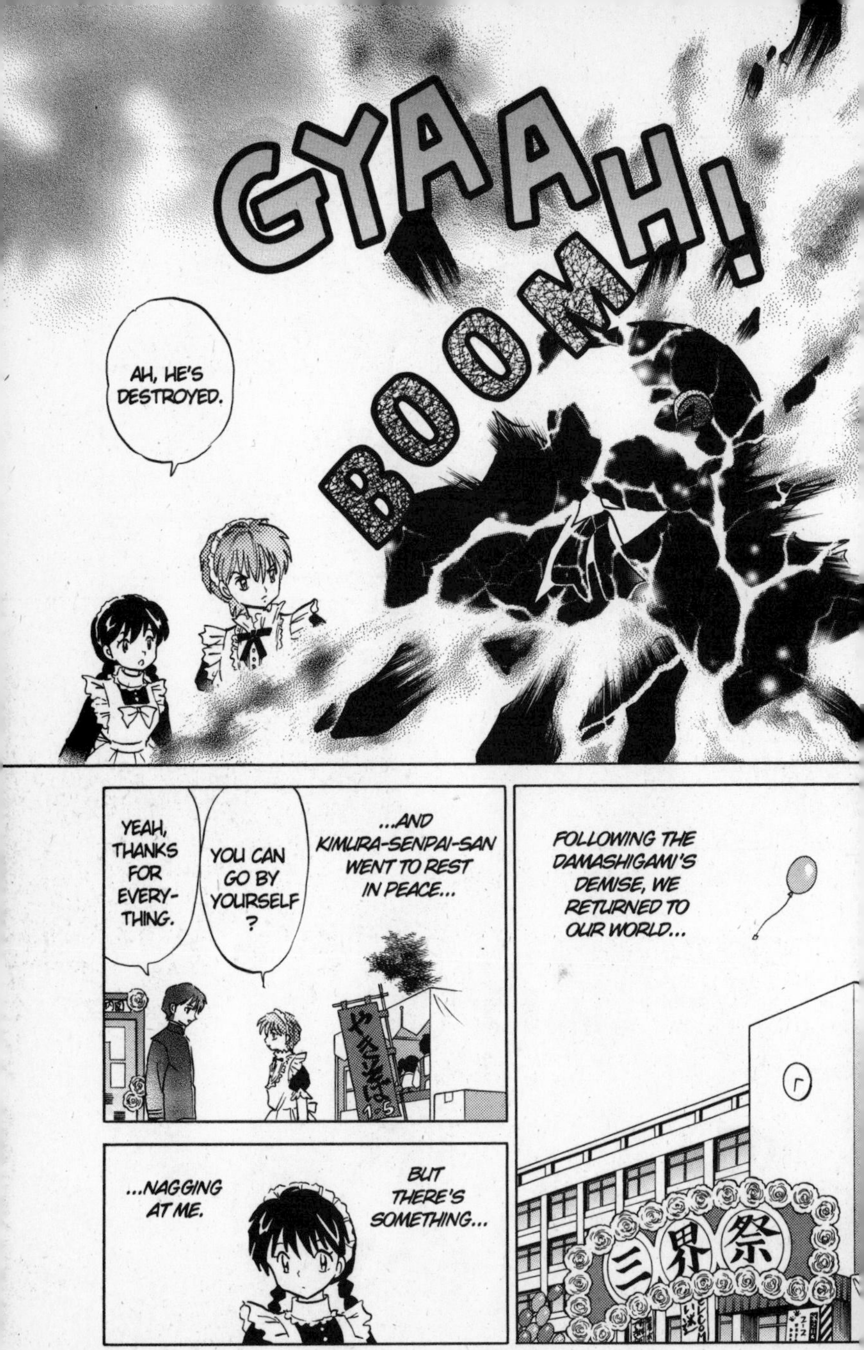
GYAAH!
BOOM
AH, HE'S DESTROYED.
FOLLOWING THE DAMASHIGAMI'S DEMISE, WE RETURNED TO OUR WORLD...
三界祭
...AND KIMURA-SENPAI-SAN WENT TO REST IN PEACE...
YOU CAN GO BY YOURSELF?
YEAH, THANKS FOR EVERYTHING.
BUT THERE'S SOMETHING...
...NAGGING AT ME.

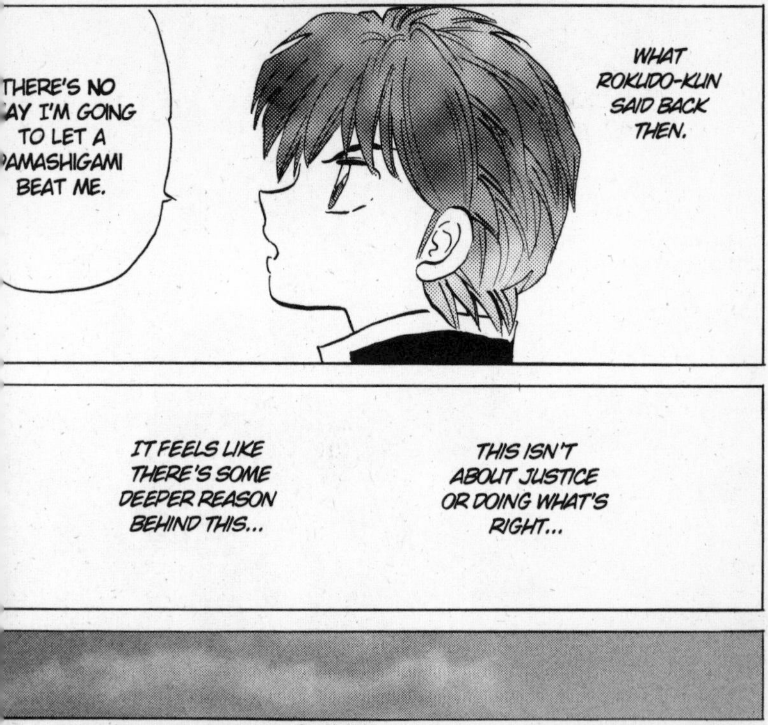
WHAT ROKUDO-KUN SAID BACK THEN.
THERE'S NO
AY I'M GOING
TO LET A
AMASHIGAMI
BEAT ME.
THIS ISN'T ABOUT JUSTICE OR DOING WHAT'S RIGHT...
IT FEELS LIKE THERE'S SOME DEEPER REASON BEHIND THIS...

Sign: Mr. Lady

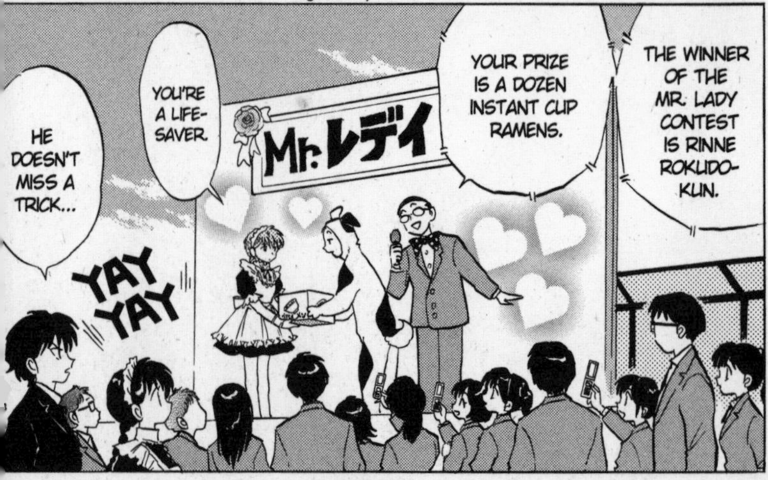
THE WINNER OF THE MR. LADY CONTEST IS RINNE ROKUDO-KUN.
YOUR PRIZE IS A DOZEN INSTANT CUP RAMENS.
Mr.レディ
YOU'RE A LIFE-SAVER.
HE DOESN'T MISS A TRICK...
YAY YAY

CHAPTER 27: DRAW ME

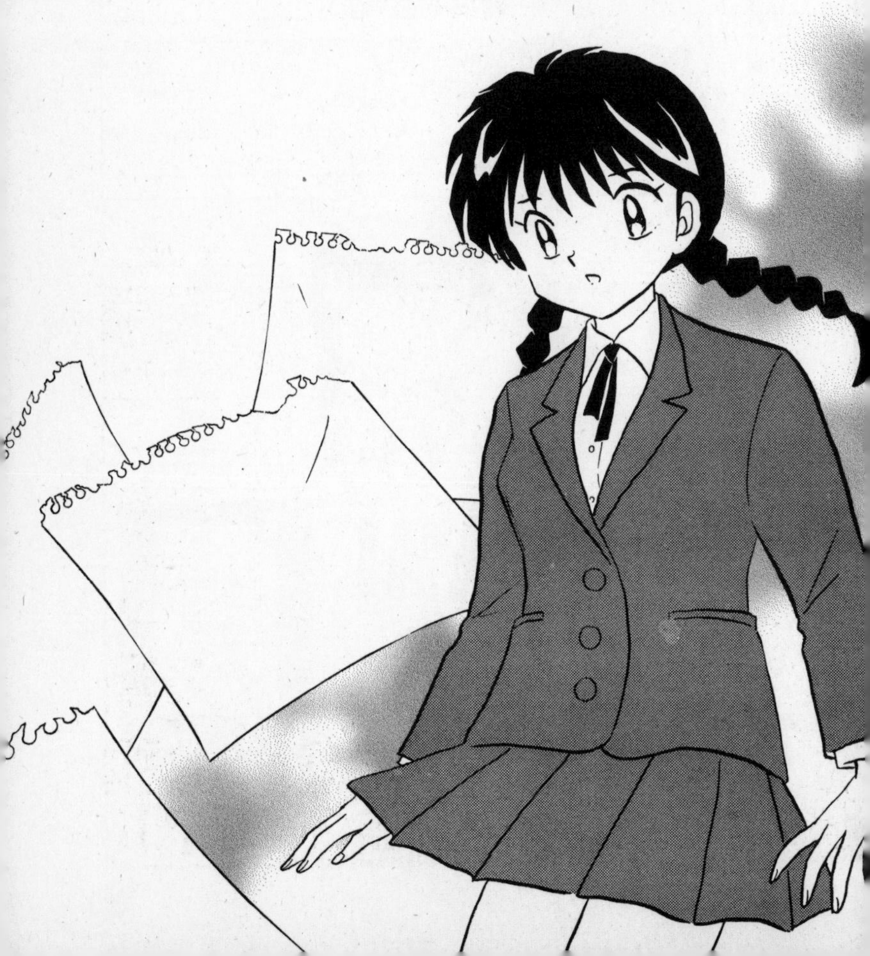

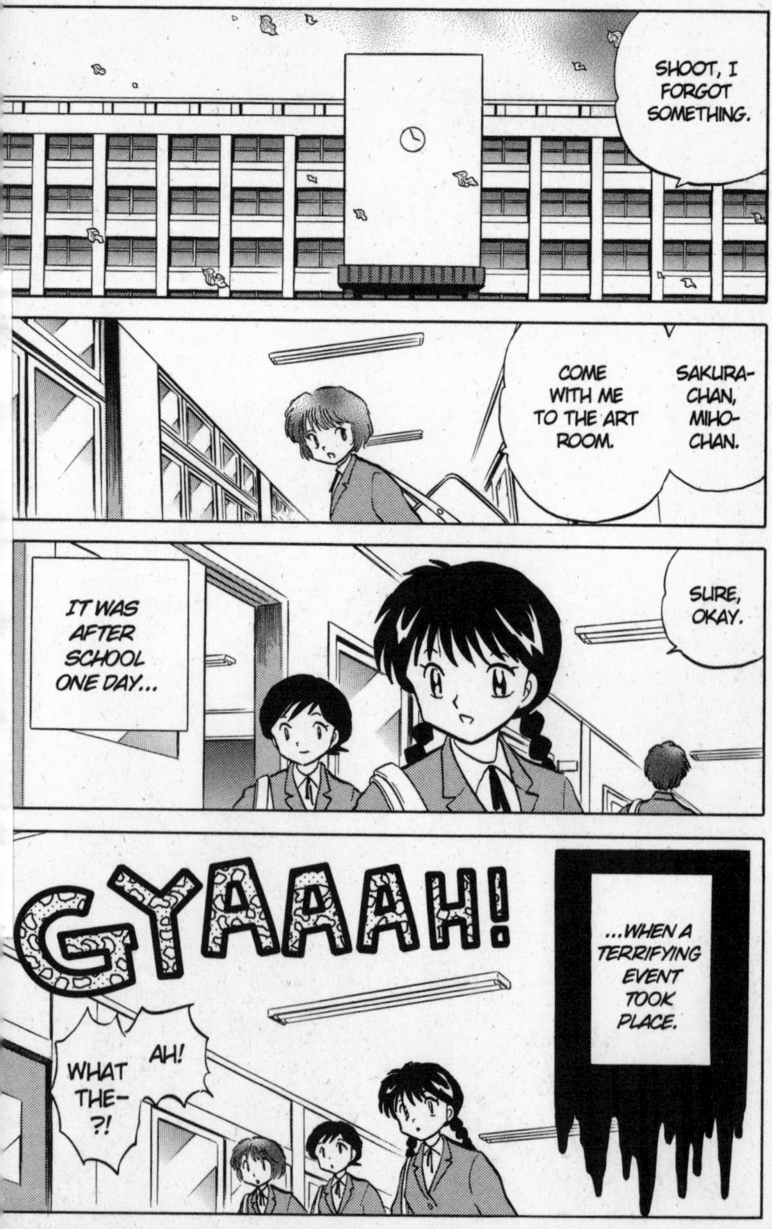
SHOOT, I FORGOT SOMETHING.
SAKURA-CHAN, MIHO-CHAN.
COME WITH ME TO THE ART ROOM.
SURE, OKAY.
IT WAS AFTER SCHOOL ONE DAY...
...WHEN A TERRIFYING EVENT TOOK PLACE.
GYAAAH!
AH!
WHAT THE-?!

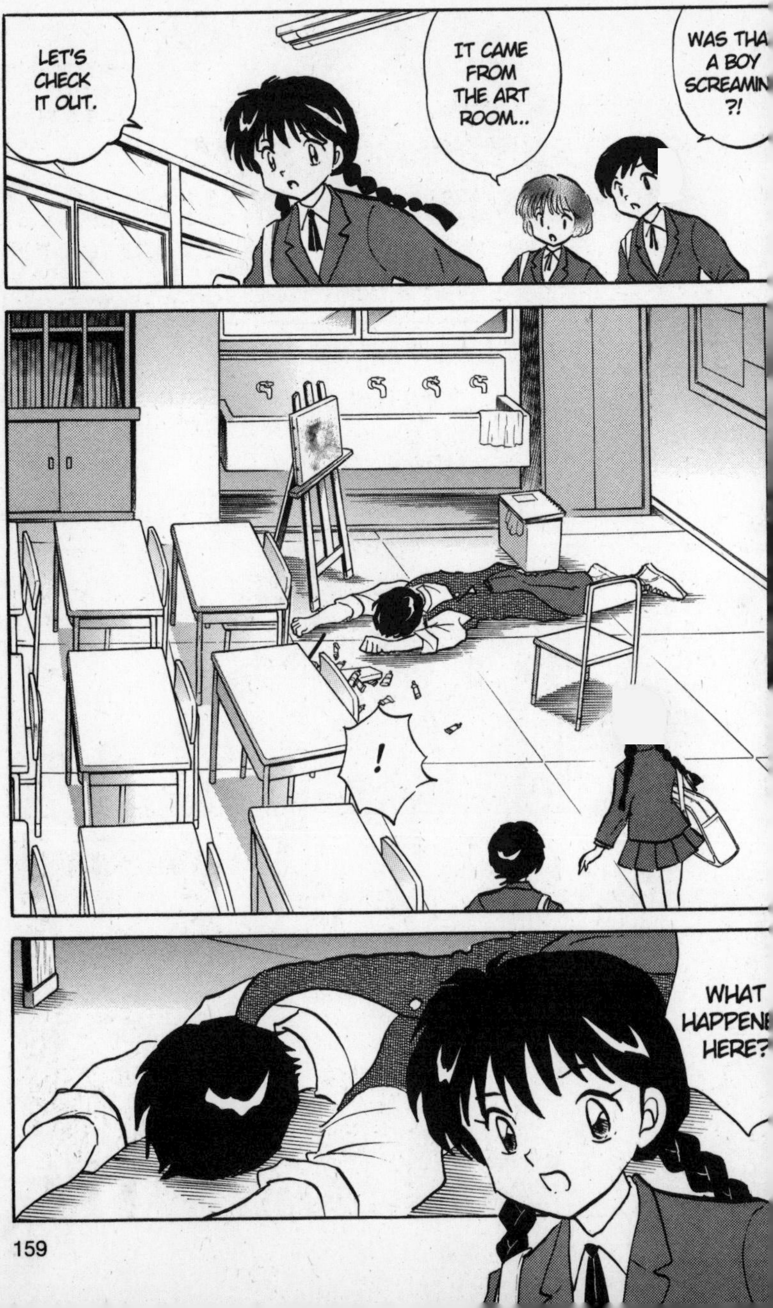
WAS THA A BOY SCREAMIN ?!
IT CAME FROM THE ART ROOM...
LET'S CHECK IT OUT.
!
WHAT HAPPENE HERE?

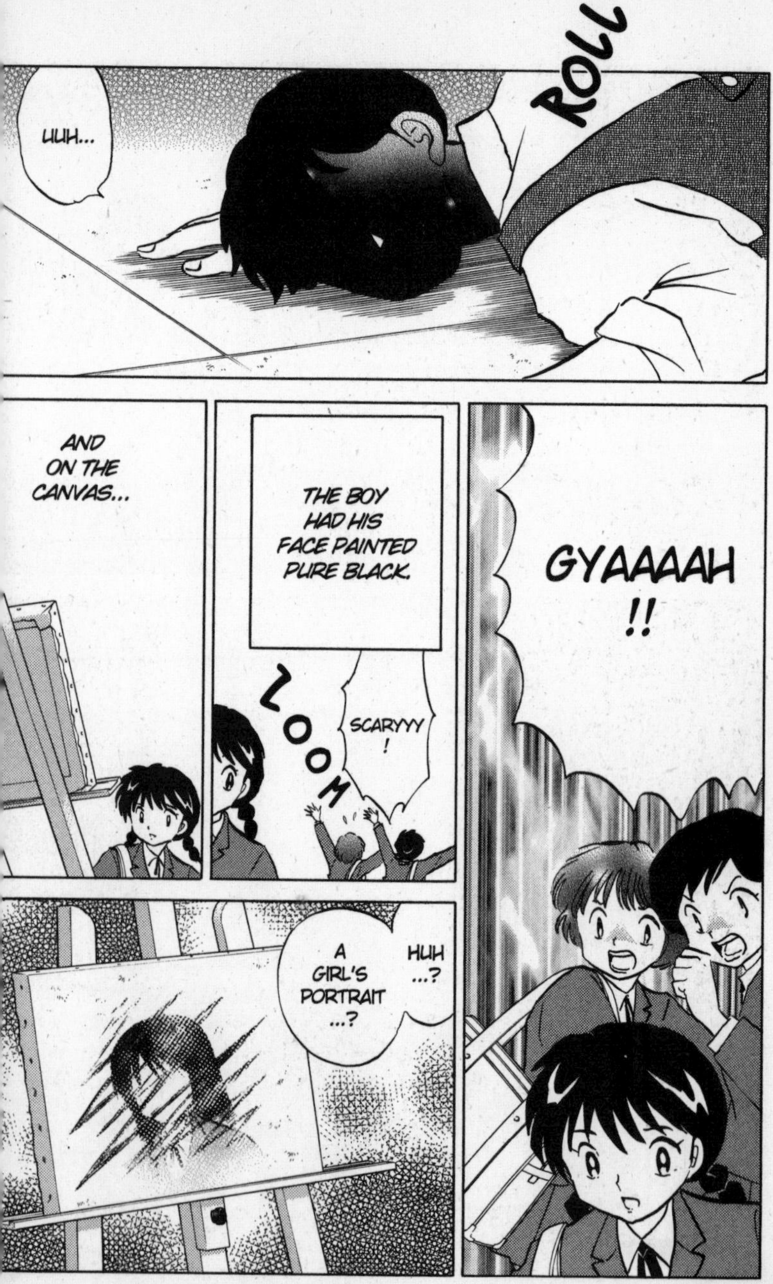
ROLL
UUH...
GYAAAAH !!
THE BOY HAD HIS FACE PAINTED PURE BLACK.
AND ON THE CANVAS...
ZOOM
SCARYYY !
HUH ...?
A GIRL'S PORTRAIT ...?

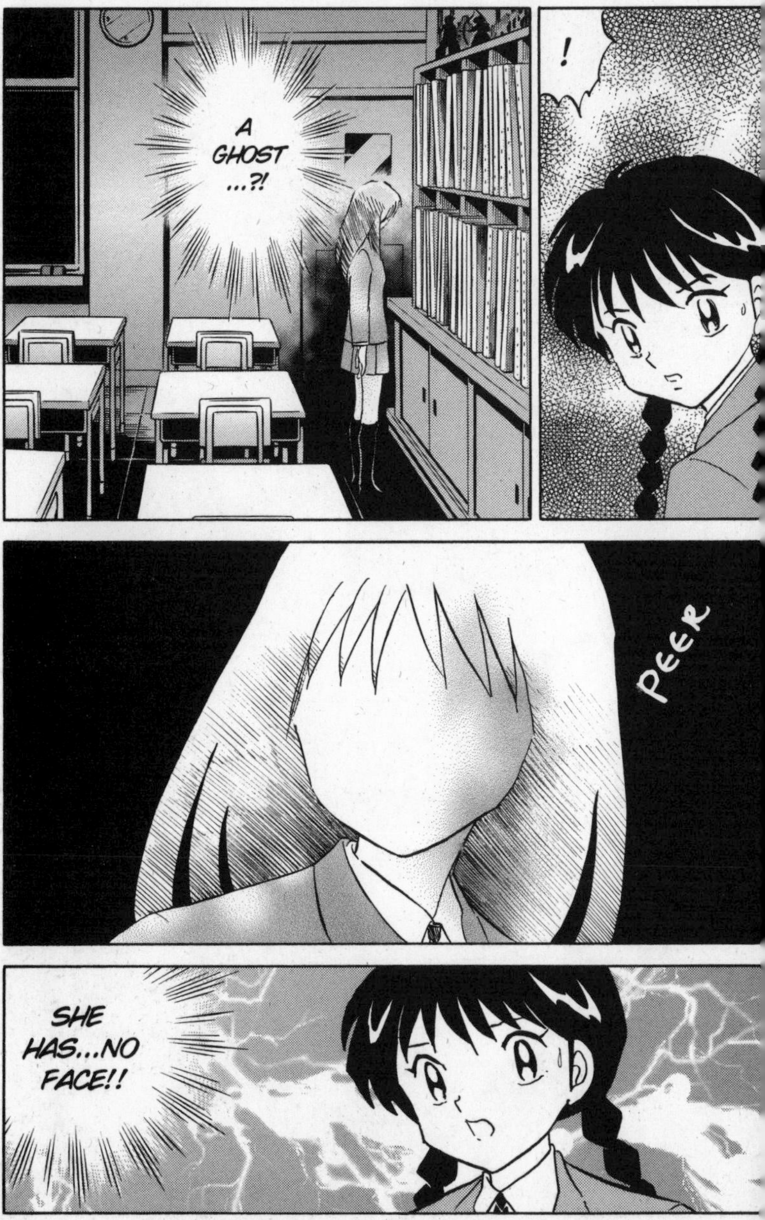
!
A GHOST ...?!
PEER
SHE HAS...NO FACE!!

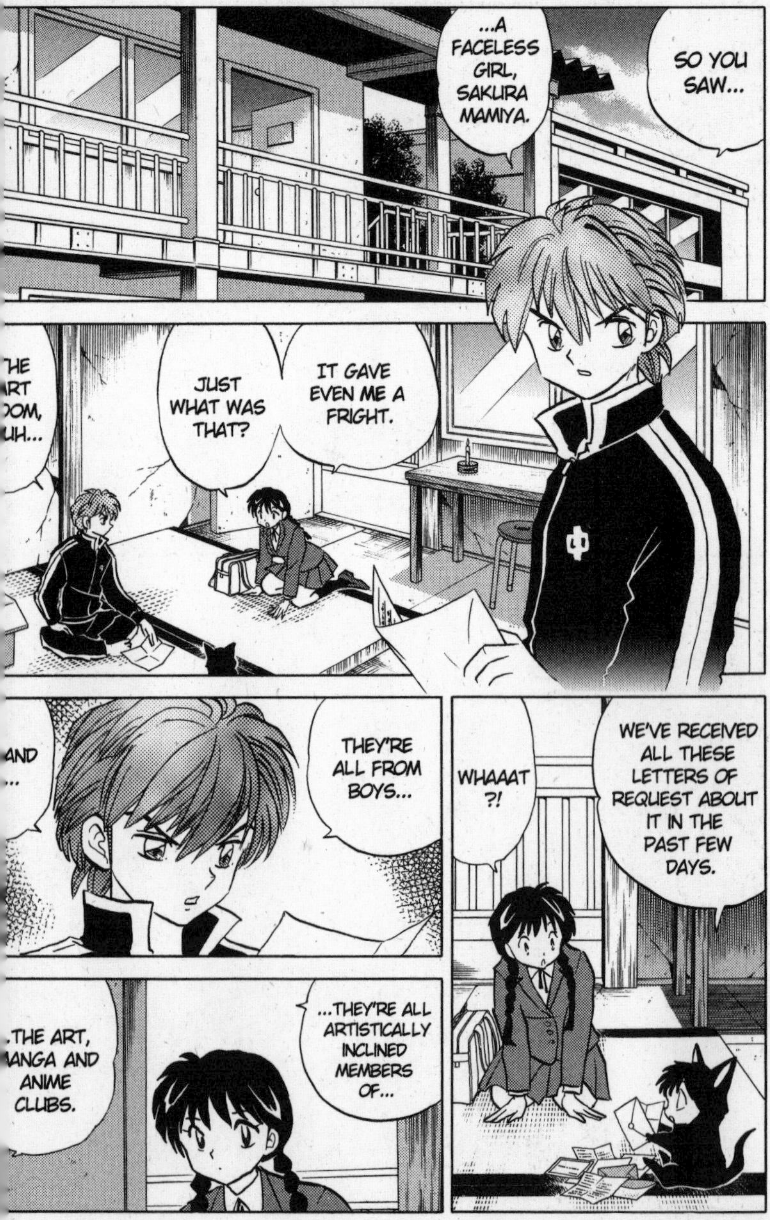
SO YOU SAW...
...A FACELESS GIRL, SAKURA MAMIYA.
IT GAVE EVEN ME A FRIGHT.
JUST WHAT WAS THAT?
HE RT OOM, UH...
WE'VE RECEIVED ALL THESE LETTERS OF REQUEST ABOUT IT IN THE PAST FEW DAYS.
WHAAAT ?!
THEY'RE ALL FROM BOYS...
AND ...
...THEY'RE ALL ARTISTICALLY INCLINED MEMBERS OF...
.THE ART, ANGA AND ANIME CLUBS.

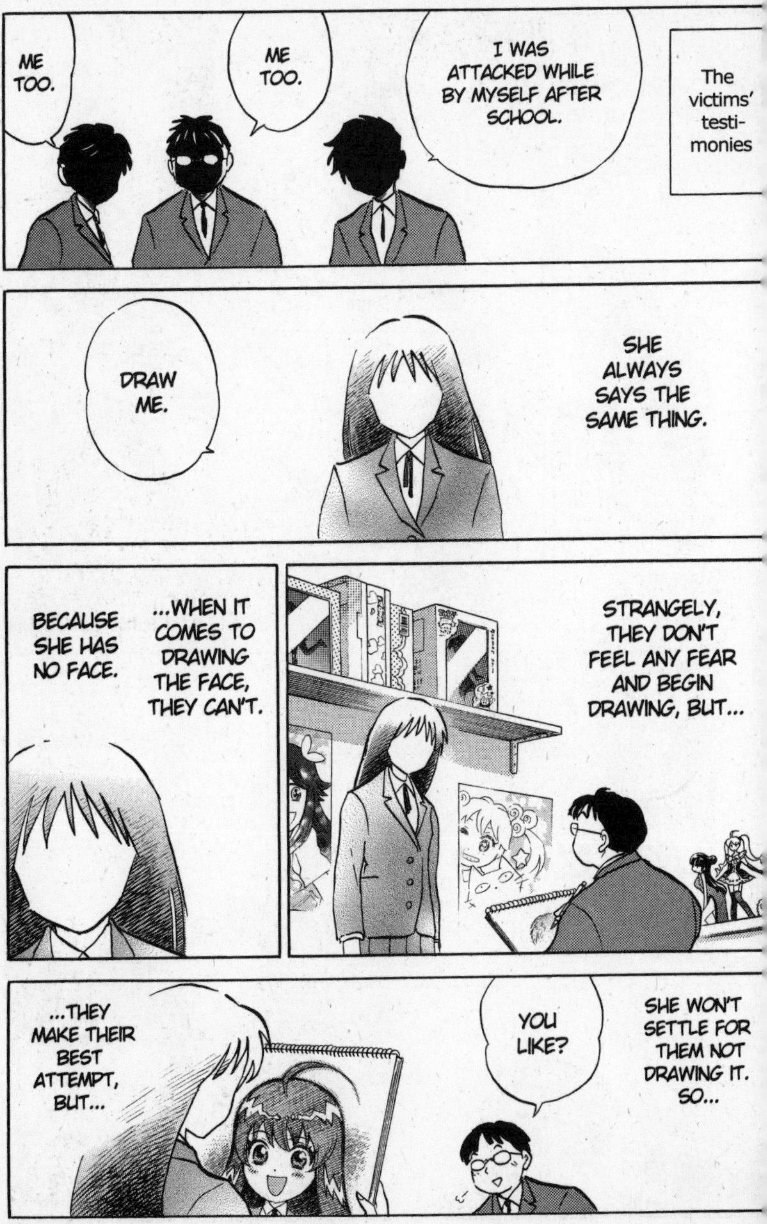
The victims' testimonies
I WAS ATTACKED WHILE BY MYSELF AFTER SCHOOL.
ME TOO.
ME TOO.
SHE ALWAYS SAYS THE SAME THING.
DRAW ME.
STRANGELY, THEY DON'T FEEL ANY FEAR AND BEGIN DRAWING, BUT...
...WHEN IT COMES TO DRAWING THE FACE, THEY CAN'T.
BECAUSE SHE HAS NO FACE.
SHE WON'T SETTLE FOR THEM NOT DRAWING IT. SO...
YOU LIKE?
...THEY MAKE THEIR BEST ATTEMPT, BUT...

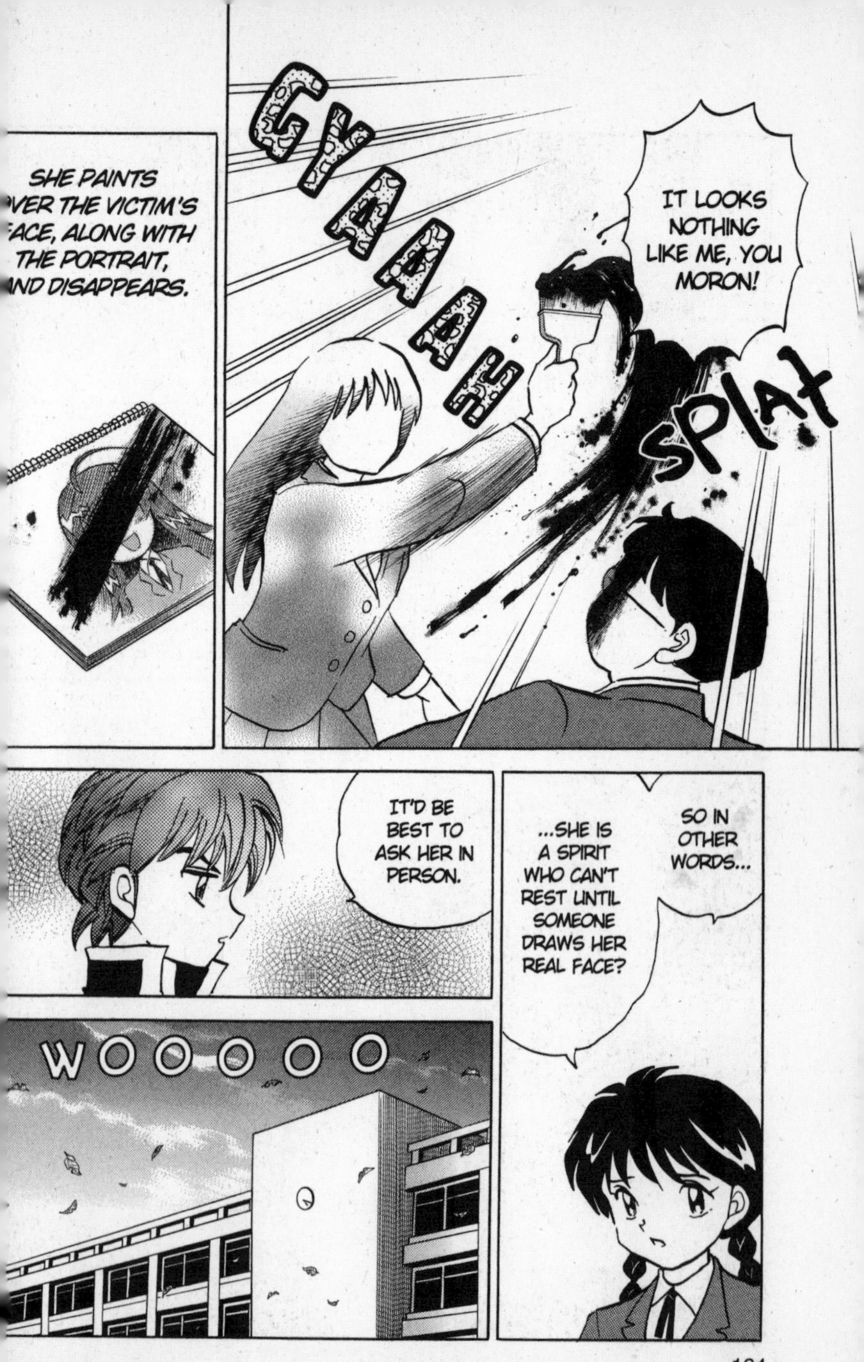
GYAAAH
IT LOOKS NOTHING LIKE ME, YOU MORON!
SPLAT
SHE PAINTS OVER THE VICTIM'S FACE, ALONG WITH THE PORTRAIT, AND DISAPPEARS.
SO IN OTHER WORDS...
...SHE IS A SPIRIT WHO CAN'T REST UNTIL SOMEONE DRAWS HER REAL FACE?
IT'D BE BEST TO ASK HER IN PERSON.
WOOOOO

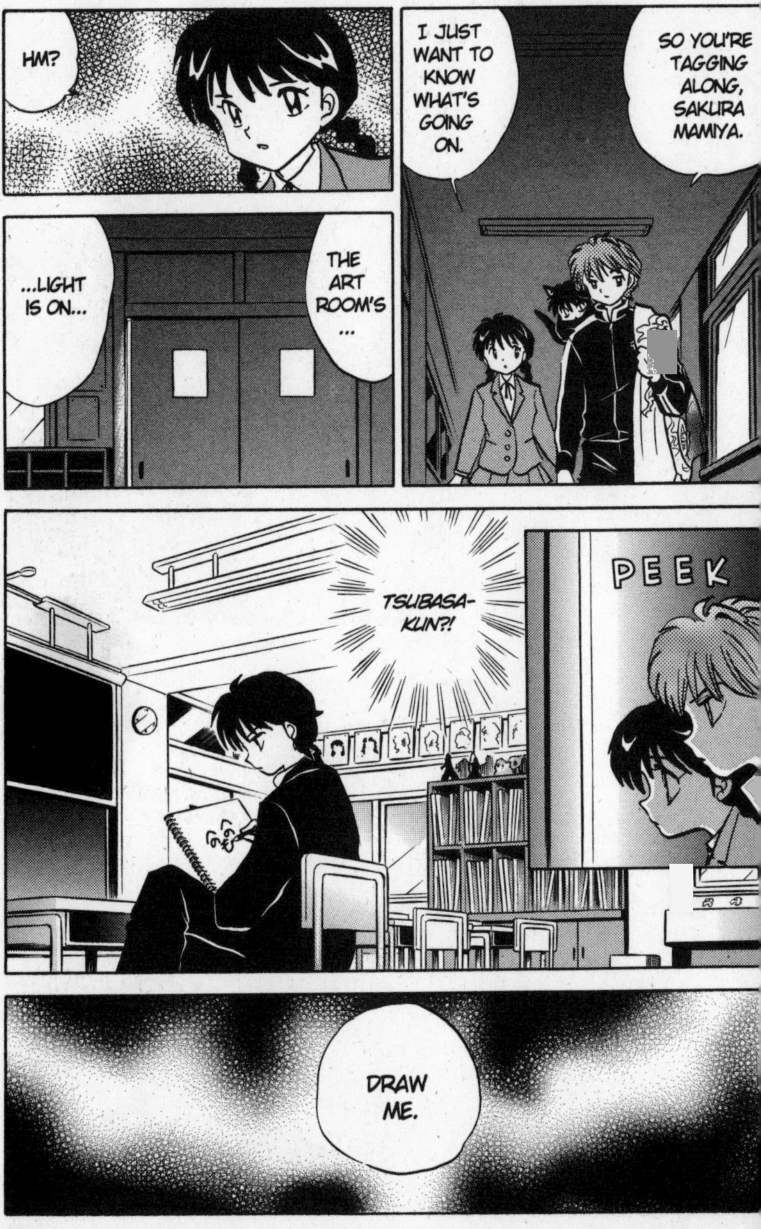
SO YOU'RE TAGGING ALONG, SAKURA MAMIYA.
I JUST WANT TO KNOW WHAT'S GOING ON.
HM?
THE ART ROOM'S ...
...LIGHT IS ON...
PEEK
TSUBASA-KUN?!
DRAW ME.

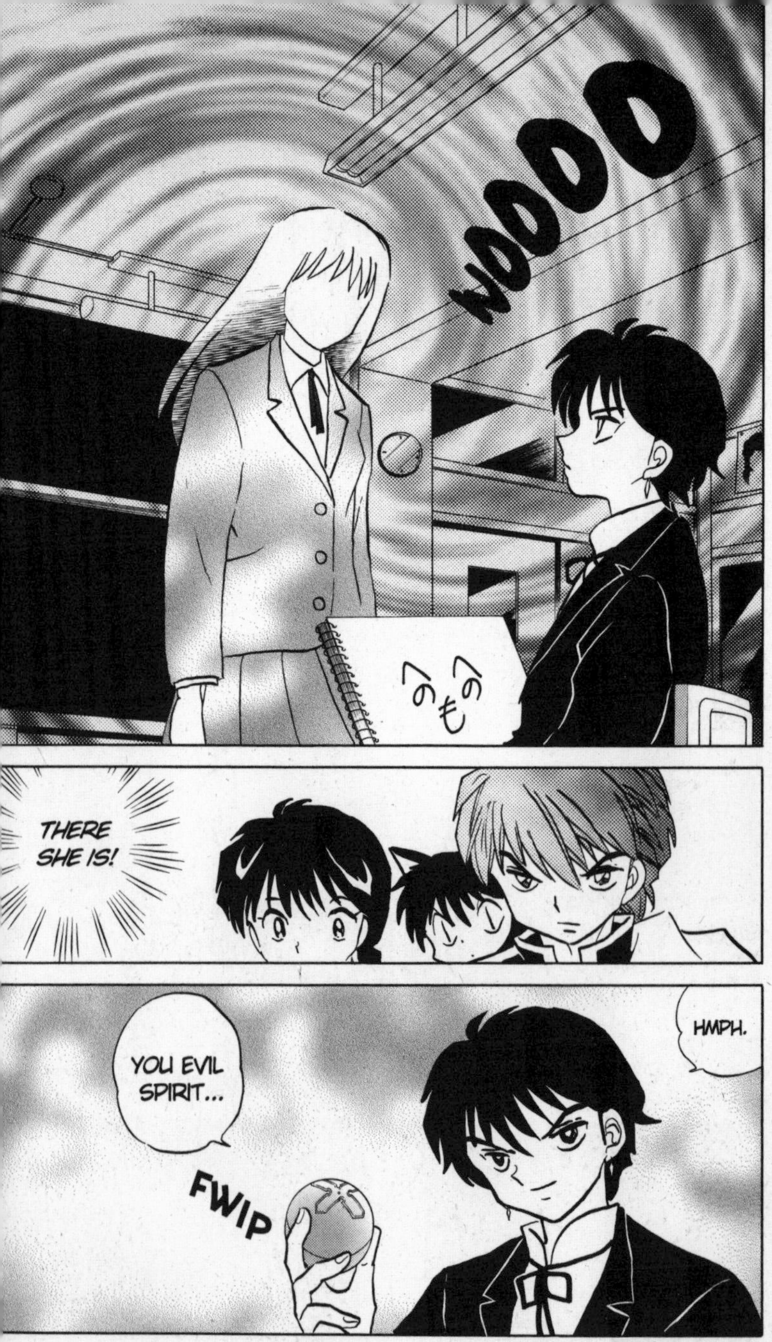
WOOOO
THERE SHE IS!
HMPH.
YOU EVIL SPIRIT...
FWIP

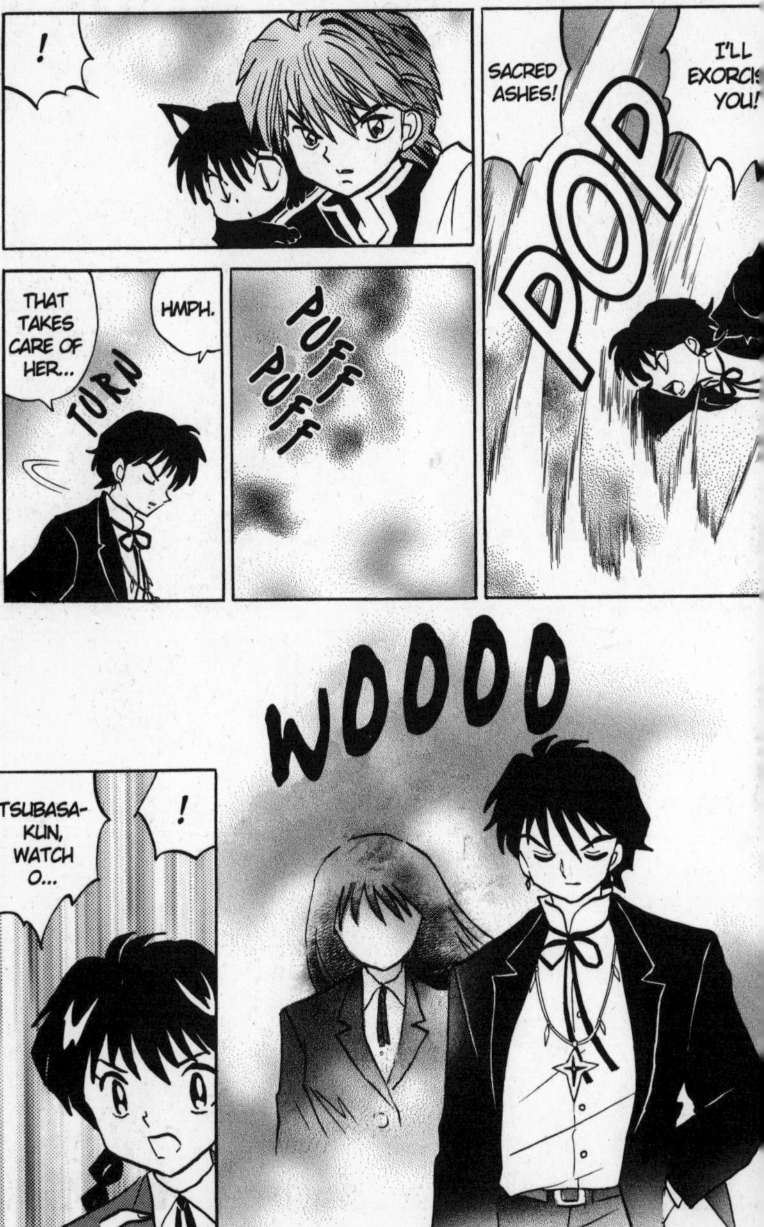
I'LL EXORCIS YOU!
SACRED ASHES!
POP
!
PUFF PUFF
HMPH.
THAT TAKES CARE OF HER...
TURN
WOOOO
!
TSUBASA-KUN, WATCH O...

HURRY UP AND GET DRAWING!!

SHOVE

HAORI OF THE UNDERWORLD!

flap

!

TCH.

fwap

THE SACRED ASHES DIDN'T WORK?!

POOMF

SPLAT

HM?!

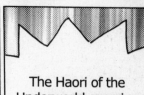

The Haori of the Underworld can give physical form to ghosts when worn inside-out.

DOES THAT MEAN THAT GIRL ISN'T A GHOST?

SHE'S GONE?!

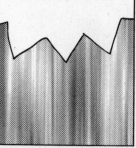

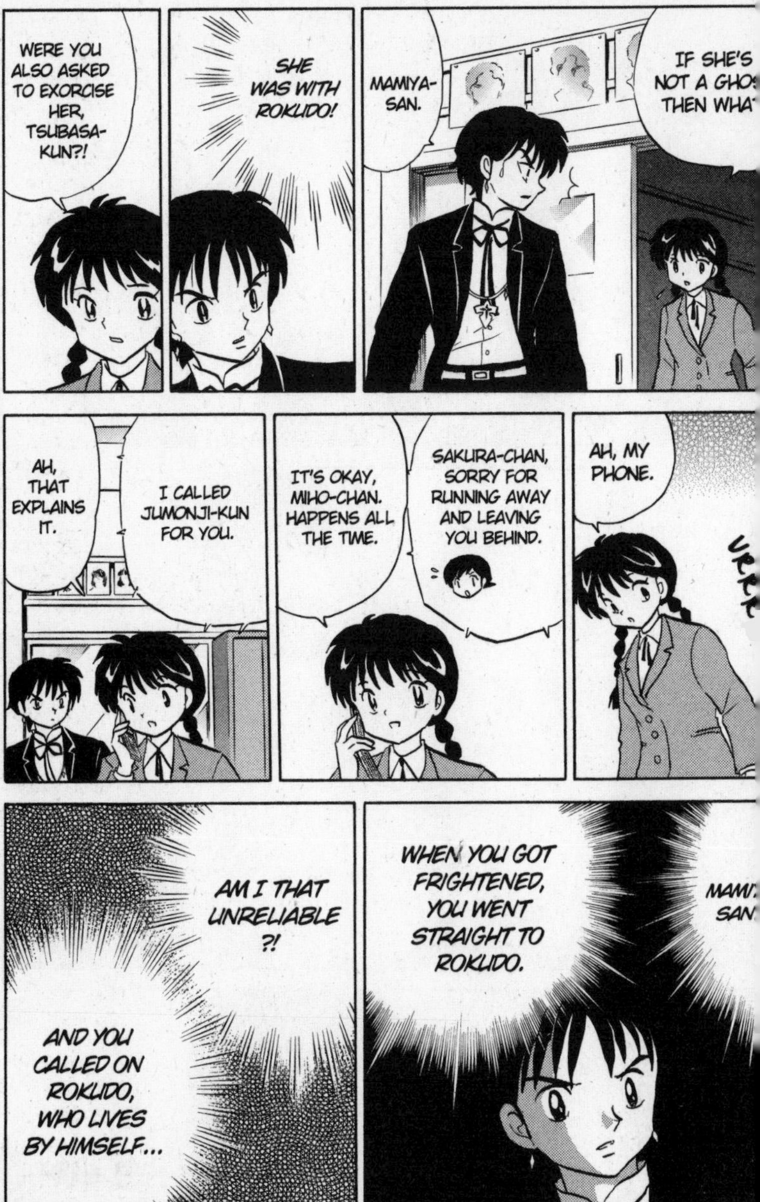
IF SHE'S NOT A GHOS THEN WHA
MAMIYA-SAN.
SHE WAS WITH ROKUDO!
WERE YOU ALSO ASKED TO EXORCISE HER, TSUBASA-KUN?!
URRR
AH, MY PHONE.
SAKURA-CHAN, SORRY FOR RUNNING AWAY AND LEAVING YOU BEHIND.
IT'S OKAY, MIHO-CHAN. HAPPENS ALL THE TIME.
I CALLED JUMONJI-KUN FOR YOU.
AH, THAT EXPLAINS IT.
MAMI SAN
WHEN YOU GOT FRIGHTENED, YOU WENT STRAIGHT TO ROKUDO.
AM I THAT UNRELIABLE ?!
AND YOU CALLED ON ROKUDO, WHO LIVES BY HIMSELF...

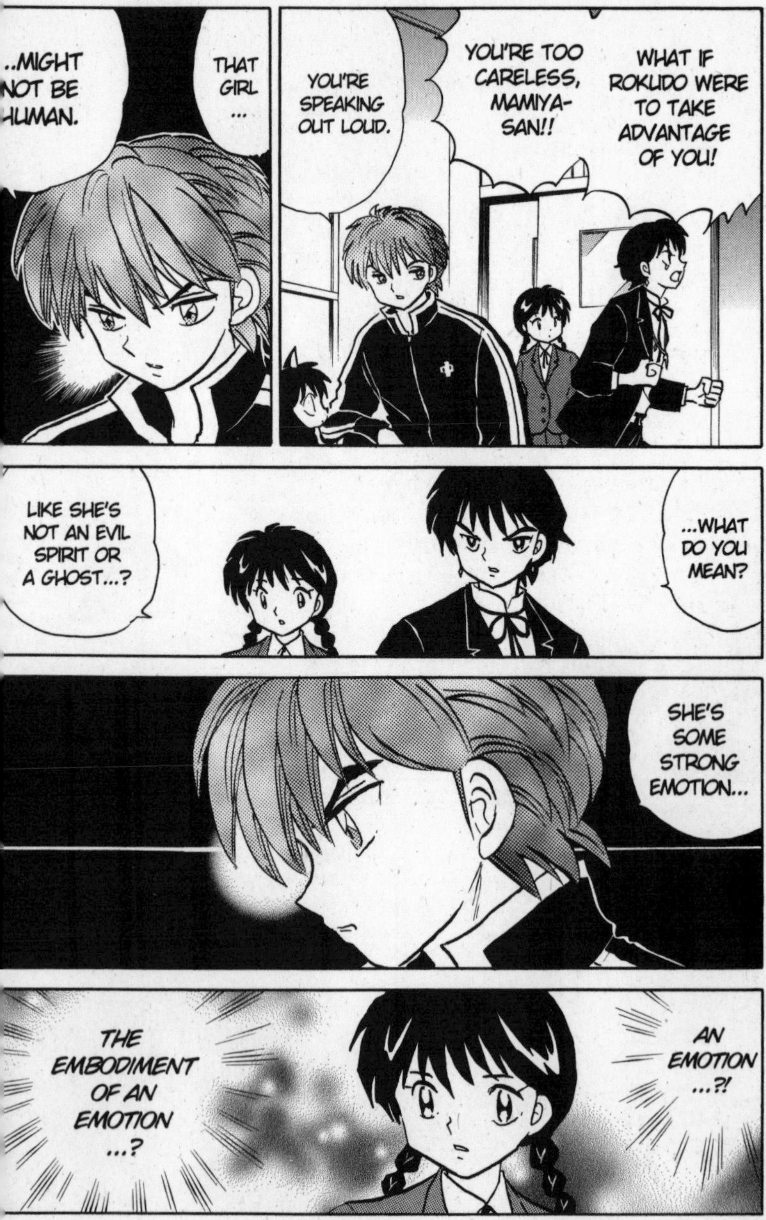
WHAT IF ROKUDO WERE TO TAKE ADVANTAGE OF YOU!
YOU'RE TOO CARELESS, MAMIYA-SAN!!
YOU'RE SPEAKING OUT LOUD.
THAT GIRL ...
..MIGHT NOT BE HUMAN.
...WHAT DO YOU MEAN?
LIKE SHE'S NOT AN EVIL SPIRIT OR A GHOST...?
SHE'S SOME STRONG EMOTION...
AN EMOTION ...?!
THE EMBODIMENT OF AN EMOTION ...?

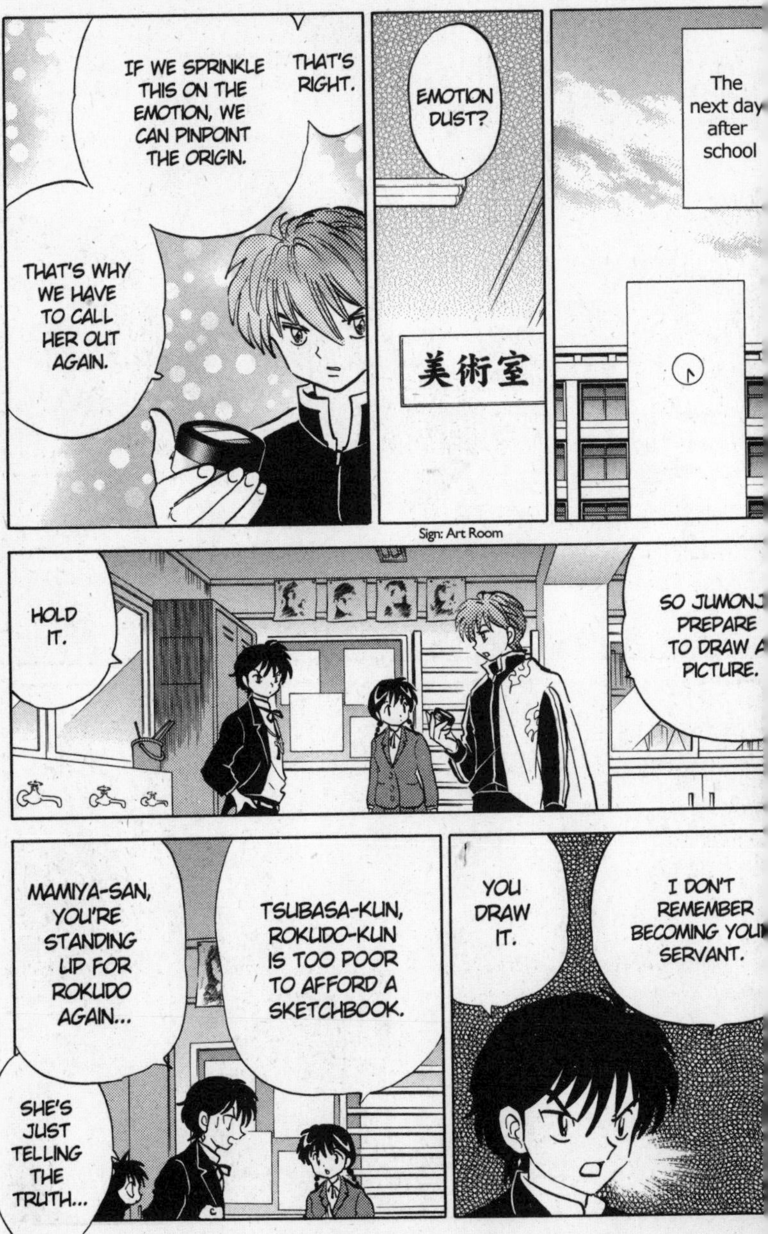
The next day after school
EMOTION DUST?
美術室
THAT'S RIGHT.
IF WE SPRINKLE THIS ON THE EMOTION, WE CAN PINPOINT THE ORIGIN.
THAT'S WHY WE HAVE TO CALL HER OUT AGAIN.
SO JUMONJ PREPARE TO DRAW A PICTURE.
HOLD IT.
I DON'T REMEMBER BECOMING YOU SERVANT.
YOU DRAW IT.
TSUBASA-KUN, ROKUDO-KUN IS TOO POOR TO AFFORD A SKETCHBOOK.
MAMIYA-SAN, YOU'RE STANDING UP FOR ROKUDO AGAIN...
SHE'S JUST TELLING THE TRUTH...

Sign: Art Room

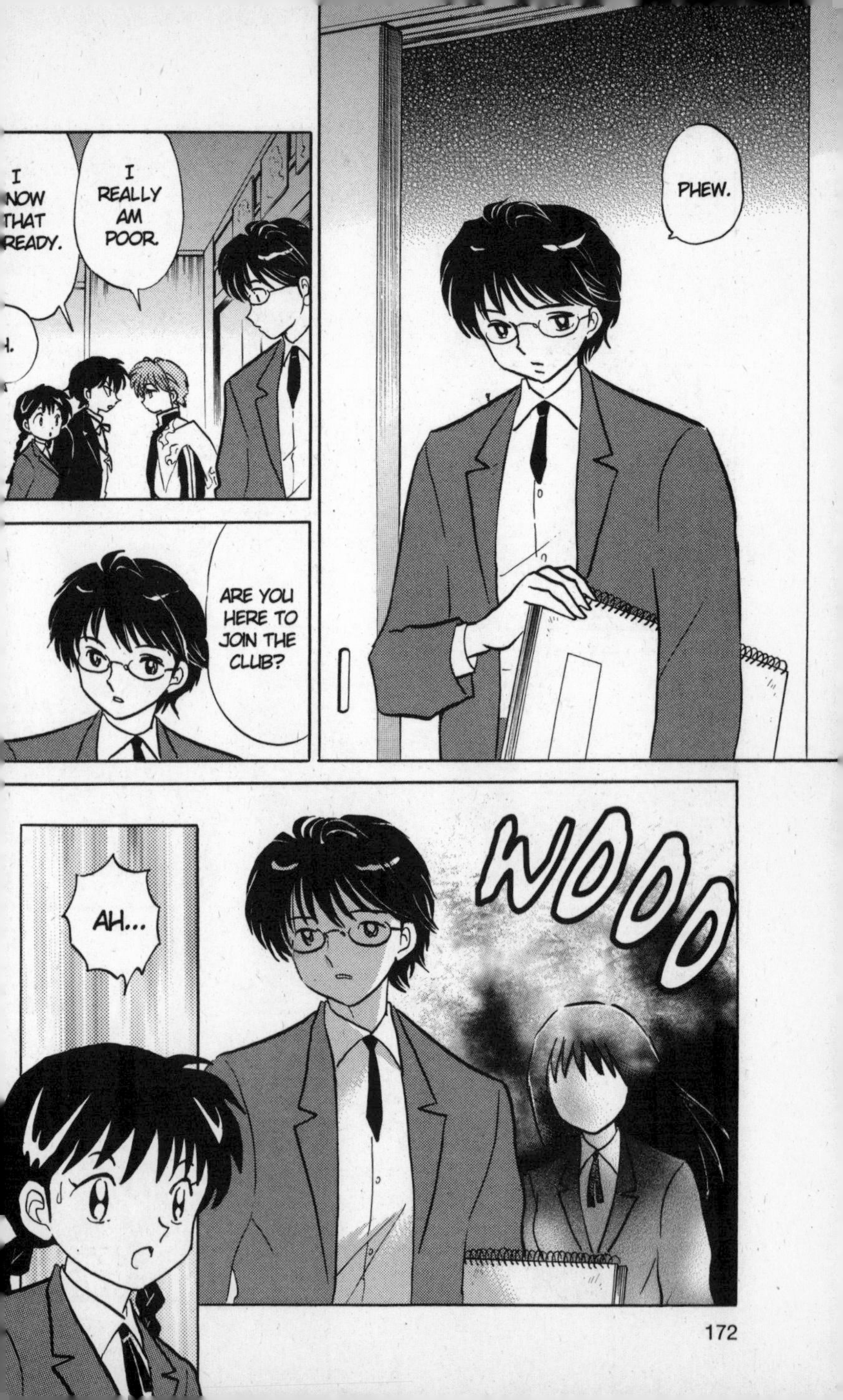
PHEW.
I REALLY AM POOR.
ARE YOU HERE TO JOIN THE CLUB?
WOOO
AH...

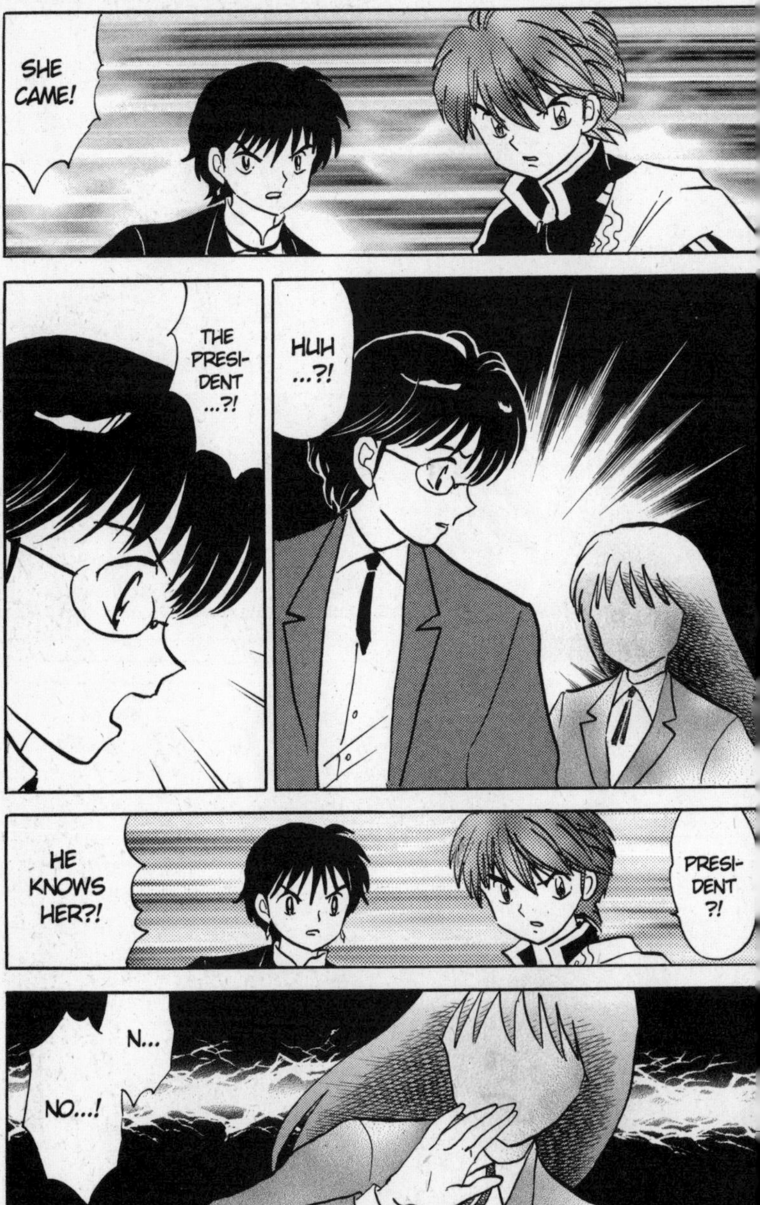
SHE CAME!
HUH ...?!
THE PRESI-DENT ...?!
PRESI-DENT ?!
HE KNOWS HER?!
N...
NO...!

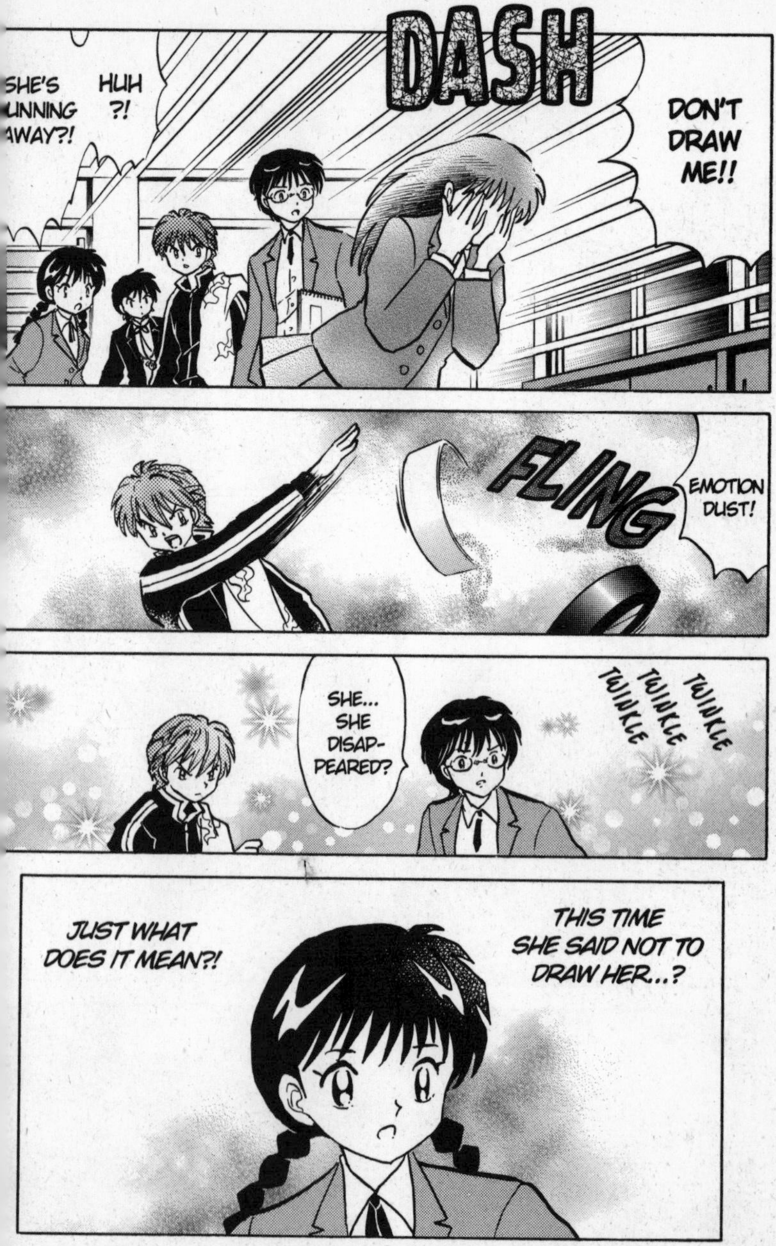
DASH
DON'T DRAW ME!!
HUH ?!
SHE'S RUNNING AWAY?!
EMOTION DUST!
FLING
TWINKLE TWINKLE TWINKLE
SHE... SHE DISAPPEARED?
THIS TIME SHE SAID NOT TO DRAW HER...?
JUST WHAT DOES IT MEAN?!

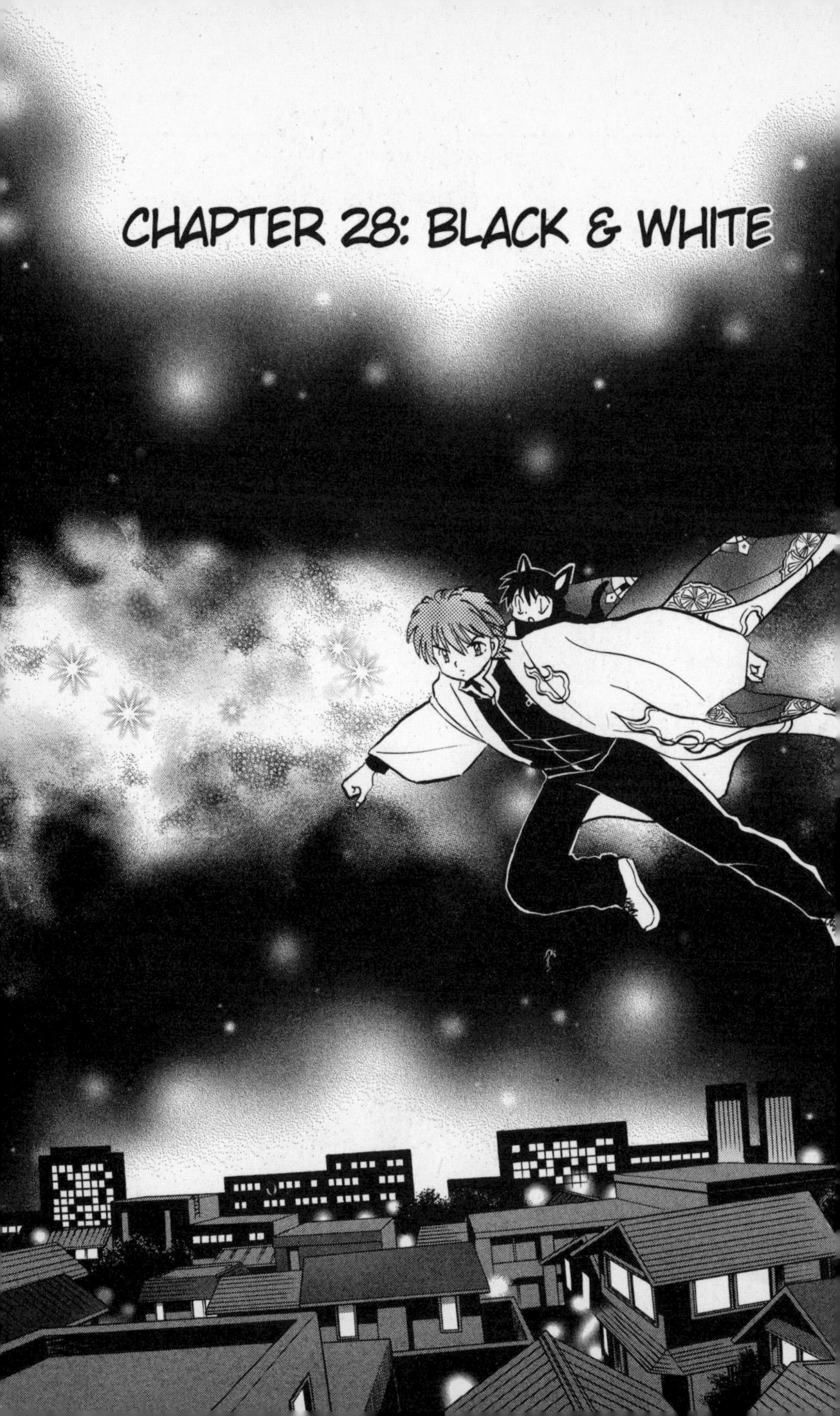
CHAPTER 28: BLACK & WHITE

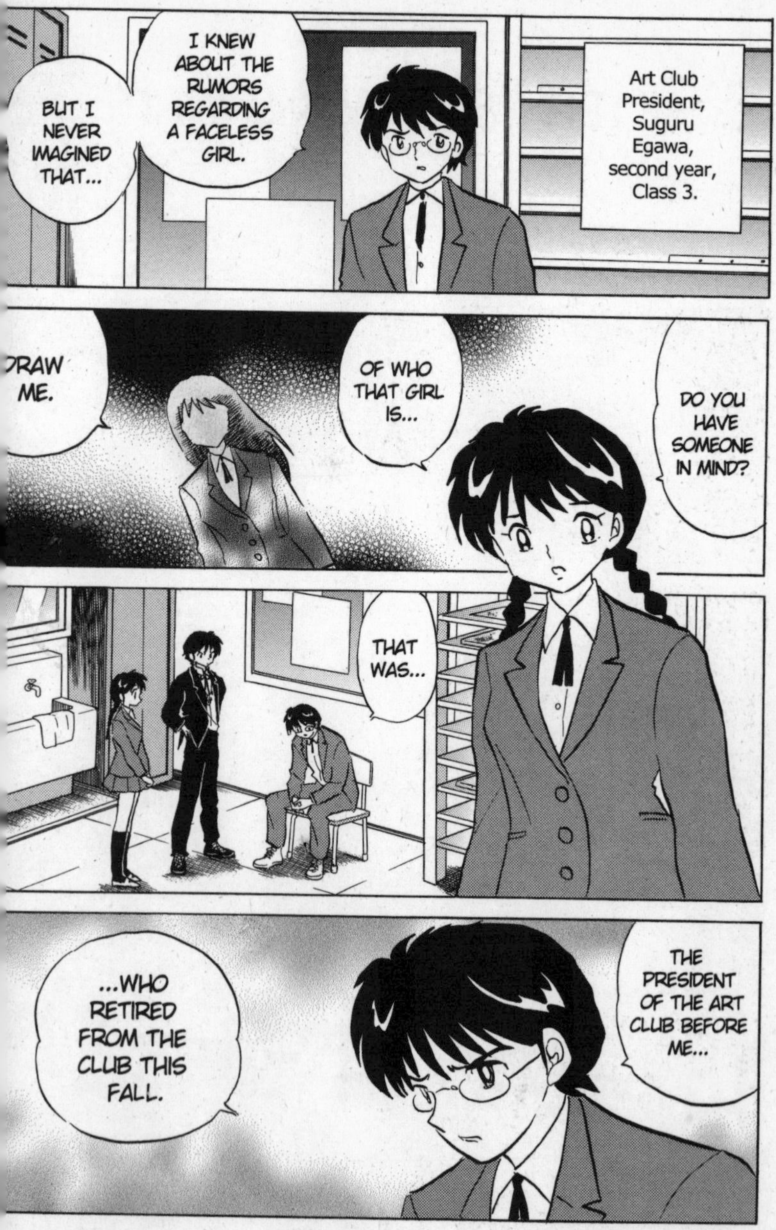

Art Club President, Suguru Egawa, second year, Class 3.
I KNEW ABOUT THE RUMORS REGARDING A FACELESS GIRL.
BUT I NEVER IMAGINED THAT...
DO YOU HAVE SOMEONE IN MIND?
OF WHO THAT GIRL IS...
DRAW ME.
THAT WAS...
THE PRESIDENT OF THE ART CLUB BEFORE ME...
...WHO RETIRED FROM THE CLUB THIS FALL.

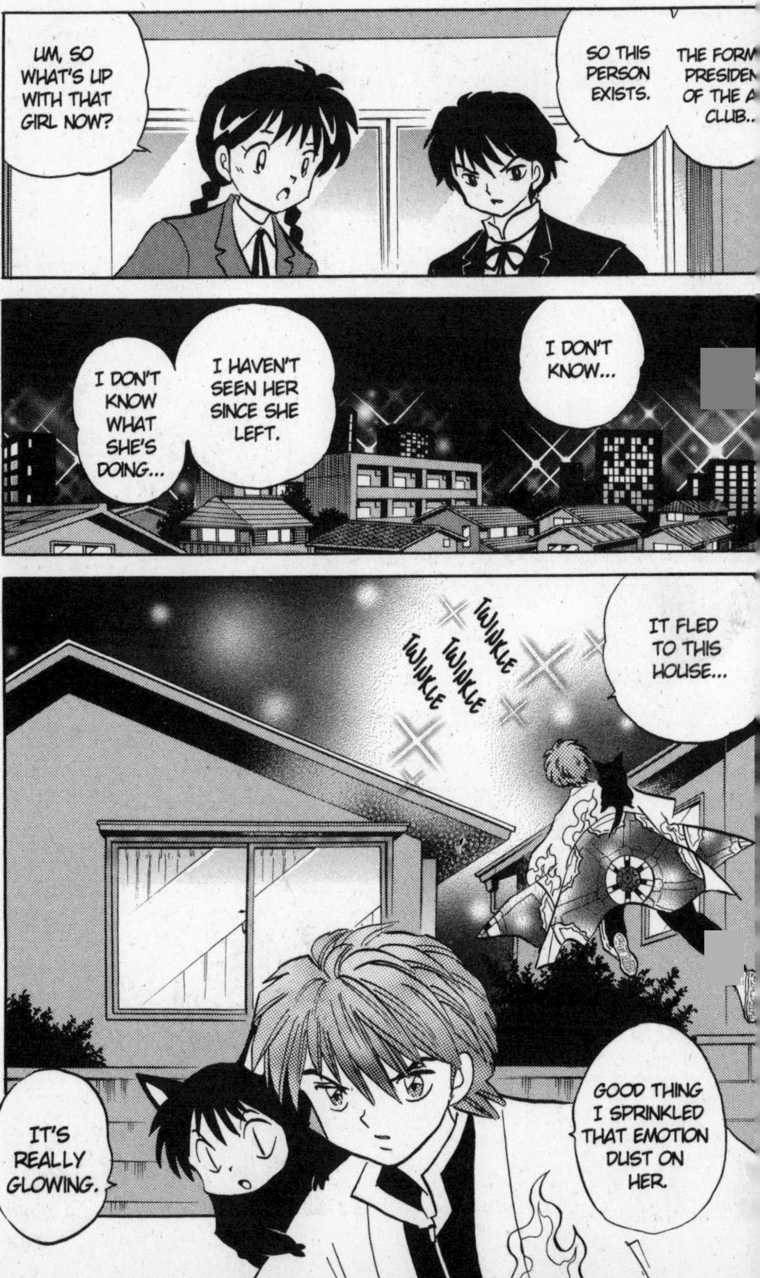
THE FORM PRESIDEN OF THE A CLUB..
SO THIS PERSON EXISTS.
UM, SO WHAT'S UP WITH THAT GIRL NOW?
I DON'T KNOW...
I HAVEN'T SEEN HER SINCE SHE LEFT.
I DON'T KNOW WHAT SHE'S DOING...
IT FLED TO THIS HOUSE...
TWINKLE TWINKLE TWINKLE
GOOD THING I SPRINKLED THAT EMOTION DUST ON HER.
IT'S REALLY GLOWING.

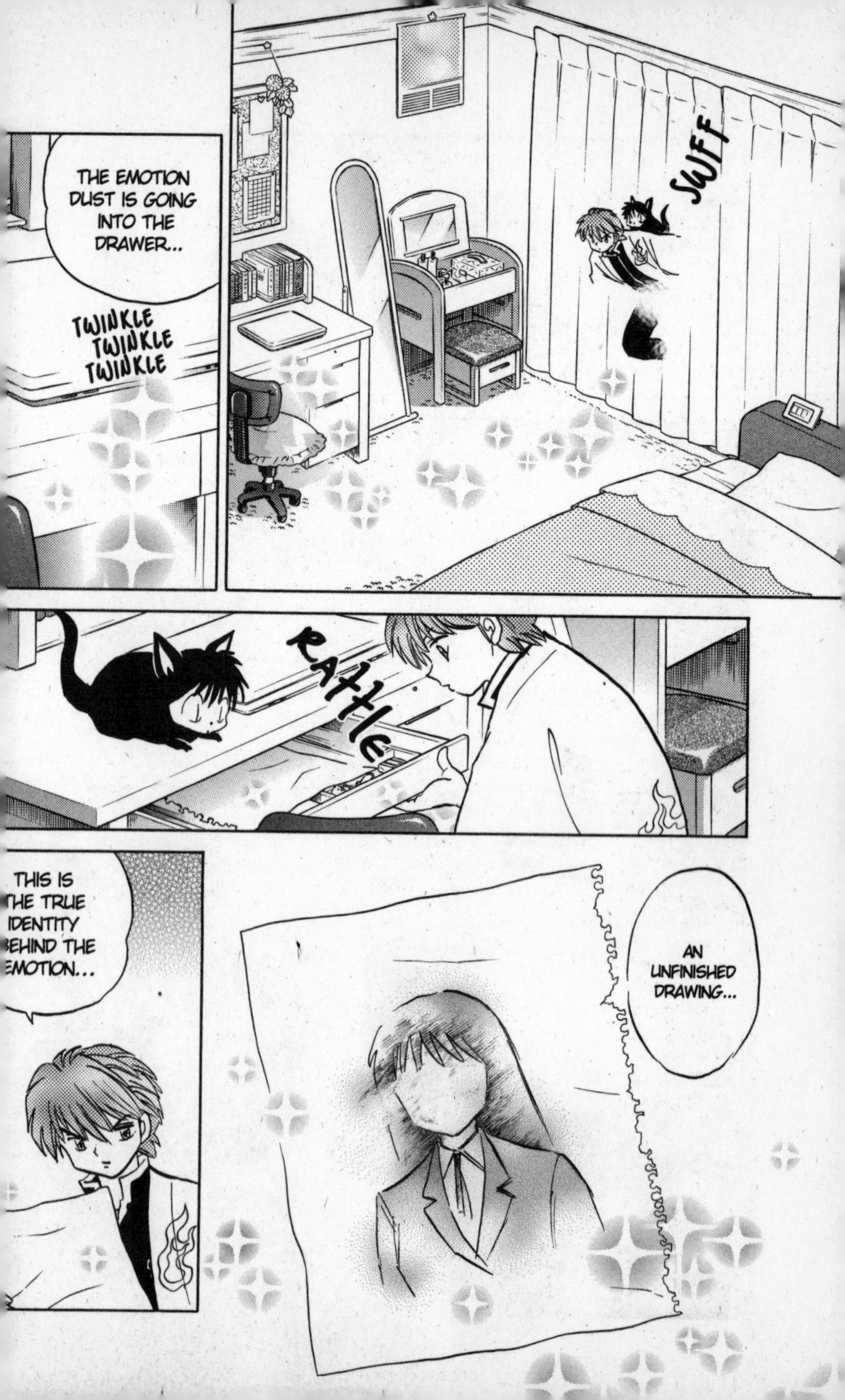
SWFF
THE EMOTION DUST IS GOING INTO THE DRAWER...
TWINKLE TWINKLE TWINKLE
RATTLE
AN UNFINISHED DRAWING...
THIS IS THE TRUE IDENTITY BEHIND THE EMOTION...

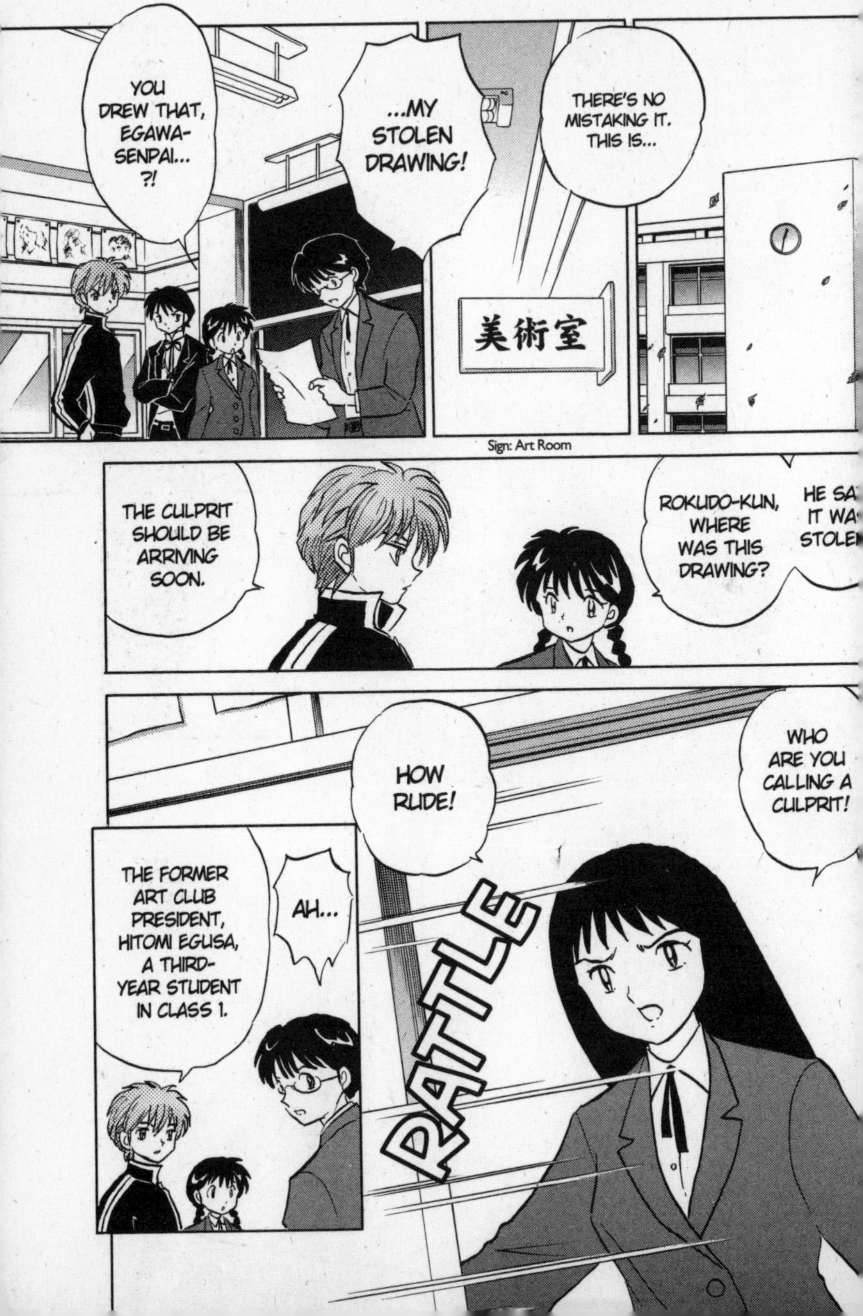
THERE'S NO MISTAKING IT. THIS IS...
...MY STOLEN DRAWING!
YOU DREW THAT, EGAWA-SENPAI...?!
美術室
Sign: Art Room
ROKUDO-KUN, WHERE WAS THIS DRAWING?
THE CULPRIT SHOULD BE ARRIVING SOON.
WHO ARE YOU CALLING A CULPRIT!
HOW RUDE!
RATTLE
AH...
THE FORMER ART CLUB PRESIDENT, HITOMI EGUSA, A THIRD-YEAR STUDENT IN CLASS 1.

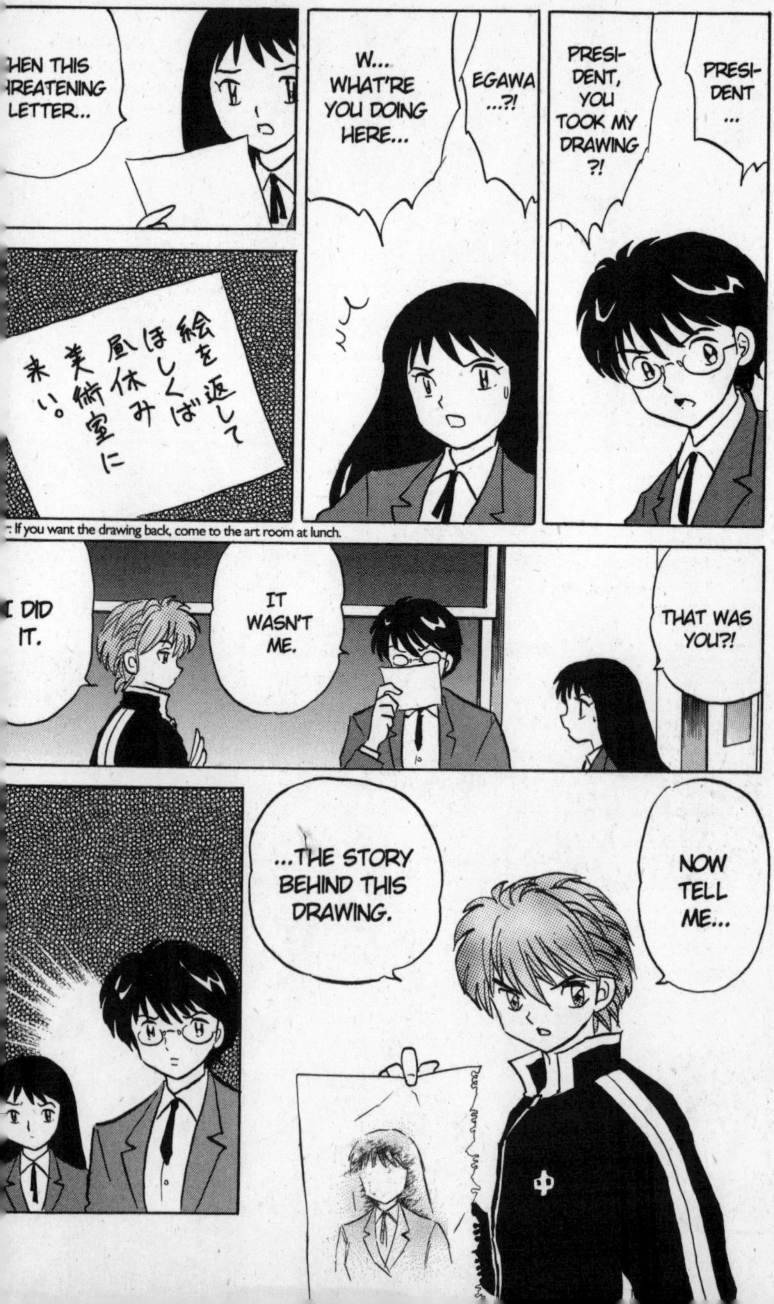
PRESI-DENT...
PRESI-DENT, YOU TOOK MY DRAWING?!
EGAWA...?!
W... WHAT'RE YOU DOING HERE...
HEN THIS HREATENING LETTER...
絵を返してほしくば昼休み美術室に来い。
: If you want the drawing back, come to the art room at lunch.
THAT WAS YOU?!
IT WASN'T ME.
DID IT.
NOW TELL ME...
...THE STORY BEHIND THIS DRAWING.

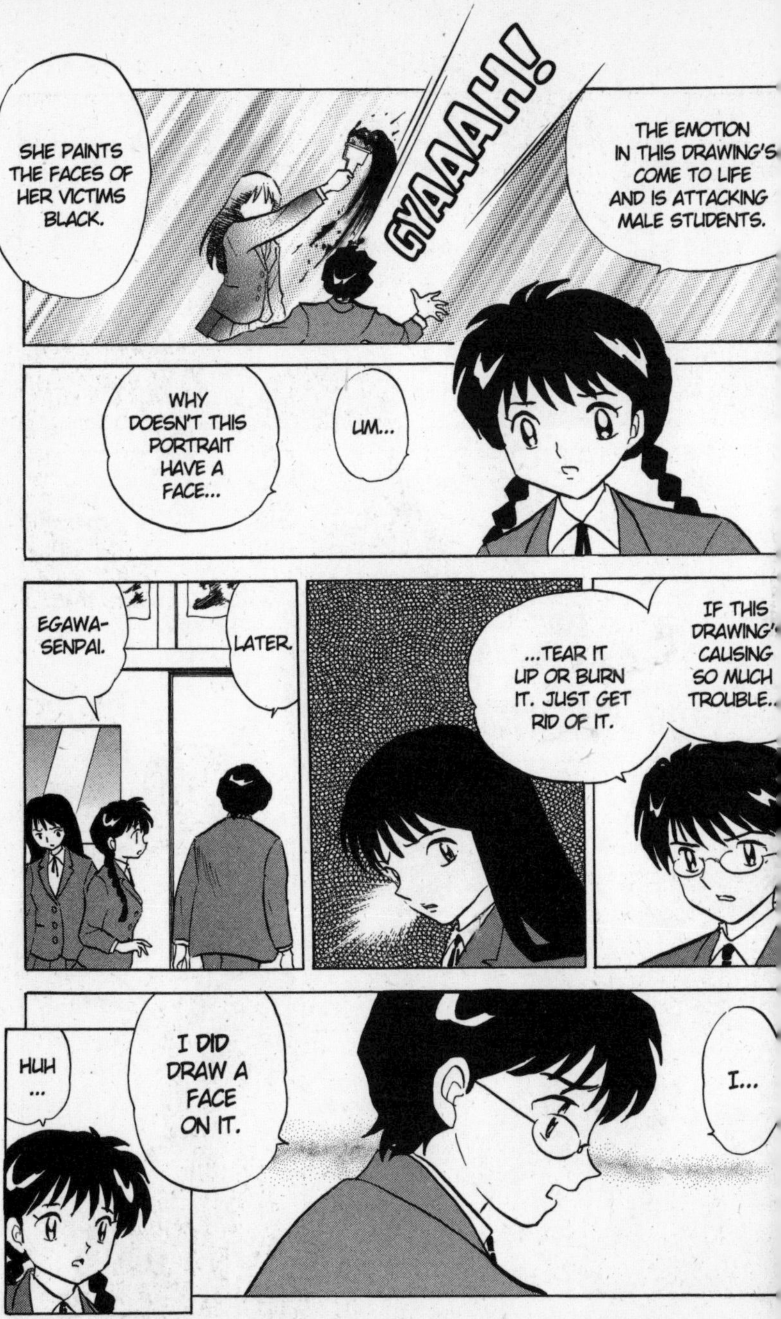
THE EMOTION IN THIS DRAWING'S COME TO LIFE AND IS ATTACKING MALE STUDENTS.
GYAAAH!
SHE PAINTS THE FACES OF HER VICTIMS BLACK.
UM...
WHY DOESN'T THIS PORTRAIT HAVE A FACE...
IF THIS DRAWING' CAUSING SO MUCH TROUBLE..
...TEAR IT UP OR BURN IT. JUST GET RID OF IT.
EGAWA-SENPAI.
LATER.
I...
I DID DRAW A FACE ON IT.
HUH ...

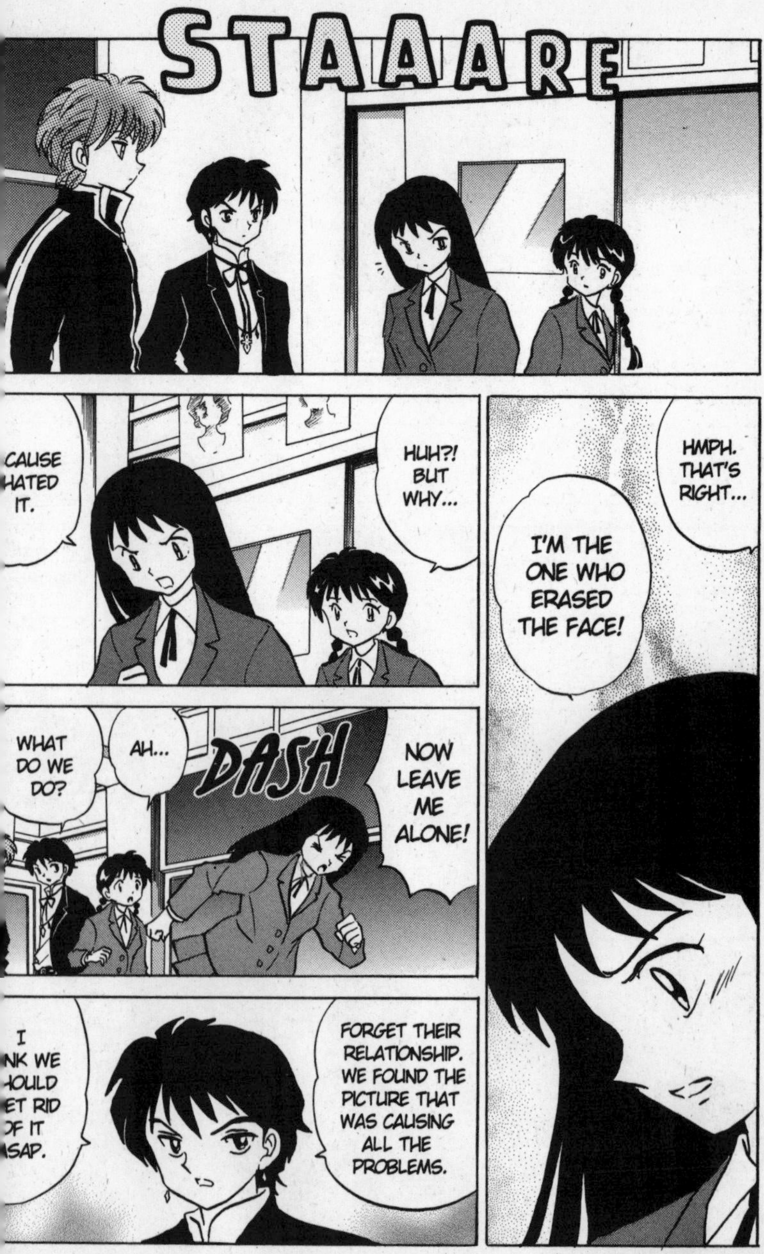
STAAARE
HMPH. THAT'S RIGHT...
I'M THE ONE WHO ERASED THE FACE!
HUH?! BUT WHY...
CAUSE HATED IT.
NOW LEAVE ME ALONE!
DASH
AH...
WHAT DO WE DO?
FORGET THEIR RELATIONSHIP. WE FOUND THE PICTURE THAT WAS CAUSING ALL THE PROBLEMS.
I NK WE HOULD ET RID OF IT SAP.

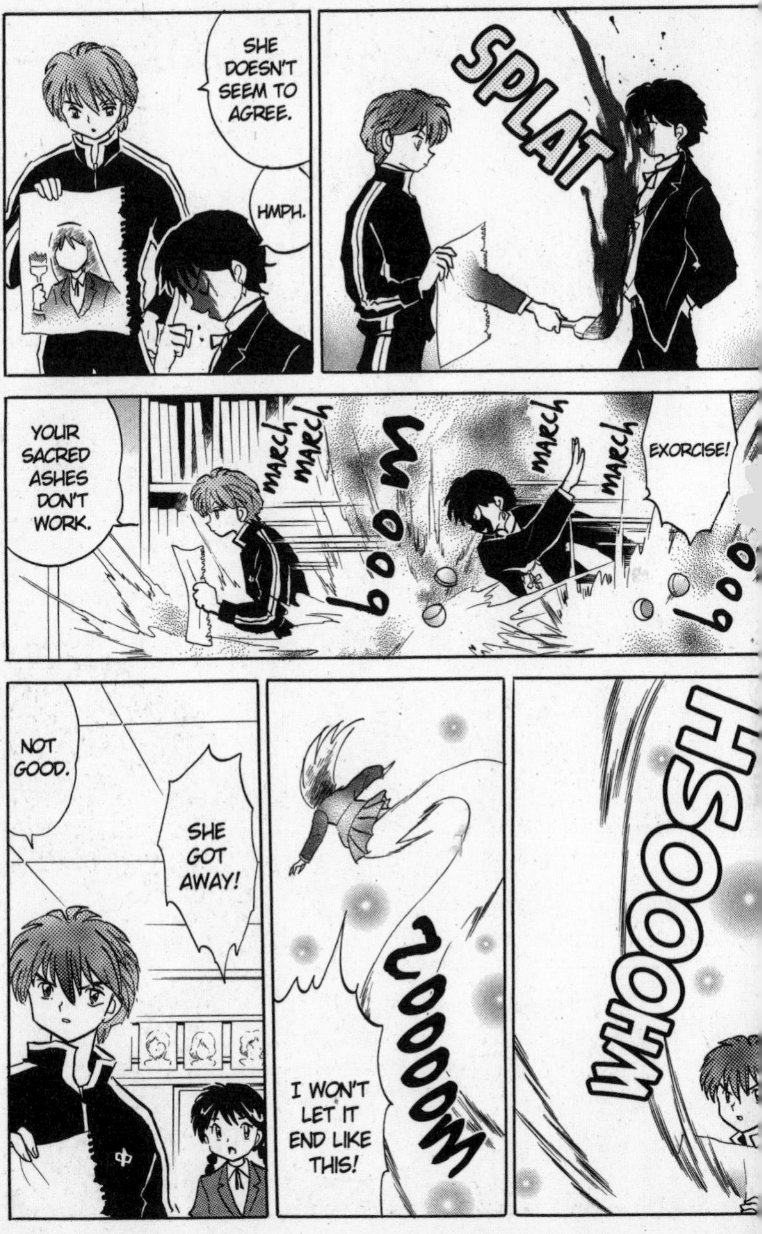
SPLAT
SHE DOESN'T SEEM TO AGREE.
HMPH.
EXORCISE!
goo
march march
goo
march march
YOUR SACRED ASHES DON'T WORK.
WHOOOSH
ZOOOOOM
I WON'T LET IT END LIKE THIS!
SHE GOT AWAY!
NOT GOOD.

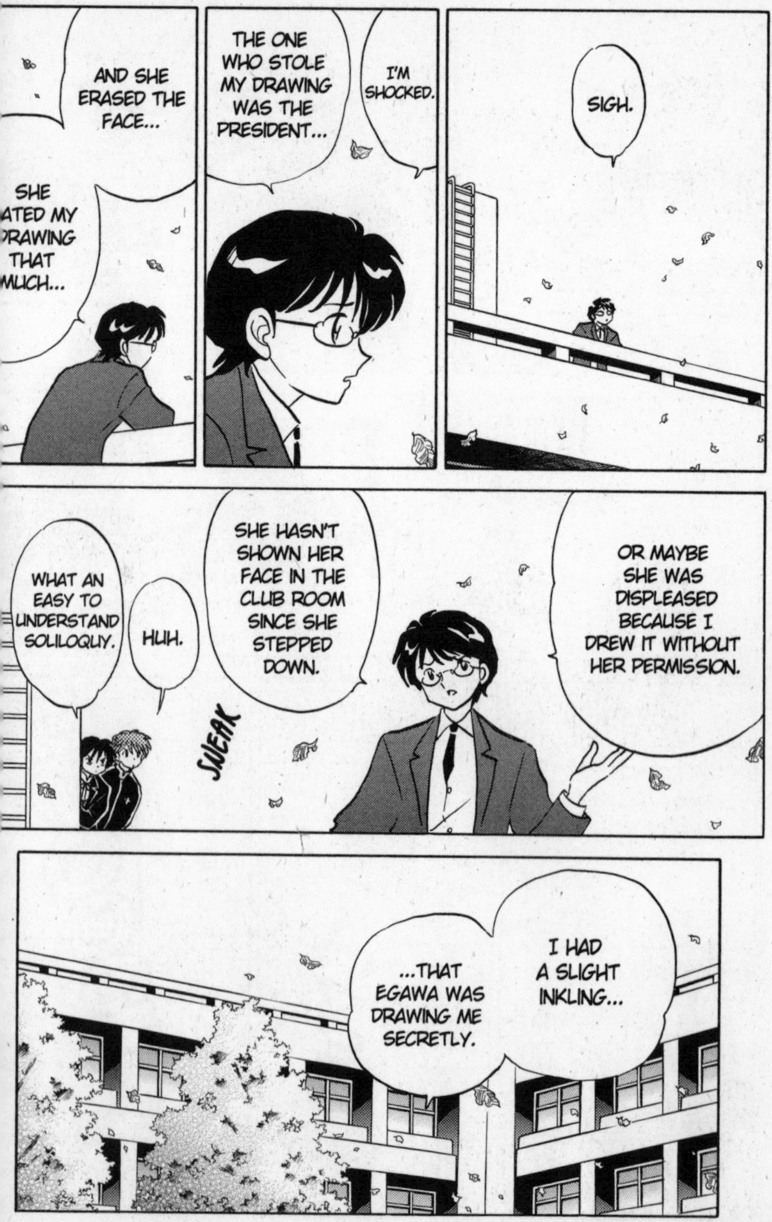
SIGH.
I'M SHOCKED.
THE ONE WHO STOLE MY DRAWING WAS THE PRESIDENT...
AND SHE ERASED THE FACE...
SHE ATED MY RAWING THAT MUCH...
OR MAYBE SHE WAS DISPLEASED BECAUSE I DREW IT WITHOUT HER PERMISSION.
SHE HASN'T SHOWN HER FACE IN THE CLUB ROOM SINCE SHE STEPPED DOWN.
SNEAK
HUH.
WHAT AN EASY TO UNDERSTAND SOLILOQUY.
I HAD A SLIGHT INKLING...
...THAT EGAWA WAS DRAWING ME SECRETLY.

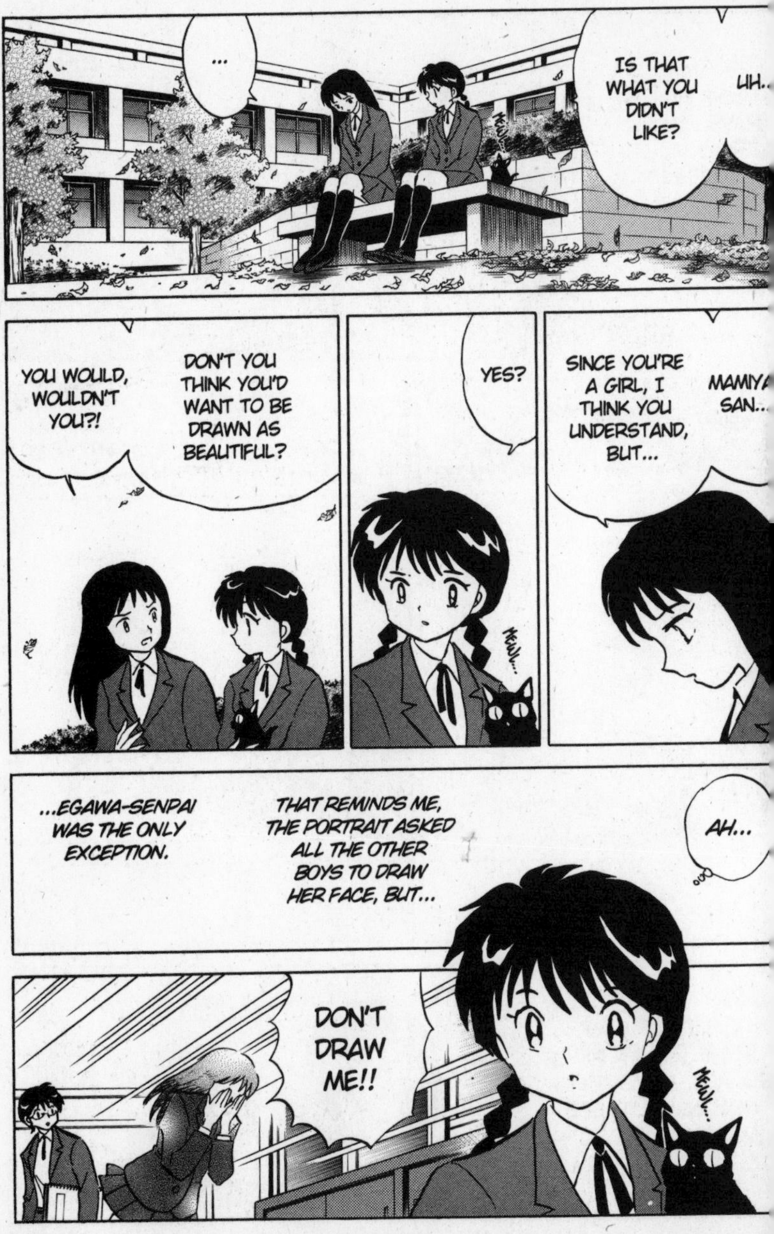
UH...
IS THAT WHAT YOU DIDN'T LIKE?
...
MAMIYA SAN...
SINCE YOU'RE A GIRL, I THINK YOU UNDERSTAND, BUT...
YES?
MEWL...
DON'T YOU THINK YOU'D WANT TO BE DRAWN AS BEAUTIFUL?
YOU WOULD, WOULDN'T YOU?!
AH...
THAT REMINDS ME, THE PORTRAIT ASKED ALL THE OTHER BOYS TO DRAW HER FACE, BUT...
...EGAWA-SENPAI WAS THE ONLY EXCEPTION.
MEWL...
DON'T DRAW ME!!

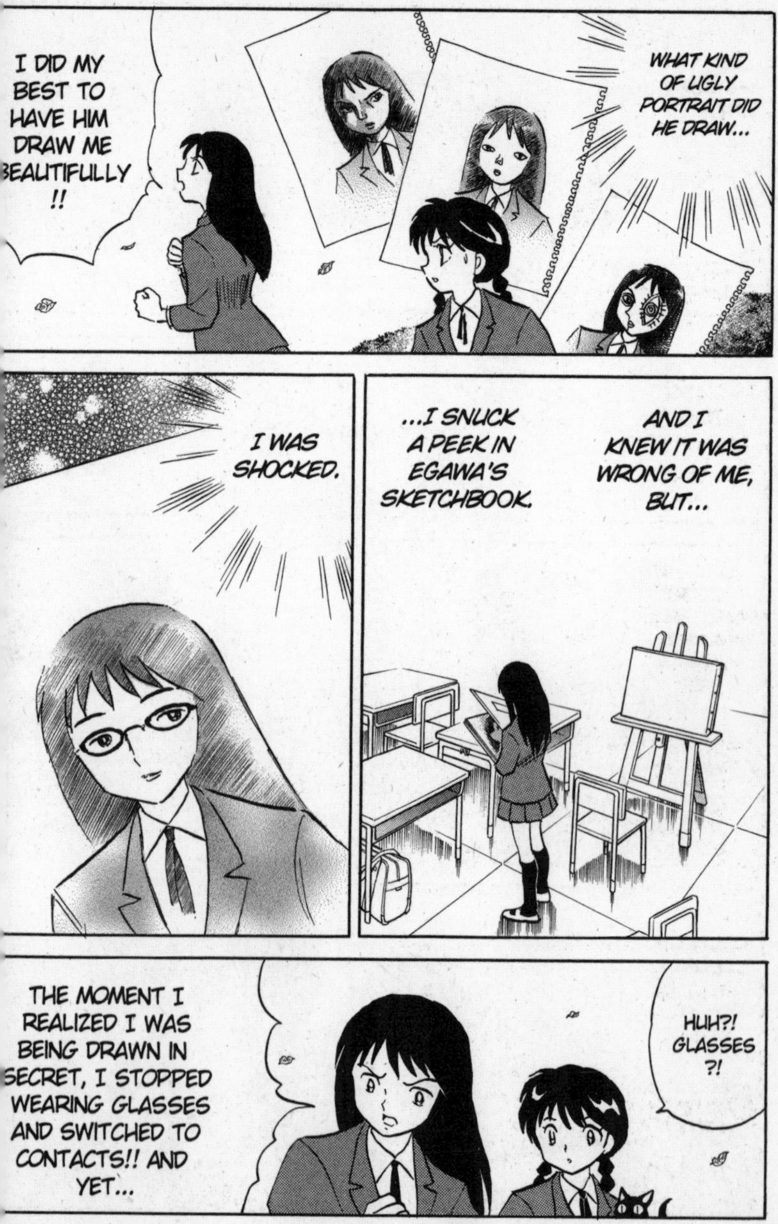
WHAT KIND OF UGLY PORTRAIT DID HE DRAW...
I DID MY BEST TO HAVE HIM DRAW ME BEAUTIFULLY!!
AND I KNEW IT WAS WRONG OF ME, BUT...
...I SNUCK A PEEK IN EGAWA'S SKETCHBOOK.
I WAS SHOCKED.
THE MOMENT I REALIZED I WAS BEING DRAWN IN SECRET, I STOPPED WEARING GLASSES AND SWITCHED TO CONTACTS!! AND YET...
HUH?! GLASSES?!

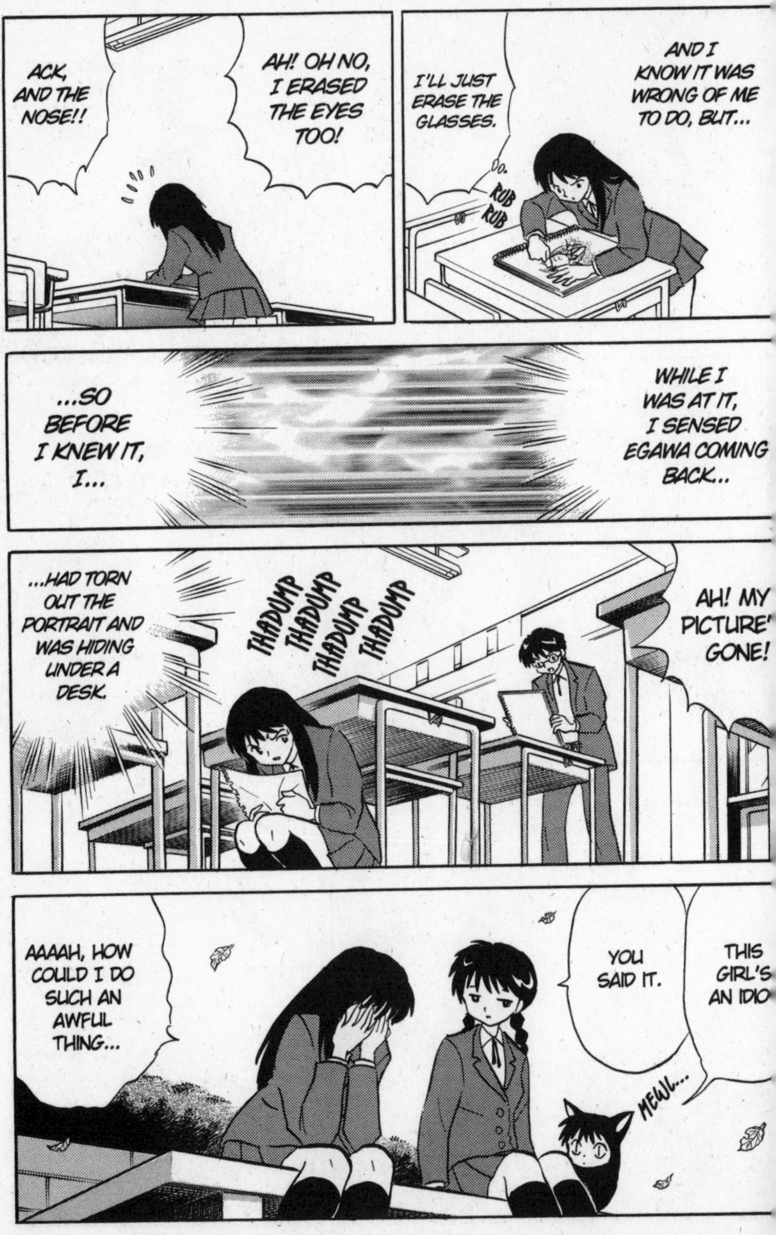
AND I KNOW IT WAS WRONG OF ME TO DO, BUT...
I'LL JUST ERASE THE GLASSES.
RUB RUB
AH! OH NO, I ERASED THE EYES TOO!
ACK, AND THE NOSE!!
WHILE I WAS AT IT, I SENSED EGAWA COMING BACK...
...SO BEFORE I KNEW IT, I...
AH! MY PICTURE' GONE!
THADUMP THADUMP THADUMP THADUMP
...HAD TORN OUT THE PORTRAIT AND WAS HIDING UNDER A DESK.
THIS GIRL'S AN IDIO
YOU SAID IT.
MEWL...
AAAAH, HOW COULD I DO SUCH AN AWFUL THING...

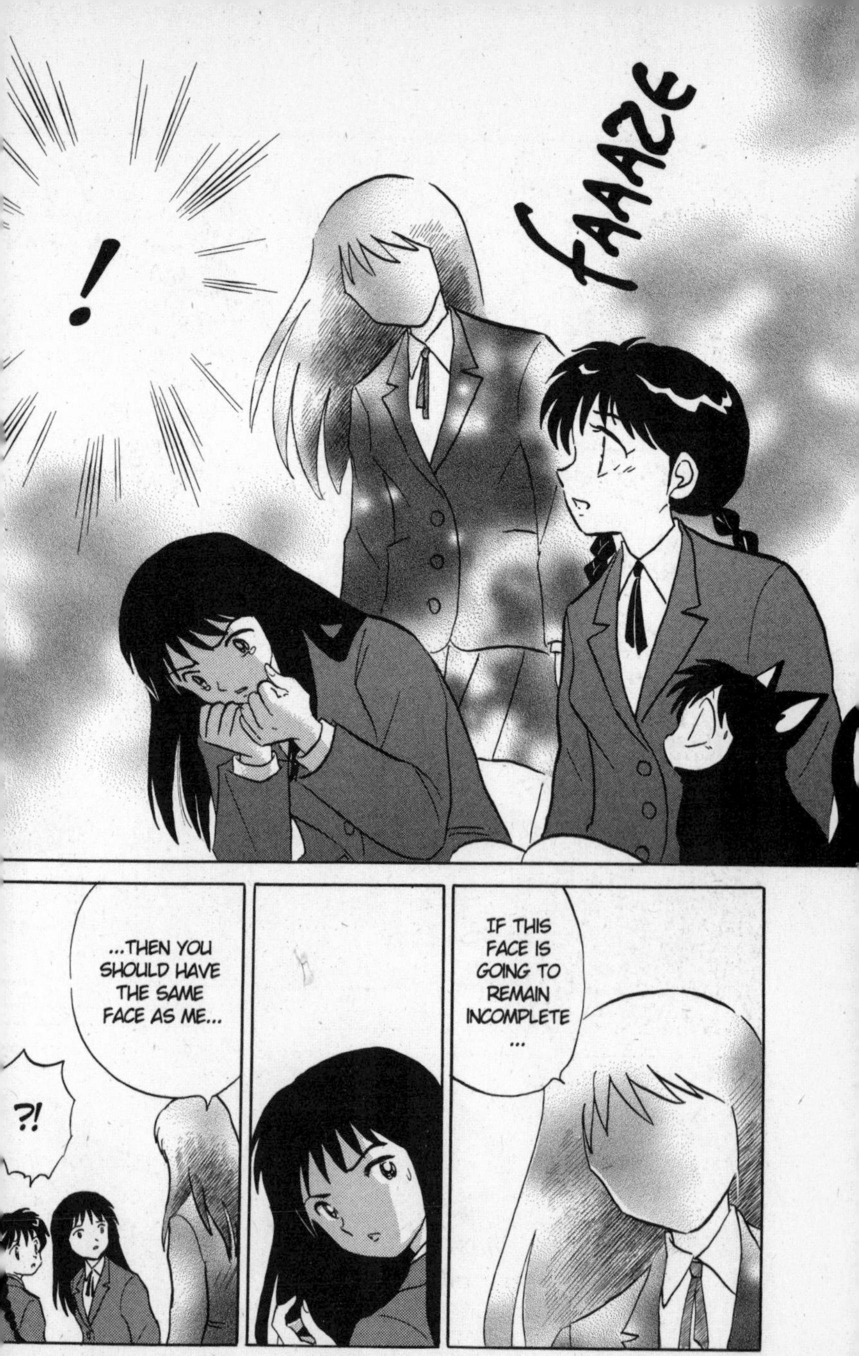
FAAAZE
!
IF THIS FACE IS GOING TO REMAIN INCOMPLETE ...
...THEN YOU SHOULD HAVE THE SAME FACE AS ME...
?!

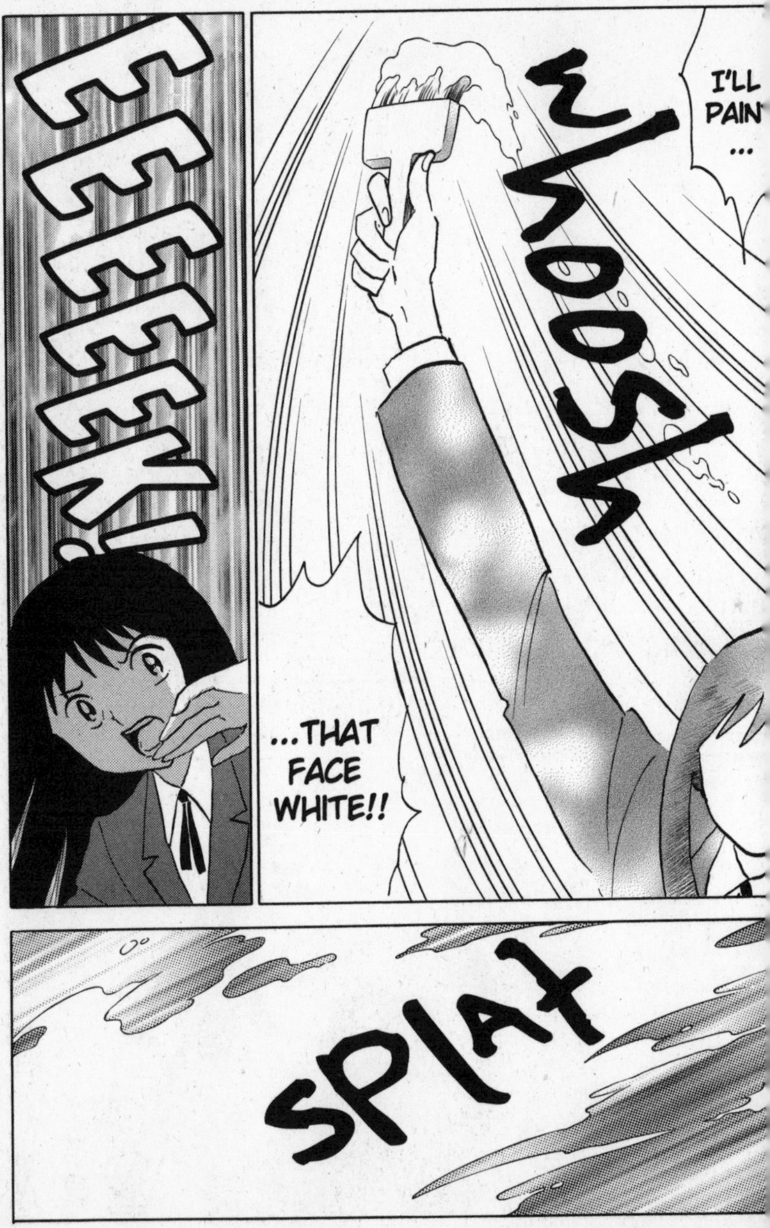
I'LL PAINT ...
WHOOSH
...THAT FACE WHITE!!
EEEEEEK!!
SPLAT

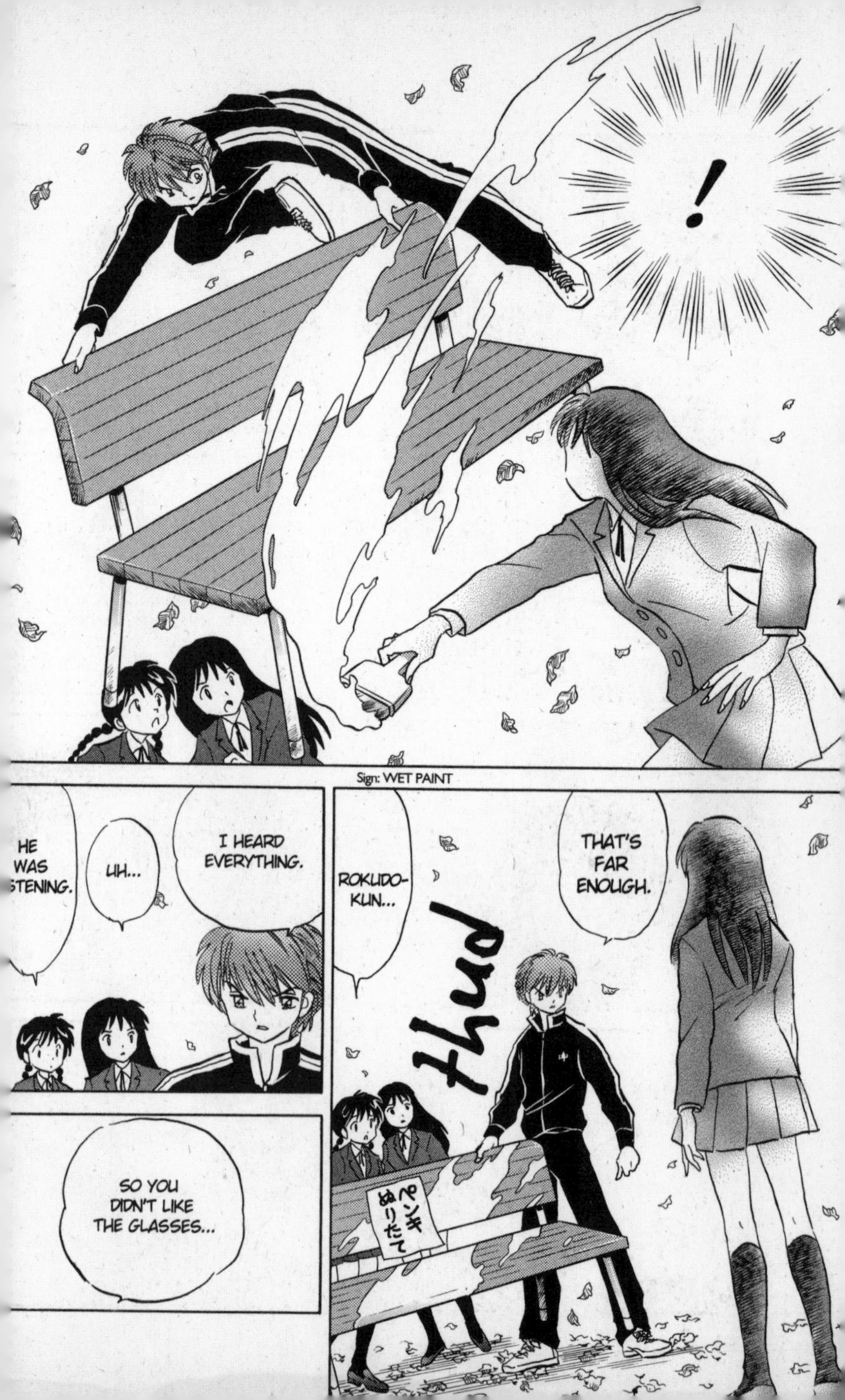
!
Sign: WET PAINT
ペンキぬりたて
THAT'S FAR ENOUGH.
thud
ROKUDO-KUN...
I HEARD EVERYTHING.
UH...
HE WAS
STENING.
SO YOU DIDN'T LIKE THE GLASSES...

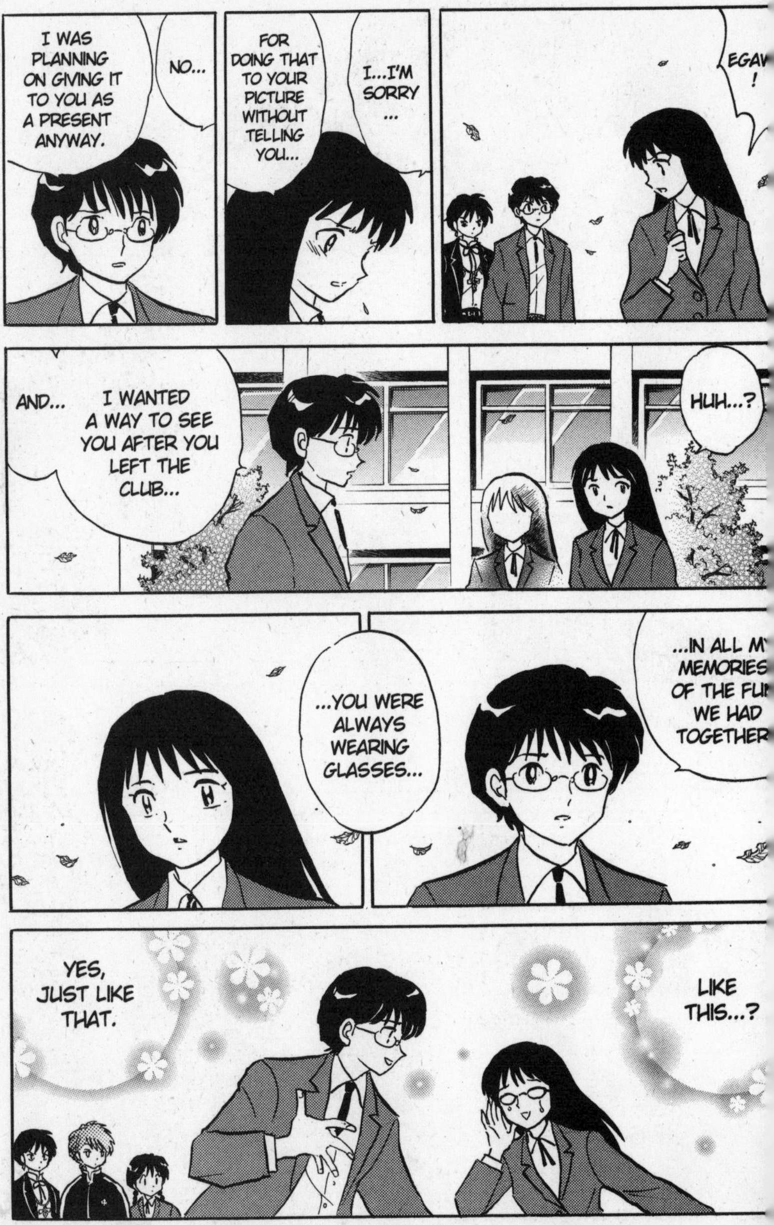
EGAW !
I...I'M SORRY ...
FOR DOING THAT TO YOUR PICTURE WITHOUT TELLING YOU...
NO...
I WAS PLANNING ON GIVING IT TO YOU AS A PRESENT ANYWAY.
HUH...?
AND...
I WANTED A WAY TO SEE YOU AFTER YOU LEFT THE CLUB...
...IN ALL M MEMORIES OF THE FU WE HAD TOGETHER
...YOU WERE ALWAYS WEARING GLASSES...
LIKE THIS...?
YES, JUST LIKE THAT.

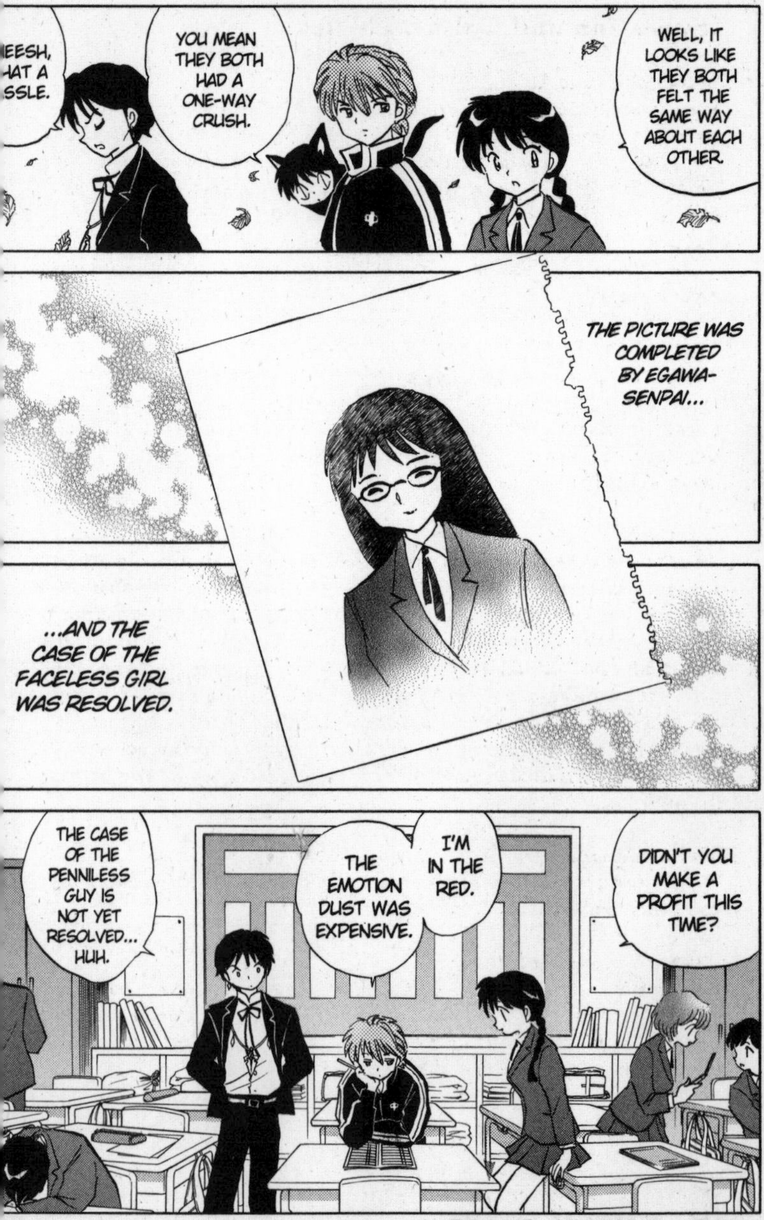
WELL, IT LOOKS LIKE THEY BOTH FELT THE SAME WAY ABOUT EACH OTHER.
YOU MEAN THEY BOTH HAD A ONE-WAY CRUSH.
EESH, HAT A SSLE.
THE PICTURE WAS COMPLETED BY EGAWA-SENPAI...
...AND THE CASE OF THE FACELESS GIRL WAS RESOLVED.
DIDN'T YOU MAKE A PROFIT THIS TIME?
I'M IN THE RED.
THE EMOTION DUST WAS EXPENSIVE.
THE CASE OF THE PENNILESS GUY IS NOT YET RESOLVED... HUH.

RIN-NE VOLUME 3 - END -

Translation and Cultural Notes

Chapter 19, page 16
When Tsubasa meets Sakura he says, "It's me. Me." In Japanese, he says, "Ore da yo. Ore."「おれだよ。 おれ。」Sakura doesn't remember who he is at first, and she asks, "Itsumi-kun?" but the original Japanese is 「俺田くん…とか？」(Oreda-kun). So the joke here is that she thinks his name is Oreda, when all he's saying is "It's me." Now, "Itsumi" kind of sounds like "It's me," and "It's me" is indeed a translation of "Ore da yo." So, "Itsumi" was used for Sakura's guess at Tsubasa's name in order to preserve the joke.

Chapter 20, page 37
Sakura uses the term *Megane-kun* to refer to the ghost of Usui-kun, the boy Rinne is trying to help. In Japan, *Megane-kun* is used simply as a nickname for someone who wears glasses. *Megane* by itself means "glasses." Also, the suffix *-kun* in this case indicates a boy. *Megane-kun* can also be translated as "Four-Eyes."

Chapter 22
"Hanako-san of the Toilet" is a well-known urban legend/ghost story in Japan. Like many such stories there are lots of variations on it, but the basic idea is that Hanako is the ghost of a schoolgirl that haunts the third floor restroom of a public school. Kids dare each other to go into the stall next to the one that's believed to be haunted, knock three times, and call out to Hanako. She might answer, or she might try to strangle the person who called to her. There are a lot of regional twists on the story that change the floor the bathroom is on, what to say to summon her, what she does if she comes, and so on. There have been a couple of movies based on this story too.

Chapter 23, page 84
The evil spirit's name *Toichi* literally means "10 percent interest every ten days." It's a term associated with loan sharks in Japan.

Chapter 27, page 165
Here Tsubasa is drawing some Japanese characters on his sketch pad. If you read Japanese, you'll see that they are the hiragana characters for *henohenomoheji*「へのへのもへじ」. This is really just a playful way of drawing faces in Japan and is often used on stick figures.

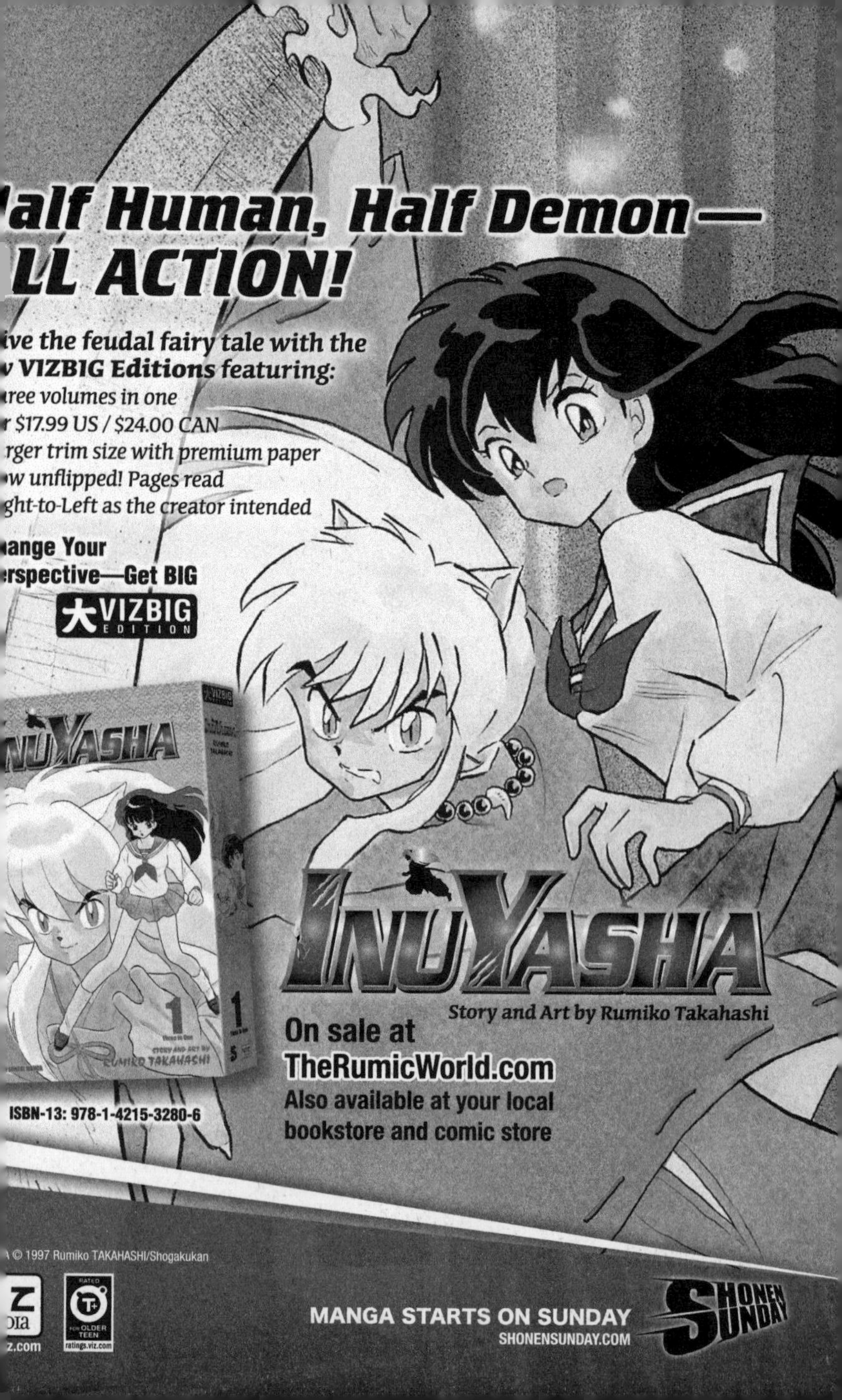
alf Human, Half Demon—
LL ACTION!
ive the feudal fairy tale with the
v VIZBIG Editions featuring:
ree volumes in one
r $17.99 US / $24.00 CAN
rger trim size with premium paper
w unflipped! Pages read
ght-to-Left as the creator intended
ange Your
rspective—Get BIG
大 VIZBIG EDITION
INUYASHA
1
STORY AND ART BY RUMIKO TAKAHASHI
ISBN-13: 978-1-4215-3280-6
INUYASHA
Story and Art by Rumiko Takahashi
On sale at
TheRumicWorld.com
Also available at your local
bookstore and comic store
© 1997 Rumiko TAKAHASHI/Shogakukan
RATED T+ FOR OLDER TEEN
ratings.viz.com
z.com
MANGA STARTS ON SUNDAY
SHONENSUNDAY.COM
SHONEN SUNDAY

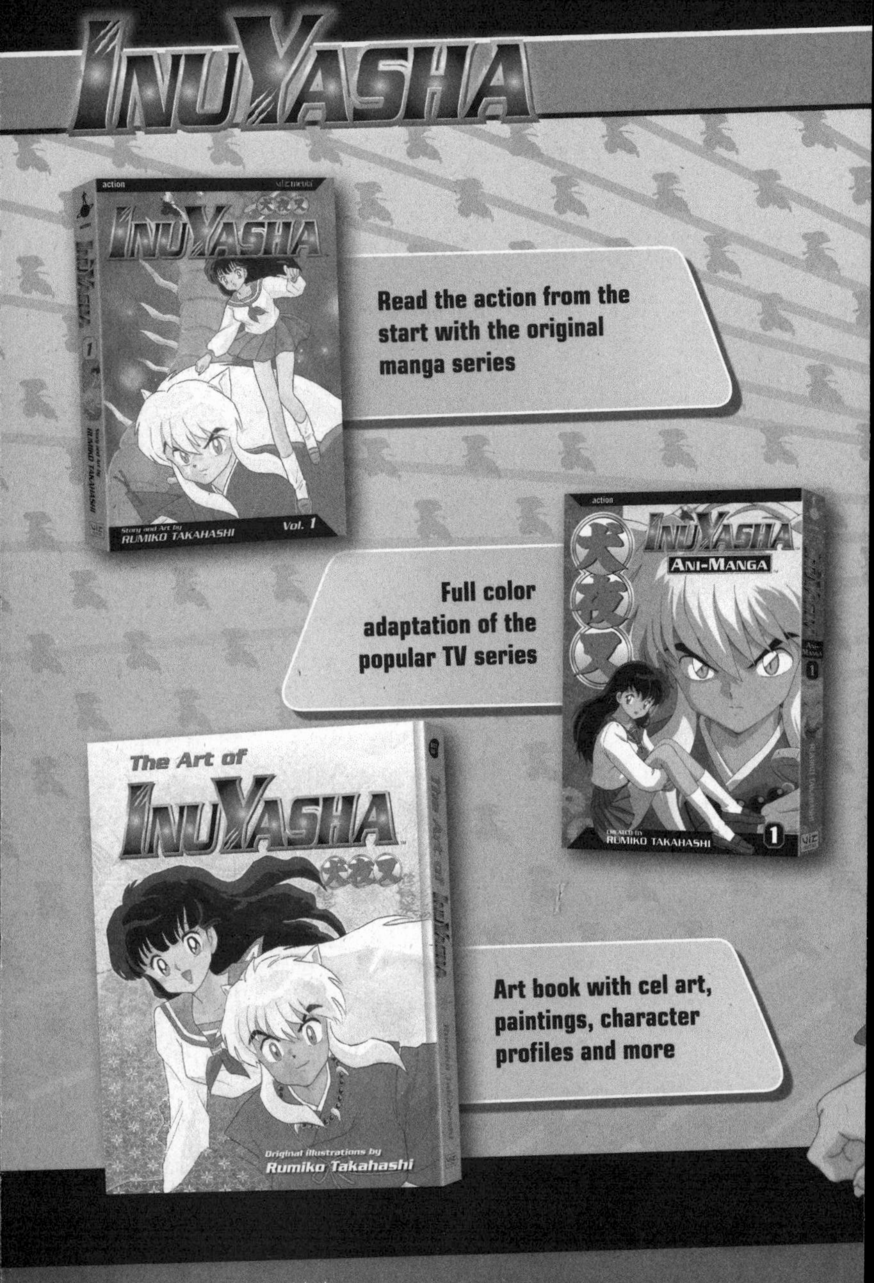

INUYASHA
action
INUYASHA
Story and Art by
RUMIKO TAKAHASHI
Vol. 1
Read the action from the start with the original manga series
action
INUYASHA
ANI-MANGA
CREATED BY
RUMIKO TAKAHASHI
1
Full color adaptation of the popular TV series
The Art of
INUYASHA
Original illustrations by
Rumiko Takahashi
Art book with cel art, paintings, character profiles and more

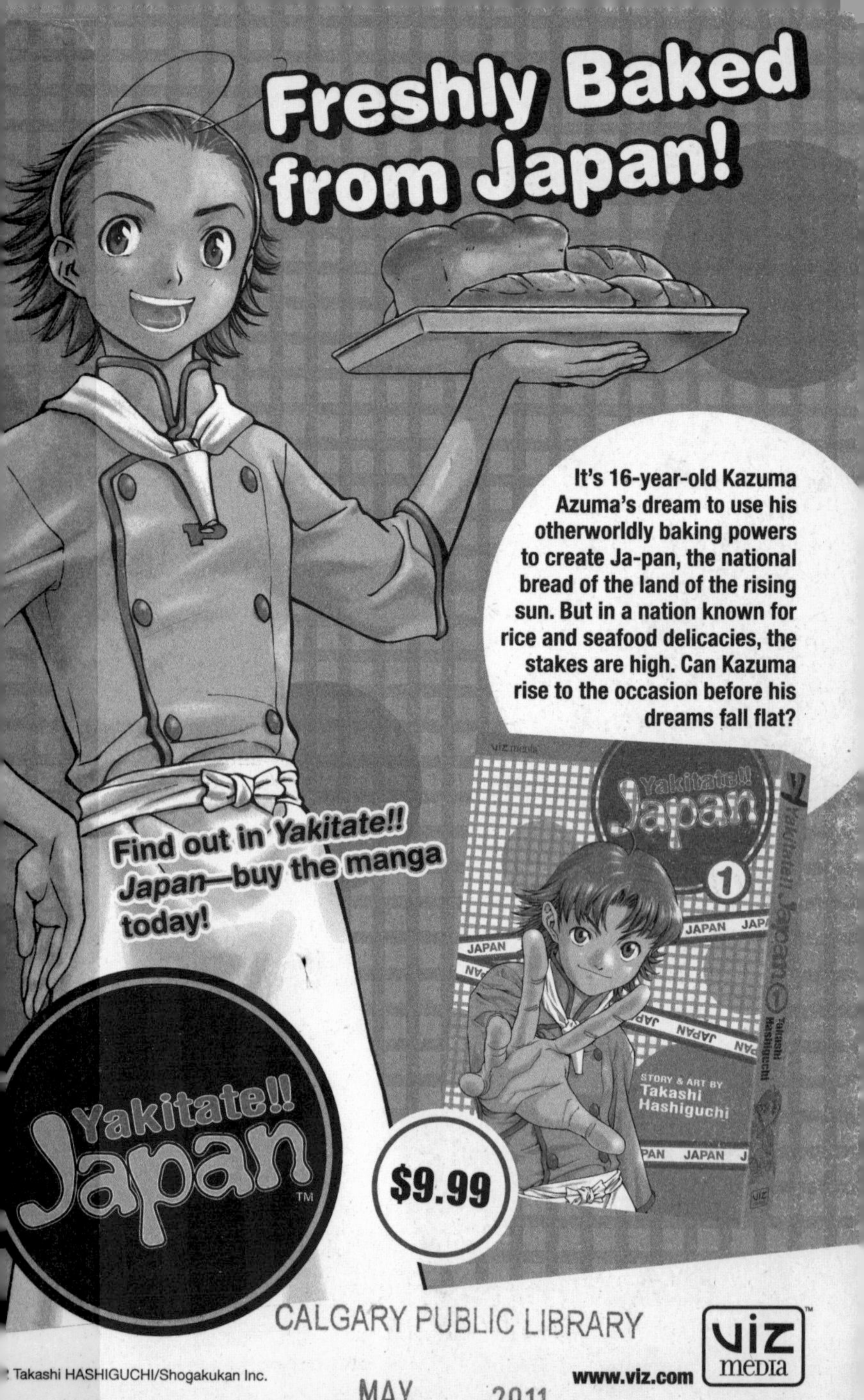
Freshly Baked from Japan!
It's 16-year-old Kazuma Azuma's dream to use his otherworldly baking powers to create Ja-pan, the national bread of the land of the rising sun. But in a nation known for rice and seafood delicacies, the stakes are high. Can Kazuma rise to the occasion before his dreams fall flat?
Find out in Yakitate!! Japan—buy the manga today!
Yakitate!! Japan™
$9.99
Yakitate!! Japan 1
STORY & ART BY Takashi Hashiguchi
© Takashi HASHIGUCHI/Shogakukan Inc.
www.viz.com
VIZ media